SAFEGUARDING
LIBERTY

SAFEGUARDING LIBERTY

The Constitution and Citizen Militias

Larry Pratt, Editor

Legacy Communications
Franklin, Tennessee

Safeguarding Liberty is a co-publication of Gun Owners Foundation, Springfield, Virginia, and Legacy Communications, Franklin, Tennessee.

Direct all inquiries for trade orders or special sales for groups or organizations to: Legacy Communications, Post Office Box 680365, Franklin, Tennessee 37068.

ISBN 1-880692-18-X

Contents

This book is dedicated to the memory of George Mason and George Washington, who exercised their right to keep and bear arms by organizing the Fairfax, Virginia militia.

Introduction

Firearms: the People's Liberty Teeth

Larry Pratt

Now that the Brady bill has become the law of the land, does that mean it has to be obeyed? Certainly, federally licensed firearms dealers must obey it because they operate under federal government authority. But what about sheriffs and police chiefs?

Many sheriffs in several states have refused to do the background check mandated by the Brady law. One such sheriff is Ray Nixon of Lincoln County, Montana. He addressed a meeting of the unorganized militia in February 1994 at a crowded meeting in Eureka.

The concern of the militia was to lawfully reinforce the sheriff in case the federal government might contemplate another Waco- or Weaver-type massacre in Lincoln County. Citing the Militia Act in Title 10 of U.S. Code and the Montana Posse Law, the members of the unorganized militia offered themselves to be deputized by the sheriff. Military service and NRA firearms certification were considered adequate qualification for membership in the sheriff's posse.

The Lincoln County unorganized militia that evening began the process of forming a lawful force to resist any tyrannical act on the part of the federal government. This was not a bunch of vigilantes or a mob that night. This was the militia of the Second Amendment and of the posse law in Montana.

The Lincoln County militia had reached the point that the colonial militias had in 1774 when they began to form and to drill. In 1774, as in 1994, there was still hope of reconciliation with the growing tyranny of the central government. But after years of encroachments on their liberties, the colonists of 1774 and the militiamen of 1994 decided to be prepared.

Meaning of Well-Regulated Militia

This helps us understand the now greatly misunderstood words of the Second Amendment which read: "A well-regulated militia being necessary for the defense of a free state, the right of the people to keep and bear arms shall not be infringed." Opponents of the individual right to keep and bear arms have greatly misunderstood the initial clause of the Second Amendment.

For many in our time, it is inconceivable to think of anything being well-regulated without a law mandating the regulation and a bureaucracy to conduct the regulation. In the 18th century, the word regulation did not at all require government involvement. The actions of the American colonists make it plain that a well-regulated militia was well-rehearsed and well-drilled without the control of the government. Indeed, the colonial well-regulated militias shot at the King's policemen (the King's soldiers were acting in the capacity we now consider a police function, but there were no police departments then).

When the Reverend Josiah Clark met the British forces at Lexington on April 19, 1775, he was serving as the elected commander of his well-regulated militia. He had well-regulated his men many a Sunday afternoon following church services. The British had made the importation of powder (semi-auto rifles?) illegal and General Gage had sent his men to confiscate colonial stockpiles, along with other war materiel such as muskets and food stores.

It is interesting to note that then, as today, the city people were disarmed first. General Gage had earlier registered firearms in Boston and then shortly thereafter he confiscated what he had just registered. He did it in the name of crime control. Throughout history the names of tyrants change, but not their methods.

Effectiveness of the Militia

The militia's of the communities outside of Boston had been alerted by messengers from Boston the night of April 18. Paul Revere was one of these messengers, although he was captured before he got very far. The British were defeated rather soundly by the militia at Lexington and the other companies that came from surrounding areas answering the call.

Today's Paul Reveres use electronic bulletin boards and computers, and appropriately enough, one of the leading such networks is the Paul Revere Bulletin Board (phone 408-947-7800.)* Gun Owners of America

---

* Paul Revere is connected to a 14.4v.32 bis modem. It will run at that speed, or at your modem's maximum speed below 14.4. Set your modem setting to N (no-parity)-8-1. Dial the number. You will be prompted to press escape twice. Do so. You will be asked to give your real name and create a password for yourself. You are now part of the network.

uses this bulletin board for legislative alerts. Paul Revere now rides on electrons, not a horse.

The day following the battle of Lexington, Lord Dunmore of Virginia ordered the looting of the colonial powder magazine in Williamsburg. He should not have been surprised at Patrick Henry's response, since the Patriot Orator had only a month before delivered his stirring call to arms at St. John's Church in Richmond before the Second Virginia Convention.

Some cautioned against using force in response to Lord Dunmore's theft, and the matter seemed to pass without colonial response. But by the end of April, news of the British attack in Lexington reached Virginia. By May 2, 1775, Patrick Henry was on the move. Stirring the Hanover Volunteers to action with a fiery speech, they elected Henry their captain, and rode off to Williamsburg. So popular was Henry's action that by the time the Hanover Volunteers got to Williamsburg their ranks had swollen to 5,000 from the cheering crowds that lined their way. The powder was compensated twice over, and shortly afterwards, Governor Dunmore, fearing for his safety, ended up on board a ship in the York River.

Well-regulated these militias were, but controlled or sanctioned by the established government they were not. The actions of the colonies indicated that they viewed militia as something that free men had an unalienable right to organize among themselves.

Revolution or War?

Were the formation of colonial militias the actions of revolutionaries? Revolutionaries are not concerned about the legitimacy of government. They appoint themselves and strike out using force. The American colonists had remonstrated for a decade before the War for Independence, asking the English King to stop the violations of the colonial charters which the kings of England had agreed to submit themselves. The colonists had complained through their own elected governments. When hostilities broke out, it was a war between a government supported by the people and a foreign government that had become illegitimate.

We should consider some of the complaints the colonists enumerated in their Declaration of Independence. It sounds so very contemporary. For example, "He [King George III] has refused his Assent to Laws, the most wholesome and necessary for the public good." Does that not apply to the refusal of many urban jurisdictions to make it easier for people to legally arm and protect themselves from the criminal element? In addition, our government virtually refuses to execute murderers and often sets them free to kill again.

Another complaint was that "He has called together legislative bodies at places unusual, uncomfortable, and distant . . ." Have you ever been to a hearing to consider legislation regulating or banning guns held during the week when the gun owners are at work? The Senate provided another example with the midnight deals cooked up by Senators Dole and Mitchell, followed by passage of the Brady bill with only three Senators present and voting.

This complaint rings true still: "He has obstructed the Administration of Justice, by refusing his assent to Laws for establishing Judiciary Powers." Juries are prohibited from hearing whatever case a defendant wishes to make. Also, the jury's power to refuse to convict someone who has broken a law if that would be an injustice has been hidden from jurors. This has made a mockery of justice.

And finally, this one could be found in almost any daily paper: "He has erected a multitude of New Offices, and sent hither swarms of Officers to harass our people, and eat out their substance."

Government, Not the People, to Be Held Suspect

The words of the founding fathers reflected the actions they took during the War of Independence. Their view of government was one of deep suspicion. The task they set for themselves in establishing a government once they had thrown off the British tyranny was to limit and restrain their own creation.

A couple of Jefferson quotes are illustrative: "When the people fear the government there is tyranny." And, "The strongest reason for the people to retain the right to keep and bear arms is, as a last resort. to protect themselves against tyranny in government."

Patrick Henry warned during the Virginia Ratifying Convention debates over adoption of the present Constitution: "Guard with jealous attention the public liberty. Suspect every one who approaches that jewel. Unfortunately, nothing will preserve it but downright force. Whenever you give up that force, you are inevitably ruined." What exactly was Henry warning of? He foresaw that the new government would dangerously centralize power unto itself. In Henry's words, it would "oppress and ruin the people."

Even a defender of the new Constitution, James Madison, (author of the Second Amendment) shared in *Federalist Paper* number 46 the same suspicion of government: "Besides, the advantage of being armed forms a barrier against the enterprises of ambition, more insurmountable than any which a simple government of any form can admit of. The governments of Europe are afraid to trust the people with arms. If they did, the people would certainly shake off the yoke of tyranny, as America did."

An ally of James Madison and George Washington, George Mason articulated his suspicion of government this way: "To disarm the people is the best and most effectual way to enslave them." Mason defined the militia as "the whole people, except for a few public officials." Noah Webster, a patriot and scholar, defined the militia similarly as "the effective part of the people at large."

Webster wrote that, "Before a standing army can rule, the people must be disarmed as they are in almost every kingdom in Europe. The supreme power in America cannot enforce unjust laws by the sword because the whole body of the people are armed, and constitute a force superior to any band of regular troops that can be, on any pretense, raised in the United States."

Militia Act of 1792

The first Congress of the United States under the new Constitution adopted the Bill of Rights. A few months later Congress enacted the Militia Act of 1792. That Act has two important lessons for understanding the meaning of the militia. First, the law required everyone covered by the act to have a military rifle and the ammunition for it. Second, military firearms were to be in peoples' homes, not in armories as in the case of the National Guard which did not exist at that time.

The Militia Act of 1792 helped put feet to the suspicions the Founders had of government. The militia was seen as a practical way of containing the dangerous potential of government.

Anti-gunners often ask regarding an AR-15 or an AK-47, "Why would anyone want a gun like that? You cannot hunt with it." Even if that were true, the answer constitutionally is, "So what?" Truly, the Second Amendment is not about hunting or target shooting as a recreation. Arguably, those pastimes are protected by the Ninth Amendment which says that "The enumeration in the Constitution of certain rights shall not be construed to deny or disparage others retained by the people."

AR-15s and other semi-automatic rifles should be in the hands of as many Americans as want them precisely because they make anti-gunners in general and many politicians in particular nervous. That was the express purpose the Founders had in mind for the Second Amendment.

Government Needs to Fear the People Again

When a government no longer fears the people, atrocities become possible such as the murder of members of Randy Weaver's family by U.S. Marshals and FBI agents. Emboldened by the lack of resistance when murdering women and children in Idaho, the Feds moved to Waco, Texas and slaughtered nearly 100 people, including four of their own agents.

Following on the heels of these acts, the government now has the audacity to insist that the militia be disarmed by the illegalization of semi-automatic rifles and shotguns. Why should they not be so bold? After all, where was the outcry when they first restricted, then outlawed new machine guns? The politicians of this century have been able to accomplish a more effective disarmament of the American militia than George III and his minions such as General Gage, Governor Dunmore and others.

The events in Lincoln County, Montana and many other similar activations of the militia in counties across America are one of the most hopeful signs for the preservation of liberty in our time. One can only speculate had there been an effective militia in Naples, Idaho which could have been mobilized after the U.S. Marshal murdered Sammy Weaver by shooting him in the back. It is entirely possible that Vicki Weaver would not have been murdered later on by an FBI trained assassin while she was holding a baby in her arms.

Had the Feds feared a militia as active as the one in Lexington on April 19, 1775, it is entirely possible that the massacre of Branch Davidians in Waco, Texas on April 19, 1993 would never have occurred.

Long live the militia! Long live freedom! Long live a government that fears the people!

The Historical Bases of
The Right to Keep and Bear Arms

David Hardy

In analyzing the right to keep and bear arms, we must constantly keep in mind that it is one of the few rights in the Constitution which can claim any considerable antiquity. Freedom of the press, for instance, had little ancestry in common law: statutes requiring a government license to publish any works on political or religious matters were in effect in England until 1695, when they were allowed to expire for economic, not libertarian, reasons.[1] Long after that date, prosecutions after-the-fact for seditious libel were common. In the Colonies, these and similar statutes were likewise enforced and offending religious material was burned in Massachusetts as late as 1723.[2] Protests against general search warrants did not become common until after 1760, and the invalidity of such warrants at common law was not recognized until the eve of the American Revolution.[3]

David T. Hardy received his Bachelor of Arts degree from the University of Arizona where he graduated *cum laude* in 1972. He received his Juris Doctorate from the University of Arizona College of Law in 1975. Hardy has written extensively in the area of law and firearms regulation. He is the co-author of a lengthy article titled: "Of Arms and the Law," *51 Chicago-Kent Law Review* 62 (1974), author of "Firearms Ownership and Regulation," *20 William and Mary Law Review,* 235 (1978) and "Gun Laws and Gun Collectors," *85 Case & Comment 3* (Jan.–Feb. 1978.) Hardy wrote a scholarly essay, "Historical Bases of the Right to Keep and Bear Arms," for the Subcommittee on the Constitution's report, *The Right to Keep and Bear Arms* (Report of the Subcommittee on the Constitution of the Committee on the Judiciary, United States Senate, 97th Congress 2nd Session). That essay is reprinted here.

---

[1] W. Churchill, *A History of the English Speaking Peoples,* p. 168 (1957). E. W. Williams, *The Eighteenth Century Constitution,* pp. 399-401 (Cambridge University, 1960). Despite existence of this censorship, freedom of press was completely omitted from the 1688 "Declaration of Rights."

[2] 1 John Tebbel, *A History of Book Publishing in the United States,* p. 45 (1972).

[3] In 1763, to be precise, when John Wilkes won substantial civil awards against ministers who issued general warrants for search and arrest of those responsible for an alleged seditious libel, G. Rude, *Wilkes and Liberty,* pp. 27-29 (1962); Churchill, supra, at 165-67. "From the 'Glorious Revolution' onwards, Secretaries of State had, for nearly a hundred years, been issuing similar warrants . . . and until April 1763, their validity had never been challenged in a Court of Law." Rude, supra, at 29.

In contrast to these rights, the right to keep and bear arms can claim an ancestry stretching for well over a millennium. The antiquity of the right is so great that it is all but impossible to document its actual beginning. It is fairly clear that its origin lay in the customs of Germanic tribes, under which arms bearing was a right and a duty of free men; in fact, the ceremony for giving freedom to a slave required that the former slave be presented with the armament of a free man.[4] He then acquired the duty to serve in an equivalent of a citizen army. These customs were brought into England by the earliest Saxons. The first mention of the citizen army, or the "fyrd," is found in documents dating to 690 A.D. but scholars have concluded that the duty to serve in such with personal armament "is older than our oldest records." (Not knowing of the earlier records, 18th century legal historians, including the great Blackstone, attributed the origin of the English system to Alfred the Great, who ruled in the late 9th century A.D.)[5]

This viewpoint of individual armament and duty differed greatly from the feudal system which was coming into existence in Europe. The feudal system presupposed that the vast bulk of fighting duties would fall to a small warrior caste, composed primarily of the mounted knight. These individuals held the primary political and military power. Thus peasant armament was a threat to the political status quo. In England, on the other hand, a system evolved whereby peasant armament became the great underpinning of the status quo and individual armament became viewed as a right rather than a threat.

This in turn significantly changed the evolution of political systems in Britain. Since so much military power lay with the private citizen, the traditional monarchy was necessarily much more a limited monarchy than an absolute one. Even after the Norman Conquest of 1066, which brought feudal systems into Britain, kings regularly appealed to the people for assistance. William Rufus, second Norman king of England, was driven to appeal to the citizenry to put down a rebellion of feudal barons. To obtain the assistance of the individual armed citizen, he promised the people of England to provide better laws than had ever been made, to rescind all new taxes instituted during his reign, and to annul the hated

---

[4] Charles Hollister, *Anglo-Saxon Military Institutions*, p. 27 (Oxford University, 1962). Hollister's excellent study is matched only by Brooks "The Development of Military Obligations in Eighth and Ninth Century England," in *England Before the Conquest*, p. 69 (Clemoes and Hughes, eds., Cambridge University, 1971).

[5] William Blackstone, *Commentaries on the Common Law of England*, Book 1, Ch. XIII; 1 J. Bagley & P. Rowly, *A Documentary History of England 1066-1540*, p. 152.

forest laws which imposed draconian punishments; inspired by his promises, the citizenry rose with their arms and defended his government against the rebels.[6] After his death, his brother, Henry I, often drilled the citizen units in person, seeking to appeal to the individual members. In short, kingship in Britain became a far more democratic affair than it would ever become on the Continent, due in major part to the individual armament of the British citizen.

The Angevin monarchs expanded this still farther. Henry II, who is considered the father of the common law, promulgated the Assize of Arms in 1181. This required all British citizens between 15 and 40 to purchase and keep arms. The type of arms required varied with wealth; the wealthiest had to provide themselves with full armor, sword, dagger and war horse, while even the poorest citizens, "the whole community of freemen," must have leather armor, helmet, and a lance.[7] Twice a year all citizens were to be inspected by the king's officials to insure that they possessed the necessary arms. Conversely, the English made it quite clear that the king was to be expected to depend exclusively upon his armed freemen. When rebellious barons forced John I to sign the Magna Carta in 1215, they inserted in its prohibitions a requirement that he "expel from the kingdom all foreign knights, crossbowmen, sergeants, and mercenaries, who have come with horses and weapons to the harm of the realm."

Henry III continued this tradition. In his 1253 Assize of Arms he expanded the age categories to include everyone between 15 and 60 years of age, and made a further modification which bordered on the revolutionary. Now, not only were freemen to be armed, but even "villeins," who were little more than serfs and were bound to the land. Now all "citizens, burgesses, free tenants, villeins and others from 15 to 60 years of age" were legally required to be armed.[8] Even the poorest classes of these were required to have a halberd (a pole arm with an axe and spike head) and a knife, plus a bow if they owned lands worth over two pounds sterling.

---

[6] H. W. C. Davis, *England Under the Normans and Angevins*, p. 75 (1957).

[7] 1 Francis Grose, *Military Antiquities Respecting a History of the British Army*, pp. 9-11 (London, 1812). "Assize" was a term which had several meanings in medieval law. In this sense it signified a proclamation or piece of legislation which was intended to modify or expand traditional law, rather than simply construe it—the earliest form of what we today would consider true legislation. W. L. Warren, *Henry II*, p. 281 (1973).

[8] Bagley & Rowley, supra, pp. 155-56.

The role of the armed citizen expanded under the rule of the four Edwards. During civil wars in Wales, Edward I discovered the utility of the Welsh longbow, an extremely potent bow (its pull was estimated to have been between 100-200 pounds, whereas today a 60-pound bow is considered extremely powerful) which could penetrate the heaviest armor. Unlike the crossbow (and to an even greater extent, the armor and horse of the mounted knight) the longbow could be made cheaply enough and maintained easily enough to become the universal armament of all citizens. While on the Continent so deadly a weapon was considered a threat to the rule of the armored knight, in Britain its use was encouraged by the monarch. At Crecy, Poitiers and Agincourt, the longbow in the hands of British commoners decimated the French armored knights. By 1369 Edward III was ordering the sheriffs of London to require "everyone of said city stronge in body, at leisure time on holidays" to use in their recreation "bowes and arrows."[9] He hardly needed the encouragement; the archery ranges outside London were so constantly swamped with arrows that no grass would grow upon them. Edward IV continued this policy, commanding that "every Englishman or Irishman dwelling in England must have a bow of his own height," and commanding that each town build and maintain an archery range upon which every citizen must practice on feast days."[10] In 1470 he banned games of dice, horseshoes, and tennis in order to force citizens to use nothing but the bow for sport.[11] He imposed price controls on bows in order to ensure that bows would be inexpensive enough for even the poorest citizen to purchase them.[12]

While the common law sought to force all commoners to possess what was then the most deadly military weapon, it also imposed only the most minimal restraints upon use of that weapon. These focused purely upon criminal misuse of the weapon or its transportation into certain highly protected areas. In 1279, for instance, those coming before the royal courts were required to "come without all force and armor."[13] The Statute of Arms, whose date of enactment is uncertain, required that spectators at tournaments attend without armament and that those participating in

---

[9] E. G. Heath, *The Grey Goose Wing*, p. 109 (1971).

[10] Robert Hardy, *The Longbow: A Social and Military History*, p. 129 (1977).

[11] *Ibid.*

[12] *Ibid.*, p. 128. These price limitations would be repeated through to the reign of Henry VIII, along with requirements for import of longbows and quotas on less expensive longbows.

[13] 7 Edward I c.2 (1279).

the tournament carry swords without points.[14] The 1328 Statute of Northampton prohibited anyone, other than the king's servants or citizens attempting to keep the peace, from coming before the king's ministers "with force and arms," or acting "in affray of the peace," and from going or riding "armed by night or by day in fairs, markets, nor in the presence of the justices nor other ministers nor in no part elsewhere. . . ."[15] In light of the common law preference for individual armament, however, English courts construed this to mean that only carrying of arms in a threatening or terrifying manner was prohibited. In the words of William Harkins in his *Pleas of the Crown*, "no wearing of arms is within the meaning of the statute, unless it be accompanied with such circumstances as are apt to terrify the people; from which it seems to follow, that persons of quality are in no danger of offending against the statute by wearing common weapons. . . ."[16] Thus the sole common law restraints upon use of armament in this period focused either upon carrying into specially protected areas or upon what today would be considered assault with a deadly weapon.

While firearms had been invented sometime before, only in the 16th century did they become truly portable with the invention of the wheel lock. This breakthrough inspired a number of attempts in Europe and England to control weaponry. The Emperor Maximilian attempted to impose bans upon wheel lock manufacture throughout his empire on the Continent; the French imposed strict controls both upon manufacture and sale of firearms and upon assembly of ammunition and making of powder.[17] The English briefly experimented with such but found them repugnant to their institutions. Henry VII had in 1503 banned the shooting of crossbows upon an extremely limited basis.[18] First, only shooting and not possession was outlawed, and that only without a license or "placarde" from the king. Secondly, an exception was made for those who shot in defense of a residence ("but if he shote aw of a howse for the lawefull defen of the same") and for lords who owned land worth 200 marks per year. Third, as might be surmised from the ban upon shooting

---

[14] 1 *Statutes of the Realm*, pp. 151, 230 (London, 1810).

[15] 2 Edw. III c.3 (1328).

[16] 1 W. Hawkins, *Pleas of the Crown*, p. 267 (6th ed., 1788). See also *Rex v. Knight*, 87 Eng. Rep. 75 (King's Bench, 1686); *Rex v. Dewhurst*, 1 State Trials (New Series) 529 (1820).

[17] L. Kennet & J. Anderson, *The Gun in America*, pp. 12, 15 (1975); N. Perring, *Giving Up the Gun*, p. 58 (1975).

[18] 19 Henry VI c.4 (1503).

5

rather than upon ownership, the purpose was to force citizens to use the longbow, which was considered a much deadlier weapon.

His successor Henry VIII was a great devotee of the longbow and early in his reign attempted to push its use by still more vigorous means. In 1511 he enacted "an act concerning shooting in longe bowes" which banned games, required fathers to purchase bows for sons between the ages of 7 and 14 and to "lern theym and bryng theym up in shootyng." From age 14 until 40 each non-disabled citizen was obliged to practice longbow shooting and also to have bow and arrows "contynually in hys house." Anyone who failed to own and use a longbow was subject to a fine. The ban upon crossbows was renewed and the property requirement for such was raised to 300 marks.[19]

In 1514 Henry extended the ban upon crossbows to include "hand-gonnes" (which at that time meant any firearm carried by hand, as opposed to cannons, rather than what are today called "pistols"), and to extend the ban to possession as well as shooting.[20] Once again the intent was to force ownership and use of the longbow in place of the less efficient firearms of the time.

Unlike his continental equivalents, Henry was soon forced to give up his attempt at gun control. In 1523 the property qualification was lowered from 300 pounds sterling to only 100 pounds, and the penalty was reduced from imprisonment and a fine to a fine only.[21] In 1541 the statute was again amended (adding in its preface a protest that despite the earlier law people "have used and yet doe daylie ryde and go in the King's highwayes and elsewhere, having with them crosbowes and little handguns") to permit ownership of the longer arms (over three-quarters of a yard or one yard in total length, depending upon type) by any citizen, and ownership of the shorter arms by citizens with over 100 pounds' worth of land.[22] It also prohibited shooting within a quarter of a mile of a town except upon a range "or for defense of his person or house," and provided that "it shall be laufull from henceforth to all gentlemen, yeomen and servingmen . . . and to all the inhabitants of citties, boroughes and markett townes of this realme of Englande to shote with any handgune, demyhake or hagbutt at anye butt or bank of earth

---

19 3 Henry VIII c.3, 13 (1511).

20 6 Henry VIII c.13 (1514).

21 14 & 15 Henry VIII c.7 (1523).

22 33 Henry VIII c.6 (1541).

. . . to have and kepe in everie of their houses any such handgune or handgunes . . . with the intent to use and shote the same at a butt or bank of earth . . . this present act or anythinge therein conteyned to the contrarie notwithstandinge." Eventually Henry gave up the entire effort and simply rescinded his firearm laws by proclamation.[23] Weapons control—at least that which limited armament rather than required it—was recognized as repugnant to the English system. Indeed, the Tudor legal commentator Sir John Fortescue would comment (in his comparison between the happy state of peasants in England, with its limited monarchy, and the unhappy state of peasants in France, with absolute monarchy) that the French peasants were so poorly off that they not only starved but could not have any "Wepen" or the means to obtain it.[24] The consciousness of English as a weapons-owning and weapons-using people, in contrast to the French and other Continentals, was beginning to take form.

Under Elizabeth I the English militia system developed still farther; indeed, it was during her reign that the phrase "militia" was first used to describe the concept of a universally armed people ready to stand in defense of their nation.[25] The militia were now mustered by bounty lieutenants and called to formal musters to display and practice with their weapons.[26] Elizabeth also sought the creation of "trained bands," which were small militia units given special training and provided with governmentally purchased arms.[27]

Her efforts largely decayed under her successor James I, who permitted repeal of some of the most important militia statutes. His successor, Charles I, paid the price. Increasing hostility from Parliament, which was now beginning to assert itself as a distinct legislative body, brought the kingdom to the brink of civil war. The king compromised,

---

[23] Perrin, supra, pp. 59-60.

[24] "Thai goncrokyd, and ben feble, not able to fight, nor to defend ye realm; nor thai have wepen, nor money to bie thaim wepen withall." Sir John Fortescue, *The Governance of England*, p. 114 (C. Plummer, ed., Oxford, 1885). The Venetian ambassador to France confirmed this in a 1537 report of peasants taken into military service: "They were brought up in slavery, with no experience of handling weapons, and since they have suddenly passed from total servitude to freedom, sometimes they no longer want to obey their master." 1 R. Laffont, *The Ancient Art of Warfare*, p. 485 (1966).

[25] Jim Hill, *The Minutemen in War and Peace*, pp. 26-27 (1968). "Militia" was apparently derived from the French word "milice" which in turn can be related to the Latin term "miles," or soldier.

[26] The foremost study of the militia system under Elizabeth is Lindsay Boynton, *The Elizabethan Militia* (1967).

[27] C. G. Cruikshank, *Elizabeth's Army*, pp. 24-25 (2d ed., 1968).

sending his best advisor to the scaffold, but when Parliament asked for control over the militia he exploded. "By God, not for an hour, you have asked that of me in this, which was never asked of a king,"[28] he replied. An unsuccessful attempt to arrest five members of Parliament on charges of treason led to the final breach. The five members were protected by the London militia, and the king was forced to flee the city and attempt to muster his own army.

As the civil war wore on, Parliament was at length driven to create the "New Model Army," a standing body of veteran troops who were predominantly Puritan.[29] They were rigorously disciplined under the leadership of Oliver Cromwell, who eventually rose to head the army, and with their aid Parliament ended as the victor in the civil war. But in July 1647 the New Model Army (alienated by a failure of pay and by the anti-Puritan measures of the Parliament) marched on London and took over the government. On December 6, 1648, troops, acting on Cromwell's orders, surrounded the Parliament building and drove off over 140 members. The remainder formed what became known as "the Rump Parliament." By 1653 even the Rump was an impediment to Cromwell and he used his troops to totally shut down parliamentary government; the army officers then selected a new Parliament composed largely of Puritan elders. A short time later Cromwell pressured its dissolution and in 1654 he replaced it with yet another Parliament, in whose election only those whose land was worth over 200 pounds sterling could vote. This Parliament in turn, named Cromwell "Lord Protector" and king of England in all but name. Yet a year later Cromwell dissolved even this Parliament and established a military dictatorship, dividing the nation into eleven districts, each headed by a major general whose duties included political surveillance, censorship of publications, and influencing future elections.[30] A major factor in the dissolution of several of these parliaments was their attempt to adopt new militia statutes; Cromwell, who controlled the "New Model Army," had little interest in permitting Parliament to reorganize the militia.

Following Cromwell's death, the English were more than happy to accept back the son of the late Charles, Charles II, as monarch. Charles

---

[28] Richard Ollard, *This War Without an Enemy*, p. 53 (1976).

[29] See generally Correlli Barnett, *Britain's Army*, pp. 89-90 (1970); Charles Firth, *Cromwell's Army* (1962).

[30] Michael Gruber, *The English Revolution*, p. 125 (1967); Barnett, supra, p. 107.

II promptly dissolved the army, offering full pay plus a bonus from his own finances, and guaranteeing work on public works projects for the demobilized troops.[31] He also sought to secure himself by a variety of legislation which people in Parliament, in their haste to welcome the end of Puritan rule, did not recognize as dictatorial. In 1661 and 1662 he expanded the definition of treason, imposed press censorship, restricted practice of religion by Puritans and others and leveled the protective walls of many towns which had sided with Parliament.[32] Instructions were also issued to the lord's lieutenant to form special militia units out of volunteers of favorable political views, "the officers to be numerous, disaffected persons watched and not allowed to assemble, and their arms seized. . . ."[33] The excessive searches for arms under that order led to Parliamentary resistance and refusal to grant a militia bill in the sessions of 1660 and 1661.[34] Only in 1662 was Charles able to obtain a militia statute pleasing to him. The 1662 statute permitted the King to appoint lieutenants for each county and major city; these lieutenants could charge persons with the responsibility of equipping and paying a militia man. But not every Englishman was required to be armed or serve, and those who were required could always hire a substitute to appear for them. The lieutenants were moreover empowered to hire persons "to search for and seize all arms in the custody or possession of any person or persons whom the said lieutenant or any two or more of their deputies shall judge dangerous to the peace of the kingdom. . . ."[35] The Calendar of State Papers for the period is filled with reports of confiscations of weapons from suspicious persons and religious independents.[36] Charles also by proclamation ordered gunsmiths to produce records of all firearms sold; importation of firearms from overseas was banned; and carriers through-

---

[31] John Childs, *The Army of Charles II*, p. 9 (1976).

[32] Joyce Malcolm, *Disarmed: The Loss of the Right to Bear Arms in Restoration England*, p. 11 (Mary Ingraham Bunting Institute, Radcliffe College, 1980).

[33] 8 *Calendar of State Papers (Domestic) Charles II*, No. 188, p. 150 (July 1660).

[34] J. R. Western, *The English Militia in the Eighteenth Century*, pp. 11-13 (1965).

[35] 14 Caar.II c.3 (1662). The political background of the passage of this enactment is discussed in Western, supra, p. 11.

[36] A few examples: "Think Fauntleroy an untoward fellow; arms for thirty or forty were found in his house last year," 68 *Calendar of State Papers (Domestic) Charles II*, No. 35, p. 44 (February 1662); [Jacob Knowles, arrested for] "dangerous designs, he having been taken on the guard with a pistol upon him," 70 *Calendar of State Papers (Domestic), Charles II*, No. 13, p. 83 (March 1662); "Hearing of a nonconformist meeting, issued warrant for the search of arms; the officers being denied entrance broke open the doors, and found 200 or 300 persons," 88 *Calendar of State Papers (Domestic) Charles II*, No. 56, p. 32.

out the realm were forbidden to transport firearms without first obtaining a license. (The resemblance between these measures and the American Gun Control Act of 1968 is astonishing.)

In 1671 this was followed with an amendment to the Hunting Act. Hunting was restricted to those who owned lands worth 100 pounds and, most importantly, those who could not hunt (who formed the vast bulk of the kingdom) were "declared to be persons by the laws of this realm, not allowed to have or keep for themselves, or any other person or persons, any guns, bows, greyhounds. . . ."[37] "Guns" were an addition to the list: All but the wealthiest of land owners could be disarmed. As Charles's reign wore on he encountered increasing opposition from Parliament and from what was becoming the Whig party. This he met by such drastic measures as moving the sitting of Parliament from London (which was quite favorable to the Whigs) to Oxford, and by arresting and executing several Whig leaders on charges of treason. Charles survived, but it was a close race.

James II, Charles's brother and successor, would not be so lucky. He continued to enforce the laws on disarmament, directing them with increasing force against Puritans and his political opponents. Moreover he used his "dispensing power" to permit Catholic officers to stay with the army. He sought to obtain permission to expand the standing army complaining that during rebellion the militia "is not sufficient for such occasions, and that there is nothing but a good force of well disciplined troops in constant pay that can defend us. . . ."[38] Parliament refused, but James kept a limited standing army on foot from his own resources. In 1686 he issued orders to six lord lieutenants complaining that "a great many persons not qualified by law, under pretense of shooting matches, keep muskets or other guns in their houses," and that he desired them to "cause strict search to be made for such muskets or guns and to seize and safely keep them until further order."[39] In Ireland he ordered General Richard Tyrconnel to disarm the populace:

A royal order came from Whitehall for disarming the population. This order Tyrconnel strictly executed as he respected the English. Although the country was infested by predatory bands, a Protestant

---

[37] 22 & 23 Car. II, c. 25 (1671).

[38] Andrew Browning, *English Historical Documents 1660-1714*, p. 81 (1953).

[39] 2 *Calendar of State Papers (Domestic) James II*, No. 1212, p. 314 (December 1686).

gentleman could scarcely obtain permission to keep a brace of pistols.[40]

These measures did James little good; in 1688 his son-in-law and daughter, William of Orange and Mary, entered the nation in a supposed "invasion" which came to be known as "the Glorious Revolution." After defection of a number of his nobility and refusal of the militia to fight, James fled to the Continent.

This left Parliament with an interesting question: Was James king and, if not, how did they go about putting William and Mary on the throne? They approached this problem by promulgating a Declaration of Rights, which listed complaints against James and argued that these had forfeited him the right to rule. After William accepted this Declaration as definitive of the rights of Englishmen, he was permitted to assume the throne and call a Parliament, which then reenacted the Declaration as the Bill of Rights.[41]

The Declaration and Bill of Rights were later said to be "the essence of the revolution";[42] only a year before the adoption of the American Bill of Rights, the great English jurist Edmund Burke would refer to the Declaration as "the cornerstone of our Constitution."[43] The Declaration listed a variety of civil liberties which James was accused of infringing. Prominent among these was the right to keep and bear arms. The form finally adopted complained that James had violated the liberties of the kingdom by keeping a standing army and moreover by causing his Protestant subjects "to be disarmed at the same time when Papists were both armed and employed contrary to law." It accordingly resolved that "the subjects which are Protestant may have arms for their defense suitable to their conditions and as allowed by law."[44] Since only slightly over one percent of the population was then Catholic, this amounted to a general right to own arms applicable to virtually all Englishmen. The possible restriction—that they be arms "as allowable by law"—was clarified by prompt amendment of the Hunting Act to remove the word "guns" from items which even the poorest Englishman was not permitted

---

[40] 3 Thomas Macaulay, *The History of England in the Accession of Charles II*, pp. 136-37 (London, 1856).

[41] 1 Gul. & Mar., sess. 2, c.2 (1689).

[42] James Jones, *The Revolution of 1688 in England*, pp. 316-17 (London, 1972).

[43] L. Brevold & R. Ross, *The Philosophy of Edmund Burke*, p. 192 (1970).

[44] 1 Gul. & Mar., sess. 2, c.2 (1689).

to own. Now all Englishmen could own arms "for their defense suitable to their conditions and as allowed by law" in the form of whatever firearms they desired.[45]

A few modern writers, none of whom cite any historical evidence, have claimed that the Bill of Rights was directed not so much at disarmament as at the fact that Catholics were permitted to be armed while the Protestants had been disarmed.[46] The statutory history of the Declaration of Rights proves beyond any doubt that this is totally incorrect. The debates in the House of Commons, as recorded by Lord Somers, the principal draftsman of the Declaration, show that the Members focused on the confiscation of private arms collections under the 1662 Militia Act. Sergeant Maynard, for instance, complains of James: "Can he sell or give away his subjects; an act of Parliament was made to disarm all Englishmen, whom the lieutenant should suspect, by day or by night, by force or otherwise—this was done in Ireland for the sake of putting arms into Irish hands." Somers condensed a speech by Sir Richard Temple to "Militia bill—power to disarm all England—now done in Ireland." A Mr. Boscawen complained of "arbitrary power exercised by the ministry—militia—imprisoning without reason; disarming—himself disarmed. . . ." Sergeant Maynard complained of the "Militia Act—an abominable thing to disarm the nation. . . ."[47]

The Lords felt even more strongly about the issue. The Commons originally passed a declaration simply declaring that "the acts concerning the militia are grievous to the subject" and that "it is necessary for the public safety that the subjects which are Protestant should provide and keep arms for the common defense; and that the arms which have been seized and taken from them be restored."[48] The Lords apparently felt this did not state the individual rights strongly enough and completely omitted the language "subjects which are Protestant may have arms for their defense suitable to their conditions and as allowed by law."[49] The language referring to the fact that Catholics were armed while the

---

[45] Joyce Malcolm, *Disarmed: The Loss of the Right to Keep and Bear Arms in Restoration England*, p. 16 (Mary Ingraham Bunting Institute, Radcliffe College, 1980).

[46] See Rohner, *The Right to Bear Arms: A Phenomenon of Constitutional History*, p. 16, *Cath. U. Law Rev.* pp. 53, 59 (1966).

[47] 2 Philip, *Earl of Hardwicke, Miscellaneous State Papers from 1501-1726*, pp. 407-17 (London, 1778).

[48] *Journal of the House of Commons from December 26, 1688 to October 26, 1693*, pp. 5, 6, 21-22 (London, 1742).

[49] Western, supra, p. 339.

disarmaments were proceeding was added only at conference, with the Lords suggesting that it was a "further aggravation" to the underlying illegality and therefore "fit to be mentioned."[50] Indeed, the modern British historian J. R. Western complains that the modifications by the House of Lords created too much of an individual right: "The original wording implied that everyone had a duty to be ready to appear in arms whenever the state was threatened. The revised wording suggested only that it was lawful to keep a blunderbuss to repel burglars."[51]

The "Glorious Revolution" also gave birth to the political philosophy which underlay the American Revolution less than a century later. The two major British parties, the Whigs and the Tories, had achieved both their essence and their names during the fight under Charles II to exclude his brother James II from the succession to the throne. One of the major points of the Whig philosophy was the need for a true militia, in the sense which England had it during the Tudor years, and the scrapping of the standing army. All the major Whig authors stressed this point; Algernon Sidney counseled that "no state can be said to stand on a steady foundation, except those whose whole strength is in their own soldiery, and the body of their own people";[52] Robert Molesworth advised that with standing armies "the people are contributors to their own misery; and their purses are drained in order to their misery,"[53] while attacking disarmament under the game laws with the argument that "I hope no wise man will put a hare or a partridge in balance with the safety and liberties of Englishmen."[54] These and other Whig authors were to be found in the library of every American political thinker during the years before the Revolution;[55] John Adams himself would estimate that ninety percent of Americans were at that time Whigs by sentiment.[56]

---

[50] *Journal of the House of Commons*, supra, p. 25.

[51] Western, supra, p. 339.

[52] Algernon Sidney, *Discourses Concerning Government*, p. 156 (3d ed., London, 1751) (Library of Congress, Rare Books Collection).

[53] Robert Molesworth, *An Account of Denmark, As It Was in The Year 1692*, p. 123 (London, 1692; reprinted Copenhagen, 1976).

[54] Francis Hotoman, *Franco-Gallia*, XXVIII (Tr. by Robert Molesworth, 1721) (Library of Congress, Rare Books Collection).

[55] But a few examples: In 1773, Harvard's library contained Harrington and Molesworth; Sidney was added by 1790. The College of New Jersey (today Princeton) boasted Sidney by 1760, as did the New York Society Library. John Adams's private library contained a two-volume edition of Sidney and Molesworth; Jefferson at various times bought several different editions of both authors. H. Colbourn, *The Lamp of Experience*, pp. 200-18 (1965).

[56] Clinton Rossiter, *The Political Thought of the American Revolution*, p. 55 (1963).

Notwithstanding this growing support for a true militia, the use of the militia system in Britain steadily declined. By 1757, when a new Militia Act was adopted, only 32,000 men, a very small part of the population, were to serve.[57] The officers were to be chosen from the more wealthy of the gentry; property qualifications were imposed for all commissioned officers. The government would issue the arms to the militia, which were to be kept under lock and key, and could be seized by the lieutenant or deputy lieutenant of the county whenever he "shall adjudge it necessary to the peace of the kingdom."[58] The Whigs considered this "select militia" as little better than a standing army: It was hardly a true "militia," an armed citizenry. In the debates over the Scottish militia act, the Lord Mayor of London argued to the Commons that the militia "could not longer be deemed a constitutional defense, under the immediate control and direction of the people; for by that bill they were rendered a standing army for all intents and purpose."[59] This background—that of a tradition of an armed citizenry met with recent infringements upon the traditional right of bearing arms—formed the background of the political views of the Framers of our own Constitution.

The American experience with citizen armament had been more extensive even than that of Britain. The early colonists brought their own arms and secured additional ones from the government. As early as September 1622, they were being armed not only with muskets but with "three hundred short pistols with firelocks."[60] Virginia in 1623 ordered that no one was to "go or send abroad without a sufficient party well armed" and each plantation was to insure that there was "sufficient of powder and ammunition within the plantation."[61] In 1631 it ordered that no one work their fields unarmed and required militia musters on a weekly basis following church services: "All men that are fittinge to bear armes, shall bring their peeces to church. . . ."[62] By 1673 the colony provided that persons unable to purchase firearms from their own

---

[57] Barnett, supra, p. 174.

[58] 30 Geo. II, c.2 (1757). This power was invoked during the waves of rioting which spread across the English nation in 1766. Tony Hayter, *The Army and the Crowd in Mid-Georgian England*, p. 158 (1978).

[59] *The North British Intelligencer*, vol. 1, p. 20 (Edinburgh, 1776) (Library of Congress, Rare Books Collection).

[60] Harold Gill, *The Gunsmith in Colonial Virginia*, p. 3 (1974).

[61] 1 William Henning, *The Statutes at Large: Being a Collection of All the Laws of Virginia from the First Session of the Legislature in the Year 1619*, p. 127 (New York, 1823).

[62] *Ibid.*, pp. 173-74.

finances would be supplied guns by the government and required to pay a reasonable price when able to do so. Similar legislation was imposed in the other colonies. The first session of the legislature of the New Plymouth colony required "that every free man or other inhabitant of this Colony provide for himself and each under him able to beare armes, a sufficient musket and other serviceable peece for war" with other equipment.[63] Similar measures were enacted in Connecticut in 1650.

When the colonies began drifting toward revolution following the elections of 1760, the colonists were thus well equipped for their role. The British government began extensive troop movements into Boston in 1768 to reduce opposition, and the town government responded by urging its citizens to arm themselves and be prepared to defend themselves against the deprivations of the soldiers. When Tories responded that this order was illegal, the colonial newspapers responded that the right of personal armament was guaranteed to every Englishman. The *Boston Evening Post* asserted that "It is certainly beyond human art and sophistry, to prove that the British subjects, to whom the privilege of possessing arms is expressly recognized by the Bill of Rights, and who live in a province where the law requires them to be equipped with arms, are guilty of an illegal act, in calling upon one another to be provided with them, as the law directs."[64] The *New York Journal Supplement* argued that the proposal "was a measure as prudent as it was legal" and "it is a natural right which the people have reserved to themselves, confirmed by the Bill of Rights, to keep arms for their own defense. . . ."[65] There can be little doubt from these passages that the American colonists viewed the English 1688 Declaration of Rights as recognizing an individual right to own private firearms for self defense—even defense against government agents.

Years passed before these proposals were actually put into effect, but the warning signs were present long before the revolution itself broke out, and some British heeded them. William Pitt, the great Whig minister and friend of the colonies, had warned that "three millions of Whigs, with arms in their hands, are a very formidable body."[66] Rather than the

---

[63] William Brigham, *The Compact with the Charter and Laws of the Colony of New Plymouth*, p. 31 (Boston, 1836).

[64] Oliver Dickerson, ed., *Boston Under Military Rule*, p. 61 (1936).

[65] *Ibid.*, p. 79.

[66] 1 William Gordon, *The History of the Rise, Progress and Establishment of the Independence of the United States*, pp. 442-43 (London, 1788) (Library of Congress, Rare Books Collection).

conciliation he called for, the result was an attempt to disarm the Americans—an attempt which brought on the Revolution. In December 1774, for instance, export of guns and powder to the colonies was prohibited.[67] When a group of British regulars quietly emptied a militia powder magazine in September of 1774, the reaction was dramatic. To some "it seemed part of a well designed plan to disarm the people";[68] others were inflamed by incorrect rumors that six colonists had been killed during the raid. Over 60,000 armed citizens turned out, heading toward Boston, prepared for war.[69] This was more men under arms than would be boasted by the entire British military establishment at the time. Fortunately for that establishment, the colonists were convinced that their actions were premature and returned to their homes. By September, a Massachusetts town had instituted "the Minutemen," a group of select militia.[70] Others formed special companies of militia—one of which in Virginia included George Washington and George Mason, who would later draft the Virginia Declaration of Rights.[71] In December the Maryland Convention called upon the colonies to form a "well-regulated militia" and illustrated what it meant by instructing all citizens between the ages of 16 and 50 to arm themselves and form into companies.[72] The following month the Fairfax Committee of Public Safety, chaired by George Washington, joined in this resolution, further defining its intent with the comment that "A well-regulated militia, composed of gentlemen, freeholders, and other freemen, is the natural strength and only security of a free government," and recommending all persons between 16 and 50 to "provide themselves with good fire-locks."[73] When Patrick Henry shortly thereafter gave his famed "give me liberty or give me death" speech, the resolution which he moved by his oration began, "Resolved, that a well-regulated militia, composed of gentlemen and freemen, is the natural strength and only security of a free government.[74]

---

[67] John Alden, *General Gage in America*, p. 224 (1948).

[68] Stephen Patterson, *Political Parties in Revolutionary Massachusetts*, p. 103 (1973).

[69] *Ibid.*

[70] *Ibid.*, pp. 104-105; Gavin, supra, p. 64.

[71] 1 Kate Rowland, *The Life of George Mason*, pp. 181, 430-32 (1892.)

[72] *Ibid.*, pp. 182-83; Donald Higginbotham, "The American Militia: A Traditional Institution with Revolutionary Responsibilities," in *Reconsiderations on the Revolutionary War*, p. 92 (1978).

[73] Rowland, supra, pp. 183, 427-28.

[74] Hezekiah Miles, republication of *The Principles and Acts of the Revolution in America*, p. 278 (New York, 1876).

16

The Colonials did not have long to wait. General Horatio Gage, military governor of Boston, was already writing to London with regard to the "idea of disarming certain counties."[75] In April of 1775, Gage made the mistake of repeating his earlier raid upon a militia arsenal. This time there was firing and a number of colonists were killed. The regulars were compelled to fight their way back to Boston, swamped under the harassing fire of militia who swarmed in on their flanks; without a last minute relief attack from Boston the entire column might have been forced to surrender by ammunition exhaustion. The British lost nearly 300 men in killed, wounded, and missing. Within a few days 16,000 militia descended upon Boston and besieged the area. During a British attack on Breeds Hill, colonial sharpshooters (one of whom commented that he fired "taking deliberate aim, as at a squirrel, and saw a number of men fall")[76] inflicted disastrous losses on British troops. Over 1,000 regulars fell, 40 percent of the attacking force and over a tenth of the entire British army in the Colonies. Officers suffered especially serious losses; one rifleman was said to have shot down twenty officers in ten minutes; every single member of Gage's staff was shot down.[77]

In the meantime the militia throughout the rest of the Colonies seized political control at the grass roots. Tories were quickly put down; British foraging parties cut off; the mechanisms of government and administration lay solidly in the hands of revolutionaries. While the British during the French and Indian War were supplied primarily from the Colonies, throughout the Revolution they would have to draw primarily from their homeland. The constant damage to British foraging parties ultimately led to a shipping problem which, one historian judges, would have ended the war by 1782 in any event.[78]

The militia played no minor role in the fighting: "Seldom has an armed force done so much with so little—providing a vast reservoir of manpower for a multiplicity of military needs, fighting (often unaided by Continentals) in the great majority of the 1,331 land engagements of the war."[79]

---

[75] 1 *The Political Writings of Thomas Paine*, p. 111 (Boston, 1856).

[76] Charles Flood, *Rise and Fight Again*, p. 61 (1976).

[77] Willard Wallace, *Appeal to Arms*, p. 43 (1951); Joe Huddleston, *Colonial Riflemen in the American Revolution*, p. 25 (1978).

[78] I. Christie, *Crisis of Empire*, p. 106 (1966).

[79] Higginbotham, supra, p. 103.

Following the war the colonies were temporarily governed under the Articles of Confederation, which permitted a federal force necessary to garrison forts and prohibited states from maintaining any standing forces. During these years a number of militia proposals were put forward to George Washington, Alexander Hamilton, Baron Steuben and Henry Knox.[80] All involved a general militia—in which essentially every free citizen would serve—and a "select militia." Steuben's proposal gave the greatest emphasis to the select militia; he would have had a small force of 21,000 select militiamen, chosen by volunteering, who would train one month out of each year. None of these proposals became law.

By 1787 the difficulties with the Articles of Confederation were becoming insurmountable, and work began on a new Constitution. As adopted, the Constitution gave Congress the power to provide "for organizing, arming and disciplining the militia" but it could "govern" only those in federal service, while the states would have the power of appointing officers and actually training the militia according to the uniform system of discipline. Militiamen would be subject to federal martial law only when called into active service.

In the state conventions called to ratify the Constitution, the proposal faced serious opposition. A major part of the opposition, later termed anti-Federalist, focused on the fact that the Constitution lacked a Bill of Rights. The British Bill of Rights was called into attention as a precedent for such a measure. In the conflicts in the states three themes relating to citizen armament soon became apparent. The first was the acceptance by both Federalist and anti-Federalist of the critical role of the armed citizen; the second was a distrust both of standing armies and of select militia, like the modern National Guard; the third was pressure for a Bill of Rights which would include provisions guaranteeing rights of individual armament.

These thoughts began to take form in Connecticut, the fourth state to ratify. An anti-Federalist article in the *Connecticut Journal* objected strongly to the failure to outlaw a standing army and went on to criticize the Constitution's militia provisions as permitting the formation of a select militia: "This looks too much like Baron Steuben's militia, by which a standing army was meant and intended."[81] In Pennsylvania the opposition

---

[80] The best study of these proposals is John McAuley Palmer's, *Washington, Lincoln, Wilson: Three War Statesmen* (1930). Palmer was responsible for locating Washington's militia plan, which had been missing from Congressional archives for over a century.

[81] 3 Merrill Jensen, ed., *The Documentary History of the Ratification of the Constitution*, p. 378 (1976).

became even stiffer as the sentiment for a Bill of Rights grew. In a pamphlet hurriedly written to support adoption of the Constitution without the Bill of Rights, Noah Webster argued that the existing universal citizen armament made a standing army of little danger. He claimed that a standing army is oppressive only when it is "superior to any force that exists among the people" since otherwise it "would be annihilated on the first exercise of acts of oppression." He advised that the general armament of Americans rendered any constitutional limitations on a standing army unnecessary:

> Before a standing army can rule, the people must be disarmed; as they are in almost every kingdom in Europe. The supreme power in America cannot enforce unjust laws by the sword; because the whole body of the people are armed and constitute a force superior to any band of regular troops that can be, on any pretense, raised in the United States.[82]

In the convention the fighting was heavy. Delegate John Smiley argued that "Congress may give us a select militia which will, in fact, be a standing army. . . . When a select militia is formed, the people in general may be disarmed."[83] (The universal hostility to a select militia forms a most convincing refutation to the current argument that the "militia" referred to in the Second Amendment is the National Guard. On the contrary, virtually every citation to such militia during the drafting and ratification period views them as an evil comparable to a standing army and stresses that only militia composed of the entire body of the populace armed and trained will protect freedom.) Ultimately, Delegate Robert Whitehill moved a series of fifteen proposed amendments which would have established a bill of rights protecting freedom of conscience, speech, press, and virtually every other right ultimately incorporated into the Bill of Rights. This proposal was not adopted in Pennsylvania but was widely read in the Colonies and formed the inspiration for later proposals.[84] Its provision of keeping and bearing arms made it very clear that the right protected was to be an individual right:

---

[82] Noah Webster, *An Examination Into The Leading Principles of The Federal Constitution Proposed by The Late Convention,* reprinted in Paul, Ford, ed., *Pamphlets on The Constitution of The United States,* p. 56 (New York, 1888).

[83] 2 Jensen, supra, p. 508.

[84] E. Dumbauld, *The Bill of Rights and What It Means Today,* p. 11 (1959).

That the people have a right to bear arms for the defense of themselves and their own state, or the United States, or for the purpose of killing game; and no law shall be passed for disarming the people or any of them, unless for crimes committed, or real danger of public injury from individuals. . . .[85]

In the Massachusetts Convention similar thoughts were expressed. Delegate Sedgwick asked whether a standing army "could subdue a nation of freemen, who know how to prize liberty, and who have arms in their hands?"[86] Sam Adams, who had done so much to bring on the revolution, spoke convincingly for the anti-Federalist position. He called for a bill of rights which would have provided "that the said Constitution shall never be construed to authorize Congress to infringe the just liberty of the press or the rights of conscience; or to prevent the people of the United States who are peaceable citizens from keeping their own arms."[87] Like the Pennsylvania minority, Adams clearly considered the right of armament as a right of individual citizens to own personal arms.

In the following months additional states ratified, bringing the total to eight. A ninth vote was needed before the necessary majority would be obtained and the Constitution would become binding upon the states which had ratified to date. That critical vote was provided by New Hampshire, which added to its ratification a recommendation for a bill of rights including the provision that "Congress shall never disarm any citizen unless such as are or have been in actual rebellion."[88] A clearer statement of an absolute individual right could not have been drafted. The major commercial state—New York—and major intellectual state—Virginia—still remained to be heard from.

The Virginia Convention set the record for legal and intellectual talent. Major participants included Patrick Henry, George Mason, James Madison and John Marshall. The major writings of the period come from Richard Henry Lee, who had in the Continental Congress moved the drafting of the Declaration of Independence. In his "Letters from the

---

[85] 2 Jensen, supra, p. 508.

[86] 2 Jonathan Elliot, ed., *Debates in The Several State Conventions on The Adoption of The Federal Constitution*, p. 97 (2d ed., 1888).

[87] Paul Lewis, *The Grand Incendiary*, pp. 359-60 (1973).

[88] Joseph Walker, *Birth of The Federal Constitution: A History of The New Hampshire Convention*, p. 51 (Boston, 1881); *Documents Illustrative of the Formation of the Union of the American States*, p. 1026 (House of Representatives Document 398: Government Printing Office, 1927).

Federal Farmer to the Republican" he warned that Congress might suddenly undermine the strength of the "yeomanry of the country" who possessed the lands, "possess arms, and are too strong a body of men to be openly offended."[89] He added "This might be done in a great measure by the Congress, if disposed to do it, by modeling the militia. Should one-fifth or one-eighth of the men capable of bearing arms be made a select militia, as has been proposed . . . and all the others put upon a plan that will render them of no importance, the former will answer all the purposes of an army, while the latter will be defenseless."[90] Like others in Connecticut and Pennsylvania, Lee feared a "select militia" similar to the modern National Guard, which he considered a betrayal of the militia tradition and similar to a standing army. In strong terms he advised:

> First, the Constitution ought to secure a genuine, and guard against a select militia, by providing that the militia shall always be kept well organized, armed and disciplined, and include, according to the past and general usage of the states, all men capable of bearing arms, and that all regulations tending to establish this general useless and defenseless, by establishing select corps of militia or distinct bodies of military men, not having permanent attachments in the community, to be avoided.[91]

He extensively criticized select militia and argued that on the contrary "to preserve liberty, it is essential that the whole body of people always possess arms, and be taught alike, especially when young, how to use them. . . ."[92] In the Convention, Patrick Henry seconded Lee's judgments. Henry joined with Lee—and with Sam Adams and others who defended individual armament—explaining that "The great object is that every man be armed" and that "Everyone who is able may have a gun."[93] While Virginia ratified, it did so with a call for a bill of rights, including a recognition "that the people have the right to keep and bear arms; that a

---

[89] Walter Bennett, ed., "Letters From the Federal Farmer to the Republican," p. 21 (1978).

[90] *Ibid.*, pp. 21-22.

[91] *Ibid.*, p. 124.

[92] *Ibid.*

[93] "Debates and Other Proceedings of The Convention of Virginia . . . taken in shorthand by David Robertson of Petersburg," p. 275 (2nd ed., Richmond, 1805).

well-regulated militia, composed of the body of the people trained to arms is the proper, natural and safe defense of a free state."[94]

From Virginia, the debate moved to New York. The New York controversy gave rise to the famed *Federalist Papers*. Since these were devoted to justifying the adoption of the Constitution without a Bill of Rights, they are at best of marginal utility in interpreting the early amendments to the Constitution. Even so, their authors stressed citizen armament as a bulwark of liberty which made adoption of the Constitution safe. Alexander Hamilton, no friend of the militia (and little friend of democracy, for that matter) attacked proposed limits on standing armies in *Federalists* 25 and 26. In *Federalist* 29 he suggested that militia could not be expected to tolerate much professional training: "little more can reasonably be aimed at with respect to the people at large than to have them properly armed and equipped." This armed but untrained citizenry, together with a select militia would ensure liberty despite a standing army: "That army can never be formidable to the liberties of the people while there is a large body of citizens, little if at all inferior to them in discipline and use of arms. . . ."

James Madison in *Federalist* 46 argued the point at greater length, stressing citizen armament and state governments as bulwarks of freedom:

> Besides the advantage of being armed, which the Americans possess over the people, the existence of subordinate governments, to which the people are attached and by which the militia officers are appointed, forms a barrier against the enterprises of ambition . . . notwithstanding the military establishments in the several kingdoms of Europe, which are carried as far as the public resources will bear, the governments are afraid to trust the people with arms.

If those people were armed and formed into militia units by subordinate governments, Madison asserted, "It may be affirmed with the greatest assurance that the throne of every tyranny in Europe would be speedily overturned in spite of the legions which surround it." To him citizen armament was not merely a matter of military service or collective defense, but a guarantee of all other freedoms, to be used if necessary, against the government.

---

[94] *Documents Illustrative of the Formation of the Union,* supra, p. 1030.

New York joined in ratifying, but by an even closer margin than most states: a shift of two votes out of fifty-seven cast would have rejected the Constitution. It proposed amendments, including a recognition "That the people have a right to keep and bear arms; that a well-regulated militia, including the body of the people capable of bearing arms, is the proper, natural, and safe defense of a free state."

Only a few weeks later, word came that North Carolina had joined Rhode Island in rejecting the proposed constitution, citing the lack of a bill of rights. Among the amendments they called for before the delegates would sign was a provision identical to the New York and Virginia "keep and bear arms" sections.

The Constitution thus went into effect with eleven ratifications. But the pressing need for a bill of rights was clear. Not only had two states repudiated the new Constitution, but five of the ratifying states had demanded such a bill and influential minorities in two more had striven unsuccessfully for it. (While freedom of speech was designated by only three ratifying states, the right to bear arms was mentioned by all five which called for a bill of rights, as well as by both groups of minority delegates and the dissenting North Carolina convention. This constitutional preference poll would suggest the ratifying conventions considered the right of private armament to be even more important than free speech.)

The Constitution carried in New York and eventually in every other state: but the anti-Federalist sentiment for a bill of rights also triumphed. Ultimately James Madison was put to the task of drafting a bill of rights. From the many proposals by the state conventions, he eventually distilled a limited number of rights deserving specific recognition, protecting the rest with the "catchall clauses" of the Ninth and Tenth Amendments. The rights given express recognition were primarily procedural. Only the First and Second Amendments created substantive rights and these were a very small number of rights: speech, press, assembly, and keeping and bearing arms. These were viewed as the critical matters upon which the federal government might not infringe, under any conditions (and even by proceeding in accord with the procedural guarantees of the Fourth, Fifth and Sixth Amendments). Madison's initial proposal for what became the Second Amendment was worded: "The right of the people to keep and bear arms shall not be infringed; a well-armed and well-regulated militia being the best security of a free country; but no person religiously scrupulous of bearing arms shall be compelled to render military service in person."

There is no doubt that Madison saw this as an individual right. His earliest drafts of the Bill of Rights did not separate those proposals into numbered amendments which would follow the Constitution. Instead, the amendments would have been inserted into the body of the Constitution at specified points. Madison did not place the right to keep and bear arms as a limitation on Congress' power over the militia, set out in Article I, section 8 of the Constitution. Instead, he grouped the right to arms with rights of freedom of religion, speech and press, to be inserted "in article first, section nine, between clauses 3 and 4." This would have put these provisions immediately following the general limitations of congressional power over citizens—outlawing suspension of habeas corpus, bill of attainder and ex post facto laws. Madison viewed his right to keep and bear arms proposal as a civil right, not a limit on federalization of the militia. Further, in an outline of a proposed speech on introduction of the Bill of Rights, Madison mentioned these "relate first to private rights," and indicated he meant to criticize the 1689 Declaration of Rights as too narrow: "No freedom of the press—conscience—GI warrants . . . attainders—arms to Protestants." Apparently he felt the 1689 recognition that "Protestants may have arms for their defense" should be extended to all, that the second amendment would broaden, not narrow, this.

Like most of his draft, the wording was both lengthy and convoluted. In the House of Representatives his proposals were edited extensively; since "the right of the people" was already contained in the provision, the comment that the militia would consist "of the body of the people" was deleted. The religious exemption was removed in view of objections that Congress might exempt too many people on these grounds and thus destroy the concept of the militia. When the proposal was submitted to the Senate, it was proposed that the right be limited to keeping and bearing arms "for the common defense," but the Senate refused the amendment, retaining it in its broadest form.[95]

Contemporaries of the first Congress clearly viewed the Second Amendment as creating an individual right. When St. George Tucker, then a professor at William and Mary School of Law and later a Justice of the Virginia Supreme Court, published a five-volume edition of Blackstone's *Commentaries* in 1803, he commented that "whenever standing armies are kept up, and the right of the people to keep and bear arms is, under any color or pretext whatsoever, prohibited, liberty, if not

---

[95] See generally, 1 J. Gobel, *History of the Supreme Court of the United States*, p. 456.

already annihilated, is on the brink of destruction. In England, the people have been disarmed, generally under the specious pretext of preserving the game."[96] He criticized the British Bill of Rights for limiting its guarantee of arms ownership to Protestants, whereas the American right was "without any qualification as to their condition or degree, as is the case in the British government."[97] William Rawle in his 1825 "View of the Constitution" suggested that:

The Prohibition is general. No clause in the Constitution could by any rule of construction be conceived to give to Congress a power to disarm the people.[98]

Tucker and Rawle had unique advantages in interpreting the Bill of Rights. Tucker had fought in the Revolutionary militia and was twice wounded in action. He was a close friend of Jefferson, an associate of Madison, and had a brother in the first Senate. Rawle was a friend of Washington and was offered the post of first Attorney General.

The Congress itself made its intent clear when the second Congress adopted the Militia Act of 1792. This required every "free able bodied white male citizen . . . who is or shall be of the age of 18 years, and under the age of 45 years," to be enrolled in the militia and "within six months thereafter, provide himself with a good musket or firelock," plus ammunition and equipment.[99] The bill remained on the books until 1903. Thus, from the subsequent enactments of Congress, as well as the contemporaneous statements of the drafters and their associates, there can be little doubt that the drafters of the Second Amendment viewed that amendment as creating an individual right to keep and carry arms for purposes ranging from self-protection to hunting to acquisition of military skills.

The right of individual citizens to keep and bear arms found early recognition by the courts, in a solid chain of precedent stretching forward for nearly two centuries. In 1813, Kentucky adopted the first general concealed weapon ban and nine years later the act was struck down as an

---

[96] 1 S. Tucker, ed., Blackstone's *Commentaries*, p. 300 (Philadelphia, 1803).

[97] *Ibid.*, p. 143.

[98] W. Rawle, *A View of the Constitution*, pp. 125-26 (2nd ed., 1829).

[99] Act of May 8, 1792. See generally J. Mahony, *The American Militia: Decade of Decision* (1960).

invasion of the right to keep and bear arms.[100] Similar statutes were later upheld in other states—upon the grounds that only one form of carrying, not all forms, were restricted.[101] The Alabama Supreme Court, for instance, added:

> We do not desire to be understood as maintaining, that in regulating the manner of wearing arms, the legislature has no limit other than its own discretion. A statute which, under the pretence of regulating, amounts to a destruction of the right, or which requires arms to be so borne as to render them wholly useless for the purpose of defense would be clearly unconstitutional.[102]

Likewise, when Georgia in 1837 enacted the first ban on pistol ownership, its supreme court promptly struck it down, holding in the process that the Second Amendment applied to the states. It explained the amendment's meaning: "The right of the whole people, old and young, men, women, and boys, and not militia only, to keep and bear arms of every description, and not merely such as are used by the militia, shall not be infringed . . . and this for the important end to be achieved, the rearing up and qualifying of a well-regulated militia, so vitally necessary to the security of a free state."[103]

Second Amendment issues rarely came before the federal courts at this time, simply because there were no federal controls on arms ownership. But the position of the United States Supreme Court was indicated in the famed *Dred Scott* case, where it held that the free black Americans were not citizens. The majority indicated that if blacks were regarded as citizens, "entitled to the privileges and immunities of citizens," they would have freedom of speech and assembly, "and the right to keep and carry arms wherever they went."[104]

Post Civil War arms enactments encountered judicial limitations arising at the individual right to keep and bear arms. Tennessee, for instance, had to amend its constitution to expressly grant legislative power to "regulate the wearing of arms." Even so, its 1870 ban on

---

[100] *Bliss v. Commonwealth*, 12 Ky. 90 (1822).

[101] *State v. Mitchell*, 3 Ind. (Blackf.) 229 (1839); *State v. Reid*, 1 Ala. 612 (1840); *State v. Buzzard*, 4 Ark. 18 (1842).

[102] *State v. Reid*, supra.

[103] *Nunn v. State*, 1 Ga. 243, 251 (1846).

[104] *Dred Scott v. Sanford*, 60 U.S. 393, 417 (1857).

26

carrying small ("pocket") pistols barely passed constitutional muster, the court warning that the legislature might not prohibit the carrying of "all manner of arms" since the power to regulate "does not fairly mean the power to prohibit."[105] Arkansas upheld a ban on pistol carrying only by construing it to apply only to pocket pistols and not to rifles, shotguns, or larger handguns. "To prohibit a citizen from wearing or carrying a war arm . . . is an unwarranted restriction upon the constitutional right to keep and bear arms. If cowardly and dishonest men sometimes shoot unarmed men with army pistols or guns, the evil must be prevented by the penitentiary and the gallows, and not by a general deprivation of a constitutional privilege."[106] A similar technique was used to construe Missouri's 1875 carrying ban to apply only to concealed carry, the court citing with approval the concept that legislatures might not limit carrying so as to make the arms useless for defense.[107]

Nor has recognition of the right to keep and bear arms been lacking in our century. City bans on handgun carrying have been struck down in North Carolina ("the right to bear arms is a most essential one to every free people and should not be whittled down by technical constructions"),[108] Tennessee,[109] and New Mexico.[110] The Michigan Supreme Court has stricken a ban on gun ownership by non-citizens with the comment that "the guarantee of the right of every person to bear arms in defense of himself means the right to possess arms for legitimate use in defense of himself (and) his property."[111] A similar statute was stricken in Colorado, its Supreme Court expressly rejecting the "collective rights" approach.[112] The U.S. Supreme Court, in *United States v. Miller*,[113] held that a court cannot merely take judicial notice that an arm is within the Second Amendment's protection, but explained:

---

[105] *Andrew v. State*, 50 Tenn. 165, 8 Am. Rep. 8 (1971). The Andrews Court went on to note that "this right was intended . . . to be exercised and enjoyed by the citizen as such, and not by him as a soldier . . ." 8 Am. Rep. at 17.

[106] *Wilson v. State*, 33 Ark. 557, 24 Am. Rep. 52 (1878).

[107] *State v. Wilforth*, 85 Mo. 528, 530 (1892).

[108] *State v. Kerner*, 181 N.C. 574, 107 S.E. 222 (1921).

[109] *Glassock v. City of Chattanooga*, 157 Tenn. 518, S.W. 2d. 678 (1928).

[110] *City of Las Vegas v. Moberg*, 82 N.M. 626, 485 P. ad 737 (1971) ("an ordinance may not deny the people the constitutionally guaranteed right to bear arms").

[111] *People v. Zerillo*, 219 Mich. 635, 189 N.W. 927 (1923).

[112] *People v. Nakamura*, 99 Colo. 262, 62, P. 2d 246 (1936).

[113] *United States v. Miller*, 307 U.S. 175, 178-79 (1939).

The Constitution as originally adopted granted to the Congress power "to provide for calling forth the Militia (etc.) . . ." With obvious purpose to assure the continuations and render possible the effectiveness of such forces the declaration and guarantee of the second amendment were made. It must be interpreted and applied with that end in view.

The signification attributed to the term "militia" appears from the debates in the Convention, the history and legislation of the colonies and states, and the writings of approved commentators. These show plainly enough that the militia comprised all males physically capable of acting in concert for the common defense . . . and further, that ordinarily when called for service these men were expected to appear bearing arms supplied by themselves and of the kind in common use at the time.

The right to keep and bear arms has found its most recent recognition in two 1980 decisions in Oregon[114] and Indiana,[115] the first striking down a very narrow arms possession ban, the second strictly limiting power to refuse carrying licenses.

In summary, the right to keep and bear arms is, in all probability, the oldest right memorialized in the Bill of Rights. Its common law right extends beyond our written records forward to the 1689 Declaration of Rights—so largely a response to individual disarmament under laws of the 1660s—and to our own Revolution, brought on primarily by British attempts at disarmament of the colonists. The recognition of the right in our Bill of Rights is a natural outgrowth of that experience and of demands for preservation of a clearly individual right to own and carry arms. It is a right reserved to "the people"—the same "people" who possess the right to assemble, and security from unreasonable searches and seizures, the "people" whom the tenth amendment distinguished from "the states." It is clearly not a right relating solely to the National Guard, which had no legal recognition prior to 1903, and whose 18th century predecessors were criticized by Richard Henry Lee and other constitutional figures as equal in danger to standing armies. Rather, it is a right reserved to individual citizens, to possess ("keep") and carry ("bear") arms for personal and political defense of themselves and their rights.

---

[114] *State v. Kessler*, 289 Ore. 359, 614 p. 2d 94 (1980).

[115] *Schubert v. DeBard*, --- Ind. App. ---, 398 N.E. 2d 1139 (1980).

The Embarrassing Second Amendment

Sanford Levinson

One of the best known pieces of American popular art in this century is the *New Yorker* cover by Saul Steinberg presenting a map of the United States as seen by a New Yorker. As most readers can no doubt recall, Manhattan dominates the map; everything west of the Hudson is more or less collapsed together and minimally displayed to the viewer. Steinberg's great cover depends for its force on the reality of what social psychologists call "cognitive maps." If one asks inhabitants ostensibly of the same cities to draw maps of that city, one will quickly discover that the images carried around in people's minds will vary by race, social class, and the like. What is true of maps of places—that they differ according to the perspective of the mapmakers—is certainly true of all conceptual maps.

To continue the map analogy, consider in this context the Bill of Rights: Is there an agreed upon "projection" of the concept? Is there even a canonical text of the Bill of Rights? Does it include the first eight, nine, or ten Amendments to the Constitution?[1] Imagine two individuals

Sanford Levinson is the Charles Tilford McCormick Professor of Law, University of Texas Law School. This essay was initially prepared for delivery at a symposium on Interpretation and the Bill of Rights at Williams College on November 4, 1988. It was first published in the *Yale Law Journal*. I should note that I wrote (and titled) this article before reading Nelson Lund's *The Second Amendment, Political Liberty, and the Right to Self-Preservation*, 39 Ala. L. Rev. 103 (1987), which begins, "The Second Amendment to the United States Constitution has become the most embarrassing provision of the Bill of Rights." I did hear Lund deliver a talk on the Second Amendment at the University of Texas Law School during the winter of 1987, which may have penetrated my consciousness more than I realized while drafting this article.

---

[1] It is not irrelevant that the Bill of Rights submitted to the states in 1789 included not only what are now the first ten Amendments, but also two others. Indeed, what we call the First Amendment was only the third one of the list submitted to the states. The initial "first amendment" in fact concerned the future size of the House of Representatives, a topic of no small importance to the Anti-Federalists, who were appalled by the smallness of the House seemingly envisioned by the Philadelphia framers. The second prohibited any pay raise voted by members of Congress to themselves from taking effect until an election "shall have intervened." See J. Goebel, 1 *The Oliver Wendell Holmes Devise History of the Supreme Court of the United States: Antecedents and Beginnings to 1801*, at 442 n.162 (1971). Had all of the initial twelve proposals been ratified, we would, it is possible, have a dramaticaly different cognitive map of the Bill of Rights. At the very least, one would neither hear defenses of the "preferred" status of freedom of speech framed in terms of the "firstness" of (what we know as) the First Amendment, nor the wholly invalid inference drawn from that "firstness" of some special intention of the Framers to safeguard the particular rights laid out there.

who are asked to draw a "map" of the Bill of Rights. One is a (stereo-) typical member of the American Civil Liberties Union (of which I am a card-carrying member); the other is an equally (stereo-)typical member of the "New Right."

The first, I suggest, would feature the First Amendment[2] as Main Street, dominating the map, though more, one suspects, in its role as protector of speech and prohibitor of established religion than as guardian of the rights of religious believers. The other principal avenues would be the criminal procedure aspects of the Constitution drawn from the Fourth,[3] Fifth,[4] Sixth,[5] and Eighth[6] Amendments. Also depicted prominently would be the Ninth Amendment,[7] although perhaps as in the process of construction. I am confident that the ACLU map would exclude any display of the just compensation clause of the Fifth Amendment[8] or of the Tenth Amendment.[9]

The second map, drawn by the New Rightist, would highlight the free exercise clause of the First Amendment,[10] the just compensation clause

---

[2] "Congress shall make no law respecting an establishment of religion . . . or abridging the freedom of speech, or of the press; or the right of the people peaceably to assemble, and to petition the Government for a redress of grievances." U.S. Constitution, Amendment I.

[3] "The right of the people to be secure in their persons, houses, papers, and effects, against unreasonable searches and seizures, shall not be violated; and no Warrants shall issue but upon probable cause, supported by Oath or affirmation, and particularly describing the place to be searched, and the persons or things to be seized." U.S. Constitution, Amendment IV.

[4] "No person shall be held to answer for a capital, or otherwise infamous crime, unless on a presentment or indictment of a Grand Jury, except in cases arising in the land or naval forces, or in the Militia, when in actual service in time of War or public danger; nor shall any person be subject for the same offense to be twice put in jeopardy of life or limb; nor shall be compelled in any criminal case to be a witness against himself, nor be deprived of life, liberty, or property, without due process of law. . . ." U.S. Constitution, Amendment V.

[5] "In all criminal prosecutions, the accused shall enjoy the right to a speedy and public trial, by an impartial jury of the State and district wherein the crime shall have been committed, which district shall have been previously ascertained by law, and to be informed of the nature and cause of the accusation; to be confronted with the witnesses against him; to have compulsory process for obtaining witnesses in his favor, and to have the Assistance of Counsel for his defense." U.S. Constitution, Amendment VI.

[6] "Excessive bail shall not be required, nor excessive fines imposed, nor cruel and unusual punishments inflicted." U.S. Constitution, Amendment VIII.

[7] "The enumeration in the Constitution, of certain rights, shall not be construed to deny or disparage others retained by the people." U.S. Constitution, Amendment IX.

[8] "[N]or shall private property be taken for public use, without just compensation." U.S. Constitution, Amendment IV.

[9] "The powers not delegated to the United States by the Constitution, nor prohibited by it to the States, are reserved to the States respectively, or to the people." U.S. Constitution, Amendment X.

[10] "Congress shall make no law . . . prohibiting the free exercise thereof [religion]. . . ." U.S. Constitution, Amendment I.

of the Fifth Amendment,[11] and the Tenth Amendment.[12] Perhaps the most notable difference between the two maps, though, would be in regard to the Second Amendment: "A well regulated militia being necessary to the security of a free State, the right of the people to keep and bear Arms shall not be infringed." What would be at most only a blind alley for the ACLU mapmaker would, I am confident, be a major boulevard in the map drawn by the New Right adherent. It is this last anomaly that I want to explore in this essay.

I. The Politics of Interpreting the Second Amendment

To put it mildly, the Second Amendment is not at the forefront of constitutional discussion, at least as registered in what the academy regards as the venues for such discussion—law reviews,[13] casebooks,[14] and other scholarly legal publications. As Professor LaRue has recently written, "the second amendment is not taken seriously by most scholars."[15]

---

[11] See supra note 8.

[12] See supra note 9.

[13] There are several law review articles discussing the Amendment. See, e.g., Lund, supra author's biography, and the articles cited in Dowlut & Knoop, *State Constitutions and the Right to Keep and Bear Arms*, 7 Okla. City U.L. Rev. 177, 178 n.3 (1982). See also the valuable symposium on Gun Control, edited by Don Kates in 49 *Law & Contemp. Probs.* 1-267 (1986), including articles by Shalhope, *The Armed Citizen in the Early Republic*, at 125; Kates, *The Second Amendment: A Dialogue*, at 143; Halbrook, *What the Framers Intended: A Linguistic Analysis of the Right to "Bear Arms,"* at 151. The symposium also includes a valuable bibliography of published materials on gun control, including Second Amendment considerations, at 251-67. The most important single article is almost undoubtedly Kates, *Handgun Prohibition and the Original Meaning of the Second Amendment*, 82 Mich. L. Rev. 204 1983. Not the least significant aspect of Kates' article is that it is basically the only one to have appeared in an "elite" law review. However, like many of the authors of other Second Amendment pieces, Kates is a practicing lawyer rather than a legal academic. I think it is accurate to say that no one recognized by the legal academy as a "major" writer on constitutional laws has deigned to turn his or her talents to a full consideration of the Amendment. But see LaRue, *Constitutional Law and Constitutional History*, 36 Buffalo L. Rev. 373, 375-78 (1988) (briefly discussing Second Amendment). Akhil Reed Amar's reconsideration of the foundations of the Constitution also promises to delve more deeply into the implications of the Amendment. See Amar, *Of Sovereignty and Federalism*, 96 Yale L.J. 1425, 1495-1500 (1987). Finally, there is one book that provides more in-depth treatment of the Second Amendment: S. Halbrook, *That Every Man Be Armed, The Evolution of a Constitutional Right* (1984).

[14] One will search the "leading" casebooks in vain for any mention of the Second Amendment. Other than its being included in the text of the Constitution that all of the casebooks reprint, a reader would have no reason to believe that the Amendment exists or could possibly be of interest to the constitutional analyst. I must include, alas, P. Brest & S. Levinson, *Processes of Constitutional Decisionmaking* (2d ed. 1983), within this critique, though I have every reason to believe that this will not be true of the forthcoming third edition.

[15] LaRue, supra note 13, at 375.

Both Laurence Tribe[16] and the Illinois team of Nowak, Rotunda, and Young[17] at least acknowledge the existence of the Second Amendment in their respective treatises on constitutional law, perhaps because the treatise genre demands more encyclopedic coverage than does the casebook. Neither, however, pays it the compliment of extended analysis. Both marginalize the Amendment by relegating it to footnotes; it becomes what a deconstructionist might call a "supplement" to the ostensibly "real" Constitution that is privileged by discussion in the text.[18] Professor Tribe's footnote appears as part of a general discussion of congressional power. He asserts that the history of the Amendment "indicate[s] that the central concern of [its] Framers was to prevent such federal interferences with the state militia as would permit the establishment of a standing national army and the consequent destruction of local autonomy."[19] He does note, however, that "the debates surrounding congressional approval of the second amendment do contain references to individual self-protection as well as to states' rights," but he argues that the presence of the preamble to the Amendment, as well as the qualifying phrase "'well regulated' makes any invocation of the amendment as a restriction on state or local gun control measures extremely problematic."[20] Nowak, Rotunda, and Young mention the Amendment in the context of the incorporation controversy, though they discuss its meaning at slightly greater length.[21] They state that "[t]he Supreme Court has not determined, at least not with any clarity, whether the amendment protects only a right of state governments against federal interference with state militia and police forces . . . or a right of individuals against the federal and state government[s]."[22]

Clearly the Second Amendment is not the only ignored patch of text in our constitutional conversations. One will find extraordinarily little

---

[16] Tribe, *American Constitutional Law* (2d ed., 1988).

[17] J. Nowak, R. Rotunda & J. Young, *Constitutional Law* (3d ed., 1986).

[18] For a brilliant and playful meditation on the way the legal world treats footnotes and other marginal phenomena, see Balkin, *The Footnote*, 83 *Nw. U.L. Rev.* 275, 276-81 (1989).

[19] Tribe, supra note 16, at 299 n.6.

[20] *Ibid.*, see also J. Ely, *Democracy and Distrust* 95 (1980) ("[T]he framers and ratifiers . . . opted against leaving to the future the attribution of [other] purposes, choosing instead explicitly to legislate the goal in terms of which the provision was to be interpreted"). As shall be seen below, see infra text accompanying note 38, the preamble may be less plain in its meaning than Tribe's (and Ely's) confident argument suggests.

[21] J. Nowak, R. Rotunda & J. Young, supra note 17, at 316 n.4. They do go on to cite a spate of articles by scholars who have debated the issue.

[22] *Ibid.* at 316 n.4.

discussion about another one of the initial Bill of Rights, the Third Amendment: "No Soldier shall, in time of peace be quartered in any house, without the consent of the Owner, nor in time of war, but in a manner to be prescribed by law." Nor does one hear much about letters of marque and reprisal[23] or the granting of titles of nobility.[24] There are, however, some differences that are worth noting.

The Third Amendment, to take the easiest case, is ignored because it is in fact of no current importance whatsoever (although it did, for obvious reasons, have importance at the time of the founding). It has never, for a single instant, been viewed by any body of modern lawyers or groups of laity as highly relevant to their legal or political concerns. For this reason, there is almost no case law on the Amendment.[25] I suspect that few among even highly sophisticated readers can summon up the Amendment without the aid of the text.

The Second Amendment, though, is radically different from these other pieces of constitutional text just mentioned, which all share the attribute of being basically irrelevant to any ongoing political struggles. To grasp the difference, one might simply begin by noting that it is not at all unusual for the Second Amendment to show up in letters to the editors of newspapers and magazines.[26] That judges and academic lawyers, including the ones who write casebooks, ignore it is most certainly not evidence for the proposition that no one cares about it. The National Rifle Association, to name the most obvious example, cares

---

[23] U.S. Constitution art. I, § 10.

[24] U.S. Constitution art. I, § 9, cl. 8.

[25] See, e.g., Legislative Reference Serv., Library of Congress, *The Constitution of the United States of America: Analysis and Interpretation* 923 (1964), which quotes the Amendment and then a comment from Miller, *The Constitution* 646 (1893): "This amendment seems to have been thought necessary. It does not appear to have been the subject of judicial exposition; and it is so thoroughly in accord with our ideas, that further comment is unnecessary." Cf. *Engblom v. Carey*, 724 F.2d 28 (2d Cir., 1983), *affg* 572 F. Supp. 44 (S.D.N.Y. 1983). *Engblom* grew out of a "statewide strike of correction officers, when they were evicted from their facility residences . . . and members of the National Guard were housed in their residences without their consent." The district court had initially granted summary judgment for the defendants in a suit brought by the officers claiming a deprivation of their rights under the Third Amendment. The Second Circuit, however, reversed on the ground that it could not "say that as a matter of law appellants were not entitled to the protection of the Third Amendment." *Engblom v. Carey*, 677 F.2d 957, 964 (2d Cir., 1982). The District Court on remand held that, as the Third Amendment rights had not been clearly established at the time of the strike, the defendants were protected by a qualified immunity, and it is this opinion that was upheld by the Second Circuit. I am grateful to Mark Tushnet for bringing this case to my attention.

[26] See, e.g., "The Firearms the Second Amendment Protects," *N.Y. Times*, June 9, 1988, at A22, col. 2 (three letters); "Second Amendment and Gun Control," *L.A. Times*, March 11, 1989, Part II, at 9 col. 1 (nine letters); "What 'Right to Bear Arms'?", *N.Y. Times*, July 20, 1989, at A23, col. 1 (national ed.) (op. ed. essay by Daniel Abrams); see also "We Rebelled to Protect Our Gun Rights," *Washington Times*, July 20, 1989, at F2, col. 4.

33

deeply about the Amendment, and an apparently serious Senator of the United States averred that the right to keep and bear arms is the "right most valued by free men."[27] Campaigns for Congress in both political parties, and even presidential campaigns, may turn on the apparent commitment of the candidates to a particular view of the Second Amendment. This reality of the political process reflects the fact that millions of Americans, even if (or perhaps *especially* if) they are not academics, can quote the Amendment and would disdain any presentation of the Bill of Rights that did not give it a place of pride.

I cannot help but suspect that the best explanation for the absence of the Second Amendment from the legal consciousness of the elite bar, including that component found in the legal academy,[28] is derived from a mixture of sheer opposition to the idea of private ownership of guns and the perhaps subconscious fear that altogether plausible, perhaps even "winning," interpretations of the Second Amendment would present real hurdles to those of us supporting prohibitory regulation. Thus the title of this essay—*The Embarrassing Second Amendment*—for I want to suggest that the Amendment may be profoundly embarrassing to many who both support such regulation and view themselves as committed to zealous adherence to the Bill of Rights (such as most members of the ACLU). Indeed, one sometimes discovers members of the NRA who are equally committed members of the ACLU, differing with the latter only on the issue of the Second Amendment but otherwise genuinely sharing the libertarian viewpoint of the ACLU.

It is not my style to offer "correct" or "incorrect" interpretations of the Constitution.[29] My major interest is in delineating the rhetorical structures of American constitutional argument and elaborating what is sometimes called the "politics of interpretation," that is, the factors that explain why one or another approach will appeal to certain analysts at certain times, while other analysts, or times, will favor quite different approaches. Thus my general tendency to regard as wholly untenable any approach to the Constitution that describes itself as obviously correct and condemns its opposition as simply wrong holds for the Second Amendment as well. In some contexts, this would lead me to label as tendentious the certainty of

---

[27] See Subcommittee on the Constitution of the Comm. on the Judiciary, *The Right to Keep and Bear Arms*, 97th Cong., 2d Sess. viii (1982) (preface by Senator Orrin Hatch) [hereinafter *The Right to Keep and Bear Arms*].

[28] See supra notes 13-14.

[29] See Levinson, *Constitutional Rhetoric and the Ninth Amendment*, 64 *Chi.-Kent L. Rev.* 131 (1988).

NRA advocates that the Amendment means precisely what they assert it does. In the original context of this article—i.e., the pages of a journal (*The Yale Law Journal*) whose audience is much more likely to be drawn from an elite, liberal portion of the public—I will instead be suggesting that the skepticism should run in the other direction. That is, we might consider the possibility that "our" views of the Amendment, perhaps best reflected in Professor Tribe's offhand treatment of it, might themselves be equally deserving of the "tendentious" label.

II. The Rhetorical Structures of the Right to Bear Arms

My colleague Philip Bobbitt has, in his book *Constitutional Fate*,[30] spelled out six approaches—or "modalities," as he terms them—of constitutional argument. These approaches, he argues, comprise what might be termed our legal grammar. They are the rhetorical structures within which "law-talk" as a recognizable form of conversation is carried on. The six are as follows:

1) textual argument—appeals to the unadorned language of the text;[31]

2) historical argument—appeals to the historical background of the provision being considered, whether the history considered be general, such as background but clearly crucial events (such as the American Revolution), or specific appeals to the so-called intentions of the Framers;[32]

3) structural argument—analyses inferred from the particular structures established by the Constitution, including the tripartite division of the national government; the separate existence of both state and nation as political entities; and the structured role of citizens within the political order;[33]

4) doctrinal argument—emphasis on the implications of prior cases decided by the Supreme Court;[34]

---

[30] P. Bobbitt, *Constitutional Fate* (1982).

[31] *Ibid.* at 25-38.

[32] *Ibid.* at 9-24.

[33] *Ibid.* at 74-92.

[34] *Ibid.* at 39-58.

5) prudential argument—emphasis on the consequences of adopting a preferred decision in any given case;[35] and, finally,

6) ethical argument—reliance on the overall "ethos" of limited government as centrally constituting American political culture.[36]

I want to frame my consideration of the Second Amendment within the first five of Bobbitt's categories; they are all richly present in consideration of what the Amendment might mean. The sixth, which emphasizes the ethos of limited government, does not play a significant role in the debate of the Second Amendment.[37]

A. Text

I begin with the appeal to text. Recall the Second Amendment: "A well regulated Militia, being necessary to the security of a free State, the right of the people to keep and bear Arms, shall not be infringed." No one has ever described the Constitution as a marvel of clarity, and the Second Amendment is perhaps one of the worst drafted of all its provisions. What is special about the Amendment is the inclusion of an opening clause—a preamble, if you will—that seems to set out its purpose. No similar clause is part of any other Amendment,[38] though that does not, of course, mean that we do not ascribe purposes to them. It would be impossible to make sense of the Constitution if we did not engage in the ascription of purpose. Indeed, the major debates about the First Amendment arise precisely when one tries to discern a purpose, given that "literalism" is a hopelessly failing approach to interpreting it. We usually do not even recognize punishment of fraud—a classic speech act—as a free speech problem because we so sensibly assume that the purpose of the First Amendment could not have been, for example, to protect the circulation of patently deceptive information to potential investors in commercial enterprises. The sharp differences that distinguish those who

---

[35] *Ibid.* at 59-73.

[36] *Ibid.* at 93-119.

[37] For the record, I should note that Bobbitt disagrees with this statement, making an eloquent appeal (in conversation) on behalf of the classic American value of self-reliance for the defense of oneself and, perhaps more importantly, one's family. I certainly do not doubt the possibility of constructing an "ethical" rationale for limiting the state's power to prohibit private gun ownership. Nonetheless, I would claim that no one unpersuaded by any of the arguments derived from the first five modes would suddenly change his or her mind upon being presented with an "ethical" argument.

[38] Cf., e.g., the patents and copyrights clause, which sets out the power of Congress "[t]o promote the Progress of Science and useful Arts, by securing for limited Times to Authors and Inventors the exclusive Right to their respective Writings and Discoveries." U.S. Const. art. I., § 8.

would limit the reach of the First Amendment to "political" speech from those who would extend it much further, encompassing non-deceptive commercial speech, are all derived from different readings of the purpose that underlies the raw text.[39]

A standard move of those legal analysts who wish to limit the Second Amendment's force is to focus on its "preamble" as setting out a restrictive purpose. Recall Laurence Tribe's assertion that that purpose was to allow the states to keep their militias and to protect them against the possibility that the new national government will use its power to establish a powerful standing army and eliminate the state militias. This purposive reading quickly disposes of any notion that there is an "individual" right to keep and bear arms. The right, if such it be, is only a state's right. The consequence of this reading is obvious: The national government has the power to regulate—to the point of prohibition—private ownership of guns, since that has, by stipulation, nothing to do with preserving state militias. This is, indeed, the position of the ACLU, which reads the Amendment as protecting only the right of "maintaining an effective state militia. . . . [T]he individual's right to bear arms applies only to the preservation or efficiency of a well-regulated [state] militia. Except for lawful police and military purposes, the possession of weapons by individuals is not constitutionally protected."[40]

This is not a wholly implausible reading, but one might ask why the Framers did not simply say something like "Congress shall have no power to prohibit state-organized and directed militias." Perhaps they in fact meant to do something else. Moreover, we might ask if ordinary readers of late 18th century legal prose would have interpreted it as meaning something else. The text at best provides only a starting point for a conversation. In this specific instance, it does not come close to resolving the questions posed by federal regulation of arms. Even if we accept the preamble as significant, we must still try to figure out what might be suggested by guaranteeing to "the people the right to keep and bear arms"; moreover, as we shall see presently, even the preamble presents unexpected difficulties in interpretation.

---

[39] For examples of this, see F. Schauer, *Freedom of Speech: A Philosophical Enquiry* (1982); Levinson, *First Amendment, Freedom of Speech, Freedom of Expression: Does It Matter What We Call It?* 80 *Nw. U.L. Rev.* 767 (1985) (reviewing M. Redish, *Freedom of Expression: A Critical Analysis* [1984]).

[40] ACLU Policy No. 47. I am grateful to Joan Mahoney, a member of the national board of the ACLU, for providing me with a text of the ACLU's current policy on gun control.

B. History

One might argue (and some have) that the substantive right is one pertaining to a collective body—"the people"—rather than to individuals. Professor Cress, for example, argues that state constitutions regularly used the words "man" or "person" in regard to "individual rights such as freedom of conscience," whereas the use in those constitutions of the term "the people" in regard to a right to bear arms is intended to refer to the "sovereign citizenry" collectively organized.[41] Such an argument founders, however, upon examination of the text of the federal Bill of Rights itself and the usage there of the term "the people" in the First, Fourth, Ninth, and Tenth Amendments.

Consider that the Fourth Amendment protects "[t]he right of the people to be secure in their persons," or that the First Amendment refers to the "right of the people peaceably to assemble, and to petition the Government for a redress of grievances." It is difficult to know how one might plausibly read the Fourth Amendment as other than a protection of individual rights, and it would approach the frivolous to read the assembly and petition clause as referring only to the right of state legislatures to meet and pass a remonstrance directed to Congress or the President against some governmental act. The Tenth Amendment is trickier, though it does explicitly differentiate between "states" and "the people" in terms of retained rights.[42] Concededly, it would be possible to read the Tenth Amendment as suggesting only an ultimate right of revolution by the collective people should the "states" stray too far from their designated role of protecting the rights of the people. This reading follows directly from the social contract theory of the state. (But, of course, many of these rights are held by individuals.)

Although the record is suitably complicated, it seems tendentious to reject out of hand the argument that one purpose of the Amendment was to recognize an individual's right to engage in armed self-defense against criminal conduct.[43] Historian Robert E. Shalhope supports this view, arguing in his article *The Ideological Origins of the Second Amendment*,[44]

---

[41] Cress, *An Armed Community: The Origins and Meaning of the Right to Bear Arms*, 71 J. Am. Hist. 22, 31 (1984).

[42] See U.S. Const. amend. X.

[43] For a full articulation of the individualist view of the Second Amendment, see Kates, *Handgun Prohibition and the Original Meaning of the Second Amendment*, 82 Mich. L. Rev. 204 (1983). One can also find an efficient presentation of this view in Lund, supra author's biography, at 117.

[44] Shalhope, *The Ideological Origins of the Second Amendment*, 69 J. Am. Hist. 599 (1982).

that the Amendment guarantees individuals the right "to possess arms for their own personal defense."[45] It would be especially unsurprising if this were the case, given the fact that the development of a professional police force (even within large American cities) was still at least a half century away at the end of the colonial period.[46] I shall return later in this essay to this individualist notion of the Amendment, particularly in regard to the argument that "changing circumstances," including the development of a professional police force, have deprived it of any continuing plausibility. But I want now to explore a second possible purpose of the Amendment, which as a sometime political theorist I find considerably more interesting.

Assume, as Professor Cress has argued, that the Second Amendment refers to a communitarian, rather than an individual, right.[47] We are still left the task of defining the relationship between the community and the state apparatus. It is this fascinating problem to which I now turn.

Consider once more the preamble and its reference to the importance of a well-regulated militia. Is the meaning of the term obvious? Perhaps we should make some effort to find out what the term "militia" meant to 18th century readers and writers, rather than assume that it refers only to Dan Quayle's Indiana National Guard and the like. By no means am I arguing that the discovery of that meaning is dispositive as to the general meaning of the Constitution for us today. But it seems foolhardy to be entirely uninterested in the historical philology behind the Second Amendment.

I, for one, have been persuaded that the term "militia" did not have the limited reference that Professor Cress and many modern legal analysts assign to it. There is strong evidence that "militia" refers to all of the people, or at least all of those treated as full citizens of the community. Consider, for example, the question asked by George Mason, one of the Virginians who refused to sign the Constitution because of its lack of a

---

[45] *Ibid.* at 614.

[46] See Daniel Boorstin's laconic comment that "the requirements for self-defense and food-gathering had put firearms in the hands of nearly everyone" in colonial America. D. Boorstin, *The Americans—The Colonial Experience* 353 (1958). The beginnings of a professional police force in Boston are traced in R. Lane, *Policing the City: Boston 1822-1855* (1967). Lane argues that as of the earlier of his two dates, "all the major eastern cities . . . had several kinds of officials serving various police functions, all of them haphazardly inherited from the British and colonial past. These agents were gradually drawn into better defined and more coherent organizations." *Ibid.* at 1. However, as Oscar Handlin points out in his introduction to the book, "to bring into being a professional police force was to create precisely the kind of hireling body considered dangerous by conventional political theory." *Ibid.* at vii.

[47] See Cress, supra note 41.

39

Bill of Rights: "Who are the Militia? They consist now of the whole people."[48] Similarly, the *Federal Farmer*, one of the most important Anti-Federalist opponents of the Constitution, referred to a "militia, when properly formed, [as] in fact the people themselves."[49] We have, of course, moved now from text to history. And this history is most interesting, especially when we look at the development of notions of popular sovereignty. It has become almost a cliche of contemporary American historiography to link the development of American political thought, including its constitutional aspects, to republican thought in England, the "country" critique of the powerful "court" centered in London.

One of this school's important writers, of course, was James Harrington, who not only was influential at the time but also has recently been given a certain pride of place by one of the most prominent of contemporary "neo-republicans," Professor Frank Michelman.[50] One historian describes Harrington as having made "the most significant contribution to English libertarian attitudes toward arms, the individual, and society."[51] He was a central figure in the development of the ideas of popular sovereignty and republicanism.[52] For Harrington, preservation of republican liberty requires independence, which rests primarily on possession of adequate property to make men free from coercion by employers or landlords. But widespread ownership of land is not sufficient. These independent yeoman should also bear arms. As Professor Morgan puts it, "[T]hese independent yeomen, armed and embodied in a militia, are also a popular government's best protection against its enemies, whether they be aggressive foreign monarchs or scheming demagogues within the nation itself."[53]

A central fear of Harrington and of all future republicans was a standing army, composed of professional soldiers. Harrington and his

---

[48] 3 J. Elliot, *Debates in the General State Conventions* 425 (3d ed., 1937) (statement of George Mason, June 14, 1788), reprinted in Kates, supra note 13, at 216 n.51.

[49] *Letters from the Federal Farmer to the Republican* 123 (W. Bennett, ed., 1978) (ascribed to Richard Henry Lee), reprinted in Kates, supra note 13, at 216 n.51.

[50] Michelman, *The Supreme Court 1985 Term—Foreword: Traces of Self-Government*, 100 *Harv. L. Rev.* 4, 39 (1986) (Harrington is "pivotal figure in the history of the 'Atlantic' branch of republicanism that would find its way to America").

[51] Shalhope, supra note 44, at 602.

[52] Edmund Morgan discusses Harrington in his recent book, *Inventing the People* 85-87 (1988) (analyzing notion of popular sovereignty in American thought).

[53] *Ibid.* at 156.

fellow republicans viewed a standing army as a threat to freedom, to be avoided at almost all costs. Thus, says Morgan, "A militia is the only safe form of military power that a popular government can employ; and because it is composed of the armed yeomanry, it will prevail over the mercenary professionals who man the armies of neighboring monarchs."[54]

Scholars of the First Amendment have made us aware of the importance of John Trenchard and Thomas Gordon, whose *Cato's Letters* were central to the formation of the American notion of freedom of the press. That notion includes what Vincent Blasi would come to call the "checking value" of a free press, which stands as a sturdy exposer of governmental misdeeds.[55] Consider the possibility, though, that the ultimate "checking value" in a republican polity is the ability of an armed populace, presumptively motivated by a shared commitment to the common good, to resist governmental tyranny.[56] Indeed, one of Cato's letters refers to "the Exercise of despotick Power [as] the unrelenting War of an armed Tyrant upon his unarmed Subjects. . . ."[57]

Cress persuasively shows that no one defended universal possession of arms. New Hampshire had no objection to disarming those who "are or have been in actual rebellion," just as Samuel Adams stressed that only "peaceable citizens" should be protected in their right of "keeping their own arms."[58] All these points can be conceded, however, without conceding as well that Congress—or, for that matter, the States—had the power to disarm these "peaceable citizens."

---

[54] *Ibid.* at 157. Morgan argues, incidentally, that the armed yeomanry was neither effective as a fighting force nor paticularly protective of popular liberty, but that is another matter. For our purposes, the ideological perceptions are surely more important than the "reality" accompanying them. *Ibid.* at 160-65.

[55] Blasi, *The Checking Value in First Amendment Theory*, 1977 *Am. B. Found. Res. J.* 521.

[56] See Lund, supra author's biography, at 111-16.

[57] Shalhope, supra note 44, at 603 (quoting 1755 edition of *Cato's Letters*). Shalhope also quotes from James Burgh, another English writer well known to American revolutionaries: "The possession of arms is the distinction between a free man and a slave. He, who has nothing, and who himself belongs to another, must be defended by him, whose property he is, and needs no arms. But he, who thinks he is his own master, and has what he can call his own, ought to have arms to defend himself, and what he possesses; else he lives precariously, and at discretion." *Ibid.* at 604. To be sure, Burgh also wrote that only men of property should in fact comprise the militia: "A militia consisting of any others than the men of *property* in a country, is no militia; but a mungrel army." Cress, supra note 41, at 27 (emphasis in original) (quoting J. Burgh, 2 *Political Disquisitions: or, An Enquiry into Public Errors, Defects, and Abuses* (1774-75). Presumably, though, the widespread distribution of property would bring with it equally widespread access to arms and membership in the militia.

[58] See Cress, supra note 41, at 34.

Surely one of the foundations of American political thought of the period was the well-justified concern about political corruption and consequent governmental tyranny. Even the Federalists, fending off their opponents who accused them of foisting an oppressive new scheme upon the American people, were careful to acknowledge the risks of tyranny. James Madison, for example, speaks in *Federalist* Number 46 of "the advantage of being armed, which the Americans possess over the people of almost every other nation."[59] The advantage in question was not merely the defense of American borders; a standing army might well accomplish that. Rather, an armed public was advantageous in protecting political liberty. It is therefore no surprise that the *Federal Farmer*, the nom de plume of an anti-Federalist critic of the new Constitution and its absence of a Bill of Rights, could write that "to preserve liberty, it is essential that the whole body of the people always possess arms, and be taught alike, especially when young, how to use them. . . ."[60] On this matter, at least, there was no cleavage between the pro-ratification Madison and his opponent.

In his influential *Commentaries on the Constitution*, Joseph Story, certainly no friend of Anti-Federalism, emphasized the "importance" of the Second Amendment.[61] He went on to describe the militia as "the natural defence of a free country" not only "against sudden foreign invasions" and "domestic insurrections," with which one might well expect a Federalist to be concerned, but also against "domestic usurpations of power by rulers."[62] "The right of the citizens to keep and bear arms has justly been considered," Story wrote, "as the palladium of the liberties of a republic; since it offers a strong moral check against the usurpation and arbitrary power of rulers; and will generally, even if these are successful in the first instance, enable the people to resist and triumph over them."[63]

We also see this blending of individualist and collective accounts of the right to bear arms in remarks by Judge Thomas Cooley, one of the

---

[59] The Federalist No. 46, at 299 (J. Madison) (C. Rossiter, ed., 1961).

[60] *Letters From the Federal Farmer to the Republican* 124 (W. Benett, ed., 1978).

[61] 3 J. Story, *Commentaries* § 1890 (1833), quoted in 5 *The Founders' Constitution* 214 (P. Kurland and R. Lerner, eds., 1987).

[62] *Ibid.*

[63] *Ibid.* Lawrence Cress, despite his forceful critique of Shalhope's individualist rendering of the Second Amendment, nonetheless himself notes that "[t]he danger posed by manipulating demagogues, *ambitious rulers,* and foreign invaders to free institutions required the vigilance of citizen-soldiers cognizant of the common good." Cress, supra note 41, at 41 (emphasis added).

most influential 19th century constitutional commentators. Noting that the state might call into its official militia only "a small number" of the eligible citizenry, Cooley wrote that "if the right [to keep and bear arms] were limited to those enrolled, the purpose of this guaranty might be defeated altogether by the action or neglect to act of the government it was meant to hold in check."[64] Finally, it is worth noting the remarks of Theodore Schroeder, one of the most important developers of the theory of freedom of speech early in this century.[65] "[T]he obvious import [of the constitutional guarantee to carry arms]," he argues, "is to promote a state of preparedness for self-defense even against the invasions of government, because only governments have ever disarmed any considerabe class of people as a means toward their enslavement."[66]

Such analyses provide the basis for Edward Abbey's revision of a common bumper sticker, "If guns are outlawed, only the government will have guns."[67] One of the things this slogan has helped me to understand is the political tilt contained within the Weberian definition of the state—i.e., the repository of a monopoly of the legitimate means of violence[68]—that is so commonly used by political scientists. It is a profoundly statist definition, the product of a specifically German tradition of the (strong) state rather than of a strikingly different American political tradition that is fundamentally mistrustful of state power and vigilant about maintaining ultimate power, including the power of arms, in the populace.

---

[64] T. Cooley, *The General Principles of Constitutional Law in the United States of America* 298 (3d ed. 1898): "The right of the people to bear arms in their own defence, and to form and drill military organizations in defence of the State, may not be very important in this country, but it is significant as having been reserved by the people as a possible and necessary resort for the protection of self-government against usurpation, and against any attempt on the part of those who may for the time be in possession of State authority or resources to set aside the constitution and substitute their own rule for that of the people. Should the contingency ever arise when it would be necessary for the people to make use of the arms in their hands for the protection of constitutional liberty, the proceeding, so far from being revolutionary, would be in strict accord with popular right and duty." Cooley advanced this same idea in *The Abnegation of Self-Government*, 12 *Princeton Rev.* 213-14 (1883).

[65] See Rabban, *The First Amendment in Its Forgotten Years,* 90 *Yale L.J.* 514, 560 (1981) ("[P]rodigious theoretical writings of Theodore Schroeder . . . were the most extensive and libertarian treatments of freedom of speech in the prewar period"); see also Graber, *Transforming Free Speech* (forthcoming, 1990) (manuscript at 4-12; on file with author).

[66] T. Schroeder, *Free Speech For Radicals* 104 (reprint ed. 1969).

[67] Shalhope, supra note 44, at 45.

[68] See M. Weber, *The Theory of Social and Economic Organization* 156 (T. Parsons, ed., 1947), where he lists among "[t]he primary formal characteristics of the modern state" the fact that: "today, the use of force is regarded as legitimate only so far as it is either permitted by the state or prescribed by it. . . . The claim of the modern state to monopolize the use of force is as essential to it as its character of compulsory jurisdiction and of continuous organization."

We thus see what I think is one of the most interesting points in regard to the new historiography of the Second Amendment—its linkage to conceptions of republican political order. Contemporary admirers of republican theory use it as a source both of critiques of more individualist liberal theory and of positive insight into the way we today might reorder our political lives.[69] One point of emphasis for neo-republicans is the value of participation in government, as contrasted to mere representation by a distant leadership, even if formally elected. But the implications of republicanism might push us in unexpected, even embarrassing, directions: Just as ordinary citizens should participate actively in governmental decision-making through offering their own deliberative insights, rather than be confined to casting ballots once every two or four years for those very few individuals who will actually make decisions, so should ordinary citizens participate in the process of law enforcement and defense of liberty rather than rely on professionalized peacekeepers, whether we call them standing armies or police.

C. Structure

We have also passed imperceptibly into a form of structural argument, for we see that one aspect of the structure of checks and balances within the purview of 18th century thought was the armed citizen. That is, those who would limit the meaning of the Second Amendment to the constitutional protection of state-controlled militias agree that such protection rests on the perception that militarily competent states were viewed as a potential protection against a tyrannical national government. Indeed, in 1801 several governors threatened to call out state militias if the Federalists in Congress refused to elect Thomas Jefferson president.[70] But this argument assumes that there are only two basic components in the vertical structure of the American polity—the national government and the states. It ignores the implication that might be drawn from the Second, Ninth, and Tenth Amendments: The citizenry itself can be viewed as an important third component of republican governance insofar as it stands ready to defend republican liberty against the depredations of the other two structures, however futile that might appear as a practical matter.

---

[69] See, e.g., *Symposium: The Republican Civil Tradition, Yale L.J.* 1493-1723 (1988).

[70] See D. Malone, 4 *Jefferson and His Times: Jefferson the President: First Term, 1801-1805*, at 7-11 (1970) (republican leaders ready to use state militias to resist should lame duck Congress attempt to violate clear dictates of Article II by designating someone other than Thomas Jefferson as President in 1801).

44

One implication of this republican rationale for the Second Amendment is that it calls into question the ability of a state to disarm its citizenry. That is, the strongest version of the republican argument would hold it to be a "privilege and immunity of United States citizenship"—of membership in a liberty-enhancing political order—to keep arms that could be taken up against tyranny wherever found, including, obviously, state government. Ironically, the principal citation supporting this argument is to Chief Justice Taney's egregious opinion in *Dred Scott*,[71] where he suggested that an uncontroversial attribute of citizenship, in addition to the right to migrate from one state to another, was the right to possess arms. The logic of Taney's argument at this point seems to be that, because it was inconceivable that the Framers could have genuinely imagined blacks having the right to possess arms, it follows that they could not have envisioned them as being citizens, since citizenship entailed that right. Taney's seeming recognition of a right to arms is much relied on by opponents of gun control.[72] Indeed, recall Madison's critique, in *Federalist* Numbers 10 and 14, of republicanism's traditional emphasis on the desirability of small states as preservers of republican liberty. He transformed this debate by arguing that the states would be less likely to preserve liberty because they could so easily fall under the sway of a local dominant faction, whereas an extended republic would guard against this danger. Anyone who accepts the Madisonian argument could scarcely be happy enhancing the powers of the states over their own citizens; indeed, this has been one of the great themes of American constitutional history, as the nationalization of the Bill of Rights has been deemed necessary in order to protect popular liberty against state depredation.

D. Doctrine

Inevitably one must at least mention, even though there is not space to discuss fully, the so-called incorporation controversy regarding the application of the Bill of Rights to the states through the Fourteenth Amendment. It should be no surprise that the opponents of gun control appear to take a "full incorporationist" view of that Amendment.[73] They

---

[71] *Scott v. Sanford*, U.S. (19 How.) 393, 417 (1857).

[72] See, e.g., Featherstone, Gardiner & Dowlut, "The Second Amendment to the United States Constitution Guarantees an Individual Right to Keep and Bear Arms," in *The Right to Keep and Bear Arms*, supra note 27, at 100.

[73] See, e.g., Halbrook, "The Fourteenth Amendment and the Right to Keep and Bear Arms: The Intent of the Framers," in *The Right to Keep and Bear Arms*, supra note 27, at 79. Not the least of the ironies observed in the debate about the Second Amendment is that NRA-

45

view the privileges and immunities clause, which was eviscerated in the *Slaughterhouse Cases*,[74] as designed to require the states to honor the rights that had been held, by Justice Marshall in *Barron v. Baltimore* in 1833,[75] to restrict only the national government. In 1875 the Court stated, in *United States v. Cruikshank*,[76] that the Second Amendment, insofar as it grants any right at all, "means no more than that it shall not be infringed by Congress. This is one of the amendments that has no other effect than to restrict the powers of the national government . . ." Lest there be any remaining doubt on this point, the Court specifically cited the *Cruikshank* language 11 years later in *Presser v. Illinois*,[77] in rejecting the claim that the Second Amendment served to invalidate an Illinois statute that prohibited "any body of men whatever, other than the regular organized volunteer militia of this State, and the troops of the United States . . . to drill or parade with arms in any city, or town, of this State, without the license of the Governor thereof. . . ."[78]

The first "incorporation decision," *Chicago, B. & O. R. Co. v. Chicago*,[79] was not delivered until 11 years after *Presser*; one therefore cannot know if the judges in *Cruikshank* and *Presser* were willing to concede that *any* of the amendments comprising the Bill of Rights were

---

oriented conservatives like Senator Hatch could scarcely have been happy with the wholesale attack leveled by former Attorney General Meese on the incorporation doctrine, for here is one area where some "conservatives" may in fact be more zealous adherents of that doctrine than are most liberals, who, at least where the Second Amendment is concerned, have a considerably more selective view of incorporation.

[74] 83 U.S. 36 (1873).

[75] 32 U.S. (7 Pet.) 243 (1833).

[76] 92 U.S. 542, 553 (1875).

[77] 116 U.S. 252, 267 (1886). For a fascinating discussion of *Presser*, see Larue, supra note 13, at 386-90.

[78] 116 U.S. at 253. There is good reason to believe this statute, passed by the Illinois legislature in 1879, was part of an effort to control (and, indeed, suppress) widespread labor unrest linked to the economic troubles of the time. For the background of the Illinois statute, see P. Avrich, *The Haymarket Tragedy* 45 (1984): "As early as 1875, a small group of Chicago socialists, most of them German immigrants, had formed an armed club to protect the workers against police and military assaults, as well as against physical intimidation at the polls. In the eyes of its supporters . . . the need for such a group was amply demonstrated by the behavior of the police and [state-conrolled] militia during the Great Strike of 1877, a national protest by labor triggered by a ten percent cut in wages by the Baltimore and Ohio Railroad, which included the breaking up of workers' meetings, the arrest of socialist leaders, [and] the use of club, pistol, and bayonet against strikers and their supporters. . . . Workers . . . were resolved never again to be shot and beaten without resistance. Nor would they stand idly by while their meeting places were invaded or their wives and children assaulted. They were determined, as Albert Parsons [a leader of the anarchist movement in Chicago] expressed it, to defend both 'their persons and their rights.' "

[79] 166 U.S. 226 (1897) (protecting rights of property owners by requiring compensation for takings of property).

anything more than limitations on congressional or other national power. The obvious question, given the modern legal reality of the incorporation of almost all of the rights protected by the First, Fourth, Fifth, Sixth, and Eighth Amendments, is what exactly justifies treating the Second Amendment as the great exception. Why, that is, should *Cruikshank* and *Presser* be regarded as binding precedent any more than any of the other "pre-incorporation" decisions refusing to apply given aspects of the Bill of Rights against the states?

If one agrees with Professor Tribe that the Amendment is simply a federalist protection of state rights, then presumably there is nothing to incorporate.[80] If, however, one accepts the Amendment as a serious substantive limitation on the ability of the national government to regulate the private possession of arms based on either the "individualist" or "neo-republican" theories sketched above, then why not follow the "incor-porationist" logic applied to other amendments and limit the states as well in their powers to regulate (and especially to prohibit) such possession? The Supreme Court has almost shamelessly refused to discuss the issue,[81] but that need not stop the rest of us.

Returning, though, to the question of Congress's power to regulate the keeping and bearing of arms, one notes that there is, basically, only one modern case that discusses the issue, *United States v. Miller*,[82] decided in 1939. Jack Miller was charged with moving a sawed-off shotgun in

---

[80] My colleague Douglas Laycock has reminded me that a similar argument was made by some conservatives in regard to the establishment clause of the First Amendment. Thus, Justice Brennan noted that "[i]t has been suggested, with some support in history, that absorption of the First Amendment's ban against congressional legislation 'respecting an establishment of religion' is conceptually impossible because the Framers meant the Establishment Clause also to foreclose any attempt by Congress to *disestablish* the existing official state churches. *Abington School Dist. v. Schempp*, 374 U.S. 203, 254 (1963) (Brennan, J., concurring) (emphasis added). According to this reading, it would be illogical to apply the establishment clause against the states "because that clause is not one of the provisions of the Bill of Rights which in terms protects a 'freedom' of the individual," *ibid.* at 256, inasmuch as it is only a federalist protection of states against a national establishment (or disestablishment). "The fallacy in this contention," responds Brennan, "is that it underestimates the role of the Establishment Clause as a co-guarantor, with the Free Exercise Clause, of religious liberty." *Ibid.* Whatever the sometimes bitter debates about the precise meaning of "establishment," it is surely the case that Justice Brennan, even as he almost cheerfully concedes that at one point in our history the "states-right" reading of the establishment clause could have been thoroughly plausible, expresses what has become the generally accepted view as to the establishment clause being some kind of limitation on the state as well as on the national government. One may wonder whether the interpretive history of the establishment clause might have any lessons for the interpretation of the Second Amendment.

[81] It refused, for example, to review the most important modern gun control case, *Quilici v. Village of Morton Grove*, 695 F.2d 261 (7th Cir. 1982), *cert. denied*, 464 U.S. 863 (1983), where the Seventh Circuit Court of Appeals upheld a local ordinance in Morton Grove, Illinois, prohibiting the possession of handguns within its borders.

[82] 307 U.S. 174 (1939).

interstate commerce in violation of the National Firearms Act of 1934. Among other things, Miller and a compatriot had not registered the firearm, as required by the Act. The court below had dismissed the charge, accepting Miller's argument that the Act violated the Second Amendment.

The Supreme Court reversed unanimously, with the arch-conservative Justice McReynolds writing the opinion.[83] Interestingly enough, he emphasized that there was no evidence showing that a sawed-off shotgun "at this time has some reasonable relationship to the preservation or efficiency of a well regulated militia."[84] And "[c]ertainly it is not within judicial notice that this weapon is any part of the ordinary military equipment or that its use could contribute to the common defense."[85] *Miller* might have had a tenable argument had he been able to show that he was keeping or bearing a weapon that clearly had a potential military use.[86]

Justice McReynolds went on to describe the purpose of the Second Amendment as "assur[ing] the continuation and render[ing] possible the effectiveness of [the Militia]."[87] He contrasted the Militia with troops of a standing army, which the Constitution indeed forbade the states to keep without the explicit consent of Congress. "The sentiment of the time strongly disfavored standing armies; the common view was that adequate defense of country and laws could be secured through the Militia—civilians primarily, soldiers on occasion.[88] McReynolds noted further that the debates in the Convention, the history and legislation of Colonies and States, and the writings of approved commentators [all] [s]how plainly enough that the Militia comprised all males physically capable of acting in concert for the common defense."[89]

It is difficult to read *Miller* as rendering the Second Amendment meaningless as a control on Congress. Ironically, *Miller* can be read to support some of the most extreme anti-gun control arguments, e.g., that

---

[83] Justice Douglas, however, did not participate in the case.

[84] *Miller*, 307 U.S. at 178.

[85] *Ibid.* at 178 (citation omitted).

[86] Lund notes that "commentaries have since demonstrated that sawed-off or short-barreled shotguns are commonly used as military weapons." Lund, supra author's biography, at 109.

[87] 307 U.S. at 178.

[88] *Ibid.* at 179.

[89] *Ibid.*

the individual citizen has a right to keep and bear bazookas, rocket launchers, and other armaments that are clearly relevant to modern warfare, including, of course, assault weapons. Arguments about the constitutional legitimacy of a prohibition by Congress of private ownership of handguns or, what is much more likely, assault rifles, might turn on the usefulness of such guns in military settings.

E. Prudentialism

We have looked at four of Bobbitt's categories—text, history, structure, and caselaw doctrine—and have seen, at the very least, that the arguments on behalf of a "strong" Second Amendment are stronger than many of us might wish were the case. This, then, brings us to the fifth category, prudentialism, or an attentiveness to practical consequences, which is clearly of great importance in any debates about gun control. The standard argument in favor of strict control and, ultimately, prohibition of private ownership focuses on the extensive social costs of widespread distribution of firearms. Consider, for example, a speech given by former Justice Lewis Powell to the American Bar Association. He noted that over 40,000 murders were committed in the United States in 1986 and 1987, and that fully sixty percent of them were committed with firearms. England and Wales, however, saw only 662 homicides in 1986, less than eight percent of which were committed with firearms.[90] Justice Powell indicated that, "[w]ith respect to handguns," in contrast "to sporting rifles and shotguns[,] it is not easy to understand why the Second Amendment, or the notion of liberty, should be viewed as creating a right to own and carry a weapon that contributes so directly to the shocking number of murders in our society."[91]

It is hard to disagree with Justice Powell; it appears almost crazy to protect as a constitutional right something that so clearly results in extraordinary social costs with little, if any, compensating social advantage. Indeed, since Justice Powell's talk, the subject of assault rifles has become a staple of national discussion, and the opponents of regulation of such weapons have deservedly drawn the censure even of conservative leaders like William Bennett. It is almost impossible to imagine that the judiciary would strike down a determination by Congress

---

[90] L. Powell, "Capital Punishment, Remarks Delivered to the Criminal Justice Section, ABA" 10 (Aug. 7, 1988).

[91] *Ibid.* at 11.

that the possession of assault weapons should be denied to private citizens.

Even if one accepts the historical plausibility of the arguments advanced above, the overriding temptation is to say that times and circumstances have changed and that there is simply no reason to continue enforcing an outmoded, and indeed dangerous, understanding of private rights against public order. This criticism is clearest in regard to the so-called individualist argument, for one can argue that the rise of a professional police force to enforce the law has made irrelevant, and perhaps even counter-productive, the continuation of a strong notion of self-help as the remedy for crime.[92]

I am not unsympathetic to such arguments. It is no purpose of this essay to solicit membership for the National Rifle Association or to express any sympathy for what even Don Kates, a strong critic of the conventional dismissal of the Second Amendment, describes as "the gun lobby's obnoxious habit of assailing all forms of regulation on 2nd Amendment grounds."[93] And yet . . .

Circumstances may well have changed in regard to individual defense, although we ignore at our political peril the good-faith belief of many Americans that they cannot rely on the police for protection against a variety of criminals. Still, let us assume that the individualist reading of the Amendment has been vitiated by changing circumstances. Are we quite so confident that circumstances are equally different in regard to the republican rationale outlined earlier?

One would, of course, like to believe that the state, whether at the local or national level, presents no threat to important political values, including liberty. But our propensity to believe that this is the case may be little more than a sign of how truly different we are from our radical forebears. I do not want to argue that the state is necessarily tyrannical; I am not an anarchist. But it seems foolhardy to assume that the armed state will necessarily be benevolent. The American political tradition is, for good or ill, based in large measure on a healthy mistrust of the state. The development of widespread suffrage and greater majoritarianism in our polity is itself no sure protection, at least within republican theory. The republican theory is predicated on the stark contrast between mere democracy, where people are motivated by selfish personal interest, and

---

[92] This point is presumably demonstrated by the increasing public opposition of police officials to private possession of handguns (not to mention assault rifles).

[93] D. Kates, "Minimalist Interpretation of the Second Amendment" 2 (draft, Sept. 29, 1986) (unpublished manuscript available from author).

a republic, where civic virtue, both in citizens and leadership, tames selfishness on behalf of the common good. In any event, it is hard for me to see how one can argue that circumstances have so changed as to make mass disarmament constitutionally unproblematic.[94]

Indeed, we have seen the brutal suppression of the Chinese student demonstrations in Tiananmen Square. It should not surprise us that some NRA sympathizers have presented that situation as an object lesson to those who unthinkingly support the prohibition of private gun ownership. "[I]f all Chinese citizens kept arms, their rulers would hardly have dared to massacre the demonstrators. . . . The private keeping of hand-held personal firearms is within the constitutional design for a counter to government run amok. . . . As the Tiananmen Square tragedy showed so graphically, AK-47s fall into that category of weapons, and that is why they are protected by the Second Amendment."[95] It is simply silly to respond that small arms are irrelevant against nuclear-armed states: Witness contemporary Northern Ireland and the territories occupied by Israel, where the sophisticated weaponry of Great Britain and Israel have proved almost totally beside the point. The fact that these may not be pleasant examples does not affect the principal point, that a state facing a totally disarmed population is in a far better position, for good or for ill, to suppress popular demonstrations and uprisings than one that must calculate the possibilities of its soldiers and officials being injured or killed.[96]

---

[94] See Lund, supra author's biography, at 116.

[95] Wimmershoff-Caplan, "The Founders and the AK-47," *Washington Post*, July 6, 1989, at A18, col. 4, reprinted as "Price of Gun Deaths Small Compared to Price of Liberty," *Austin American Statesman*, July 11, 1989, at A11. Ms. Wimmershoff-Caplan is identified as a "lawyer in New York" who is "a member of the National Board of the National Rifle Association." *Ibid.* One of the first such arguments in regard to the events at Tiananmen Square was made by William A. Black in a letter, "Citizens Without Guns," *New York Times*, June 18, 1989 at D26, col. 6. Though describing himself as "find[ing] no glory in guns [and] a very profound anti-hunter," he nonetheless "stand[s] with those who would protect our right to keep and bear arms" and cited for support the fact that "none [of the Chinese soldiers] feared bullets: the citizens of China were long ago disarmed by the Communists." "Who knows," he asks, "what the leaders and the military and the police of our America will be up to at some point in the future? We need an armed citizenry to protect our liberty."

As one might expect, such arguments draw heated responses. See Rudlin, "The Founders and the AK-47 (Cont'd)," *Washington Post*, July 20, 1989, at A22, col. 3. Jonathan Rudlin accused Ms. Wimmershoff-Caplan of engaging in Swiftian satire, as no one could "take such brilliant burlesque seriously." Neal Knox, however, endorsed her essay in full, adding the Holocaust to the list of examples: "Could the Holocaust have occurred if Europe's Jews had owned thousands of then-modern military Mauser bolt action rifles?" See also *Washington Post*, July 12, 1989, at A22, for other letters.

[96] See Lund, supra author's bio, at 115: "The decision to use military force is not determined solely by whether the contemplated benefits can be successfully obtained through the use of available forces, but rather is determined by the *ratio* of those benefits to the

III. Taking the Second Amendment Seriously

There is one further problem of no small import: If one does accept the plausibility of any of the arguments on behalf of a strong reading of the Second Amendment, but, nevertheless, rejects them in the name of social prudence and the present-day consequences produced by finicky adherence to earlier understandings, why do we not apply such consequentialist criteria to each and every part of the Bill of Rights?[97] As Ronald Dworkin has argued, what it means to take rights seriously is that one will honor them even when there is significant social cost in doing so. If protecting freedom of speech, the rights of criminal defendants, or any other part of the Bill of Rights were always (or even most of the time) clearly costless to the society as a whole, it would truly be impossible to understand why they would be as controversial as they are. The very fact that there are often significant costs—criminals going free, oppressed groups having to hear viciously racist speech and so on—helps to account for the observed fact that those who view themselves as defenders of the Bill of Rights are generally antagonistic to prudential arguments. Most often, one finds them embracing versions of textual, historical, or doctrinal argument that dismiss as almost crass and vulgar any insistence that times might have changed and made too "expensive" the continued adherence to a given view. "Cost-benefit" analysis, rightly or wrongly, has come to be viewed as a "conservative" weapon to attack liberal rights.[98] Yet one finds that the tables are strikingly turned when the Second Amendment comes into play. Here it is "conservatives" who argue in effect that social costs are irrelevant and "liberals" who argue for a notion of the "living Constitution" and "changed circumstances" that

---

expected costs. It follows that any factor increasing the anticipated cost of a military operation makes the conduct of that operation incrementally more unlikely. This explains why a relatively poorly armed nation with a small population recently prevailed in a war against the United States, and it explains why governments bent on the oppression of their people almost always disarm the civilian population before undertaking more drastically oppressive measures."

[97] See D. Kates, supra note 93, at 24-25 n.13, for a discussion of this point.

[98] See, e.g., Justice Marshall's dissent, joined by Justice Brennan, in *Skinner v. Railway Labor Executive Ass'n.*, 109 S. Ct. 1402 (1989), upholding the government's right to require drug tests of railroad employees following accidents. It begins with his chastising the majority for "ignor[ing] the text and doctrinal history of the Fourth Amendment, which require that highly intrusive searches of this type be based on probable cause, not on the evanescent cost-benefit calculations of agencies or judges," *ibid.* at 1423, and continues by arguing that "[t]he majority's concern with the railroad safety problems caused by drug and alcohol abuse is laudable; its cavalier disregard for the Constitution is not. There is no drug exception to the Constitution, any more than there is a communism exception or an exception for other real or imagined sources of domestic unrest." *Ibid.* at 1426.

would have the practical consequence of removing any real bite from the Second Amendment.

As Fred Donaldson of Austin, Texas, wrote, commenting on those who defended the Supreme Court's decision upholding flag-burning as compelled by a proper (and decidedly non-prudential) understanding of the First Amendment, "[I]t seems inconsistent for [defenders of the decision] to scream so loudly" at the prospect of limiting the protection given expression "while you smile complacently at the Second torn and bleeding. If the Second Amendment is not worth the paper it is written on, what price the First?"[99] The fact that Mr. Donaldson is an ordinary citizen rather than an eminent law professor does not make his question any less pointed or its answer less difficult.

For too long, most members of the legal academy have treated the Second Amendment as the equivalent of an embarrassing relative, whose mention brings a quick change of subject to other, more respectable, family members. That will no longer do. It is time for the Second Amendment to enter full scale into the consciousness of the legal academy. Those of us who agree with Martha Minow's emphasis on the desirability of encouraging different "voices" in the legal conversation[100] should be especially aware of the importance of recognizing the attempts of Mr. Donaldson and his millions of colleagues to join the conversation. To be sure, it is unlikely that Professor Minow had those too often peremptorily dismissed as "gun nuts" in mind as possible providers of "insight and growth," but surely the call for sensitivity to different or excluded voices cannot extend only to those groups "we" already, perhaps "complacent[ly]," believe have a lot to tell "us."[101]

I am not so naive as to believe that conversation will overcome the chasm that now separates the sensibility of, say, Senator Hatch and myself as to what constitues the "right[s] most valued by free men [and women]."[102] It is important to remember that one will still need to join up sides and engage in vigorous political struggle. But it might at least help to make the political sides appear more human to one another. Perhaps

---

[99] Donaldson, "Letter to the Editor," *Austin American Statesman*, July 8, 1989, p. A19, col. 4.

[100] See Minow, *The Supreme Court 1986 Term—Foreword: Justice Engendered*, 101 *Harv. L. Rev.* 10, 74-90 (1987). "We need settings in which to engage in the clash of realities that breaks us out of settled and complacent meanings and creates opportunities for insight and growth." *Ibid.* at 95; also see Getman, *Voices*, 66 *Tex. L. Rev.* 577 (1988).

[101] And, perhaps more to the point, "you" who insufficiently listen to "us" and to "our" favored groups.

[102] See supra note 27 and accompanying text.

"we" might be led to stop referring casually to "gun nuts" just as, maybe, members of the NRA could be brought to understand the real fear that the currently almost uncontrolled system of gun ownership sparks in the minds of many whom they casually dismiss as "bleeding-heart liberals." Is not, after all, the possibility of serious, engaged discussion about political issues at the heart of what is most attractive in both liberal *and* republican versions of politics?

The Unalienable Right to Self-Defense and the Second Amendment

David Hardy

I. Introduction

The process of legal interpretation traditionally begins with the intent of the drafter of a document or the intent of those who approved it. In the case of the Second Amendment, which provides that a "well regulated militia, being necessary to the security of a free State, the right of the people to keep and bear arms, shall not be infringed,"[1] this principle is not easily applied. Here we must speak not of the drafter of the document, but of the drafters; not of its origin, but of its origins; not of its background, but of its backgrounds. The Second Amendment is divisible into two portions—the first referring to a militia as necessary to a free state, the second to a right of the people to keep and bear arms—and each has an entirely different background, purpose and constituency.

The origins of the two separate clauses lie in two different reactions to the seventeenth-century doctrine of royal absolutism. Although the supporters of absolutism claimed support from antiquity, the fact is that it was a relatively new doctrine in the seventeenth century. To be sure, monarchy as an institution had a long history, but kings were content to rule by simple physical power. William the Conqueror, in establishing his control over England, saw no great problem with rendering one third of his kingdom desert and killing about the same proportion of his new subjects. His grandson saw little wrong at the time with eliminating the Archbishop of Canterbury, and his sons in turn murdered their own half-brother. Any of these kings, if asked for the natural law basis of his kingship, might well have replied that "might makes right."

David Hardy is a staff attorney, Office of the Solicitor, United States Department of the Interior, Washington, D.C. The views expressed are solely those of the author and do not necessarily represent those of his department. In addition to this paper, Hardy has written several other articles on this subject—which also appear in this book.

---

[1] U.S. Const., Amend. II.

While the kings themselves were not overly concerned with natural law, medieval theologians were. Christian theology generally did not accept an absolute right of kings. St. Thomas Aquinas had argued that while power in the abstract is of divine origin, its function is to achieve justice. A ruler who fails to achieve justice is not properly a ruler but a tyrant, and the people are justified in setting him aside. That is, to an extent, individuals have a right of self-defense against a government which perverts the purposes of the divine grant of power.

> It must not be thought that such a multitude is acting unfaithfully and deposing the tyrant, even though it had previously subjected itself to him in perpetuity, because he himself has deserved that the covenant with his subjects should not be kept, since, in ruling the multitude, he did not act faithfully as the office of a king demands.[2]

In the early seventeenth century, this view was challenged, first in France, and then by importation in England. The argument was advanced that the king as a specific individual had an absolute grant of power. The most widespread English writing of this type was probably King James's *The Trew Law of Free Monarchies*.[3] James found support for absolute monarchy in Samuel's revelation to the Israelites that a king would hold absolute dominion over them.[4] Although the context was hardly a divine endorsement of such government, James contended the Israelites bound all subsequent men to accepting a king on those terms. James also invoked David's tolerance of Saul's oppression, and Paul's injunction to obey higher powers[5] as support for his claim that Christians were duty-bound to acquiesce even to persecution. James's work was followed by Sir Robert Filmer's *Patriarcha*,[6] in which Filmer argued that monarchies stemmed from the original family at the Creation, and that therefore a

---

[2] Aquinas, *De Regimine Principum* (or *On Kingship*), bk. 1, ch. VI (Phelan-Eschmann, trans.). Aquinas drew a distinction between individual tyrannicde, which he maintained led to anarchy, and the collective actions of an entire people, in rejecting the tyrant's rule. He suggests that the Scriptural admonitions to suffer persecution rather than resist, see, e.g., 1 Peter 2:18-19, are meant to deter the former but not the latter means of dealing with a tyrant.

[3] James I, *The Trew Law of Free Monarchies* (1598), reprinted in "The Political Works of James I," at 53-70 (C. McIlwain, ed., 1918), reviewed by G. Sensabaugh, *That Grand Whig, Milton*, 6-9 (1952).

[4] 1 Samuel 13:11-18.

[5] Romans 13:1-7.

[6] *Patriarcha and Other Political Works of Sir Robert Filmer*, 49-126 (P. Laslett, ed., 1949).

man could no more lawfully oppose his monarch than he could oppose his father within the household. He concluded that it is "unnatural for the multitude to choose their governors, or to govern or to partake in the government."[7]

To Filmer and the other theoreticians of royal absolutism, the king was subject to no man-made law because he was the ultimate fountainhead of man-made law. While he was subject to divine law, only a superior could judge him, and his only superior was God. Thus, the only sanctions for a royal violation of divine law must await the final judgment, and no man may take action against the king based upon his violation of any law, human or divine.

One of the corollaries of absolutism was the doctrine of non-resistance, which achieved widespread acceptance within the Anglican church, and essentially taught that no man could oppose the king or take up arms against the king under *any* circumstances. This doctrine maintained that it is never acceptable to take up arms or dispossess the king, no matter what his actions. No exceptions were permitted. As Abednego Seller wrote in 1689, it was "the duty of every Christian, in things lawful, *actively* to obey his Superior; in things unlawful, to *suffer* rather than obey, and in any case, or upon any pretense whatsoever not to resist."[8]

II. Reaction to Absolutism:
the Classical Republic and the Militia

The response to absolutism and non-resistance was not long in coming, and, like the doctrine of royal absolutism, it came to England as an import. But the revival of republicanism had its birth, not in monarchical France, but in the Italian republic of Florence. J. G. A. Pocock has brilliantly chronicled its origins.[9] Florence was, in the first years of the fifteenth century, menaced by Giangaleazzo Visconti, absolute ruler of Milan, whose resident propagandists portrayed his role as a revival of the Roman Empire, an inspiring image to the war-torn and fragmented Italian city-states of his day. The Florentines, who included many of the greatest

---

[7] *Ibid.* at 93.

[8] G. Sensabaugh, *supra* note 3, at 129 (quoting A. Seller, *The History of Passive Obedience Since the Reformation*, preface [Amsterdam, 1689]).

[9] See generally J. Pocock, *The Machiavellian Moment: Florentine Political Thought and the Atlantic Republican Tradition* (1975).

minds of the age, responded by championing their own government as a revival of the Roman Republic and condemning Visconti as a resurgent Julius Caesar, a man who would destroy a stable republic and initiate oppression, decadence and anarchy.

Paralleling this development was another intellectual shift. For millennia, philosophers had debated whether the thinking man best spends his life in activity—chiefly political activity—or in contemplation. To the Greeks, the active life was often seen as superior: indeed, man was seen as only capable of full life while participating in the affairs of state. This view was shared by the Romans of the Republican period. But under the late Empire a view that the thinking man's function was to withdraw from the world gained credit. Early Christian writers shared this view—understandably, given that they stood a far greater chance of being executed for their faith than of being able to reform the Empire by it. But beginning with St. Thomas Aquinas and his popularization of Aristotle—lost to Western Europe for a millennium—the concept that a Christian best lives his faith by an active life gained force.

The Florentine revival of republican ideals gave a sudden impetus to this approach. A Christian's highest earthly role is that of a statesman, not a hermit; he is to be not only pious, but *pius* in the Roman sense—patriotic, respectful of institutions, but opposing evil rather than withdrawing from its presence.

The foremost of the Florentine republicans was a statesman and militia organizer named Niccolò Machiavelli. Machiavelli may today seem a strange person to cite as an authority on ethics or the virtues of a republic: most would associate him with his work *The Prince*, which is quite—for lack of a better word—Machiavellian. But in his other works, chiefly the *Discourses* and the *Art of War*, he wholeheartedly endorsed the republic as the highest form of government, best able to endure bad, and take advantage of good, fortune. One of its strongest points, he wrote, was that it alone could safely arm all its citizens and form them into a militia.[10] The militia became the central focus of Machiavelli's republic, and for a good reason. Early republicans were greatly influenced by the writings of Polybius, a second-century B.C. historian who praised the Roman Republic of his day. Yet Polybius had also argued that republics, like all other forms of government, must decay as freedom led

---

[10] See N. Machiavelli, *The Prince and the Discourses*, 44-46 (Mod. Library ed., 1950) (1513); N. Machiavelli, *The Art of War*, 30-31 (E. Farnsworth, trans., rev. ed., 1965) (1521).

to prosperity, prosperity to decadence, and decadence to weakness.[11] The Florentines aimed at denying this criticism and proving that long-term stability was possible. The militia ideal became Machiavelli's means of escape from this cycle. Not only would it render the republic militarily powerful, it would ensure the citizenry against decadence by maintaining their public spirit and self-reliance. They would remain citizen-soldiers, not urban mobs:

> [I]t is certain that no subjects or citizens, when legally armed and kept in due order by their masters, ever did the least mischief to any state. . . . Rome remained free for four hundred years and Sparta eight hundred, although their citizens were armed all that time; but many other states that have been disarmed have lost their liberties in less than forty years.[12]

Machiavelli came into English thought mainly through James Harrington, who sought to apply his theory to the English situation and to refute thereby the claims of the royal absolutists of his day.[13] Harrington, writing in the 1650s, denied the claim of royal absolutists that government is a moral extension of the original family. Instead, he argued, government is the outcome of sociability, that is, the instinct implanted into all human beings by their Creator which leads them to behave in a restrained and non-beastly fashion. A proper government is "the true and perfect image of the soul of man,"[14] the "infusion of the soul or faculties of a man into a multitude."[15] It marks man's instinctive transformation from herd into a people, from anarchy into "rule of right." "The body of a man, not actuated or led by the soul, is a dead thing out of pain or misery; but the body of a people, not actuated or led by the soul of government, is a living thing in pain and misery."[16]

---

[11] Polybius elaborated on Aristotle's concept of three types of government—monarchy, aristocracy and democracy, with their dangerous counterparts—tyranny, oligarchy and chaos—by arguing that *all* governments pass through similar stages in an unending cycle. Tribal despotism becomes legal kingship, but then degenerates into tyranny. This is followed by aristocracy, which (degenerating into oligarchy) is toppled by democracy. But democracy becomes mob-rule—which is ended by despotism, thus restarting the cycle. Polybius, *Histories*, bk. VI, ch. 4-10.

[12] N. Machiavelli, *The Art of War*, supra note 10, at 30.

[13] Harrington's major works were *Oceana* published in 1656 and *The Prerogative of Popular Government* published in 1658. The best current collection is *The Political Works of James Harrington* (J. Pocock, ed., 1977).

[14] *Ibid.* at 838.

[15] *Ibid.*

[16] *Ibid.*

Harrington based his opposition to royal absolutism—indeed, to monarchy in any form—on several principles. First, he invoked Scripture to prove that Israel had originally been an agrarian republic based on a militia. He pointed out that the Greek translators of the Septuagint even used the term *ecclesia* to describe the assembly of tribes.[17] This term related to the political assemblies of the Greek republics. The very necessity for a covenant with God—and the divine *criticism*, without contrary *action*, of the Israelites' choice of a king[18]—indicated to Harrington that the Creator desired His laws to be accepted by a republic of His people, not imposed against their will. *"[T]his is the law which Moses set before the children of Israel.* Neither did God in this case make use of his omnipotent power, nor Christ in the like. . . ."[19]

At a second level, Harrington argued that the question of the *form* of government is innately practical. If the question is

> whether a ship or an house be the more natural, and then it will be easy to resolve that a ship is the more natural at sea, and an house at land. In like manner, where one man or a few men are landlords [landowners], monarchy must doubtlessly be the more natural, and where the whole people are the landlords, a commonwealth. . . .[20]

To Harrington, the English monarchy had been rendered unnatural by its own actions. The feudal monarch's power had rested upon his ownership of land, which he gave to the nobility in exchange for their mustering the people (by dividing their land among them in exchange for similar agreements) to fight for him. But Henry VII, whose reign ended the murderous civil wars known to history as the War of the Roses, realized that the power of the nobility posed a threat to his throne. He induced the nobility to vote away their own military powers, banning the maintenance of private armies and replacing feudal military duties with militia duties owed directly to county officials appointed by the king.

Harrington went on to say that the destruction of the nobility left the real power in the hands of the king and of the people, which must eventually come into conflict. In that conflict, the people would have the

---

[17] Numbers 10:3; Judges 20-2.

[18] 1 Samuel 8:8.

[19] J. Pocock, supra note 13, at 422.

[20] *Ibid.* at 564-65.

advantages of numbers, money and military force. Thus Henry VII's actions made an English republic inevitable, albeit after a delay of almost two centuries. The monarch could only hold his throne by a standing army, yet an army large enough to hold the nation would inevitably bankrupt the king.

Harrington's major contribution to republican thought, however, came with his discussion of the form the republic should take. To his mind, government could only be stable where political, military and economic power were all in the same hands. Thus he projected a republic where all landowners would vote and would serve in the militia. (To Harrington and most later republicans, a person who owned no land was simply not "free"; his vote would really be at the disposal of his employer). The militia could safely be given enormous power, since it had nothing to gain by revolution: composed as it was of voting property owners, its members could only lose if elected government were overthrown or private property confiscated.[21]

To the English republicans, the militia became the only safe means of collective self-defense. Moreover, the militia institution gave the republic a unique advantage. As Harrington observed, "[m]en accustomed unto their arms and their liberties will never endure the yoke."[22] Henry Neville added, "Democracy is much more powerful than aristocracy, because the latter cannot arm the people for fear they should seize upon the government."[23]

For all of this, the classical republicans went without honor in their own land. By the early eighteenth century, the English militia system was on the wane. Warfare had become more technical with the introduction of new methods by Maurice of Nassau and others. The huge medieval armies were breaking down into small company-sized units. They required far more diligent training than had ever been undertaken.[24] Militia systems were notoriously short on training and discipline.

Thus, beginning in the 1690s, the views of the classical republicans received lip service in England and no more. As Thomas Macaulay, the great nineteenth-century historian, pointed out, every year the Parliament

---

[21] *Ibid.* at 424-25.

[22] *Ibid.* at 443.

[23] C. Hill, *Some Intellectual Consequences of the English Revolution* 27 (1980) (citing Neville, Plato Redivus or *A Dialogue Concerning Government*).

[24] M. Roberts, *The Military Revolution 1560-1660*, Inaugural Lecture delivered before the Queen's University of Belfast 9-11 (copy in possession of author).

heard speeches on the vices of a standing army, following which every year Parliament authorized it.[25] "At length these declamations became too ridiculous to be repeated. The most old-fashioned, the most eccentric, politician could hardly, in the reign of George the Third, contend that there ought to be no regular soldiers. . . ."[26] (We can see a similar process in 1 Chronicles 21-28 and 2 Chronicles 26:11-15, where even divine opposition did not lead to a return to the militia!)

Macaulay overstated his case. In the American colonies, the preference for a militia became accepted by almost all thinkers. By the mid-eighteenth century, Americans generally accepted the premise that militias were characteristic of a free people, and their replacement or suppression by a standing army inevitably indicated the advance of tyranny. Thus it is not surprising that the attempt to import standing armies into the colonies in the 1760s in the wake of the Stamp Act crisis played a major role in bringing on the American Revolution. When, in spring, 1775, the actual war broke out, it followed the republican scenario for the onset of oppression. The fighting at Lexington and Concord bridge was a militia-standing army conflict, brought on by a British raid on a militia arsenal. It might have remained a local conflict, but for the raid on the Williamsburg militia arsenal a few days later, which drove Virginia and Massachusetts into alliance.

III. The Right to Arms and the Unalienable Right of Self-Defense

The background of the militia concept is important to understanding its role as a form of *national* self-defense for a republic, which in turn defines why it is "necessary to the security of a free State." But the drafters of the Bill of Rights did not stop with this statement: they added the positive guarantee that "the right of the people to keep and bear arms, shall not be infringed." To understand this addition, we have to go beyond classical republican thought, for classical republicanism was not

---

[25] 3 T. Macaulay, *The History of English from the Accession of James the Second* 47 (London, 1856).

[26] *Ibid.*

the only—or even the most important—form of political insight available at the foundation of our Republic.[27]

In its purest form, classical republicanism viewed a free nation as one free from internal tyranny and external invasion or domination. We would probably agree that this is the beginning, but not the end, of a definition of a free nation. It is also vital to secure certain natural rights, even against an elective government. In its earliest form, classical republicanism would not have accepted this. Harrington himself had argued that his republic should have an established church: he saw no reason why a national majority, as any other group or congregation, should not be as free to choose a church. The emphasis upon what benefits the state, as opposed to individual liberties, is obvious.[28] (Harrington does not even seem to care which religion was established; one is left with the suspicion he would not have minded if his republic established the worship of the "official" gods of Rome, so long as the resulting idolatry benefitted the government.) Thus classical republican thought emphasized the individual only as a component of the state, albeit of a free state.

Thus it should not be surprising that a second response to royal absolutism arose and eventually came to supplant classical republicanism. It is hard to assign a particular name to this second response. It has been called Enlightenment thought, but it far antedates the Enlightenment, and some of its advocates repudiated certain parts of the Enlightenment. It could be called Jeffersonianism, but it antedates Thomas Jefferson. Some historians have called it the radical movement, but the people at the time did not think of themselves as radical, and today they would be thought of as profoundly conservative. For our purposes, we will call it Jeffersonianism, notwithstanding the anomaly that it begins several centuries before Thomas Jefferson was born.

The seeds of Jeffersonianism are found in Thomas Hobbes, a contemporary of Harrington whose most famed work was *Leviathan*. (*Leviathan*, by the way, offended almost everyone in England. The Tories felt that it undermined the power of the king by basing monarchy on a contract theory; the Whigs felt that it gave a king too much power, by making the contract irrevocable.)

---

[27] The distinction drawn here between the origin of the militia portion of the Second Amendment in the classical republican movement, and the origin of its right-to-arms portion in later Jeffersonian thought, is an expression of a position first taken by the author in Hardy, *The Second Amendment and the Historiography of the Bill of Rights*, 4 J.L. & Pol., 1 (1987).

[28] J. Pocock, supra note 13, at 752.

To Hobbes, the origin of government did not lie in sociability. Rather it lay in the darker side of human nature. To him, men were basically selfish, often violent individuals. Life in a state of nature, as he put it, would be "nasty, brutish, and short."[29] Men, in order to deal with this, created a sovereign.[30] (Hobbes is often seen as supporting absolute monarchy, but in fact he does not specify that the sovereign power must be a monarch.) Men create a sovereign power for one purpose, and that is to protect them from harm—in particular, murder.[31]

This grant is absolute and irrevocable to Hobbes, with one exception. This is vital because in it, Hobbes, traditionally viewed as a spokesman for absolutism, recognizes for the first time in specific terms the doctrine of *unalienable* rights. Hobbes's one exception to the sovereign power is the right to self-defense, because no man may lawfully covenant to yield his own life to a sovereign whose sole purpose is to preserve that life.

> [T]here be some Rights, which no man can be understood by any words, or other signes to have abandoned, or transferred. As first a man cannot lay down the right of resisting them, that assault him by force, to take away his life. . . . The same may be sayd of Wounds, and Chayns, and Imprisonment. . . .
>
> A Covenant not to defend my selfe from force, by force, is alwayes voyd. For (as I have shewed before) no man can transferre, or lay down his Right to save himselfe from Death.[32]

Hobbes has been criticized as saying that man's one unalienable right is to kick the executioner before being dragged away. Nonetheless, he does recognize for the first time, not only the notion of rights, but rights that specifically cannot be alienated in any covenant made with the sovereign power.

From Hobbes's time onward the definition of unalienable rights expanded. It took force from the concept of common law rights, derived from legal custom and tradition. Few legal dicta, for example, have had

---

[29] T. Hobbes, *The Leviathan* 65 (Prometheus Books, reprint, 1988) (1651).

[30] *Ibid.*, at 89-90.

[31] It is often assumed that Hobbes saw protection from homicide as the sole purpose of a government; a careful reading will show, however, that he included protection against physical and property harm in general as among those purposes. Of all early political writers, none requires a more careful reading than Hobbes, whose distinctions and definitions are often quite subtle.

[32] T. Hobbes, supra note 29, at 68, 72.

the impact of Chief Justice Coke's in the famous *Dr. Bonham's Case*, when he said with regard to the common law that

> in many cases, the common law will . . . controul Acts of Parliament, and sometimes adjudge them to be utterly void: for when an Act of Parliament is against common right and reason, or repugnant, or impossible to be performed, the common law will controul it, and adjudge such Act to be void. . . .[33]

The major impetus behind the common law right of arms for self-defense came from the 1689 English Declaration of Rights. Its section on arms was an outgrowth of various royal attempts to disarm the people of England following the Civil War of the mid-seventeenth century. The two major disarmament statutes were the 1662 Militia Act,[34] which authorized militia lieutenants to confiscate arms from anyone judged "dangerous to the Peace of the Kingdom";[35] and the 1671 Hunting Act,[36] which prohibited gun ownership by all but major landowners (those owning land worth a hundred pounds sterling a year in rental).[37]

Under Charles II and later James II, these Acts were vigorously enforced. "Think Fauntleroy an untoward fellow; arms for thirty or forty were found at his house . . . ,"[38] reads a 1662 report; in 1686 James

---

[33] *Dr. Bonham's Case*, 77 Eng. Rep. 646, 652 (1610). The concept of a common law which rises above statutory law seems strange to the modern legal mind. However, to Coke and his successors (particularly Sir Matthew Hale), the common law was the product, not of the wisdom of any one legislator or legislature, but of the experience of countless lawgivers over innumerable centuries. As Coke declared in *Calvin's Case*:

> [W]e are but of yesterday . . . and our days upon the earth are but as a shadow, in respect of the old ancient days and times past, wherein the laws have been by the wisdom of the most excellent men, in many successions of ages, by long and continual experience, (the trial of right and truth) fined and refined, which no one man, (being of so short a time) albeit he had in his head the wisdom of all the men in the world, in any one age could ever have effected or attained unto. And therefore . . . no man ought to take upon him to be wiser than the laws.

Calvin's Case, 77 Eng. Rep. 377, 381 (1609). In practical terms, the common lawyer's assertions were meant to combat the attempts of the Stuart kings to import, by proclamation or legislation, the civil law of the continent, which favored monarchical power. See generally J. Pocock, *The Ancient Constitution and the Feudal Law: A Study of English Historical Thought in the Seventeenth Century* (rev. ed., 1987).

[34] 13 & 14 Car. 2, ch. 3 (1662). The Act was expanded somewhat the following year, 15 Car. 2, ch. 4 (1663).

[35] 13 & 14 Car. 2, ch. 3, § 14, sched. 1.

[36] 22 & 23 Car. 2, ch. 25 (1671).

[37] The best survey of this legislation and its implementations is found in Malcolm, *The Right of the People to Keep and Bear Arms: The Common Law Tradition*, 10 Hast. Const. L.Q. 285 (1983).

[38] 68 Calendar of State Papers (Domestic), Charles II, No. 35, at 44 (Feb. 1662).

ordered royal officials to conduct "strict search" for arms owned by those not legally entitled to them.[39] But in 1688, James II was overthrown in a bloodless revolution which came to be known as the Glorious Revolution. Parliament replaced him with his daughter and son-in-law, William and Mary, who took power as joint sovereigns. They were required before accepting the throne to take an oath to uphold the ancient rights of Englishmen. In order to define at a minimum what those rights were, Parliament promulgated the Declaration of Rights.[40]

Among the "ancient Rights and Liberties" was the following statement: "That the Subjects which are Protestants, may have Arms for their Defence suitable to their Conditions, and as allowed by Law."[41] The most significant phrase is "Arms for *their* Defence." It had been proposed in the House of Commons to use the words "common defence" in that phrase.[42] The House of Lords rejected this and prevailed.[43] Parliament was prepared to recognize that the individual had the right to arms for his or her own defense, not just for that of the state. Whatever other debate there was over this provision was laid to rest when this author discovered in the Library of Congress a book last printed two centuries ago.[44] This contained the papers of Lord Somers, who was present during the parliamentary debates. His notes showed clearly that Parliament was concerned about the fact that they themselves had been disarmed. Sir Richard Temple's speech he summarized as "Militia Act: Power to Disarm all England."[45] Sgt. Maynard ("Sergeant" was then a legal title) was quoted as saying, "An Act was made to disarm all Englishmen whom the Lieutenant should suspect by day or night,"[46] and adding, "Militia Act: An Abominable Thing to Disarm the Nation."[47] There can thus be no doubt that the Declaration of Rights meant to recognize an individual right to own arms for self-defense.

---

[39] 2 Calendar of State Papers (Domestic), James II, No. 1212, at 314 (Dec. 6, 1686).

[40] 1 W. & M., sess. 2, ch. 2 (1689).

[41] *Ibid.*

[42] *Journal of the House of Commons from Dec. 26, 1688, to Oct. 26, 1693,* at 5-6, 21-22 (London, 1742) (Library of Congress, Rare Books Collection).

[43] J. Western, *Monarchy and Revolution: The English State in the 1680's,* at 339 (1972).

[44] 2 Phillip, Earle of Hardwicke, *Miscellaneous State Papers from 1501 to 1726* (London, 1778) (Library of Congress, Rare Books Collection).

[45] *Ibid.,* at 416.

[46] *Ibid.*

[47] *Ibid.*

Blackstone's *Commentaries* took this provision and tied it into the natural law of self-defense. He noted:

> The fifth and last auxiliary right of the subject, that I shall at present mention, is that of having arms for their defence . . . which is also declared by the same statute 1 W. & M. st. 2, c. 2, and it is indeed, a public allowance under due restrictions, of the natural right of resistance and self-preservation. . . .[48]

So Blackstone saw the right to arms as having two bases in the natural law: one was resistance against a tyrant, and the second was self-preservation.

The common law was not, of course, the only source of rights to the colonists. Indeed, many must have agreed with Washington that they should rejoice that their rights were not governed by the principles of the dark ages of legal superstition. Many Americans drew inspiration from the civil jurists of the period who had specifically dealt with the question of self-defense as a natural right. Their doctrine stemmed essentially from the traditional view of suicide as a sin and perhaps the ultimate sin. To them, a failure to defend yourself against an unlawful aggression amounted to suicide by inaction. If a person's life is the gift of the Creator and he cannot destroy it by action, he cannot destroy it by inaction or negligence. If life is not the private property of the person living, then it is not his to destroy or allow to be destroyed: you may voluntarily acquiesce to robbery; you may not voluntarily acquiesce to murder.

Some jurists did equivocate. Pufendorf felt that if a person is menaced and has no dependents, then perhaps he has the luxury of deciding that he will not employ violence to resist violence.[49] But even Pufendorf conceded that the moment a man has dependents, he is morally bound to fight, since at that point the issue of violence is no longer a matter of one act of violence offsetting another. It is a matter of a desertion of your duties toward other people, toward your family and dependents, and thus a violation of his views of natural law.[50]

---

[48] 1 W. Blackstone, *Commentaries* *144.

[49] Pufendorf, *De Jure Naturae et Gentium* (or *The Law of Nature and Nations*), bk. II, ch. V, §§ 1 & 2.

[50] *Ibid.*

In summary, there were two major responses to royal absolutism. One was classical republicanism, with its stress on the militia and political rights keyed to property ownership, but which did not place heavy emphasis on natural law. The other was Jeffersonianism, as I term it here, emphasizing individual rights, including the right to self-defense and the right to means with which to accomplish it, drawing largely upon the natural right of self-defense.

IV. Rights to Arms and Self-Defense Under the American Constitutions

In 1776 the Continental Congress recommended that the newly independent states adopt new constitutions to reflect their status.[51] While not all states heeded the call, enough did so as to enable us to track precisely the points of interaction between the classical republican and the Jeffersonian views of government and rights. A careful look at the constitutional efforts of the time shows clearly the split between militia-guarantee clauses and right-to-arms clauses. Draftsmen influenced by classical republicanism (as evidenced by linkage of property ownership to political rights) uniformly sought militia clauses; Jeffersonians (evidenced by their extension of political rights to all taxpayers) stressed individual rights to arms and self-defense.

The first American state constitution—that of Virginia—is also the clearest example. Virginia's 1776 convention was presented with its two major models. The first was prepared by Thomas Jefferson and, as might be expected, was thoroughly Jeffersonian.[52] It did not key upon the linkage of land ownership and the franchise. Any taxpayer, under Jefferson's proposal, would have been able to vote or run for office. As he explained to the Governor, "I was for extending the right of suffrage (or in other words the rights of a citizen) to all who had a permanent intention of living in the country. . . . Whoever intends to live in a country must wish that country well. . . ."[53] This would have set

---

[51] First Continental Congress, Resolution of May 10, 1776, reprinted in 1 B. Schwartz, *The Roots of the Bill of Rights* 229 (1980).

[52] Thomas Jefferson wrote three drafts of his proposal. See 1 "The Papers of Thomas Jefferson" 337-64 (J. Boyd, ed., 1950). He apparently sent copies of the third draft to George White and Edmund Pendleton to convey to the Virginia convention. *Ibid.* at 364 n.

[53] Letter from Thomas Jefferson to Edmund Pendleton (Aug. 26, 1776), reprinted in 1 "The Papers of Thomas Jefferson," supra note 52, at 503, 504.

Harrington spinning in his grave. Jefferson's severance of land ownership from voting rights marked his complete departure from Harrington's ideal republic. Jefferson went on, in his bill of rights drafts, to omit completely any mention of the militia. Instead, he put in a provision that "[no] freeman shall ever be debarred the use of arms."[54] This is as absolute a statement of an individual arms right as has ever been drafted.

The second proposal advanced in Virginia was far more Harringtonian. This was put forward by George Mason, a militia colonel who was predominantly a classical republican.[55] It recognized the triangular relationship of land, franchise and militia duty. It would have required ownership of land worth a thousand pounds sterling to run for the lower House, and twice that to run for the upper. There was no specific mention of an individual right to defense, but a clause that stated "a well regulated militia, composed of the body of the people, trained to arms, is the proper, natural, and safe defence of a free state."[56] This is purely the classical republican, the legacy of Harrington and his followers. Mason's draft carried the day, and Virginia adopted a declaration of rights with a militia recognition and no individual right to arms.

A few months later Pennsylvania adopted its constitution and broke with Virginia's model. John Adams assures us that their bill of rights was "taken almost verbatim" from the Virginia document, which by then was available in Philadelphia.[57] "Almost," though, is the critical word. Pennsylvania had just experienced its own political revolution. The Philadelphia merchants, the traditional gentry, were in fact heavily tied to England and would not support independence. The patriot forces had to hijack the political machinery and did so with speed and daring. They declared, through various committees of safety, that a new convention would be held pursuant to the orders of Congress. They then walked out of the state legislature. Although they were a minority, this action deprived the legislature of a quorum, so that it was unable to take action in opposition. Finally, they required members of the convention to swear

---

[54] The provision appears in all three of Jefferson's drafts. 1 "The Papers of Thomas Jefferson," supra note 52, at 344, 353, 363.

[55] See 1 "The Papers of George Mason" 267-85 (R. Rutland, ed., 1970); 1 "The Papers of Thomas Jefferson," supra note 52, at 366-72.

[56] 1 "The Papers of George Mason," supra note 55, at 284. Although the militia article first appeared in the committee draft, it appears that Mason is its author. Rutland indicates that its "wording . . . is characteristically" that of George Mason and is "similar to his admonition in the 'Plan for Embodying the People' of 6 Feb. 1775." Ibid. at 286.

[57] Diary of John Adams (June 23, 1779), reprinted in "The Works of John Adams" 220 (C. Adams, ed., 1850-56 & reprint, 1969).

loyalty to the new government and stacked the representation toward the western end of the state, which was wholly in favor of independence. The result was that the convention was dominated by independence supporters, who were Jeffersonians nearly to a man.[58] This was immediately obvious from their product. It is interesting to note the contrast between how Virginia and Pennsylvania opened their constitutions. Virginia primarily stressed the nature of government: "[G]overnment is, or ought to be, instituted for the common benefit, protection, and security of the people, nation, or community. . . ."[59] Pennsylvania stressed not the collective society, but the individual and natural law: "[A]ll government ought to be instituted and supported for the security and protection of the community as such, and to enable the individuals who compose it to enjoy their natural rights, and the other blessings which the Author of existence has bestowed upon man. . . ."[60] The Pennsylvania constitution also would have enfranchised any taxpayer over the age of twenty-one, breaking Harrington's traditional link. It contained no militia clause; in place of the militia clause found in the Virginia document, it provided in section 13 "[t]hat the people have a right to bear arms for the defence of themselves and the state."[61] The rationale for this is apparent from another change it made to the Virginia model. Whereas Virginia had prefaced its bill of rights with a vague reference to the need for "safety," Pennsylvania declared: "[A]ll men are born equally free and independent, and have certain natural, inherent and inalienable rights, amongst which are, the enjoying and defending life and liberty. . . ."[62]

Thus as early as 1776, Americans had two models for a constitution: the Virginia/George Mason model, which stressed the militia and the benefits of a free state, and the Pennsylvania/Jeffersonian model, which stressed the right to keep and bear arms and unalienable rights which included defense of life. The Pennsylvania/Jeffersonian model ultimately triumphed. Only Maryland thereafter followed Virginia's lead, recognizing the militia rather than the right to arms, and also limiting political rights

---

[58] Harding, *Party Struggles Over the First Pennsylvania Constitution,* in "Annual Report of the American Historical Association for the Year 1894," at 371, 371-76 (1895).

[59] Va. Const. of 1776, pt. 1, § 3. The Virginia Constitution, as well as the constitutions referenced in footnotes 60-75 *infra,* can be found in *The Federal and State Constitutions, Colonial Charters, and Other Organic Laws* (F. Thorpe, ed., 1909).

[60] Pa. Const. of 1776, preamble.

[61] *Ibid.* at pt. 1, § 13.

[62] *Ibid.* at p. 1, § 1.

to major landowners. (Indeed, it is estimated only one-tenth of taxpayers could run for office under her 1776 constitution.) North Carolina in 1776 and Massachusetts in 1780 recognized a right of the people to bear arms, albeit with the qualification "for the defence of the State"[63] or "for the common defence."[64] The latter qualifier is probably explained by the fears of John Adams, drafter of the Massachusetts language, that an unlimited right to arms would protect not only use "in private self-defence, or by partial orders of towns, counties, or districts" but also use for riot or mob rule.[65] As it was, Jeffersonian-inclined towns in Massachusetts protested that "we deem it an essential privilege to keep Arms in our Houses for our Own defense."[66] Still more popular was the unlimited individual-right language of Pennsylvania, sometimes made even stronger by addition of for "defence of themselves and the State," which was adopted by Kentucky in 1792,[67] Indiana in 1816,[68] Mississippi in 1817,[69] Connecticut in 1818,[70] Missouri in 1820,[71] and in most later states. Pennsylvania's decision to preface its bill of rights with a recognition of the right of "defending life" was followed by most of these states, as well as by New Hampshire in 1784,[72] Vermont in 1786,[73] Ohio in 1802,[74] and New Jersey in 1844.[75]

The debates over state bills of rights were but a prelude to the great constitutional controversies of 1787 to 1791. The decision of the Constitutional Convention to go beyond its instructions and draft, not amendments to the Articles of Confederation, but an entirely new constitution, was praiseworthy; their failure also to draft a bill of rights

---

[63] N.C. Const. of 1776, pt. 1, art. 17.

[64] Mass. Const. of 1780, pt. 1, art. 17.

[65] J. Adams, 3 *A Defence of the Constitutions of Government of the United States of America*, reprinted in 6 *The Works of John Adams*, supra note 57, at 197.

[66] *The Popular Sources of Political Authority: Documents on the Massachusetts Convention of 1780*, at 624 (O. & M. Handlin, eds., 1966).

[67] Ky. Const. of 1792, art. XII, § 23.

[68] Ind. Const. of 1816, art. 1, § 20.

[69] Miss. Const. of 1817, art. I, § 23.

[70] Conn. Const. of 1818, art. I, § 17.

[71] Mo. Const. of 1820, art. XIII, § 3.

[72] N.H. Const. of 1784, pt. 1, art. II.

[73] Vt. Const. of 1786, ch. 1, § 1.

[74] Ohio Const. of 1802, art. VIII, § 1.

[75] N.J. Const. of 1844, art. I, § 1.

was not. When the various state conventions met to vote on ratification of the new Constitution, the lack of a bill of rights became a focal point of opposition. This in turn led to specific proposals for such a set of guarantees. As these strongly reflected the Jeffersonian viewpoint, it is not surprising that most emphasized an individual right to arms and gave the militia ideal little emphasis.

The first demand for a bill of rights came from a minority in the Pennsylvania convention. As I have mentioned previously, the 1776 Pennsylvania Constitution was a model of Jeffersonian thought, drafted while the Philadelphia merchant gentry were temporarily powerless. In the years since 1776, this gentry had returned to power, and in 1787 they controlled that state's ratifying convention. As a result, only a minority report contained a call for a bill of rights. It demanded recognition:

> That the people have a right to bear arms for the defence of themselves and their own State or the United States, or for the purpose of killing game; and no law shall be passed for disarming the people or any of them unless for crimes committed, or real danger of public injury from individuals. . . .[76]

The Pennsylvania minority report was widely reprinted throughout the states and became the rallying cry of supporters of a bill of rights. When Madison drafted the Bill of Rights a few years later, he considered minority proposals from Pennsylvania along with those from other states.[77]

In Massachusetts, radical and Jeffersonian Sam Adams unsuccessfully proposed a guarantee "that the said Constitution be never construed to authorize Congress to infringe the just liberty of the press, or the rights of conscience; or to prevent the people of the United States, who are peaceable citizens, from keeping their own arms. . . ."[78]

In New Hampshire, the move for a bill of rights finally won. New Hampshire demanded a guarantee that "Congress shall never disarm any Citizen unless such as are or have been in Actual Rebellion."[79] New

---

[76] J. McMaster & F. Stone, *Pennsylvania and the Federal Constitution of 1787-1788*, at 462 (1888).

[77] See I. Brant, *James Madison: Father of the Constitution* 264 (1950).

[78] Debates and Proceedings in the Convention of the Commonwealth of Massachusetts, Held in the Year 1788, at 86 (Boston, 1856); P. Lewis, *The Grand Incendiary: A Biography of Samuel Adams* 361 (1973).

[79] 2 *Documentary History of the Constitution of the United States of America* 143 (1894).

Hampshire's 1788 decision gave the Constitution its nine ratifications it needed to go into effect. But the critical states of Virginia and New York remained. Without their concurrence, the proposed Constitution would have little hope of survival.

Virginia contained a most unusual mixture of personalities. George Mason and Thomas Jefferson, whose 1776 constitutional thinking differed so widely, now agreed on the necessity of a bill of rights. Others, whose thoughts were generally republican in nature, now sided with Jeffersonians and began stressing individual rights to arms. Patrick Henry argued "[t]he great object is, that every man be armed,"[80] and Richard Henry Lee suggested that "to preserve liberty, it is essential that the whole body of the people always possess arms, and be taught alike, especially when young, how to use them. . . ."[81] The shift in thinking is best illustrated by George Mason's changing views. Prior to 1787, he had uniformly stressed the militia concept and ignored the right to arms.[82] Yet when he addressed British attempts to undermine the militia, he now treated these as merely the first step toward total civilian disarmament.[83] When Britain conspired to enslave the colonists, he charged, she planned to "disarm the people";[84] this was begun with an attack on the militia, following which Americans would "sink gradually" into a disarmed state.[85] Thus Virginia's convention had to placate both republicans and Jeffersonians, and the republicans were for the first time accepting the Jeffersonian emphasis on individual arms ownership. The solution was simple: take both a recognition of the militia and a guarantee of the right to bear arms, and splice them together, separated by a comma. Both Jeffersonians and republicans will achieve their ends. Virginia thus called for a guarantee that "the people have a right to keep and bear arms; that a well-regulated militia, composed of the body of the people trained to arms, is the proper,

---

[80] 3 *The Debates in the Several State Conventions on the Adoption of the Federal Constitution* 386 (J. Elliot, 2d ed., n.d. & reprint, 1974) [hereinafter Elliot].

[81] *Letters from the Federal Farmer to the Republican* 124 (W. Bennett, ed., 1978).

[82] See text accompanying *supra* notes 55, 56. Mason's militia emphasis is hardly surprising. Since 1675, Mason's ancestors, and then Mason himself, had commanded their county's militia; in 1774 he had chaired the Fairfax committee meeting which created the first "Independent company" of American militia. 1 K. Rowland, *The Life of George Mason* 8, 33, 181 (1892).

[83] 3 Elliot, supra note 80, at 380.

[84] *Ibid.*

[85] *Ibid.*

natural, and safe defence of a free state."[86] New York followed, using virtually the same words.

With those calls for a bill of rights, the First Congress was hard put to ignore America's rights. Congressman James Madison, by one of the great paradoxes of history, became the father of the Bill of Rights. This is a paradox because Madison spent most of his career arguing that there was no need for a bill of rights and it might be dangerous to have one.[87] However, under some persuasion from local constituents opposed to establishments of religion (in particular, being imprisoned for unlicensed preaching in Virginia, it being impossible to get a license unless you were of the established church), Madison saw the light.[88] He began to draft a bill of rights, pieced together from the demands of the several states.[89] He followed Virginia's proposal almost to the letter, omitting a few phrases.[90]

There is no question which of the two components, militia or right to bear arms, predominated in Madison's mind. The clearest proof of this is the organization he gave to his creation. While the Constitution said it might be amended, the form of amendments was not specified. In fact, one of Madison's opponents in the First House thought the amendments would have to be written in on the original, signed copy of the Constitution and argued that amending it would require defacing an

---

[86] *Ibid.* at 659.

[87] Madison had argued against a bill of rights in his contributions to the *Federalist* papers. *See The Federalist No. 46*, at 238 (J. Madison) (Modern Library ed., 1947). At the Virginia convention, he argued that "A bill of rights would be a poor protection for liberty." 4 B. Schwartz, *supra* note 51, at 764. Even after introducing his bill of rights, he informed Jefferson, "My own opinion has always been in favor of a bill of rights. . . . At the same time I have never thought the omission of a material defect, nor been anxious to supply it even by subsequent amendment, for any other reason than that it is anxiously desired by others." Letter from James Madison to Thomas Jefferson (Oct. 17, 1788), reprinted in 11 *The Papers of James Madison* 295, 297 (R. Rutland & C. Hobson, eds., 1977). Yet this and later tendencies to downplay the bill of rights as an improvement on the Constitution may have been an attempt to avoid accusations of inconsistency. No one could complain if Madison, who had expressed his personal beliefs that a bill of rights was unnecessary, was later to advocate one simply because his constituents demanded it.

[88] In the 1770s, Virginia courts frequently convicted Baptist ministers for preaching in unlicensed houses of worship, preaching without the required ordination in the established Anglican church, or failure to attend established services. Madison was a witness to, and personally outraged by, these prosecutions. L. Levy, *The Establishment Clause* 3 (1986). Running for the first House in 1788, Madison was alarmed by reports that his opponents had been gaining ground among non-Anglicans by arguing that he would oppose constitutional amendments protecting religious liberty. He countered with a letter to the influential minister George Eve, promising to support a bill of rights; Eve in turn became a staunch Madison supporter, stressing to his fellow Baptists the depth of Madison's commitment to religious freedom. R. Ketcham, *James Madison* 276-77 (1970).

[89] 12 *The Papers of James Madison* 58 (R. Rutland & C. Hobson, eds., 1979).

[90] See I. Brant, supra note 77, at 265.

important document! Madison proposed to organize his amendments in the manner of a modern pocket-part. Instead of having ten or twelve numbered amendments, he would have drafted each proviso as a statement that certain words shall be inserted in certain points in certain constitutional clauses. If Madison had seen the Second Amendment primarily as a limitation on the militia, he would have placed it after the statement of the congressional power over the militia in article I, section 8. He did not. He instead grouped the future Second Amendment, together with the future First Amendment, to be inserted in article I, section 9, which set out the limitations on the power of Congress and contained the limited existing guarantees of civil liberties.[91]

Madison's attempt to satisfy everyone met with success. The classical republicans had no objection to a recognition that the militia was a natural defense of a republic. The Jeffersonians were in favor of the guarantee of the right to keep and bear arms. There can be little doubt that the Jeffersonians saw Madison's language as encompassing their earlier demands for an individual right to arms. One Massachusetts newspaper, in an article reprinted in the *Philadelphia Independent Gazetteer* on August 20, 1789, described Madison's ideas as incorporating the earlier proposals of Samuel Adams, including his prohibition on "prevent[ing] the people of the United States, who are peaceable citizens, from keeping their own arms."[92] Tench Coxe, a close friend of Madison, published an article in *The Federal Gazette and Philadelphia Evening Post* for June 18, 1789, which summarized Madison's arms guarantee as follows: "[T]he people are confirmed by the next article in the right to keep and bear their private arms."[93] That Coxe's explanation was available to the First Congress, and met with Madison's approval, is obvious. Madison's papers show that Coxe sent him a copy, and that he replied with gratitude and a note that the article had already been reprinted in the local newspapers.[94]

Henry St. George Tucker, a brilliant individual and Revolutionary veteran who was appointed to the Bench both by Madison and by

---

[91] 1 *Annals of the Congress of the United States* 451 (J. Gates, ed., 1789), reprinted in 5 B. Schwartz, supra note 51, at 1026.

[92] *The Philadelphia Independent Gazetteer*, Aug. 20, 1789, at 2, col. 2.

[93] *The Federal Gazette & Philadelphia Evening Post*, June 18, 1789, at 2, col. 1.

[94] Letter from Tench Coxe to James Madison (June 18, 1789) reprinted in 12 *The Papers of James Madison, supra* note 89, at 239, 239-40; Letter from James Madison to Tench Coxe (June 24, 1789), reprinted in 12 *The Papers of James Madison, supra* at 257.

Jefferson, in the early 1800s brought out the first American edition of Blackstone. St. George Tucker linked the Second Amendment to the natural right of self-defense when he explained, "This may be considered as the true palladium of liberty. . . . The right of self-defence is the first law of nature. . . ."[95] William Rawle, a friend of Washington and Franklin, who was rumored to have been offered the first post of Attorney General of the United States, in his 1825 book, *View of the Constitution*, likewise explained, "The prohibition is general. No clause in the Constitution could by any rule of construction be conceived to give Congress a power to disarm the people."[96] It is remarkable that these early commentaries so universally ignored the militia clause, or relegated it to a secondary priority when compared to the individual right to arms.

V. Rights to Arms and Self-Defense in the Courts

A. The Right to Arms

The natural right of self-defense was unchallenged in the early years of the Republic. The same was not true of the right to arms. On that subject, three lines of case law developed in the early United States. The first and earliest ones simply recognized that, indeed, the Second Amendment or its state analog guaranteed an individual right to keep and bear arms subject to some limitations.[97] The first major question to arise was whether prohibiting concealed carrying of weapons was a proper limitation or not. The courts split on this subject. Kentucky, for instance, struck down its 1813 concealed weapons law on the ground that no restrictions upon arms were constitutional.[98] Louisiana upheld its enactment, reasoning that since only concealed carrying was banned, it was still possible to carry arms in a way appropriate to self-defense.[99]

The second chain of cases developed in the Reconstruction period and essentially said there is an individual right to keep and bear arms, but that

---

[95] 1 *Blackstone's Commentaries* 300 (St. George Tucker, ed., 1803 & photo. reprint, 1969).

[96] W. Rawle, *A View of the Constitution of the United States of America* 125 (Philadelphia, 2d ed., 1829).

[97] See, e.g., *Bliss v. Commonwealth*, 12 Ky. (2 Litt.) 90 (1822); *State v. Chandler*, 5 La. Ann. 489, 52 Am. Dec. 599 (1850); *State v. Reid*, 1 Ala. 612 (1840); *State v. Mitchell*, 3 Black. 229 (Ind., 1833) (per curiam); *State v. Buzzard*, 4 Ark. 18 (1842); *Aymette v. State*, 21 Tenn. (2 Hum.) 154 (1840); *Nunn v. State*, 1 Ga. 243 (1846).

[98] *Bliss v. Commonwealth*, 12 Ky. (2 Litt.) 90 (1822).

[99] *State v. Chandler*, 5 La. Ann. 489, 52 Am. Dec. 599 (1850).

the type of arms must be suitable to the militia.[100] Therefore, the state can prohibit certain arms, like cane guns, daggers and similar weapons, which are not basically a military type of arms but used, as one court put it, "in quarrels and broils."[101] These cases involved a mixture, and perhaps a confusion, of the Jeffersonian and republican objects, recognizing an individual right only to the extent it serves a collective national purpose.

The third view did not actually arise until *City of Salina v. Blaksley*.[102] The Founders had been dead for almost a century before this interpretation was suggested. This approach claims that the Second Amendment only relates to a militia, the militia is the National Guard, and therefore the Second Amendment is basically meaningless. This view has since gained acceptance by many federal courts,[103] none of which have cared to engage in any serious research. The one Supreme Court decision cited for this proposition, *United States v. Miller*,[104] actually does not support this post-1905 view. Jack Miller, who was by profession a bank robber, was prosecuted for possessing a shotgun with the barrel beneath the legally required eighteen inches. The district court dismissed the case, based on the Second Amendment, without taking evidence. The government appealed to the United States Supreme Court, which reversed. The Court essentially said that it was not within judicial notice whether such a shotgun is suitable for militia duty[105] and remanded the case for this finding. Clearly the Court did not require that a person be a member of the National Guard. Jack Miller was in fact a bank robber, not one had contended that he was a member of a National Guard unit, let alone acting in the course of duty. The Supreme Court in fact does not use the words "National Guard" in the opinion and nowhere suggests that upon remand the district court should inquire into Miller's National Guard status—but only into the nature of the firearm. *Miller* is thus in line with

---

[100] See, e.g., *Andrews v. State*, 50 Tenn. (3 Heisk.) 165 (1871); *English v. State*, 35 Tex. 473 (1872); *Fife v. State*, 31 Ark. 455 (1876); *Dabbs v. State*, 39 Ark. 353 (1882); cf. *State v. Rosenthal*, 75 Vt. 295, 55 A. 610 (1903); *State v. Wilforth*, 74 Mo. 528 (1881) and cases cited therein. See generally, *The Right to Bear Arms for Private and Public Defense*, 1 Cent. L.J. 260-61, 273-75, 285-87, 295-96 (1874).

[101] *English v. State*, 35 Tex. 473, 475 (1871).

[102] 72. Kan. 230, 83 P. 619 (1905).

[103] See, e.g., *Eckert v. Philadelphia*, 477 F.2d 610 (3d Cir., 1942) (per curiam); *Cases v. United States*, 131 F.2d 916 (1st Cir., 1942), *cert. denied*, 319 U.S. 770 (1943); *United States v. Tot*, 131 F.2d 261 (ed Cir., 1942), *rev'd*, 319 U.S. 463 (1943).

[104] 307 U.S. 174 (1939).

[105] *Ibid.* at 178.

the Reconstruction cases, which it cites, and not with the post-1905 collective rights view.

B. The Right to Self-Defense

While the individual and fundamental right to self-defense went unchallenged in the early Republic, it is unfortunately subject to frequent challenge and restriction at present. The modern tendency to question so basic a natural right is attributable to a number of factors. The first is a tendency to view the government as a universal protector of all things, and the individual as an inferior and erring subset of this juridical idol. This is illustrated by the controversy over the prosecution of Bernhard Goetz for shooting several armed individuals who accosted him on the New York subway. Following his acquittal on assault charges, one columnist decried his action as linked to "the crazy passions of vigilantism [sic]" and closed with the prayer that the nation be spared "a widening spell of lawlessness in which self-styled vigilantes may decide what you and I deserve."[106] Whether or not one believes that Goetz acted in necessary self-defense, it is impossible to claim that he was hunting down now-harmless individuals to repay them for past offenses. Classifying his response to a perceived robbery as vigilanteeism assumes that protection from crime—as well as the assessment of punishment for completed crimes—is the *sole prerogative* of government, and that a citizen whose safety is endangered by criminal attack has no right to protect himself should the government fail to offer aid.

A second factor undermining the fundamental right of self-defense is the increasing tendency toward determinism as a means of explaining behavior—which denies the possibility of moral choice—and of moral relativism—which denies the possibility of morals at all. As one commentator recently noted:

> When President Ronald Reagan called the Soviet Union "the evil empire," right-thinking persons joined in an angry chorus of protest against such provocative rhetoric. At other times Mr. Reagan has said that the United States and the Soviet Union "have different *values*" [italics added], an assertion that those same persons greet at worst with silence and frequently with approval. I believe he thought he was saying the same thing in both instances,

---

[106] *Washington Post*, June 19, 1987, at A25, col. 2.

and the different reaction to his different words introduces us to *the* most important and most astonishing phenomenon of our time, all the more astonishing in being almost unnoticed: there is now an entirely new language of good and evil, originating in an attempt to get "beyond good and evil" and preventing us from talking with any conviction about good and evil anymore. . . .

The new language is that of *value* relativism, and it constitutes a change in our view of things moral and political as great as the one that took place when Christianity replaced Greek and Roman paganism. . . .

Good and evil now for the first time appeared as values, of which there have been a thousand and one, none rationally or objectively preferable to any other.[107]

This of course leads to a manner of moral equivalence between the criminal's attack and the victim's defense. If a murderer is merely displaying his lack of control or displaying the residuum of his own abuse as a child, a rapist acting out his repressed Freudian anger, or a robber attempting to better his lot in a difficult world, a victim who suffers from none of these and who fights such a sufferer is certainly guilty of intolerance and insensitivity.

The net result is illustrated by several cases that have subverted the rights of self-defense and to arms. Massachusetts is a case in point. In *Commonwealth v. Davis*,[108] the Massachusetts Supreme Court, notwithstanding a state constitutional provision that recognizes the right of the people to keep and bear arms, concluded there is no right to keep and bear arms in the State of Massachusetts. The Massachusetts court simply quotes the guarantee and, without looking at its history, concludes that it is directed to maintaining a militia.[109] Then it notes that "our militia, of which the backbone is the National Guard, is now equipped and supported by public funds."[110] The opinion must stand as one of the more remarkable exercises in judicial nullification: apart from the questionable reasoning, the court's claim that the National Guard is the "backbone" of

---

[107] A. Bloom, *The Closing of the American Mind* 141-43 (1987).

[108] 369 Mass. 886, 343 N.E.2d 847 (1976).

[109] *Ibid.* at 887-88, 343 N.E.2d at 848-49.

[110] *Ibid.* at 888, 343 N.E.2d at 849.

the militia, not the entirety of it, suggests that the court was aware of the flaws in its reasoning process.

A year earlier, the same court had handed down *Commonwealth v. Shaffer.*[111] Roberta Shaffer resided in a one-story ranch home with her two children. She was separated from her husband and in the process of being divorced. She was having breakfast with her fiancé—an ex-mental patient who was extremely violent and had severely beaten her before and threatened to kill the children—when an argument ensued. At one point the fiancé rose and said, "Never mind, I'll take care of you right now." The defendant threw a cup of tea at him and ran into the basement, where the children were having breakfast. The fiancé shouted down, "If you don't come up these stairs, I'll come down and kill you and the kids." He came down, and she fatally shot him. She was tried and found guilty of manslaughter. The court held she was not entitled to the standard jury instruction on self-defense, that she need not retreat from her own home. The common law rule was that a victim must generally retreat before using deadly force, but that in his or her own house, the victim was deemed to have retreated "to the wall." The Massachusetts Supreme Court conceded that the exception to the retreat requirements is the majority rule, but concluded:

> This has never been the law of the Commonwealth, and we see no reason to adopt it now. . . . [T]he right to use deadly force by way of self-defense is not available to one threatened until he has availed himself of all reasonable and proper means to avoid combat. . . . [T]his rule has equal application to one assaulted in his own home.[112]

The District of Columbia offers another example. The District of Columbia has banned the possession of unlicensed handguns and frozen

---

[111] 367 Mass. 508, 326 N.E.2d 880 (1975).

[112] *Ibid.* at 511, 326 N.E.2d at 883. A digression: At common law, the retreat requirement would never have come into play in a case such as this. A citizen had nearly an absolute right to kill a felon, either to prevent the commission of a felony or to prevent the escape of a felon. The self-defense privilege was thus superfluous when a felony was committed. It would only be pled where the person killed was *not* a felon—in, for example, mutual combat between persons with no criminal record. Here, the retreat requirement made sense: otherwise-law-abiding citizens should be required to break off a fight, if practical, rather than escalating it. The great narrowing of rights to use deadly force to prevent felonies or the escape of a felon has led to the use of the self-defense privilege, with its restrictions, in contexts where the common law never applied those restrictions.

registrations for a dozen years.[113] Residents are permitted to possess a rifle or shotgun with appropriate police registration, provided they keep it unloaded and disassembled or trigger locked.[114] Thus, even these cannot be used for self-defense. It is also illegal to possess tear gas, Mace, any irritant spray and any electrical shocking device or stun gun.[115] These statutes were upheld against a Second Amendment challenge in *Sandidge v. United States.*[116] The Court of Appeals of the District of Columbia held that the right to keep and bear arms applies only to a state's right to raise and regulate a militia, and noted that D.C. has no militia.[117]

Compare this with another interesting D.C. case, *Warren v. District of Columbia.*[118] Three women lived in a two-level apartment. Two rapists broke in and began beating and raping the one below; the two upstairs heard this and called the police. The dispatcher told them that help was on the way. In fact, the dispatcher radioed the police car in the area that there was a suspicious situation but did not mention that a crime was in progress. The women upstairs saw a police car drive around the building and depart. They called the dispatcher again and were assured that this time help would be on the way. The dispatcher this time logged the request as "investigate the trouble" but did not bother to signal the police car at all. The women upstairs cried down to their roommate below, shouting that help was coming. The rapists downstairs heard them and came upstairs, and, as the court notes, the women were then beaten and gang-raped for the following fourteen hours. Not unexpectedly, they sued the District of Columbia. Not unexpectedly, the court held they had no right of action, because "a government and its agents are under no general duty to provide public services, such as police protection, to any particular individual citizen."[119] The court noted in horror that submitting the case to the jury would have let the jurors "join in the responsibility of judging the adequacy of a public employee's performance in office."[120]

---

[113] D.C. Code § 22-3204 (1981).

[114] D.C. Code §§ 6-2311, 6-2372 (1981).

[115] D.C. Code §§ 6-2303(c)-(D), 6-2311 (1981).

[116] 520 A.2d 1057 (D.C., 1987), *cert. denied*, 484 U.S. 868 (1987).

[117] 520 A.2d at 1058.

[118] 444 A.2d 1 (D.C., 1981).

[119] *Ibid.* at 3 (quoting trial judge's opinion).

[120] *Ibid.* at 8 (Appendix).

VI. Conclusion

The Second Amendment to our Constitution embodies not one but two concepts. The first, a recognition that the militia is the proper defense of a free state, is not a guarantee of a right in any sense, collective or individual. It is a statement of a principle of classical republicanism, a recommendation as to how the newly created national government should function. Its essential purpose was to ensure the collective defense of the nation, not to reserve rights for the nation's citizens. As such, its position in the Bill of Rights remains an anomaly, probably inspired by Madison's need to placate classical republicans in his home state of Virginia. Whatever its inspiration, it should be apparent that this provision was not the primary thrust of the amendment. At the federal level, proposals for a right to arms were the driving force behind the Second Amendment, with the militia recognition surfacing as a proposed addition only with the Virginia ratifying convention, at the eleventh hour of our constitutional process.

The other portion of the Second Amendment derives its origin from the natural right of individual self-defense which, in turn, reflects the right of every human being to defend his or her life against illegal attack. It is all but indisputable that this is the most fundamental of all natural rights, and accordingly some have maintained that such defense is not merely a right but a moral duty: Failure to so defend is tantamount to suicide by inaction. A person may act morally in transferring property without resistance, but one who voluntarily becomes a homicide victim is a party to destruction of that which he did not create and does not own.

Twentieth-century courts have often abandoned these principles. By overlooking the distinction between the two provisions of the Second Amendment and by treating its description of the militia as its exclusive purpose, courts have effectively nullified its right-to-arms provision. The same courts have often imposed unusual restrictions upon the right of self-defense and, paradoxically, repudiated any enforceable duty of the sovereign to defend its citizens. The result is a government which will neither allow its citizens to defend their own lives nor itself assume the responsibility for defending them.

On Liberty

R. A. I. Munday

"Arms," wrote the Scottish **Whig** Andrew Fletcher in the wake of the Glorious Revolution, "are the only true badges of liberty."[1] They were the ultimate surety of the Bill of Rights, without which the "true, ancient and indubitable rights"[2] of the citizen were but vacant and unenforceable pleadings—as Fletcher, who had been under sentence of death when he joined William of Orange at the Hague, well knew. "The possession of arms," he declared, "is the distinction of a free man from a slave."[3]

It was upon the right and power of the people to resist the oppression of the state that the constitution was founded. "'Tis no great harm if the people, by help of their arms, should happen to defend themselves against tyranny and oppression," observed the Country Party author of *The Claims of the People of England* [4] in 1701; Blackstone, setting out "the absolute rights of individuals" in his definitive constitutional *Commentaries*,[5] saw recourse to arms as the necessary final means "to vindicate these rights." The liberty to possess arms, the "fifth and last auxiliary right" of the subject, was indeed the expression of "the natural right of resistance and self-preservation, when the sanctions of society and the laws are found insufficient to restrain the violence of oppression"; a political right, balancing the power of the citizen against the government. "Every one knows," observed the Earl of Egmont in Parliament in 1753,[6] "that both the Revolution and our present happy establishment were founded upon the principle of resistance."

That principle was carried from England to her colonies. "Guard with jealous attention the public liberty," warned Patrick Henry in the Virginia

---

[1] Andrew Fletcher, *A Discourse of Government with relation to Militias* (Edinburgh, 1698), p. 47.

[2] W&M Sess. 2, c. 2.

[3] [Andrew Fletcher] *Speeches of a Member of Parliament which began at Edinburgh on the 6th of May, 1703* (Edinburgh, 1703), p. 307.

[4] Anon., *The Claims of the People of England, Essayed, in a Letter from the Country,* in: *A Collection of State Tracts, Publish'd during the Reign of King William III* (London, 1701), p. 15.

[5] William Blackstone, *Commentaries on the Laws of England* (4th Edition, Oxford, 1770), vol. I, pp. 143-44.

[6] *The Parliamentary History of England,* vol. XIV, 1747-1753, (London, 1813), col. 1281-2.

Convention in 1788.[7] "Suspect every one who approaches that jewel. Unfortunately nothing will preserve it, but downright force: whenever you give up that force, you are inevitably ruined." Henry reiterated: "The great object is, that every man be armed";[8] the strength of the American constitution resided, as his contemporary Joel Barlow observed in 1792, in "not only *permitting* every man to arm, but *obliging* him to arm."[9] Such sentiments, and the turns of phrase of Fletcher and his contemporaries, were voiced again in London in 1774 by James Burgh:

> No kingdom can be secured otherwise than by arming the people. The possession of arms is the distinction between a free man and a slave. . . . Why may not the nobility, gentry and freeholders of England be trusted with the defence of their own lives, estates, and liberties, without having guardians and keepers assigned to them? . . . Why may not a competent number of firelocks be kept in every parish, for the young men to exercise with on holy days, and rewards offered to the most expert, to stir up their emulation.[10]

In 1859, the year in which the National Rifle Association was formed to fulfill that provision, John Stuart Mill published his great essay *On Liberty*, in which he recorded the traditional concept of resisting the "highly dangerous"[11] power of central government. In England, he observed,

---

[7] Speech in the Virginia Convention, June 5, 1788, *Patrick Henry, Life, Correspondence & Speeches* (New York, 1891), vol. III, p. 436.

[8] Speech in the Virginia Convention on June 14, 1788, *ibid.*, p. 530. For a discussion of the history of the right to keep and bear arms in America, see *The Right to Bear Arms: Report of the Subcommittee on the Constitution of the Committee on the Judiciary, United States Senate* (97th Congress, 2nd Session, Washington, D.C., 1982); Robert Shalhope, "Ideological Origins of the Second Amendment," *Journal of American History*, vol. 69, no. 3 (Bloomington, Ind., 1982); Steven Halbrook, *That Every Man Be Armed* (Albuquerque, N.Mex., 1984); Robert Shalhope, "The Armed Citizen in the Early Republic," *Law & Contemporary Problems* (Durham, N.C., 1986).

[9] J. Barlow, *Advice to the Privileged Orders in the Several States of Europe, Resulting from the Necessity and Propriety of a General Revolution in the Principle of Government* (London, 1792), p. 32.

[10] J. Burgh, *Political Disquisitions* (London, 1774), p. 390; p. 416. The latter citation is a virtual quotation from J. Trenchard and W. Moyle, *An Argument Shewing, That a Standing Army is Inconsistent with a Free Government, and Absolutely Destructive to the Constitution of the English Monarchy* (London, 1697), p. 21.

[11] J. S. Mill, *On Liberty* (Edn. Dent, London, 1910) p. 65.

. . . there is considerable jealousy of direct interference, by the legislative or executive power, with private conduct; not so much from any just regard for the independence of the individual, as from the still subsisting habit of looking on the government as representing an opposite interest to the public.[12]

It was his own view that the innate human tendency to dominate was "hardly ever kept under restraint by anything but want of power";[13] and through to the First World War, the executive in Britain was kept under that restraint. Before 1914, as A. J. P. Taylor has observed, a "sensible, law-abiding Englishman could pass through life and hardly notice the existence of the state, beyond the post office and the policeman."[14]

The monolithic nation-in-arms of the Great War was to be a far remove from the liberal tradition of the independent, armed citizenry; and on the eve of the conflict, the underlying motives of those who advocated conscription had been called in question. "They do not mention the foe within," remarked A. G. Gardiner of the conscriptionists in *Pillars of Society?* in 1913, "but he is in their minds much more than the enemy without. A drilled and disciplined proletariat is their hope against an insurgent democracy."[15] The "enemy within" was certainly the concern of the government after the revolutions of 1917, and with the war's end the executive was loathe to relax its new-found authority. "The legacy of the war," as Lord Blake has remarked, "was a permanent accretion in the powers of the state, which never returned to their pre-1914 level. The same was to be true of 1939-45."[16] In 1920, those powers were deployed to rein in what Sir Eric Geddes termed "the unthinking mass of labour."[17] Gun controls were introduced, while stands of arms were held ready for the use of those whom Bonar Law defined as "friends of the government,"[18] in the event of crisis. It was the fulfillment of what Sir

---

[12] *Ibid.*, pp. 71-72.

[13] *Ibid.*, p. 77.

[14] A. J. P. Taylor, *English History 1914-45* (Oxford, 1965), p. 1.

[15] A. G. Gardiner, essay on Lord Milner, in *Pillars of Society?* (London, 1913), p. 333. See also V. G. Kiernan, "Conscription and Society in Europe Before the War of 1914-18" in *War & Society: Historical Essays in Honour and Memory of J. R. Western*, ed. M. R. D. Foot (London, 1973).

[16] Foreword to James Bishop, *The Illustrated London News Social History of the First World War* (London, 1982).

[17] PRO CAB 25/20, cited in *Handgunner* 43, p. 9.

[18] Cited in *Handgunner* 43, p. 9.

Walter Raleigh, three centuries before, had described as a maxim of the "sophistical or subtle tyrant":

> To unarm his people, and store up their weapons, under pretense of keeping them safe, and having them ready when service requireth, and then to arm them with such, and as many as he shall think meet, and to commit them to such as are sure men.[19]

In 1920, the House of Commons was not without those who recognized the constitutional significance of the Firearms Act. Major Barnes, MP, recalled that,

> We certainly owe much of our liberty today, and the fact that we do not need, and I hope never will need, to resort to armed resistance, to the fact that some 200 or 300 years ago there were people who found it necessary to take up arms against the State.[20]

Lt. Cdr. Kenworthy, MP, concerned at the political trend which the Firearms Bill exemplified, called the attention of the House to the fact that they had "here a chance at any rate of stopping one more attempt to set up a petty police bureaucracy in this country." Kenworthy declared:

> I very much object to power being given to the police to judge whether a person is fit to have a firearm or not. I hope the Committee will not give such a power to them . . . . giving the right to the police to decide a point of this kind is quite a new development in this country, and is contrary to English practice. In England the police are very respected public servants; on the Continent they are petty officials with tremendous powers, which they use to the full and are not conducive to the free development of those nations. We do not want that kind of thing here.[21]

Lt. Cdr. Kenworthy recalled how, over the centuries from the reign of Henry VII, centralizing governments had sought to deprive the people of the power to resist by taking away their arms. "I do not know whether

---

[19] W. Raleigh, *The Works of Sir Walter Raleigh, Kt., Now First Collected: to which are prefixed The Lives of the Author*, ed. Oldys and Birch (Oxford, 1829), vol. VIII, *Miscellaneous Works*, p. 25.

[20] *Parliamentary Debates [Hansard]* (London, 1920), col. 671.

[21] *Ibid.*, col. 659.

this Bill is aimed at any such goal as that," Kenworthy said, but advised that if this were the object it would be futile:

> . . . the great weapon of democracy today is not the halberd or the sword or firearms, but the power of withholding their labour. I am sure that the power of withholding his labour is one of which certain Members of our Executive would very much like to deprive him. But it is our last line of defence against tyranny.[22]

The Earl of Winterton responded for the government, that Kenworthy had:

> . . . the most extraordinary theories of constitutional history and the law. His idea is that the State is an aggressive body, which is endeavoring to deprive the private individual of the weapons which heaven has given into his hands to fight against the State.[23]

Winterton expressed deep concern at the notion of a citizenry armed against "the forces of the State," and warned darkly that "There are other people who hold those views in this country, and it is because of the existence of people of that type that the Government has introduced this Bill."[24] People of "that type," the type of Blackstone and of the Framers of the Bill of Rights, were the enemies of the new, bloated post-war state. Lt. Cdr. Kenworthy, MP, was investigated by the Special Branch.

In the most heavily armed democracy in the world, the fears of the British government were not reflected. Switzerland went through the experience of a general strike in 1918 without the strikers once taking recourse to the service rifles which they kept in their homes. Switzerland still maintained Patrick Henry's principle "that every man be armed," and continued to see the militia in the classic terms once used by James Burgh in Britain, as "the only proper security of a free people . . . both against foreign invasion and domestic tyranny."[25] Even the General Secretary of the International Peace Bureau in Bern had commented, early in the Great War, that should the aims of his organization ever be

---

[22] *Ibid.*, col. 658-59.

[23] *Ibid.*, col. 662-63.

[24] *Ibid.*, col. 663.

[25] J. Burgh, *op. cit.*, p. 389.

fulfilled and armies be banished from the Earth, "Switzerland ought merely to do away with the ammunition," her militia "being otherwise the best school of civic virtues."[26] As much as when Machiavelli had described the Swiss as *armatissimi e liberissimi* [27] most armed and most free—the armed citizenry was still seen in the post-war world as the security and expression of democracy. Henri Guisan, the Swiss commander-in-chief in the Second World War, observed in 1938 that the militia represented "not only the duty but the right of the citizen: it is the sign of the free man"[28]—expressing in the most tangible sense the devolution of power among the citizenry. As John Trenchard and the MP Walter Moyle had stated in London in 1697, "the Sword and Sovereignty always march hand in hand."[29]

In Europe after the Great War, Swiss democracy was an exception— the Sword elsewhere was ever more visibly marching in the hands of the state. It is one of the ironies of history that contemporary opponents often have more in common with each other than they do with their own progenitors and successors—and so fear of Bolshevism and then of national socialism in the West was met by measures which ever more bore the stamp of the authoritarian corporate state. Like Britain, Norway introduced gun controls, fearful of what cause the liberal "Ring of Rifles Around the Parliament," that had stood for independence from Sweden, might now espouse. In Denmark, where the organized rifle movement traced back to emulation of Britain's National Rifle Association in 1860, and where civilian corps of motorcycle-mounted machine gunners had possessed more automatic weapons than the Danish army in 1914 (when they covered the latter's mobilization), the government now sought to abolish the rifle corps. They were not in any sense politically extremist or dangerous, it was admitted in the Danish Parliament; but it was simply felt that national defense should be the business not of the individual citizen, but of the state. In 1937 the corps were disbanded; to their country's rue on April 9, 1940.

Across Europe, the state Prometheus was bursting the shackles of democracy; parliaments trailed pathetically behind, to offer a sorry sham

---

[26] J. Grande, *A Citizens' Army* (London, 1916), p. 106.

[27] Niccolò Machiavelli, *Il Principe* ch. 12, (Venezia, 1537), p. 24.

[28] Henri Guisan, *Notre Peuple et son Armée* (Zurich, 1938), p. 11.

[29] J. Trenchard and W. Moyle, *An Argument Shewing, That a Standing Army is Inconsistent with a Free Government, and Absolutely Destructive to the Constitution of the English Monarchy* (London, 1697), p. 7.

of constitutional consecration. The British government, determining to emulate America's faintly absurd 1934 "Gangster Weapons Law," introduced a new Firearms (Amendment) Bill in 1936, to get rid of what the Home Secretary, Sir John Simon, called "the weapon which we are informed is used by gangsters on the other side of the water."[30] At Second Reading, Mr. Lunn, MP, recalled the proceedings of the Home Office committee upon whose recommendations the bill was based:

> The only reason why I could ever think of why I was made a member of [the Committee] is that we were in such small numbers on this side of the House in the last Parliament that it was difficult to find Members who could take part in the many committees that were set up by the Government at that time. Perhaps I knew as little about firearms as any Member of the House. I never remembered having handled a firearm until I became a member of the Departmental Committee. I have had a long experience in this House and have found that it is not necessary that a Member should know a great deal about a subject to be able to speak about it and take part in a debate.[31]

Mr. Lunn was duly impressed by "the wonderful evidence we have heard from many people of experience . . . who knew much about the subject of the danger of firearms to the public," and was now ready to enact a law on the basis of the belief "that the public will be safeguarded from some of the dangers which may happen if we do not pass the Measure."[32] Such was now the intellectual rigor of the Mother of Parliaments.

If the legislative momentum of the expanding state was straining Parliamentary committees in the 1930s, today it has stampeded ahead. It is now the common complaint of Members of Parliament that they simply cannot keep abreast of the pace of new lawmaking. They are reduced, as William Ross, MP, observed to his colleagues in 1988, to "cannon fodder, and trot cheerfully through whichever Lobby they are directed,"[33] drilled by the Whips to crowd through legislation on debates unheard. The

---

[30] House of Commons, *Official Report [Hansard]*, vol. 312, 1936, col. 168.

[31] *Ibid.*, col. 167.

[32] *Ibid.*, col. 168.

[33] *Hansard*, Standing Committee F, February 4, 1988, col. 10.

guillotined debate on the 1988 Firearms Act, and the contemptuous disregard of the government for evidence which did not suit their plans, was symptomatic of the decrees of the Promethean state. "Men that are above all fear," John Trenchard and Thomas Gordon had observed in *Cato's Letters* at the beginning of the 18th century, "soon grow above all shame."[34] In the one-and-a-half-party system of Margaret Thatcher's Britain, the unbridled power of the executive became grotesquely apparent: When on the Report stage of the 1988 Firearms Bill the Deputy Speaker of the House of Commons ruled that divisions of the House were unnecessary because of a clear government majority, the Labour MP Frank Cook pointed out that on that principle, there was no point in Parliament now voting on anything.[35] The democracy of two, to which the system of party discipline has reduced Westminster, could only function in a hung Parliament. With a 100-seat majority for one party and team loyalty further ensured by the ever broadening office patronage of a revolving-door Cabinet, there has been no more challenge to the executive. The "opposition" as a meaningful term was broken with the unions. Like Charles I after 1629, Mrs. Thatcher was effectively able to rule without Parliament.

Yet for all its nominal power, the achievements of the unbridled executive have in many ways been worse than fatuous. The ever-increasing preoccupation with "law, order, and internal security" (the objects of the Firearms Bill, as the Earl of Feversham had described them in 1936)[36] has scarcely yielded a more peaceable society. In the name of "control," which has supplanted the outmoded concept of liberty in the British polity, the state has taken more and more responsibility away from its subjects; and found them less and less responsible.

It was for the principles of a past conservatism that Henry Bellingham, MP, stood, when he observed that "where it is not absolutely necessary to legislate, it is very necessary not to legislate."[37] The Tory Party now has become the Court Party of the new executive; and the old principles which Bellingham enunciated must seek instead a new Country Party. Labour, which has been a party in quest of a policy, has more than its

---

[34] J. Trenchard and T. Gordon, *Cato's Letters: Or, Essays on Liberty, Civil & Religious, & Other Important Subjects* (London, 1755), vol. I, p. 255.

[35] *Hansard*, May 25, 1988, col. 469.

[36] House of Lords, *Official Report*, vol. 99, 1936, col. 604.

[37] Firearms (Amendment) Bill, Standing Committee F, 1988, cited in *Handgunner* 44, p. 11.

leaders might care to admit in common with the philosophy of the present government; for the essence of Thatcherism as of socialism is the Marxist doctrine of material determinism. When in 1988 the Home Office attributed to objects the misdeeds of men, and decided to ban "weapons which are an acknowledged threat,"[38] Mr. Hattersley was as obliged as Mr. Hurd to agree, and cede more power to the state. Perhaps so were the Social Democrats—it is hard to know. For if "social democracy" is more than an impressionistic tautology and denotes the grafting of socialist onto liberal principles, it is a contradiction in terms. Socialism is predicated upon the weakness of the individual, and the way in which his actions are determined by his material surroundings; democracy is founded on the notion of the individual's strength and independence of decision. One cannot have it both ways.

There are individuals on both sides of the House of Commons who stand for the principles of the old constitutional balance, and the check on the power of the executive; but there is no Country Party. The House of Lords, in theory a brake on the whims of government, is scarcely more independent. On October 19, 1988, the Firearms Bill again gave proof of the power of party discipline. There were some 40 Peers sitting in the Chamber when an amendment was proposed to permit disabled people to use limited capacity self-loading rifles. When the Division bells rang, 27 of those 40 voted in favor of the amendment; and *197 against it*. Loyal to the government line even if they had not attended to the issue upon which they were voting, those well-drilled Peers at least came away with some credit. They could claim that they did not knowingly approve arguments like those of Lord Nelson, that cripples should be barred the use of those firearms because they "would probably have a harder job to hold on to the rifle than an able bodied person if someone wanted to steal it";[39] or of Lord Attlee, who postulated the peril to society of "a disabled person who was also mentally unstable."[40] It was upon such sick fantasy, of a disabled person lurching round like Quasimodo with a Kalashnikov, that a law would be approved in the Upper House of British democracy.

It was the optimistic notion of Benjamin Disraeli in 1844 that a grander form of democracy than Parliament was now emerging: "The representation of the Press is far more complete than the representation

---

[38] Government White Paper, *Firearms Act 1968, Proposals for Reform*, HMSO 1987, p. 9.

[39] House of Lords, *Official Report*, Oct. 19, 1988, col. 1134.

[40] *Ibid.*, col. 1131.

of Parliament . . . discussion is pursued on fairer terms, and often with more depth and information."[41] A century and a half later, Disraeli's vision of an ever-broadening presentation of viewpoints through the press has been sorely disappointed. There are indeed today some writers of outstanding merit whose articles in the daily papers have made them household names, and who with a free hand can publish general opinion pieces expressing the unconventional or unfashionable; but news reportage functions on a different dynamic. In that domain a commercial formula operates, from the gutter right through to what used to be called the "quality" press. Its method was succinctly expressed in a line from the editorial of *The Sun* after the Hillsborough football stadium deaths: "After the tears and the disbelief comes the anger."[42] First, the emotional wallowing in someone else's private grief; then, outraged indignation from which comes the crusading demand that Something-Must-Be-Done. Analysis generally counts for less than anger in the call for action; it is crusades which sell newspapers, in a serialized real-life adventure fantasy, from week to week. Thus it was that the Hungerford killings sold papers, at a time when no ferries were capsizing and people were bored with AIDS.

The crusading dynamic of the daily press is inevitably and inexorably authoritarian in its tendency. Whatever happy misfortune comes along to make a story, there must be a further "control" to solve the problem. The broader representation of views which Disraeli imagined has proven, at most, no wider than the narrow spectrum of party politics; the premises upon which the papers agree are more significant than the points upon which they differ. The independent reputation of the *Times* as the "Thunderer" is long gone, replaced with the commercial tabloid formula exemplified in front pages like that mostly devoted to a photograph of the ocean with bits of Space Shuttle flotsam; the *Independent* has yet to live up to its name; the *Guardian* has been let down by some of its stylistic reporting, and the quality of the *Daily Telegraph* by its editorials. The only refuge of independence of thought in the British press has been in its periodicals.

William Ross, MP, was careful to distinguish, in the Standing Committee on the Firearms Bill, between public opinion and media

---

[41] Benjamin Disraeli, *Coningsby* (1844); (Edn. Oxford, 1982), p. 312.
[42] *The Sun*, April 17, 1989, p. 6.

opinion; and he recalled[43] that he had not received a single letter supporting the proposals for further gun "control" legislation. Frank Cook, MP, in the same committee also noted the myriad representations of those opposed to the bill, but contrasted this with the Gallup single-question poll which registered a 76 percent majority in favor of the banning of all firearms. The "public opinion" which Gallup monitored, apparently, was not that which was sufficiently motivated by the issue to write a letter. When asked, however, it does not take much motivation to condemn the unfashionable; and the daily crusade, if not the leader of public opinion, is at least the leader of fashion. At the point at which such fashion gains the force of mandate, one sees what Alexis de Tocqueville defined as the "tyranny of the majority."[44]

When John Stuart Mill published his essay *On Liberty* in 1859, the "tyranny of the majority" was a recognized concept, "now generally included among the evils against which society requires to be on its guard."[45] It is a notion, however, which has since fallen out of our political vocabulary. We have returned, without the innocence, to what Mill depicted as the naive belief that with the emergence of representative government, a constitutional balance against the executive was no longer necessary—that "the nation did not need to be protected against its own will." It was the naiveté of the days "when popular government was a thing only dreamed about"; experience had revealed a more complex reality, namely that "the power of the people over themselves" was "not the government of each by himself, but of each by all the rest."[46] The perils of this power were manifold:

. . . when society is itself the tyrant—society collectively over the separate individuals who compose it—its means of tyrannizing are not restricted to the acts which it may do by the hands of its political functionaries. Society can and does execute its own mandates: and if it issues wrong mandates instead of right, or any mandates at all in things with which it ought not to meddle, it practises a social tyranny more formidable than many kinds of political oppression, since, though not usually upheld by such

---

[43] *Hansard*, Standing Committee F, Feb. 4, 1988, col. 17.

[44] Alexis de Tocqueville, *La Démocratie en Amérique* (1835/40).

[45] *On Liberty*, p. 68.

[46] *Ibid.*, p. 67.

extreme penalties, it leaves fewer means of escape, penetrating much more deeply into the details of life, and enslaving the soul itself. Protection, therefore, against the tyranny of the magistrate is not enough: There needs protection also against the tyranny of the prevailing opinion and feeling; against the tendency of society to impose, by other means than civil penalties, its own ideas and practices as rules of conduct on those who dissent from them; to fetter the development, and, if possible, prevent the formation, of any individuality not in harmony with its ways, and compel all characters to fashion themselves upon the model of its own. There is a limit to the legitimate interference of collective opinion with individual independence: and to find that limit, and maintain it against encroachment, is as indispensable to a good condition of human affairs, as protection against political despotism.[47]

Mill placed a high premium on the painstaking demonstration of reasoned justification for any intrusion into individual liberty:

> . . . an opinion on a point of conduct, not supported by reasons, can only count as one person's preference; and if the reasons, when given, are a mere appeal to a similar preference felt by other people, it is still only many people's liking instead of one.[48]

The appeal to the Gallup poll would not have impressed Mill; nor would the arguments for preemptive legislation with which the present government has characteristically tried to sugar the unpalatable. Douglas Hogg's contention that "If we fail to introduce reassuring measures, it is inevitable that there will soon be increased pressure for the government to go further,"[49] abdicated what John Stuart Mill saw as the essential responsibility of the government of a free society. The central criticism of the bill which Hogg was then pushing through Parliament was, as Tory backbenchers as well as the Opposition noted, its arbitrariness: The government persistently declined to apply or respond to reasoned argument in the formulation of law. It was the ultimate peril which Mill had predicted:

---

[47] *Ibid.*, p. 68.

[48] *Ibid.*, p. 69.

[49] *Hansard*, Standing Committee F, Feb. 9, 1988, col. 59.

In England, from the peculiar circumstances of our political history, though the yoke of opinion is perhaps heavier, that of the law is lighter, than in most other countries of Europe . . . [In England] The majority have not yet learnt to feel the power of government their power, or its opinion their opinion. When they do so, individual liberty will probably be as much exposed to invasion from the government, as it already is from public opinion.[50]

Unchecked by reason, the arbitrary will of society had led, Mill showed, to the burning of magicians and heretics; harnessed by the Leviathan state, it has given us the purges and pogroms of the twentieth century. It is fashionable to look upon regimes like those of South Africa or Nazi Germany as aberrant; but they are more interesting for the ways in which they have typified the twentieth-century state than for their singularities. When once the restraint of reasoned justification of each and every executive imposition is cast off, there are no bounds which tyranny may not pass.

Tyranny, like liberty, is a word which has gone out of fashion. Popular modern liberalism prides itself in having advanced beyond the harsh precepts of violence upon which those concepts were balanced. Though the nineteenth century notion of progress is much scoffed at, we are certainly in a millenarian mood—with international barriers coming down, the Iron Curtain itself being swept aside, totalitarian societies liberalizing, even South Africa reforming. If the present euphoria had any historical perspective, it would give a new lease on life to the Whig interpretation of history; but it does not. If one wishes to believe that all was peace and light in Europe before the confrontation of NATO and the Warsaw Pact, one cannot afford to look back at Europe's past. One has, as the campaign to abolish the militia in Switzerland has asserted,[51] to look to the future, renouncing force.

Patrick Henry's warning, that liberty depended on force, and "whenever you give up that force you are inevitably ruined," is unwelcome today; East and West are meeting peacefully. But we might do well to consider that the meeting is both philosophically as well as physically on the Elbe—the Warsaw Pact countries have westernized their expectations;

---

[50] *On Liberty*, pp. 71-72.

[51] *Cf. passim*, R. Brodmann, A. Gross, M. Spescha et al., *Unterwegs zu einer Schweiz ohne Armee* (Basel, 1986).

we have orientalized our institutions. It is a combination better suited to a capitalist benevolent despotism than to liberal democracy.

Germany is an unpropitious heartland for the new European democracy. Bismarck's precept that whatever the merits of liberty, control was better, has been the historical norm of German policy; and it is also the Prussifying tendency of the European Community, which with new *Lebensraum* in the east now promises to stretch from the Atlantic to the Urals. German liberties have been short-lived: 1848; the constitutional vision of the brother of the Prince Consort, Duke Ernst II of Saxe-Coburg-Gotha; Weimar; the Federal Republic before Baader-Meinhof. Terrorism occasioned the latest coronation of control, and was the former's success and reward; the indirect but most far-reaching sense in which terrorism can be sponsored by a state.

The new gun "controls" which Germany waved as a talisman against terrorism in 1972 are in the long tradition of draconian but futile Central European *Jagdgesetze*, which with cyclic monotony have mounted over the centuries to peaks of grotesque severity, before more enlightened rulers in the mold of Joseph II of Habsburg have periodically scrapped them as useless. The system of controls which Germany introduced in 1972 was that which the Weimar Republic had rejected because "in the interests of public morale and regard for the law, only practicably enforceable measures should be implemented."[52] In the quest of control, Germany, and with her Europe, has now forgotten the dangers which follow when one discredits the law; and that when one moves into the society of the Sheriff of Nottingham, one is lucky if one meets nobody worse than Robin Hood.

The liberal constitutional balance of the citizen against the state which was seen in Britain and America as the surest guarantee of stability as well as of liberty, is alien to the Central European tradition; but it is the latter which dominates our time. As Dr. Erik Buxbaum of the Austrian Ministry of the Interior has put it with uncommon candor: "a firepower superiority of private individuals over the executive is to be avoided at all costs."[53]

"If weapons are a token of power," the Swiss maintain, "then in a democracy they belong in the hands of the people."[54] But even in

---

[52] Deutsches Reichsgericht, March 11, 1929; cited in *Zur Waffengesetzgebung im in- und Ausland*, (Pro Tell, Hochdorf, 1979).

[53] *Öffentliche Sicherheit*, Jan.-Feb. 1989, p. 8, (Vienna, 1989).

[54] Pro Tell, e.g., in *Pflicht, Recht, Privileg* (Hochdorf, 1986).

Switzerland, there have been some authoritarian bureaucrats and ambitious politicians tempted by the German philosophy of control; and it took ten years for the Swiss to regain independence lost to German pressure to pursue their gun legislation policy in 1978. More discreetly but more effectively that Prussian influence is manifest today in Brussels and in Strasbourg, the token of a return to the autocratic power of the state once deplored by James Madison:

> Notwithstanding the military establishments in the several kingdoms of Europe, which are carried as far as the public resources will bear, the governments are afraid to trust the people with arms.[55]

The United States itself no longer presents the contrast depicted by Madison. The gun control movement in America has a patrician air that was well exemplified in the Bush administration. In 1990, as the House Armed Services Committee reconsidered whether it was worth preserving the long-neglected National Board for the Promotion of Rifle Practice, the role of the militia in the American political tradition was scarcely recalled. "Whenever a people . . . entrust the defence of their country to a regular, standing army," the *Independent Gazetteer* had warned the "Yeomanry of Pennsylvania" two centuries ago,[56] "the power of the country will remain under the direction of the most wealthy citizens . . . your liberties will be safe as long as you support a well regulated militia." To the American plutocracy, which the Swiss cultural historian Jacob Burckhardt saw assuming the trappings of gentrification even a hundred years ago,[57] that is a rather remote concern. "Today," Senator Edward Kennedy has declared, "firearms are not appropriate for daily life in the United States."[58]

For the duration of recorded history, serfdom has been the norm for most of mankind. There was no reason to imagine that liberal democracy had brought us to a new estate that would last forever. But as now the

---

[55] James Madison, *The Federalist* No. 46 [45]; *The Federalist, A Collection of Essays, Written in Favour of the New Constitution, As Agreed upon by the Federal Convention, September 17, 1787* (New York, 1788), vol. II, pp. 90-91.

[56] *Independent Gazetteer*, Jan. 29, 1791, quoted in Halbrok, *op. cit.*, p. 83.

[57] Jacob Burckhardt, *Weltgeschichtliche Betrachtungen*, ed. Kröner, p. 10.

[58] Quoted in Robert Shalhope, "Ideological Origins of the Second Amendment," *Journal of American History*, vol. 69, no. 3 (Bloomington, Ind., 1982), p. 613.

state, paternalistic or otherwise, asserts its dominance, we have the consolation that the one sure fact of history is change. The political trend of our time also has its term, defined, if by nothing else, by its own poverty. "A State which dwarfs its men, in order that they may be more docile instruments in its hands even for beneficial purposes," John Stuart Mill observed, "will find that with small men no great thing can really be accomplished; and that the perfection of machinery to which it has sacrificed everything will avail it nothing."[59] It is in adversity, moreover, that the independent will has always been tempered. "What country can preserve its liberties," Thomas Jefferson demanded, "if their rulers are not warned from time to time that their people preserve the spirit of resistance?"[60] In adversity and isolation, Winston Churchill remarked in 1941, "this is the lesson: never give in, never give in, *never, never, never, never*—in nothing, great or small, large or petty—never give in except to convictions of honour and good sense."[61]

[59] *On Liberty*, p. 170.

[60] Letter from Thomas Jefferson to William S. Smith, Nov. 13, 1787, in: Thomas Jefferson, *Writings* (New York, 1984), p. 911.

[61] Winston Churchill, War Speeches: vol. II, *The Unrelenting Struggle* (London, 1942), p. 275.

The Militia Is Not the National Guard

David Hardy

Many people today claim the militia has been replaced by the 50 state National Guard organizations which comprise an important part of our military's reserve. This is not the case, as the following essay will show.

> *To my mind, our institutions are best served by having a small regular army as a nucleus, (for) garrison duty, and the first line of defense; then for the support to be first called out, the organized militia, commonly called the "National Guard"; then, for the third line, the national volunteer reserve, that, under the provisions of this bill, have seen military service and are trained in the art of war. Then comes the reserve militia, which includes all the able-bodied men between the ages of 18 and 45.[1]*
>
> *The Constitution ought to secure a genuine, and guard against a select, militia, by providing that the militia shall always be kept well organized, armed and disciplined, and include, according to the past and general usage of the states, all men capable of bearing arms.*

Richard Henry Lee,
sponsor of the Declaration of
Independence, member of the federal
Constitutional Convention, Senator
in the first Congress (1787).

David Hardy received his Bachelor of Arts degree from the University of Arizona where he graduated *cum laude* in 1972. He received his Juris Doctorate from the University of Arizona College of Law in 1975. Mr. Hardy has written extensively in the area of law and firearms regulation. He is co-author of a lengthy article titled "Of Arms and the Law," 51 *Chicago-Kent Law Review* 62 (1974), author of "Firearms Ownership and Regulation." 20 *William and Mary Law Review*, 235 (1978), and "Gun Laws and Gun Collectors," 85 *Case & Comment* 3 (Jan.-Feb. 1978).

---

[1] 35 Cong. Record 7711 (June 30, 1902). As discussed in the text, the volunteer reserve was dropped from the bill.

(a) The militia of the United States consists of all able-bodied males at least 17 years of age and, except as provided in section 13 of title 32, under 45 years of age who are, or have made a declaration of intention to become, citizens of the United States. . . . (b) The classes of the militia are: 1) the organized militia, which consists of the National Guard and the Naval Militia; and 2) the unorganized militia, which consists of members of the militia who are not members of the National Guard or the Naval Militia.

10 United States Code section 311 (1983)

Almost any debate over the keeping and bearing of arms is certain to elicit the remark "but the constitutional militia is the National Guard." If the person making the remark is asked to produce proof or reasoning for the claim, their reply will generally be a more or less elaborate version of "Everyone knows it is." That the most limited research into our history and statutes proves otherwise has not restricted the popularity of this strange species of "proof."

The fact of the matter is that the National Guard is a comparatively recent creation, and clearly not an organization which the Framers of the Constitution had in mind when they drafted the militia clause in 1787, nor when they drafted the Second Amendment in 1789. Secretary of War Knox's return at the close of the Revolutionary War referred to three classes of troops: the "Continental Lines," or regular army, the "State Forces," which were primarily regular troops, and the "militia," by which he designated groups of the general population who had fought when called upon to do so.[2] Even the term "National Guard" did not enter the English language until after most of the Framers were dead. Its adoption came gradually in the years after Lafayette's American tour of 1824—the purpose being to honor that hero, who had after our Revolution formed the "Garde Nationale" in France.[3] Even this merely gave certain militia units—not by any means the entire militia—a popular name. Such units were merely constituted under state law, for whatever purposes the state envisioned; they had no legal status. That status was not achieved until our own century, as will be discussed below.

Any examination of federal militia law must begin with the Militia Act of 1792, 1 Statutes at Large 271, which *was* enacted while the Framers lived—indeed it was enacted by the Second Congress while the Bill of Rights was still in the course of ratification by the states. This Act, required "every free able-bodied white male citizen of the respective

---

[2] Walter Millis, *Arms and Men* 31 (1956).

[3] *Ibid.*, p. 89.

states, resident therein, who is or shall be of the age of 18 years, and under the age of 45 years," to be enrolled in the militia and to obtain, within six months, "a good musket," bayonet and twenty-four rounds of ammunition. The law itself was both brief and vague (it had, for example, no punishment clause to deal with violations) precisely because militia matters were handled in the first instance by the states, under much more detailed statutes which did define dates of mustering and organizational details. The 1792 Act enjoyed a remarkable longevity—it remained law for no fewer than 111 years; its only major amendment came in 1862 when militia status was extended to all "able-bodied males" regardless of color. During its existence, the nature of this militia was extolled by Washington, Jefferson, Madison and others.[4] To be sure, most of these recommended improvements aimed at turning the largely paper army created by the 1792 Act into a true citizen army modeled on that of Switzerland.[5] None of these proposals gained much support. A true citizen army requires a substantial investment in training time, and is generally only found where a republic is threatened by invasion—conditions found in Switzerland throughout its history, in Israel, and some other nations today, but not in the United States of the nineteenth century.[6] The origins of the repeal of the 1792 Act are found in a much different setting.

By the 1890s, the colonization movement was widespread in Europe and becoming accepted in the United States. It became apparent that the United States was (1) likely to want to acquire overseas colonies and (2) likely to become involved in fighting over them. That the only conflicts which did erupt were the Spanish-American War and the lesser conflicts that grew out of it should not obscure the fact that war with the British over involvement in Venezuela, the Japanese over Hawaii, and the Germans over Samoa all appeared likely at times.[7] For conflicts such as these a militia was unsuited. The result was a debate between advocates

---

[4] John McAuley Palmer, *Washington, Lincoln, Wilson: Three War Statesmen* (1930). A thorough collection of quotations from these and other presidents may be found at 35 Congressional Record App. 39495.

[5] See authorities cited note 3, supra.

[6] During the War of 1812, the United States was subjected to three major invasion thrusts—land attack from Canada, plus amphibious assaults on New Orleans and raiding in the Chesapeake Bay. None did any measurable damage (the burning of Washington was an affront, but its impact upon national strength hardly measurable) and all three were repelled—the last two almost entirely by efforts of the existing militia.

[7] Russell Weigley, *Towards an American Army* 146 (1962).

of a relatively small professional army and those of a citizen army.[8] The outcome was that neither party got much of what it desired. The nation would neither spare the money for a professional army nor the time for a citizen army. The only possible compromise was an upgraded form of an organized militia, a formalized and strengthened National Guard, which was to substitute for a regular army—not for a militia.

The compromise took the legal form of the Act of January 21, 1903, usually known from its sponsor as "the Dick Act,"[9] The Dick Act repealed the Militia Act of 1792, although it did retain the definition of the militia of the United States as including all able-bodied male citizens between the ages of 18 and 45. It divided this militia into two parts: "The organized militia, to be known as the National Guard of the State, Territory, or the District of Columbia," and the remainder of the militia, "to be known as the Reserve Militia." While the Dick Act thus recognized a "National Guard" and divided the militia into two parts, it also concentrated its federal benefits (in the form of training, money grants and surplus arms) upon the organized militia.

It is clear from the debates over the Dick Act that the Congress understood the term "militia" to include much more than the National Guard. One of the bill's sponsors explained: "In my remarks on this occasion it is not my purpose to discuss the militia, in its widest sense, as including the whole military force of the nation. I shall confine myself to the great body of our citizens who . . . have been enrolled for instruction and discipline as a reserve force. . . ."[10] Another representative explained the overall plan:

> To my mind, our institutions are best served by having a small regular army as a nucleus, (for) garrison duty, and the first line of defense; then for the support to be first called out, the organized militia, commonly called the "National Guard"; then, for the third line, the national volunteer reserve, that, under the provisions of this bill, have seen military service and are trained in the art of war. Then comes the reserve militia, which includes all the able-bodied men between the ages of 18 and 45.[11]

---

[8] *Ibid.*, pp. 145-215.

[9] 32 Stat. 755.

[10] 35 Cong. Rec. 7711 (June 30, 1902).

[11] *Ibid.*, App. 387. As discussed in the text, the volunteer reserve was dropped from the bill.

On the Senate side, this understanding was echoed by the bill's chief sponsor: "The old law makes every able-bodied man of the country a member of the militia, and provides no further organization. This bill separates and makes a class which can be called into active service."[12] A feature of the original bill did, however, attract criticism. The section in question sought to create a "national volunteer reserve," similar to the present army reserve, composed of recent veterans and commanded by officers holding army commissions. One Senator complained that, as the officers were not chosen by the states, this "is a direct infringement of the constitutional authority given to the states," citing the constitutional provision which reserved to the states the appointment of militia officers.[13] The bill's chief sponsor replied that these reserve troops "are not militia. They are volunteers," while another Senator added "while this reserve is a part of the militia, in the sense that all men are a part of the militia who are between the ages of 18 and 45, it is not a part of the militia in any other sense."[14] Another Senator conceded that if "this is part of the militia system, it would undoubtedly be in violation of its (the Constitution's) letter. . . . There is no possible question about the fact that it is not a part of the militia, so far as the letter goes."[15] The provision was stricken from the bill as finally enacted. The history of the 1903 Act thus makes it quite clear that Congress, in replacing the 1792 Act, did not intend to supplant the 1792 statute's definition of the militia as virtually all able-bodied citizens. Nor did Congress believe that the National Guard it was creating was to be *the* militia, but only a *part* of the militia trained for instant response. As the chief Senate sponsor explained: "The National Guard is in full organization; it is already created, and would naturally be first called upon if wanted for a limited time, and *then the militia would be called upon*" (emphasis supplied).[16]

The benefits extended to the organized militia were expanded in the National Defense Act of 1916.[17] The constitutional provisions requiring that the militia be officered by state-commissioned officers was evaded by provisions denying federal pay while in federal service or training to

---

[12] 36 Cong. Rec. 125 (Dec. 9, 1902).

[13] *Ibid.,* p. 299.

[14] *Ibid.,* pp. 300, 303.

[15] *Ibid.,* p. 354.

[16] *Ibid.,* p. 305.

[17] Act of June 3, 1916, 39 Stat. 166.

any officers not also approved by federal authorities. Even with this federalization, the 1916 law retained the designation of "the militia of the United States" as including all able-bodied male citizens of military age, although that portion not in the National Guard was henceforth to be known as "the Unorganized Militia." That the Congress clearly understood what was done here became apparent in the debates the following year: "Every able-bodied male citizen outside the regular army as here described is by this act of the last Congress placed in the militia."[18]

One major barrier to use of the National Guard remained, however. The Constitution authorizes Congress to provide "for calling forth the militia to execute the laws of the Union, suppress insurrections, and repel invasions." The three purposes were obviously chosen so as to keep the militia from being required to serve overseas—American laws can only be executed, insurrections against those laws suppressed, and invasions repelled, on American soil. The Attorney General of the United States had thus in 1912 ruled quite explicitly that the militia could not be compelled to serve outside the United States save in the most narrow of cases (hot pursuit of, or a "spoiling attack" upon, invaders). "These three occasions, representing necessities of a strictly domestic character, plainly indicate that the services of the militia can be rendered only upon the soil of the United States or its territories."[19]

The 1916 statute most ineffectively dealt with this limitation. The President was given the power to simply draft members of the organized militia into the regular army. When this power was exercised upon our entry into World War I, however, the existing National Guard units were dissolved and merged into various regular army units; and many Guard officers lost their commissions and served as enlisted men in the Regular Army. A good deal of bitterness was thereby created. But the dilemma was clear. If the National Guard was the constitutional "militia," it could not be called into foreign service; if it was not the constitutional militia, nor yet the Army, what constitutional warrant did Congress have to provide for its aid? The Constitution authorized the Congress to provide for the organizing and arming of a militia, and to raise and support armies (provisions known as the "militia clause" and the "army clause"), but had no provision for a third sort of organization.

---

[18] 55 Cong. Rec. 3852 (June 19, 1917).

[19] Opinion of the Attorney General, February 17, 1912. The opinion is reprinted at 55 Cong. Rec. 3851-52.

In the 1933 National Guard Act this problem was addressed. The answer was to technically fit the National Guard into the Army clause. The House report on the 1933 Act made this intent quite clear:

. . . the Organized Militia or National Guard has always been administered under the militia clause of the Constitution. For years, this condition has been most unsatisfactory. . . . Because of the fact that the National Guard was organized under the militia clause of the Constitution, it had to be drafted for the World War. . . .

Repeated discussions and studies among the membership of the National Guard produced in 1926 crystallized sentiment which is expressed in what is known as "resolution of 14" of the National Guard Convention . . . :

"That we hereby reaffirm our position heretofore declared with regard to our status, that we favor appropriate amendments to the National Defense Act so that the federally recognized National Guard shall at all times, whether in peace or in war, be a component of the Army of the United States. . . ."[20]

"(A War Department) report further developed the fact that Congress had the power under the Army provisions of the Constitution to amend the National Defense Act so as to set up a reserve organization as a part of the Army of the United States, which should comprise the men and officers of the National Guard of the States. . . ."[21] The report summarized the 1933 National Guard Act concisely: "The primary purpose of this bill is to create the National Guard of the United States as a component of the Army of the United States, both in time of peace and of war, reserving to the States their right to control the National Guard or Organized Militia absolutely under the militia clause of the Constitution in time of peace."[22] In short, the National Guard of the United States was not to be the Militia of the United States, although the states might have leave to treat it (or any other person, logically) as their own militia under their own laws. As one commentator, writing only a few years later, noted in the *Harvard Law Review*: "The 1933 Act proved conclusively that a well-regulated militia is impossible of attainment

---

[20] Act of June 15, 1933, 48 Stat. 153.

[21] House of Representatives Report No. 141, 73d Congress, 1st Sess. (1933).

[22] *Idem.*

under the militia clause, and can be organized only by resort to the plenary and untrammelled powers under the army clause."[23] Congress clearly recognized the distinction: "Every National Guard man who takes the oath takes it with the understanding that he is part of the regular army and subject to the same obligations that may be imposed upon the regular army,"[24] one thing which no Framer of the Constitution would ever have said of the militia.

In short, from a standpoint of constitutional law, the National Guard and related groups are not primarily militia groups and certainly not *the* militia referred to in the Constitution. Their present organization is the result of a conscious legislative effort to evade the restrictions the Framers placed upon use of the militia. Moreover, the present 10 U.S.C. section 311, which continues the 1903 recognition of the unorganized militia of the United States as including essentially all able-bodied citizens (without limiting the right of the states to expand the militia of the state to an even larger extent) clearly rules out a claim that the National Guard is the one and only "militia of the United States." In the words of the Subcommittee on the Constitution of the Senate Judiciary Committee:

> That the National Guard is not the "militia" referred to in the second amendment is even clearer today. Congress had organized the National Guard under its power to "raise and support armies" and not its power to "Provide for organizing, arming and disciplining the Militia." This Congress chose to do in the interests of organizing reserve military units which were not limited in deployment by the strictures of our power over the constitutional militia, which can be called forth only "to execute the laws of the Union, suppress insurrections and repel invasions." The modern National Guard was specifically intended to avoid status as the constitutional militia, a distinction recognized by 10 U.S.C. §311(a).[25]

---

[23] Wiener, *The Militia Clause of the Constitution*, 54 *Harv. L. Rev.* 181, 209 (1940).

[24] 86 Cong. Rec. 9985 (August 7, 1940).

[25] "The Right to Keep and Bear Arms," Report of the Subcomm. on the Constitution of the Senate Comm. on the Judiciary, 97th Congress, 2d Sess., at 11 (1982).

The Right of the Individual to Keep and Bear Arms as a Federally Protected Right

Paul B. Paskey

The Second Amendment to the United States Constitution provides: "A well-regulated Militia, being necessary to the security of a free State, the right of the people to keep and bear arms shall not be infringed."

Not all of those who have taken an oath to support and defend the United States Constitution share this view. According to Representative John Bryant, a Democrat from Texas, "No one needs an automatic [sic] weapon except cowards and criminals and weirdos who have to own one to feel like a man." These comments were made during debates over provisions in the House Crime Bill to ban the manufacture and sale of thirteen different types of semiautomatic "assault weapons" and all detachable box magazines with a capacity greater than seven rounds. These provisions were defeated by a vote of 247 to 177; however, the House did adopt a seven-day waiting period for the purchase of hand-guns.[1]

The United States Senate voted in July 1991 to ban the domestic manufacture or sale of nine types of semiautomatic weapons, including the Colt AR-15 rifle, as well as adopt a five-day waiting period for the purchase of handguns.[2] The Senate bill would also criminalize the possession of any of these weapons without possession of the original federal purchase record form.[3] Senator Daniel P. Moynihan of New York has offered, as a crime-reduction measure, a bill to ban the manufacture and importation of three different calibers of pistol ammunition,[4] including the 9mm round used in the United States military's newest sidearm.

Federal action against firearms is not confined to legislation only. In June 1981 the city of Morton Grove, Illinois banned the possession of all operable handguns, with minor exceptions, within its city limits. This

---

[1] *USA Today*, October 18, 1991, p. A1, col. 6.

[2] *New York Times*, July 12, 1991, p. A1, col. 1 (city ed.).

[3] S.1241, 101st Cong., 1st Sess. (1991).

[4] S.51, 101st Cong., 1st Sess. (1991).

decision was upheld by the United States Seventh Circuit Court of Appeals.[5]

In 1982 the Bureau of Alcohol, Tobacco, and Firearms issued a ruling that broadened the United States Code definition of machine gun, subject to federal excise taxation, to include weapons which had not previously functioned as machine guns (e.g. the Colt AR-15), but which possessed design features which would facilitate full automatic firing by simple modification or elimination of existing component parts. This ruling was upheld by the United States Eleventh Circuit Court of Appeals.[6]

The State of New Jersey banned possession of any weapons defined as "assault firearms," including the Colt AR-15 rifle, as of July 1, 1991. That State required owners of an "assault firearm" to sell it out of state, turn it in to police without compensation, or render it inoperable by removing the firing pin and reporting this to the state.[7] On July 30, 1991, the city council of New York City passed an ordinance, at the request of Mayor David Dinkins, banning possession of "assault weapons." These prohibited weapons include any firearm manufactured with a bayonet mount or flash suppressor, including the Colt AR-15 rifle. Owners of these weapons, already registered under the Sullivan Law, had ninety days from the signing of the bill to remove their weapons from the city or face fines of up to $5,000 and jail terms of up to one year, as well as confiscation of their previously legally owned weapon.[8]

Also in July 1991, the president of the American Bar Association, in a message to its membership, stated that now is the time for measures to control availability of military assault weapons.[9] Syndicated columnist George Will has also expressed concern about the right to individual ownership of firearms such as assault weapons. He counselled gun control advocates to ". . . face the need to deconstitutionalize the subject by repealing the embarrassing [second] amendment."[10]

---

[5] *Quilici v. Village of Morton Grove*, 522 F.Supp. 1169 (N.D. Ill. 1981), *affd.* 695 F.2d 261 (7th Cir. 1982), *cert. den.* 464 U.S. 863 (1983).

[6] *S. W. Daniel, Inc. v. United States*, 831 F.2d 253, 254 (11 Cir. 1987).

[7] *New York Times*, July 9, 1991, p. B1, col. 5 (city ed.). (The specter of covert registration of these firearms through back-tracing of BATF forms in particular, and firearms registration in general, are beyond the scope of this paper.)

[8] *New York Times*, July 31, 1991, p. B1, col. 6 (city ed.).

[9] J. Curtin, "A Message from the President," *A.B.A. Journal*, July 1991, p. 8.

[10] George Will, "The Constitution and Guns," *The Virginia Pilot & Ledger*, March 21, 1991, p. 15, col. 1.

A study of the text, context, and history of the Second Amendment, as well as related Supreme Court case precedents, leads to one conclusion. The right to keep and bear arms is an individual right and is protected by the Second Amendment against infringement by the federal government. Congress may, in its discretion, under the power of the Militia Clauses, broadly or narrowly define these arms so long as they are suitable for militia use and are interchangeable with those provided to the army.

A study of the text, context, and history of the Fourteenth Amendment to the United States Constitution, as well as relevant Supreme Court case precedents, demonstrates that, just as the individual right to peaceably assemble and petition the federal government, guaranteed by the First Amendment, is a privilege and immunity of United States citizenship, then so, too, is the individual right to keep and bear those same arms guaranteed by the Second Amendment also a privilege and immunity of United States citizenship. Both are therefore protected against state infringement by the Fourteenth Amendment.

Even if the individual right to keep and bear arms suitable for militia use were not a privilege and immunity of United States citizenship, that right is still statutorily protected against state infringement. Under the enumerated powers of the Militia Clauses, Congress is required to provide for the organizing, arming, and disciplining of the militia. The people of the United States are its militia. Therefore, the same militia arms prescribed for use by the federal government for the militia, and, thus, for the individual citizen who is a militia member, are also protected by the Supremacy Clause against infringement by state governments.

Second Amendment Text

What protection, if any, is afforded by the Second Amendment against federal action which would ban the possession, manufacture, and sale of "assault weapons," handguns, ammunition, or high-capacity, detachable box magazines? According to Chief Justice Marshall, writing the opinion in *Barron v. Mayor and City of Baltimore* (1833),[11] the Bill of Rights is applicable only to the federal government and not to the states. Thus, it would apply to any legislation passed by the Congress of the United

---

[11] *Barron v. Mayor and City of Baltimore*, 32 U.S. (7 Pet.) 243 (1833).

States, as well as to any acts of federal courts and federal administrative agencies.

The key to understanding the extent of the right of the people to keep and bear arms is to understand the plain meaning of the text. The text consists of two clauses: an introductory clause, or preamble, and a statement of the right guaranteed.

David Hardy concludes that the United States Constitution

> . . . embodies not one but two concepts. The first, a recognition that the militia is the proper defense of a free state, is not a guarantee of a right in any sense, collective or individual. It is a statement of classical republicanism, a recommendation as to how a national government should function. Its essential purpose was to ensure the collective defense of the nation, not to reserve rights for the nation's citizens. As such, its position in the Bill of Rights remains an anomaly, probably inspired by Madison's need to placate classical republicans in his home state of Virginia. Whatever its inspiration, it should be apparent that this provision was not the primary thrust of the amendment. At the federal level, proposals for a right to arms were the driving force behind the second amendment, with the militia provision surfacing as a proposed addition only with the Virginia ratifying convention, at the eleventh hour of our constitutional process.
>
> The other portion of the second amendment derives its origin from the natural right of self-defense which, in turn, reflects the right of every human being to defend his or her life against illegal attack. It is all but indisputable that this is the most fundamental of all natural rights, and accordingly some have maintained that such defense is not merely a right but a moral duty: failure to so defend is tantamount to suicide by inaction. A person may act morally in transferring property without resistance, but one who voluntarily becomes a homicide victim is a party to destruction of that which he did not create and does not own.[12]

Sanford Levinson notes that legal analysts who wish to limit the force of the Second Amendment focus on its preamble as setting out a restrictive purpose. He writes:

---

[12] David Hardy, *The Unalienable Right to Self-Defense and the Second Amendment*, 8 J. Christian Jurisprudence 87, pp. 109-10 (1990).

Recall Laurence Tribe's assertion that the purpose was to allow states to keep their militias and protect them against the possibility that the new national government will use its power to establish a powerful standing army and eliminate the state militias. This purposive reading quickly disposes of any notion that there is an "individual" right to keep and bear arms. The right, if any such be, is only a state's right. The consequence of this reading is obvious: the national government has the power to regulate—to the point of prohibition—private ownership of guns, since that has, by stiplation, nothing to do with preserving state militias.[13]

Another collectivist interpretation of the right of "the people" to keep and bear arms follows: The right to keep and bear arms is dependent on a militia being necessary for the security of a free state; however, today our freedom is protected by a standing army. Hence, there is no need for the people to keep and bear arms. According to Stephen Halbrook,

This interpretation appears to reduce the amendment to a conditional or hypothetical syllogism, with its first premise as follows: If a well-regulated militia is necessary to the security of a free state (p), then the right of the people to keep and bear arms shall not be infringed (q); that is p implies q. . . . Yet denial of the antecedent, should it be expressed in the second premise, fails to imply the opposite conclusion; that is, even if a militia were not necessary for the existence of a free state, the people still have a right to keep and bear arms. . . . In sum, the syntax of the proposition that makes up the Second Amendment necessitates that the right to keep and bear arms is absolute and is not dependent on the needs of the militia; the contrary view . . . commits the [logical] fallacy of denying the antecedent and is therefore a miscontruction.[14]

If the Framers had contemplated only the guarantee to the states to have the right to have militias and to their organized militiamen to keep and bear arms, then language such as "the right of the select militia to

---

[13] Sanford Levinson, *The Embarrassing Second Amendment*, 99 Yale L.J., pp. 637, 644 (1989).

[14] Stephen Halbrook, *That Every Man Be Armed: The Evolution of a Constitutional Right*, pp. 85-86 (1984).

keep and bear arms" would have been sufficient.[15] Nevertheless, Article I, section 8 of the Constitution provided for both the existence and armament of the organized militia. Yet, in order to have a militia, the right of the militia members to keep and bear arms must be guaranteed.

Second Amendment Context

Even if the preamble were regarded as limiting the purposes of the text, the Framers guaranteed to "the people" the right to keep and bear arms. First, some rights receive a lesser degree of protection (e.g., the Fourth Amendment guarantees "the right of the people . . . against unreasonable searches and seizures. . . .") Some are guaranteed in the most absolute and imperative terms. The First Amendment specifies that "Congress shall make no law . . . abridging freedom of speech, or of the press; or of the right of the people to peaceably assemble, and to petition the government for a redress of grievances. The Second Amendment prescribes that the right of the people to keep and bear arms shall not be infringed."[16]

Second, the context of the Second Amendment in the Constitution and the Bill of Rights must be examined to determine precisely who "the people" are whose rights are being protected. It was "the people" who ordained and established the Constitution of the United States. Unlike in England, where the sovereignty lay in the king in parliament, sovereignty lay in "the people" rather than in their representatives.

This phrase also appears in the First, Fourth, Ninth and Tenth Amendments. According to Professor Levinson, it would be

> . . . difficult to know how one might plausibly read the Fourth Amendment as other than a protection of individual rights, and it would approach the frivolous to read the assembly and petition clause as referring only to the right of the state legislature to meet and pass a remonstrance directed to Congress or the President against some government act. The Tenth Amendment is trickier,

---

[15] *Ibid.*, p. 85.

[16] W. Rumble, "James Madison on the Value of the Bill of Rights," *Constitutionalism*, pp. 122, 137 (Pennock and Chapman, eds., 1979), cited in Stephen Halbrook, supra note 15, p. 84.

though it does differentiate between "states" and "the people" in terms of retained rights.[17]

Thus, the argument that "the people" refers to the "sovereign citizenry," collectively organized, fails.[18]

Contextually, it is less difficult to understand "militia" and "arms." First, the militia and the land and naval forces of the United States are clearly distinguished in both the text of the Constitution[19] and the Bill of Rights.[20] The militia is not the "standing army" which Congress has the power to raise. The Militia Clauses grant to Congress the power to (1) provide for the calling forth of the militia to execute the laws of the Union, suppress insurrections, and repel invasions,"[21] and (2) "provide for organizing, arming, and disciplining the militia . . . and reserving to the States respectively . . . the authority of training the militia according to the discipline prescribed by Congress."[22] It is through these powers, among others, that "[t]he United States guarantee to every State in this Union a Republican Form of Government; and shall protect each of them against Invasion. . . ."[23] Thus, Congress has the power to prescribe "arms" for the militia. Nevertheless, it has no power to define the militia because "the people" are the militia.

History of the Second Amendment

Ancient Israel was defended by a militia. God told Moses that it would be comprised of the "children of Israel, . . . every male . . . from twenty years old and upward, all that are able to go to war in Israel."[24] The priestly tribe of Levi was not part of the census of the other Israelites and was not required to serve.[25] Thus, the clergy, men below the age of

---

[17] Levinson, supra note 13, p. 645.

[18] Cress, *An Armed Community: The Origins and Meaning of the Right to Bear Arms*, 71 J. Am. Hist., pp. 22, 31 (1984) cited in Levinson, supra note 13, p. 645.

[19] Compare U.S. Const. art. I, sec. 8, cl. 12 with U.S. Const. art. I, sec. 8, cl. 15 and 16.

[20] U.S. Const. amend. V.

[21] U.S. Const. art. I, sec. 8, cl. 15.

[22] U.S. Const. art. I, sec. 8, cl. 16.

[23] U.S. Const. art. IV, sec. 2.

[24] Numbers 1:2-3.

[25] See Numbers 1:49-50.

twenty years, and men unable to fight were not mustered. The organization of the militia paralleled that of the civil structure of the nation with leaders over groups of ten, fifty, one hundred, one thousand and so forth.[26]

Further, the people armed themselves,[27] at first with swords, spears and shields.[28] Later, after the Philistines' strict iron monopoly over Israel prevented the people from rearming, slings as well as bows and arrows became the equipment that each man furnished.[29] Since the same weapons borne in battle were kept by the men, they were also available to defend their homes and families.[30]

Although this citizen army had to muster when it was summoned, it did not have to fight.[31] In fact, if the militia was displeased with the king's conduct, they could and did assert their right to refuse service and return to their homes.[32] For this reason, the kings of Israel sought to render the militia impotent.

The militia was the army of Israel for more than four centuries until King David called for a peacetime census of the militia to incorporate them into a select militia that would serve as part of a standing army on a rotating basis. God was displeased with this peacetime call-up of the militia and struck Israel with a plague. David's reign ended shortly thereafter.[33] With his abdication came the rise of monarchial absolutism, the division of the kingdom and the eventual fall of the house of David to the Babylonians.

Early English monarchs also required their subjects to arm themselves for defense of the realm from attacks from both without and within.[34] Later English monarchs, known, at times, for their absolutism, sought to deprive religious groups, lower economic classes, and colonized peoples of their arms in an effort to perpetuate and enhance both the economic and political power of the ruling class. The Magna Carta, the English

---

[26] James Jordan, "The Israelite Militia," elsewhere in this volume.

[27] See Numbers 31:3, 32:20.

[28] See Judges 5:8; 1 Samuel 13:19-22.

[29] James Jordan, supra note 30, p. 33.

[30] See Exodus 22:2-3.

[31] See Exodus 30:11-16.

[32] See 1 Kings 12:16.

[33] See James Jordan, supra note 30, pp. 34-35.

[34] See generally Stephen Halbrook, supra note 14, pp. 9-14.

Declaration of Rights of 1689, and the American Declaration of Independence, are examples of documents which resulted from revolts against the various forms of oppression inherent in monarchial absolutism. The right of individuals to keep and bear arms, recognized in such documents as the Declaration of Rights of 1689,[35] also found expression in numerous common law judicial decisions as well as in the commentaries of English jurists, most notably William Blackstone.[36]

Prior to the Glorious Revolution of 1688, Charles II sought an absolute prohibition on the possession of firearms by commoners. Yet common law cases both before and after 1688, as well as the Bill of Rights of 1689, recognized the right from time immemorial of individuals to keep and bear arms for legal purposes. To circumvent these decisions and statutes, game laws were enacted which permitted hunting only by wealthy land owners. This was a pretext for depriving serfs of alternate food sources in order to force them to work for their landlords as well as depriving them of arms for revolt.[37]

Blackstone commented on the purpose of the game laws as follows:

> 3. For prevention of idleness and dissipation in husbandmen, artificers and others of lower rank; which would be the unavoidable consequence of universal license. 4. For prevention of popular insurrections and resistance to government, by disarming the bulk of the people: which last is a reason oftener meant, than avowed, by makers of the forest and game laws.[38]

The American jurist, St. George Tucker, publisher of the American edition of Blackstone's works, commented concerning this passage: "Whoever examines the forest and game laws in the British code, will readily perceive that the right of keeping arms is effectually taken away from the people of England."[39] Whether or not contemporary efforts to ban hunting are merely a pretext for disarming our citizenry is beyond the scope of this work.

---

[35] See supra note 18.

[36] Stephen Halbrook, supra note 14, p. 37. See E. Kruschke, *The Right to Keep and Bear Arms: A Continuing American Dilemma*, pp. 8-9 (1985) (discussion of legal requirements for people to keep arms to defend the nation as well as serve in the posse comitatus). See generally Stephen Halbrook, supra note 15, pp. 37-54 (development of English common law).

[37] Stephen Halbrook, supra note 14, p. 53.

[38] 2 Blackstone, *Commentaries*, p. 412.

[39] 1 Blackstone, *Commentaries*, p. 144, n.41 (St. George Tucker, ed., 1803).

115

Blackstone set forth the absolute rights of individuals, as their expression developed through the common law of England. He wrote:

> . . . we have taken a short view of the principal absolute rights which pertain to every Englishman. But in vain would these rights be declared, ascertained, and protected by the dead letter of the laws, if the constitution had provided no other method to secure their actual enjoyment. It has therefore established certain auxiliary subordinate rights of the subject, which serve principally as outworks or barriers to protect and maintain inviolate the three and great primary rights, of personal security, personal liberty, and private property. These are:
> 1. The constitution, powers and privileges of parliament;
> 2. The limitation of the king's prerogative. . . .
> 3. . . . applying to the courts of justice for redress of injuries. . . .
> 4. . . . the right of petitioning the king, or either house of parliament, for a redress of grievances. . . .
> 5. The fifth and last auxiliary right of the subject, that I shall at present mention, is that of having arms for their defence, suitable to their condition and degree, and such as are allowed by law. Which is also declared by the same statute 1 W.&M.st. 2c.2 [Bill of Rights], and it is indeed a public allowance under due restrictions, of the natural right of resistance and self-preservation, when the sanctions of society and laws are found insufficient to restrain the violence of oppression.
>
> In these several articles consist the rights, or, as they are frequently called, the liberties of Englishmen. . . . So long as these remain inviolate, the subject is perfectly free; for every species of compulsive tyranny and oppression must act in opposition to one or the other of these rights, having no other object upon which it can possible be employed. . . . And, lastly, to vindicate these rights, when actually violated or attacked, the subjects of England are entitled, in the first place, to the regular administration and free course of justice in the courts of law; next, to the right of petitioning the king and parliament for redress of grievances; and, lastly, to the right of having arms for self-preservation and defence.[40]

---

[40] 1 Blackstone, *Commentaries*, pp. 140-44.

Will and Ariel Durant wrote that democracy in America "began with the advantage of a British heritage: Anglo-Saxon law, which, from Magna Carta onward, had defended the citizens against the state; and Protestant-ism, which had opened the way to religious and mental liberty."[41] The Americans who fought and won the Revolution of 1776 were strongly influenced by their view that the common law, as established in ancient tradition, the Bill of Rights of 1689, judicial construction, defined the rights of Englishmen and by their Biblical heritage, as well. For example, the separation of governmental powers into judicial, legislative, and executive branches, embodied in both the English and American systems, are found in Scripture.[42] These traditions formed the framework for the Constitution and, later, the Bill of Rights.

That this would be the view of the Framers of the Constitution is not surprising. More than two thousand years before the birth of this nation, ancient Israel was established as a nation by means of a written charter. According to Helen Silving, late Professor of Law at the University of Puerto Rico, the national charter of ancient Israel was the original model for the theory and the practice of the establishment of societies and governments that were based on the consent of the people.[43] That charter marked the beginning of their national identity and was ratified by the consent of the people.[44]

The Declaration of Independence not only embodied the consent of the people necessary for it to be considered a national charter, but it also marked the beginning of the nation as well. The Constitution incorporates the Declaration of Independence by implicitly referring to the Declara-tion.[45] Thus, the sovereign people's right to reconstitute government, by force of arms, if necessary, if that government fails to secure for them their inalienable rights is still guaranteed.

The former colonists who drafted these documents were aware that Parliament had passed legislation to disarm the Irish and the Scots, exempting only those who remained loyal to the Crown. The British army conducted general searches for arms and shot offenders on sight.[46] This

---

[41] W. Durant and A. Durant, *The Lessons of History*, p. 76 (1968).

[42] See Isaiah 33:22.

[43] Helen Silving, *Sources of Law*, pp. 239-42 (1968).

[44] See Exodus 19:5-8; 32:15-16.

[45] See Herbert Titus, *The Declaration, the Constitution, and the Laws of Nature and Nature's God* (October 1991).

[46] R. Wilkinson-Latham, *Swords*, pp. 72-73 (1978) (citing the Disarming Act following the Scottish Rebellion of 1715 and the Act for the Abolition and Proscription of Scottish Dress of

oppression enabled the Crown to subjugate these people although resentment and, in the case of Ireland, hatred, remain to this day.

They were also aware that restrictive British firearms legislation and policy were instrumental in disarming disloyal Indians in the colonies so that they might be more easily conquered. They knew that these same policies had been used to disarm colonists in the wake of Bacon's Rebellion in 1676[47] and again in their Revolution that ended colonial rule a century later.[48]

With the victory of an armed populace over a European standing army came the battle over the proposed Constitution. The Constitution institutionalized the dual-army system that evolved during the Revolution. The historic militias would remain; however, the federal government would have ample power to raise and support armies. The Federalists achieved an impressive victory in permitting the federal government to maintain a peacetime army. They also wanted a federalized militia; however, in this they were only potentially successful. A federalized militia would depend on the laws passed by Congress implementing its authority over the militia.[49]

Anti-Federalists were less concerned with military effectiveness than they were with maintaining the proper constitutional balance between the people, the states, and the federal government. They disapproved of concurrent federal control over the militia. This was a dramatic departure from past practice. It had the potential for undermining the militia's local character and destroying state autonomy. The Anti-Federalists also opposed a standing army which could be used by their new rulers to oppress the people.[50]

1746, in response to the Rebellion of 1745); Kennett and Anderson, *The Gun in America*, pp. 20-22 (1975) (citing the Act for the Better Security of the Government, by Disarming the Papists); 7 W.&M., c.5 (Ireland, 1695), and a supplementary act, 13 George II, c.6 (Ireland, 1739); also citing anti-Scottish acts, I George I, ac. 5 (1714), I George I, c. 54 (1715), and 19 George II, c. 39 (1746), cited in Stephen Halbrook, supra, note 145, at 54.

[47] See *Ibid.*, pp. 55-57.

[48] See generally *Ibid.*, pp. 58-64.

[49] See A. Millet and P. Maslowskey, *For the Common Defense*, pp. 88-89 (1984).

[50] Richard Henry Lee, a senator who voted on the Bill of Rights that he helped to draft, wrote:
    To preserve liberty, it is essential that the whole body of the people always possess arms, and be taught alike, especially when young, how to use them. . . . It is true, the yeomanry of the country possess the lands, the weight of property, possess arms, and are too strong body of men to be openly offended . . . [but] they may in twenty or thirty years be, by means imperceptible to them, totally deprived of that weight and strength. This may be done in great measure by Congress, if disposed to do it, by modeling the militia. Should one-fifth or one-eighth part of the men capable of bearing arms be made into a select militia, as has been proposed . . . and all the others put upon a plan which will render them of no importance, the former will answer all the purposes of an army and the latter will be defenseless. . . . I see no provision made for calling out the posse

Yet, the Federalists were able to rebut their opponents' arguments and prevail, assuring their fellow citizens that the people would never be disarmed.[51] It was their view that was adopted in the Constitution and was ratified by the states. Nevertheless, state conventions also demanded and got a Bill of Rights, which included the Second Amendment.

With regard to the militia, Congress foiled the Federalist designs. President George Washington and Secretary of War Henry Knox urged Congress to reorganize the militia under federal control. Congress delayed action until the spring of 1792, in its second session, when it passed the Calling Forth Act and the Uniform Militia Act. The Calling Forth Act

---

comitatus for executing the laws of the union, but provision is made for congress to call forth the militia for the execution of them—and the militia in general, or any select part of it, may be called out under military officers, instead of the sheriff to enforce an execution of federal laws, in the first instance, and thereby introduce an entire military execution of the laws.
— Richard Henry Lee, "Letters of a Federal Farmer (1787-88)," *Pamphlets on the Constitution of the United States*, pp. 305-6.
George Mason, author of the Virginia Constitution and Bill of Rights, addressed the Virginia ratifying convention:

> An instance within the memory of some of this House, will show us how our militia may be destroyed. Forty years ago, when the resolution of enslaving America was formed in Great Britain, the British Parliament was advised by an artful man, who was governor of Pennsylvania, to disarm the people—that was the most effectual way to enslave them—but they should not do it openly; but to weaken them and let them sink gradually, by totally disusing and neglecting the militia.

—3 J. Elliot, *Debates in the Several State Conventions*, p. 380 (2d ed., 1836).

[51] Noah Webster wrote:

> Another power in government is a military force. But this, to be efficient, must be superior to any force that exists among the people, or which they can command; otherwise, this force would be annihilated on first exercise of acts of oppression. Before a standing army can rule, the people must be disarmed, as they are in almost every kingdom in Europe. The supreme power in America cannot enforce unjust laws by the sword, because the whole body of the people are armed and constitute a force superior to any band of regular troops that can be, on any pretence, raised in the United States.

— 2 Noah Webster, "An Examination into the Leading Principles of the Federal Constitution Proposed by the Late Convention Held at Philadelphia," *Pamphlets on the Constitution of the United States*, p. 56 (1888).
James Madison wrote:

> The only refuge left for those who prophesy the downfall of the State governments is the visionary supposition that the federal government may previously accumulate a military force for the projects of ambition. . . . The highest number to which, according to, the best computation, a standing army can be carried in any country does not exceed one-hundredth part of the whole number of souls; or one twenty-fifth part of the number of those able to bear arms. This proportion would not yield, in the United States, an army of more than twenty-five or thirty thousand men. To these would be opposed a militia amounting to near half a million of citizens with arms in their hands. . . . It may well be doubted whether a militia thus circumstanced could ever be conquered by such a proportion of regular troops. Those who are best acquainted with the late successful resistance of this country against British arms will be most inclined to deny the possibility of it. Besides the advantage of being armed, which the Americans possess over the people of almost every other nation, the existence of subordinate governments forms a barrier against the enterprises of ambition, more unsurmountable than any which a simple government of any form can admit of. Notwithstanding the military establishments in the several kingdoms of Europe, which are carried as far as the public resources will bear, the governments are afraid to trust the people with arms.

— *The Federalist* No. 46, pp. 320-22 (J. Madison) (J. Cooke, ed., 1809).

delegated Congress's authority to the President to call forth the militia. In case of invasion by a foreign nation or Indian tribe, the President would be free "to call forth such number of militia of the state or states most convenient to the . . . scene of action, as he may judge necessary. . . ."[52] However, should it become necessary to call forth the militia to execute the laws or suppress insurrection, a federal judge had to certify that duly constituted authorities were unable to meet the threat and the President could then act for up to thirty days after commencement of the next session of Congress, but only after first commanding "such insurgents to disperse, and retire peaceably to their abodes. . . ."[53] Thus, by restraining the authority granted to the President, Congress addressed Anti-Federalist fears of a despotic federal government.

The Militia Act, which remained the basic militia law until 1903, required that "every free able-bodied white male citizen of the respective states . . . the age of eighteen years and under the age of forty-five years . . . be enrolled in the militia . . . company, within whose bounds such citizen shall reside. . . ."[54] It also required each man to provide himself with a good rifle or musket and bayonet as well as a belt, cartridge box with twenty-four cartridges, and knapsack. It standardized musket bore size, which would remain standard for the United States military until the 1870s, to that "sufficient for balls of the eighteenth part of a pound [.58 caliber]. And every citizen so enrolled and providing himself with the arms, ammunition, and accoutrements required . . . shall hold the same exempted from all suits, distresses, executions or sales, for debt or for payment of taxes."[55]

Dragoons were to provide their own horse and saddle, boots and spurs, two pistols with twelve cartridges, cartridge box, and saber. Artillerymen were to furnish themselves "with all the equipments of a private in the infantry, until proper ordnance and field artillery is provided."[56] Finally, the Act outlined a tactical organization states might adopt at their discretion, in order to facilitate integration of militia units and army units during time of war, both tactically and logistically.

From the Federalist perspective, the law had serious flaws. It failed to provide for a select militia in each state or for federal control over

---

[52] Calling Forth Act, ch. 28, 1 Stat. 264 (1792).

[53] *Ibid.*, p. 264.

[54] Uniform Militia Act, ch. 33, 1 Stat. 271 (1792).

[55] *Ibid.*, pp. 271-72.

[56] *Ibid.*, p. 272.

officers and training. Further, it imposed no penalties on either states or individuals who failed to comply. By failing to establish uniform, interchangeable units, Washington's vision of a nationalized militia was killed.[57]

Further, upon close examination of this Act, there is great insight into what was contemplated in the Second Amendment, given that most of the congressmen who passed it had voted for the Amendment in the previous session. First, the militia was not part of the army; however, they were required to be armed with the same caliber rifles or muskets and bayonets. Second, pistols were authorized for the militia, although Congress chose not to specify the caliber as they had with the rifle and musket. Third, militia members were required to provide all the equipment necessary for them to carry out their military duties, including ammunition for their weapons, cartridge boxes for their ammunition and bayonets. Fourth, crew-served weapons, such as field artillery, were not to be provided by the people individually but by the state or federal governments. Finally, every citizen enrolled in the militia was immune from judgments against his arms and equipment, both public and private. This Act remained the law of the land until the early 1900s.

Second Amendment Cases

No restrictive firearms legislation was passed until 1934, when Congress passed the National Firearms Act. In an effort to disarm gangsters of the 1930s, this act prohibited manufacturing, importing or dealing in rifles or shotguns with a barrel length of less than 18 inches, machine guns or silencers for any firearm without approval of the Secretary of the Treasury and payment of an annual tax to the Commissioner of Internal Revenue. The Act also prohibited individuals from owning or transferring these devices without having approval of the Secretary and having paid a tax for each device of $200 (the equivalent of 10 twenty-dollar gold pieces) to the Commissioner for a stamp to affix to the written order.[58]

Jack Miller, a professional bank robber, was prosecuted for interstate transportation of an unregistered shotgun whose barrel length was less than 18 inches and for failure to possess a stamp-affixed written order for the firearm. A district court judge dismissed based on the Second

---

[57] See A. Millet and P. Maslowskey, supra note 49, pp. 89-90.

[58] National Firearms Act, ch. 757, 73 Stat. 1236-40 (1934) (codified as amended at 18 U.S.C. sec. 921-26 (1991).

Amendment. The government appealed to the Supreme Court, which reversed. In *U.S. v. Miller* (1939),[59] Justice McReynolds delivered the opinion of the Court:

> In the absence of any evidence tending to show that possession or use of a "shotgun having a barrel of less than 18 inches in length" at this time has some reasonable relationship to the preservation or efficiency of a well-regulated militia, we cannot say that the Second Amendment guarantees the right to keep and bear such an instrument.[60]

Justice McReynolds next cited the Militia Clauses. He then stated, "With the obvious purpose to assure the continuation and render possible the effectiveness of such forces the declaration and guarantee of the Second Amendment were made. It must be interpreted and applied with that end in view."[61]

He then contrasted the militia which states were to maintain and train with troops they were forbidden to keep without the consent of Congress.[62] Based on the

> debates in the Conventions, the history and legislation of the Colonies and States, and the writings of approved commentators . . . the Militia comprised all males physically capable of acting in concert for the common defense. . . . And further, that ordinarily when called for service these men were expected to appear bearing arms supplied by themselves and of the kind in common use at the time.[63]

In the body of his opinion, Justice McReynolds cited Blackstone who pointed out "that King Alfred first settled on a national militia in this kingdom" and then traced the subsequent development and use of such forces.[64]

---

[59] *U.S. v. Miller*, 307 U.S. 174 (1939).

[60] *Ibid.*, p. 178.

[61] *Ibid.*

[62] See U.S. Const. art. 10.

[63] *Miller*, 307 U.S. 174, p. 179.

[64] 2 W. Blackstone, *Commentaries* 409, cited in *Miller* 307 U.S. 174, p. 179.

Two other "approved commentators" were cited in footnote 3 of the opinion.[65] One was Justice Joseph Story, a James Madison appointee, who wrote of the Second Amendment in 1833:

> The importance of this article will scarcely be doubted by any persons who have duly reflected on the subject. The militia is the natural defense of a free country. . . . The right of the citizens to keep and bear arms has justly been considered as the palladium of the liberties of a Republic; since it offers a strong moral check against the usurpation and arbitrary powers of rulers and will generally, even if these are successful in the first instance, enable the people to resist and triumph over them.
>
> A similar provision in favor of protestants (for to them it is confined) is to be found in the bill of rights of 1688, it being declared "the subjects, which are protestants, may have arms for their defense suitable to their condition, and as allowed by law." But under various pretenses the effect of this provision has been greatly narrowed; and is at present in England more nominal than real as a defensive privilege.[66]

The other "approved commentator" cited by Justice McReynolds was Thomas Cooley. In 1898, he wrote of the Second Amendment:

> Among the other safeguards to liberty should be mentioned the right of the people to keep and bear arms [1 Bl. Com. 143]. A standing army is peculiarly obnoxious in any free government. . . . The alternative to a standing army is a "well-regulated militia"; but this cannot exist unless the people are trained to bearing arms. The Federal and State constitutions therefore provide that the right of the people to keep and bear arms shall not be infringed; but how far it may be in the power of the legislature to regulate the right we shall not undertake to say. Happily there neither has been, nor, we may hope, is there likely to be much occasion for examination of that question by the Courts.[67]

---

[65] *Miller*, 307 U.S. 174, FN 3, p. 182.

[66] 3 J. Story, *Commentaries on the Constitution*, pp. 746-47 (1833).

[67] 1 Thomas Cooley, *Constitutional Limitations*, pp. 728-29 (W. Carrington, ed., 1927).
Thomas Cooley had even more to say concerning the Second Amendment:
The right is general. It may be supposed from the phraseology of this provision that the right to keep and bear arms was guaranteed only to the militia; but this

The legislature has given the Court the occasion to examine the question of the right to keep and bear arms. *Miller* stands for the proposition that the people, in their capacity as individual citizens, are guaranteed the right to keep and bear any arms that are suitable for militia use.

U.S. v. Verdugo-Urquidez (1990).[68] buttresses this view that the right to keep and bear arms protects the rights of individual citizens. It held that the Fourth Amendment does not apply to the search and seizure of property owned by a non-resident alien and located in a foreign country by United States agents. In his textual analysis of the Fourth Amendment, Chief Justice Rehnquist wrote that

> "the people" seems to have been employed as a term of art employed in selected parts of the Constitution. The Preamble declares that the Constitution is ordained and established by "the people of the United States." The Second Amendment protects "the right of the people to keep and bear arms, and the Ninth and Tenth Amendments provide that certain rights and powers are reserved to the people." See also U.S. Const. Amdt. 1 ("Congress shall make no law . . . abridging . . . the right of the people to peaceably assemble"); Art. I sec. 2 cl. 1 ("The House of Representatives shall be composed of Members chosen every second Year by the people of the several states") (emphasis added). While this textual exegesis is by no means conclusive, it suggests that "the people" protected by the Fourth Amendment, and by the First and Second Amendments, and to whom rights and powers are reserved under the Ninth and Tenth Amendments, refers to a class of persons who are part of a national community or who have developed sufficient

---

would be an interpretation not warranted by the intent. The militia, as has been explained elsewhere, consists of those persons who, under law, are liable to the performance of military duty, and are officered and enrolled for service when called upon. . . . [I]f the right were limited to those enrolled, the purpose of the guarantee might be defeated altogether by action or the neglect to act of the government it was meant to hold in check. The meaning of the provision undoubtedly is, that the people, from whom the militia must be taken, shall have the right to keep and bear arms, and they need no permission or regulation of law for the purpose. But this enables the government to have a well-regulated militia; for to bear arms implies something more than mere keeping; it implies the learning to handle and use them in a way that makes those who keep them ready for their efficient use; in other words, it implies the right to meet for voluntary discipline in arms, observing in so doing the laws of public order.

—Thomas Cooley, *General Principles of Constitutional Law*, pp. 298-99 (1898).

[68] *U.S. v. Verdugo-Urquidez*, 110 S.Ct. 1056 (1990).

connection with this country to be considered part of that community.[69]

Clearly, the right of the people, as individuals, to keep and bear arms, ammunition for those arms, cartridge boxes for the ammunition, including high capacity magazines of the type used by the United States military, and all other associated military equipment is protected against infringement by the federal government.

Fourteenth Amendment Privilege and Immunity

What protection, if any, is afforded by the United States Constitution against state action which would ban the possession, manufacture and sale of "assault weapons," handguns, ammunition, or high capacity, detachable magazines? Section 1 of the Fourteenth Amendment says: "All persons born or naturalized in the United States and subject to the jurisdiction thereof, are citizens of the United States and of the State wherein they reside. No State shall make or enforce any law which shall abridge the privileges or immunities of the citizens of the United States. . . ." The text defines national citizenship. It defines state citizenship in terms of national citizenship. Then it provides that the "privileges or immunities" of United States citizens shall not be abridged by the states.

Article IV, section 2, of the Constitution provides that "The Citizens of each State shall be entitled to all Privileges and Immunities of the Citizens of the several States." Although these privileges and immunities are not defined, Justice Washington interpreted the clause in 1823 to protect against state infringement those privileges

> which are, in their very nature, fundamental; which belong of right to citizens of all free governments. [These] may [all be] comprehended under the following general heads: Protection by the government, the enjoyment of life and liberty, with the right to acquire and possess property of every kind, and to pursue and obtain happiness and safety; subject nevertheless to such restraints as the government may prescribe for the general good of the whole.[70]

---

[69] *Ibid.*, pp. 1060-61.
[70] *Corfield v. Coryell*, 6 Fed. Cas. 546, 551 (No. 3230) (C.C.E.D.Pa. 1823).

The Framers of the Fourteenth Amendment sought to interpose the federal government as a shield between these well-defined privileges and immunities of national citizens, which would now include blacks, and the state legislatures, particularly those which had replaced pre-Civil War slave codes with similar post-Civil War black codes.[71] Section 5 of the Amendment granted to Congress the power to enforce its provisions through appropriate legislation.[72]

In the *Slaughterhouse Cases* (1873),[73] the Court's first decision interpreting the amendment, it was held that laws enacted by the Louisiana legislature establishing a slaughterhouse monopoly did not violate the Fourteenth Amendment's privileges and immunities clause.

In his majority opinion, Justice Miller focused on the text, rather than the history, which "speaks only of the privileges and immunities of the citizens of the United States, and does not speak to those of the citizens of the several States. . . ."[74] He went on to say that, in regard to the potentially far-reaching effect of the amendment,

> when the effect is to fetter and degrade State governments by subjecting them to the control of Congress, . . . it radically changes the whole theory of the relations of the States and Federal governments to each other and of both of these to the people. . . .
>
> We are convinced that no such results were intended. . . .
>
> But lest it be said that no such privileges and immunities be found . . . we venture to suggest some which owe their existence to the Federal government. . . .
>
> . . . The right to peaceably assemble and petition for redress of grievances, the privilege of the writ of habeas corpus, are rights of the citizen guaranteed by the Federal Constitution.[75]

In *U.S. v. Cruikshank* (1876),[76] Chief Justice Waite noted that a citizen is subject to two sovereignties; however, there "need be no conflict between the two. . . . They are established for different purposes and

---

[71] See generally Stephen Halbrook, supra note 14, pp. 107-15.

[72] "The Congress shall have the power to enforce, by appropriate legislation, the provisions of this article" (U.S. Const. art. 14, sec. 5).

[73] *Slaughterhouse Cases*, 83 U.S. (16 Wall) 36 (1873).

[74] *Slaughterhouse Cases*, 83 U.S. (16 Wall) 36, p. 74.

[75] *Ibid.*, pp. 74-75.

[76] *U.S. v. Cruikshank*, 92 U.S. 542 (1876).

126

have different jurisdictions. . . . The citizen . . . owes allegiance to the two . . . and within their respective spheres must pay the penalties . . . for disobedience to its laws. In return, he can demand protection from each within its own jurisdiction."[77]

The Chief Justice then stated that the right of the people to assemble for lawful purposes was not created by the First Amendment and that the people must look to the States for its protection. Nevertheless, "[t]he right of the people peaceably to assemble for the purpose of petitioning Congress for a redress of grievances, or for anything else connected with the powers or duties of the national government, is an attribute of national citizenship . . . under the protection of and guaranteed by, the United States."[78]

Then the Chief Justice took aim at the Second Amendment. He stated that "bearing arms for a lawful purpose . . . is not a right granted by the Constitution. Neither is it in any way dependent upon it for its existence. . . . This . . . amendment[s] . . . has no other effect than to restrict the powers of the national government, leaving the people to look for their protection" to the States.[79]

Presser v. Illinois (1886)[80] held valid a state statute prohibiting all bodies of men, other than regularly organized state militia or United States troops, from associating, drilling or parading with arms in any city without a license from the state governor. In addressing this issue, Justice Wood thought it "clear that the sections under consideration, which only forbid bodies of men to associate . . . or to drill or parade in cities and towns unless authorized by law, do not infringe the right of the people to keep and bear arms."[81] He then cited *Cruikshank* as the "conclusive answer to the contention" that the Second Amendment "prohibits the legislation in question" since it "is a limitation on the power of Congress . . . and not upon that of the state."[82]

Justice Wood then began to reverse himself, acknowledging that:

---

[77] *Ibid.*, pp. 550-51.

[78] *Ibid.*, p. 552.

[79] *Ibid.*, p. 553.

[80] *Presser v. Illinois*, 116 U.S. 252 (1886).

[81] *Ibid.*, pp. 264-65.

[82] *Ibid.*, p. 265.

all citizens capable of bearing arms constitute the . . . reserve militia of the United States as well as the states, and . . . that states cannot, even laying the constitutional provision aside, prohibit the people from keeping and bearing arms, so as to deprive the United States of their rightful resource for maintaining public security, and disable the people from performing their duty to the general government.[83]

The plaintiff alleged that the sections in question abridged the privileges and immunities of United States citizenship. Justice Wood cited *Cruikshank's* view that only if the purpose of the assembly was to petition the government for a redress of grievances was the right protected by the United States. Then he concluded, "[t]he right voluntarily to associate together as a military company or organization, or to drill or parade with arms, without, and independent of, an act of congress or law of the state authorizing the same is not an attribute of national citizenship."[84]

The final opinion by the Supreme Court on direct applicability of the Second Amendment to the states was *Miller v. Texas* (1894).[85] The appellant asserted that Texas statutes prohibiting the carrying of weapons and authorizing arrest without a warrant of any person violating that law were in conflict with the Second and Fourth Amendments. While noting that "the restrictions of these amendments operate only upon Federal power," citing *Cruikshank*, the court left open the possibility that the Second and Fourth Amendments might apply to the states through the Fourteenth Amendment: "If the Fourteenth Amendment limited the power of States as to such rights, as pertaining to citizens of the United States, we think it was fatal to this claim that it was not set up in the trial court."[86] Just three years later the due process clause of the Fourteenth Amendment was held to protect the right to just compensation against state abridgement, marking the beginning of incorporation of federal protection of Bill of Rights' provisions against the states.[87]

---

[83] *Ibid.*, p. 265.

[84] *Ibid.*

[85] *Miller v. Texas*, 153 U.S. 535 (1894).

[86] *Ibid.*, p. 538.

[87] *Chicago B. & Q.R. Co. v. Chicago*, 166 U.S. 226 (1897).

Commentators[88] and cases[89] cite *Cruikshank* and *Presser* for the proposition that the Second Amendment "expresses a limitation that is applicable to the Congress and the National Government only and has no application to the States."[90] Insofar as they apply it to the general right[91] to keep and bear arms for lawful purposes, they are correct. However, like the right to assemble for any lawful purpose, which may be bifurcated to protect and guarantee assembling and petitioning the national government or anything else connected with its powers and duties,[92] so is the right to keep and bear arms for any lawful purpose.

All citizens able to bear arms constitute the reserve, or unorganized, militia of the United States and the states. The Supreme Court acknowledged this in *Perpich v. Department of Defense* (1990).[93] Members of the organized militia, and, implicitly, members of the unorganized militia, lose their state status when called to active federal duty.[94] The Court went on to quote from *Tarble's Case* (1871), in which an earlier Court stated that, "No interference with the execution of this power of the National government in the formation, organization, and government of its arms by any State officials could be permitted without greatly impairing the efficiency, if it did not utterly destroy, this branch of public service."[95]

This is entirely consistent with the Court's view in *Presser* that any prohibition on the people's keeping and bearing arms would disable the people from performing their duty to the national government.[96] It is the right to voluntarily associate together as a military organization which, according to the Court, is not an attribute of national citizenship, not the right to keep and bear arms protected by the Second Amendment.[97]

---

[88] Laurence Tribe, *American Constitutional Law* sec. 5-2, p. 299 (2d ed., 1988).

[89] See *Quilici v. City of Morton Grove*, 532 F.Supp. 1169 (N.D. Ill. 1981), affd. 695 F.2d 261 (7th Circ. 1982), *cert. den.* 646 U.S. 863 (1983); *Fresno Rifle and Pistol Club v. Van de Kamp*, 746 F. Supp. 1415 (E.D.Cal. 1990).

[90] See Thomas Cooley, supra note 67.

[91] *Fresno Rifle and Pistol Club v. Van De Kamp*, 746 F. Supp. 1415, 1417 (E.D.Cal. 1990).

[92] See *Cruikshank*, supra note 77.

[93] *Perpich v. Department of Defense*, 110 S.Ct. 2418, 2423 (1990).

[94] *Ibid.*, pp. 2426-27.

[95] *Tarble's Case*, 80 U.S. (13 Wall.) 397, 408 (1871), cited in *Perpich*, supra note 93, p. 2429.

[96] See *Presser*, supra note 82.

[97] See *Presser*, supra note 83.

The right of the people to keep and bear arms protected by the Second Amendment is as much a privilege and immunity of United States citizenship as the right of the people to peaceably assemble and petition for redress of grievances protected by the First Amendment.[98] Both are auxiliary rights described by Blackstone as being necessary to vindicate the fundamental rights of life, liberty, and property.[99] It is even more critical that the shield of federal protection be provided to this privilege and immunity of national citizenship. A state, in its plenary power, might prohibit its citizens from peaceably assembling and petitioning its own government. Yet it could not prohibit its citizens from peaceably assembling and petitioning the federal government without violating the Fourteenth Amendment. Were a state, in its plenary power, to prohibit keeping and bearing arms for lawful purposes, the people would be disabled from performing their duty as United States citizens. It must be concluded that the Framers of the Fourteenth Amendment intended no such result.

Preemption of State Law

If a state were to ban private ownership of all arms, there would still be statutory federal protection for arms suitable for militia use, even without this Fourteenth Amendment protection. When the Congress acts within an enumerated power, the preemption of conflicting state or local laws flows from the Supremacy Clause of Article VI of the United States Constitution.[100] This view was affirmed in *Gibbons v. Ogden* (1824),[101] where Chief Justice John Marshall observed that as "to such acts of the State Legislature as do not transcend their powers, but . . . interfere with, or are contrary to the law of Congress, made in pursuance of the constitution, . . . [i]n every such case, the act of Congress . . . is supreme. . . ."[102]

In 1903, Congress passed the Dick Act, repealing the Militia Act of 1792. This Act reorganized the militia into two classes: the original militia, consisting of the National Guard unit of the states, territories, and

---

[98] See *Slaughterhouse*, supra note 73.

[99] See 1 Blackstone, supra note 44.

[100] "This Constitution . . . shall be the supreme law of the land: and the judges in every State, shall be bound thereby, anything in the Constitution or laws of any State notwithstanding" (U.S. Const. art. VI).

[101] *Gibbons v. Ogden*, 22 U.S. (9 Wheat) 1 (1824).

[102] *Ibid.*, p. 221.

the District of Columbia, and the unorganized militia, consisting of all able-bodied male citizens of the states, territories, and the District of Columbia, aged eighteen to forty-five.[103] Two years later the Act was amended to establish the National Board for the Promotion of Rifle Practice to encourage marksmanship skills among our citizenry. The Secretary of War was authorized to sell service rifles and ammunition, at cost, from U.S. arsenals to rifle clubs formed under regulations prepared by the Board and approved by the Secretary.[104] Similar legislation is in force today.[105]

The arms currently prescribed for use in the civilian marksmanship training program, pursuant to Congressional power granted in the Militia Clauses, are as listed in the Code of Federal Regulations.[106] Therefore, any of these service rifles or pistols or their commercial equivalents should be exempt from infringement by state statute because of preemption of federal law. The Supreme Court, after their exhaustive study of the militia and Militia Clauses in *Perpich*, would most likely agree. In

---

[103] Dick Act, ch. 196, 32 Stat. 775-780 (1903).
No longer would a man be required to furnish his own weapon nor would there remain any protection from private creditors or tax collectors. The federal government would furnish weapons to the organized militia, thus bringing to pass what Richard Henry Lee feared most, a select militia. See Sanford Levinson, supra note 13, p. 650 (discussion of statist concept of civil government as repository of the legitimate means of violence).

[104] Act to Promote Rifle Practice, ch. 196, 33 Stat. 986-87 (1905).

[105] 10 U.S.C. sec. 4307-13 (1990).

[106] 32 C.F.R. 543.52, cited in *Fresno Rifle and Pistol Club v. Van de Kamp*, 746 F.Supp. 1415, 1426 (E.D.Cal. 1990).
1. U.S. Rifle, caliber .30 M-1 as issued by the U.S. Army, or a commercial rifle of the same type and caliber, or either rifle if chambered for 7.62 mm.
2. U.S. Rifle, caliber 7.62 mm M-14 or a commercial equivalent of the same type and caliber.
3. U.S. Rifle, caliber 5.56 mm M-16 or a commercial rifle of the same type.
4. U.S. pistol, caliber .45 M-1911 or M-1911A1 or a commercial pistol of the same type.
Arguably, to this list must be added the U.S. rifle, caliber 5.56 mm M-16A2 or a commercial rifle of the same type and the U.S. pistol, caliber 9 mm M-9 or a commercial pistol of the same type. These weapons are currently issued to the United States Army and National Guard. Further, it may be argued that the taxing and licensing requirements of the National Firearms Act of 1934 do not apply to the fully automatic versions of these service rifles since these requirements are an infringement on the right of the people to keep and bear arms suitable for militia use. Although weapons capable of fully automatic fire are of doubtful utility in the hands of individual riflemen, that right is still protected by the Second Amendment. Were Congress to delete the rifles capable of fully automatic fire from 32 C.F.R. 543.52, such an act would be void as a pretext.
Judges must be educated as to their responsibilities as members of the militia and as to the law of the land. The United States District Court Judge ruling on the constitutionality of the California Roberti-Roos Assault Weapons Control Act of 1989 had no notice that the Colt AR-15, one of the firearms defined as an "assault weapon" by the Act, is the commercial equivalent of the Colt M-16. He said, "Based on the Court's limited knowledge of firearms, it does not appear that any of the legislatively banned weapons in question here qualify as a weapon" listed in 32 C.F.R. 544.52.

their opinion, they stated that the Constitution "recognizes the supremacy of federal power in military affairs."[107]

Conclusion

The United States Constitution protects the individual right to keep and bear arms. The arms protected are not those suitable for sporting purposes only but those suitable for militia use. Professor Levinson's concern that *"Miller* can be read to support . . . the most extreme arguments, e.g., that an individual has the right to keep and bear bazookas, rocket launchers and other armaments . . ."[108] is clearly without merit. As has been shown, it was never contemplated that the right to keep and bear arms would extend to such crew-served weapons. Certain assault rifles (and bayonets)[109] are another matter. The M-16 service rifle (as well as its commercial equivalent, the Colt AR-15) is the quintessential militia arm. Since it is the individual weapon authorized by Congress to be issued to the troops in the employ of the federal government, it is precisely that arm, at a minimum, which, along with its ammunition and accoutrements, enjoys Second Amendment and Fourteenth Amendment protection. The same protection should apply to, at a minimum, the .45 ACP service pistol. Arguably, this same protection should be extended to any weapon of the same caliber as that used by the United States military.

Yet, the Second and Fourteenth Amendments grant the people no rights. "[A]ll men are created equal; . . . they are endowed by their Creator, with certain unalienable rights; . . . life, liberty, . . . pursuit of happiness. . . . [T]o secure these rights, governments are instituted among men, deriving their just powers from the consent of the governed."[110] If the right to keep and bear arms were granted by the United States Constitution, then, by amendment, that right could be denied. This is not what the Framers contemplated.

Rights exist first. Governments are instituted to secure and protect these rights. Nevertheless,

---

[107] *Perpich*, supra note 93, p. 2428.

[108] Sanford Levinson, supra note 13, pp. 654-55.

[109] See supra note 106 (each rifle listed has an integral bayonet mount).

[110] The Declaration of Independence, paragraph 2 (U.S. 1776).

whenever any form of government becomes destructive to those ends, it is the right of the people to alter or abolish it, and to institute a new government, laying its foundation on such princi- ples, and organizing its powers in such a form, as to them shall seem most likely to effect their safety and happiness.[111]

These rights are to be vindicated, when actually violated or attacked, by first appealing to the courts for justice, next petitioning the executive and legislature for redress of grievances, and, finally, resorting to the use of arms to reconstitute government in order to secure these rights.

First, the jury box. Then, the ballot box. As a last resort, the cartridge box. It was for this last purpose that the United States Constitution protects the individual right of the people to keep and bear arms.

---

[111] *Ibid.*

The Second Amendment: Toward An Afro-Americanist Reconsideration

Robert J. Cottrol
Raymond T. Diamond

> *It would give to persons of the negro race, who were recognized as*
> *citizens in any one State of the Union, the right to enter every other*
> *state whenever they pleased, . . . and it would give them the full*
> *liberty of speech in public and in private upon all subjects upon which*
> *its own citizens might speak; to hold public meetings upon political*
> *affairs,* and to keep and carry arms wherever they went.[1]

Introduction

The often strident debate over the Second Amendment[2] is like few others in American constitutional discourse and historiography. It is a constitutional debate that has taken place largely in the absence of Su-

Copyright Robert J. Cottrol and Raymond T. Diamond, 1991. This article was delivered as a paper at the 1990 annual meeting of the American Society for Legal History, at the Harvard Legal History Forum, at a faculty seminar at Northwestern University Law School, at the 1991 joint annual meeting of the Law and Society Association and the International Law and Society Association, and at the 1991 annual meeting of the American Political Science Association. The authors would like to acknowledge the helpful comments made in those forums. The authors would like to acknowledge the research assistance of Jan McNitt, Boston College Law School, 1991; Richard J. Fraher, Rutgers (Camden) School of Law, 1993; Roderick C. Sanchez, Rutgers (Camden) School of Law, 1992; Adrienne I. Logan, Tulane University School of Law, 1992; and Willie E. Shepard, Tulane University School of Law, 1992. This paper has benefitted from the criticism and helpful comments of Akhil R. Amar, Michael Les Benedict, Barbara Black, Maxwell Bloomfield, Ruth Colker, Michael Cutis, Robert Dowlut, Kermit Hall, Natalie Hull, Don B. Kates, Jr., Barbara K. Kopytoff, Sanford Levinson, Joyce Lee Malcolm, John Stick and Robert F. Williams. The authors would also like to acknowledge summer research grants from Boston College Law School, Rutgers (Camden) School of Law, and Tulane University School of Law which contributed to the writing of this paper. Robert J. Cottrol is Associate Professor, Rutgers (Camden) School of Law, A.B. 1971, Ph.D., 1978, Yale University; J.D. 1984, Georgetown University Law Center. Raymond T. Diamond is Associate Professor, Tulane University School of Law, A.B. 1973, Yale University; J.D. 1977, Yale Law School.

---

[1] *Dred Scott v. Sanford*, 60 U.S. (19 How.) 393, 417 (1857) (emphasis added).

[2] "A well regulated Militia, being necessary to the security of a free State, the right of the people to keep and bear arms shall not be infringed." U.S. Const. amend. II.

preme Court opinion.[3] It is historical controversy where the Framers' intentions have best been gleaned from indirect rather than direct evidence.[4] It is a scholarly debate that members of the academy have been until recently somewhat reluctant to join,[5] leaving the field to

---

[3] The Supreme Court has directly ruled on Second Amendment claims in only four cases. See *United States v. Miller*, 307 U.S. 174 (1939); *Miller v. Texas*, 153 U.S. 535 (1894); *Presser v. Illinois*, 116 U.S. 252 (1886); *United States v. Cruikshank*, 92 U.S. 542 (1876). Proponents of the collective rights theory have frequently cited these cases as supportive of their views. It is more accurate to describe the first three cases as having recognized the individual right, but also as having construed the Second Amendment as a bar to federal, but not state or private, infringement of the right. See infra Part III. *United States v. Miller* limited the Second Amendment's protection to weapons useful for militia duty. See infra Part IV. Since then, a number of lower federal courts have heard Second Amendment claims, often dismissing them on grounds that the Amendment has not been incorporated into the Fourteenth Amendment, which would make it binding on the states. Other courts have dismissed the claims by employing the collective rights theory. Almost all of these cases involved persons involved in criminal activity who were also convicted of firearms charges and thus are not really a good test of the extent to which the Second Amendment protects the rights of the public at large. See, e.g., *United States v. Three Winchester 30-30 Caliber Lever Action Carbines*, 504 F.2d 1288 (7th Cir., 1974) (statute prohibiting possession of firearms by previously convicted felon does not infringe upon Second Amendment). In a recent case in which a federal court sustained a general prohibition against handgun ownership, the Supreme Court refused to consider the case on appeal. See *Quilici v. Village of Morton Grove*, 695 F.2d 261 (7th Cir., 1982), cert. denied, 464 U.S. 863 (1983).

If the federal jurisprudence concerning the Second Amendment is somewhat thin, it should be noted that there is extensive case law concerning analogous provisions in state bills of rights. Indeed it is likely, should the Supreme Court ever seriously consider the question, that it might borrow Second Amendment doctrine from the state courts. For some recent constructions of state right to keep and bear arms provisions see, e.g., *Hoskins v. State*, 449 So. 2d 1269 (Ala. Crim. App., 1984) (statute prohibiting a person convicted of committing a crime of violence from owning or possessing a pistol does not deny right to keep and bear arms); *Rabbitt v. Leonard*, 413 A.2d 489 (Conn. Super. Ct., 1979) (statute permitting revocation of pistol permit for cause and providing notice of revocation and opportunity for de novo postrevocation hearing does not violate citizen's right to bear arms); *State v. Friel*, 508 A.2d 123 (Me., 1986) (statute prohibiting possession of a firearm by a convicted felon does not violate constitutional right to keep and bear arms); *People v. Smelter*, 437 N.W.2d 341 (Mich. Ct. App., 1989) (statute prohibiting possession of stun guns does not impermissibly infringe upon right to keep and bear arms); *State v. Vlacil*, 645 P.2d 677 (Utah, 1982) (statute making it a Class A misdemeanor for any noncitizen to own or possess a dangerous weapon is not unconstitutional). For a historical discussion of state right to keep and bear arms provisions, see generally Stephen P. Halbrook, *A Right to Bear Arms: State and Federal Bills of Rights and Constitutional Guarantees* (1989).

[4] The debates in the House of Representatives over what became the Second Amendment (it was originally proposed as the Fourth Amendment) centered on a clause excepting conscientious objectors from militia duty. The original text of the Amendment read: "A well regulated militia, composed of the body of the people, being the best security of a free state, the right of the people to keep and bear arms shall not be infringed; but no person religiously scrupulous shall be compelled to bear arms." *The Founders' Constitution*, 210, (Phillip B. Kurland and Ralph Lerner, eds., 1987). The House debate, focusing on the religious exemption, sheds little light on the individual versus collective rights debate, although the phrase "body of the people" used to describe the militia does suggest the idea of a militia of the whole. Still, the best evidence of the Framers' intentions in this matter comes from the surrounding history and the comments of the constitutional Framers generally with respect to the composition of the militia. See infra Part I.

[5] See Sanford Levinson, *The Embarrassing Second Amendment* [which appears elsewhere in this book—Ed.] 99 *Yale L.J.* pp. 637, 639-42 (1989) (discussing the reluctance of most constitutional scholars to treat the Second Amendment as a subject worthy of serious scholarly or pedagogical consideration). Recently, however, one scholar has examined the Second Amendment within the context of the Bill of Rights as a whole. See Akhil Amar, *The Bill of Rights as a Constitution*, 100 *Yale L.J.*, p. 1131 (1991). In Amar's view, the Bill of Rights was designed with both populist and collective concerns in mind. It was designed to protect both the right of the people and to prevent

independent scholars primarily concerned with the modern gun control controversy.[6] In short, the Second Amendment is an arena of constitutional jurisprudence that still awaits its philosopher.

The debate over the Second Amendment is ultimately part of the larger debate over gun control, a debate about the extent to which the Amendment was either meant to be or should be interpreted as limiting the ability of government to prohibit or limit private ownership of firearms.

---

potential tyranny from an overreaching federal government. Amar sees the purpose of the Second Amendment as preventing Congress from disarming freemen, so that the populace could resist tyranny imposed by a standing army. *Ibid.*, pp. 1162-73.

[6] See, e.g., David I. Caplan, *Restoring the Balance: The Second Amendment Revisited,* Fordham Urb. L.J. 31 (1976) (current efforts to limit firearm possession undermine the Second Amendment's twin goals of individual and collective defense); Robert Dowlut, *Federal and State Constitutional Guarantees to Arms,* 15 *U. Dayton L. Rev.* 59 (1989) (laws seeking to disarm the people violate the Second Amendment); Robert Dowlut, *The Right to Arms: Does the Constitution or the Predilection of Judges Reign?,* 36 L. Rev. 65 (1983) (interpretation of the Second Amendment is controlled by the Framers' intent to guarantee the individual right to keep and bear arms rather than a more narrow judicial interpretation); Keith A. Ehrman & Dennis A. Henigan, *The Second Amendment in the Twentieth Century: Have You Seen Your Militia Lately?,* 15 Dayton L. Rev. 5 (1989) (Second Amendment's historical origins erect no real barrier to federal or state laws affecting handguns); Richard E. Gardiner, *To Preserve Liberty—A Look at the Right to Keep and Bear Arms,* 10 L. Rev. 63 (1982) (advocates of gun control have twisted the original and plain meaning of the Second Amendment); Alan M. Gottlieb, *Gun Ownership: A Constitutional Right,* 10 Ky. L. Rev. 113 (1982) (modern antipathy to firearms has influenced interpretation of the Second Amendment as a collective right); David T. Hardy, *The Second Amendment and the Historiography of the Bill of Rights,* 4 & Pol. 1 (1987) (the Second Amendment has a dual purpose stemming from the merger of the militia and the right to bear arms provisions); Maynard H. Jackson, Jr., *Handgun Control: Constitutional and Critically Needed,* 8. Cent. L.J. 189 (1977) (Second Amendment is central to any discussion of the legal merits of gun control); Nelson Lund, *The Second Amendment, Political Liberty and the Right to Self-Protection,* 39 *Ala. L. Rev.* 103 (1987) (suggesting a Second Amendment jurisprudence consistent with modern treatment of the Bill of Rights such that handgun regulation be reasonably tailored to public safety); James A. McClure, *Firearms and Federalism,* 7 *Idaho L. Rev.* 197 (1970) (Second Amendment precludes federal interference but leaves to debate the issue of state regulation of handguns); Robert J. Riley, *Shooting to Kill the Handgun: Time to Martyr Another American "Hero,"* 51 *J. Urb. L.* 491 (1974) (construing the Second Amendment as a surpassable barrier to handgun control by finding the handgun a weapon of marginal military utility); Jonathan A. Weiss, *A Reply to Advocates of Gun Control Law* 52 *J. Urb. L.* 577 (1974) (placing the Second Amendment in context of the Bill of Rights, provides an inviolable right to bear arms and an absolute bar to government restriction).

Two advocates of the individual rights theory who are outside the academy, but have nonetheless been quite instrumental in influencing the constitutional debate among law teachers and historians, are Donald B. Kates, Jr. and Stephen P. Halbrook. See, e.g., Donald B. Kates, Jr., *Handgun Prohibition and the Original Meaning of the Second Amendment,* 82 h. L. Rev. 204 (1983) (Second Amendment right to bear arms, applicable against both federal and state government, does not foreclose, but limits, gun control options); Donald B. Kates, Jr., *The Second Amendment: A Dialogue,* 49 *Law & Contemp. Probs.* 143 (1986) (Second Amendment substantially limits the arbitrariness of granting gun permits); Stephen P. Halbrook, *That Every Man Be Armed: The Evolution of a Constitutional Right* (1984) [hereinafter Halbrook, *That Every Man Be Armed*] (the right of citizens to keep and bear arms has deep historical roots and overly restrictive interpretations of the Second Amendment are associated with reactionary concepts including elitism, militarism and racism); Stephen P. Halbrook, *The Jurisprudence of the Second and Fourteenth Amendments,* 4 Geo. Mason U. L. Rev. 1 (1981) (the fundamental character of the Second Amendment and the increasingly restrictive forms of gun control legislation necessitate Supreme Court precedent on the status of the Amendment's applicability to the states); Stephen P. Halbrook, *What the Framers Intended: A Linguistic Analysis of the Right to "Bear Arms,"* 49 *Law & Contemp. Probs.* 151 (1986) (Second Amendment right to bear arms is incompatible with the suggestion of no right to bear arms without state or federal permission).

Waged in the popular press,[7] in the halls of Congress,[8] and increasingly in historical and legal journals,[9] two dominant interpretations have emerged. Advocates of stricter gun controls have tended to stress the Amendment's Militia Clause, arguing that the purpose of the Amendment was to ensure that state militias would be maintained against potential federal encroachment. This argument, embodying the collective rights theory, sees the Framers' primary, indeed sole, concern as one with the concentration of military power in the hands of the federal government, and the corresponding need to ensure a decentralized military establishment largely under state control.[10]

---

[7] See, e.g., Daniel Abrams, *What 'Right to Bear Arms'?*, *N.Y. Times*, July 20, 1989, p. A23; Robert J. Cottrol, *It's Time to Enforce the Second Amendment*, *Plain Dealer* (Cleveland, Feb. 17, 1990, p. 5B; Ervin N. Griswold, *Phantom Second Amendment Rights*, *Wash. Post*, Nov. 4, 1990, p. C7; Sue Wimmershoff-Caplan, *The Founders and the AK-47*, *Wash. Post*, July 6, 1989, p. A18. Even former Chief Justice Warren Burger has used this arena to opine on the subject. See Warren Burger, *The Right to Keep and Bear Arms*, *Parade Mag.*, Jan. 14, 1990, p. 4.

For one interesting example of a writer who (reluctantly) supports the individual rights interpretation of the Second Amendment and who, as a member of the gun control group Handgun Control, Inc., is also a strong advocate of stricter gun control, see columnist Michael Kinsley, *Slicing Up the Second Amendment*, *Wash. Post*, Feb. 8, 1990, p. A25. More recently, conservative columnist George Will, also an advocate of stricter gun control, has stated that "The National Rifle Association is perhaps correct and certainly plausible in its 'strong' reading of the Second Amendment protection for private gun ownership." Will argues for repeal of the Second Amendment on the grounds that the right is not as important as it was 200 years ago.

Will also makes the interesting observation that "The subject of gun control reveals a role reversal between liberals and conservatives that makes both sides seem tendentious. Liberals who usually argue that constitutional rights (of criminal defendants, for example) must be respected regardless of inconvenient social consequences, say that the Second Amendment right is too costly to honor. Conservatives who frequently favor applying cost-benefit analysis to constitutional construction (of defendants' rights, for example) advocate an absolutist construction of the Second Amendment." See George Will, *Oh That Annoying Second Amendment: It Shows No Signs of Going Away*, *Phil. Inquirer*, March 22, 1991.

Although the Second Amendment and gun control debates involve far more than a simple liberal/conservative dichotomy, there are numerous exceptions on both sides; Will's point is well taken. If we accept the conventional view that the National Rifle Association is a predominantly conservative organization and that advocates of gun control tend to be politically liberal, we can see rather interesting role reversals. For example, the NRA has attacked firearms bans in public housing, bans which mainly affect people who are poor and black, while liberal groups have generally remained silent on the issue.

[8] See "The Right to Keep and Bear Arms: Report of the Subcomm. on the Constitution of the Comm. on the Judiciary," S. Rep. No. 522, 97th Cong., 2d Sess. 3 (1982) [hereinafter "Subcommittee Report"].

[9] See *ibid.*; see also Lawrence Delbert Cress & Robert E. Shalhope, *The Second Amendment and the Right to Keep and Bear Arms: An Exchange* 71 *J. Am. Hist.* 587 (1984) (debate whether correct interpretation of Second Amendment rests on rights to bear arms or communal prerogatives implied in Militia Clause); Joyce Lee Malcolm, *The Right of the People to Keep and Bear Arms: The Common Law Tradition*, 10 *Hastings Const. L.Q.* 285 (1983), reprinted in *Firearms and Violence: Issues of Public Policy*, pp. 391-95 (Donald B. Kates, Jr., ed., 1984) (proper reading of Second Amendment extends to every citizen right to keep and bear arms for personal defense); Robert E. Shalhope, *The Ideological Origins of the Second Amendment*, 69 *J. Am. Hist.* 599 (1982) (armed citizen and militia existed as distinct, yet interrelated, elements within American republican thought).

[10] See, e.g., Jackson, supra note 6, p. 194 (the purpose of the Second Amendment was to maintain the militia, not to provide an individual right to bear arms); Roy G. Weatherup, 1 *Standing Armies and Armed Citizens: An Analysis of the Second Amendment*, 2 *Hastings Const. L.Q.* 961, 963,

Opponents of stricter gun controls have tended to stress the Amendment's second clause, arguing that the Framers intended a militia of the whole—or at least the entire able-bodied white male—population, expected to perform its duties with privately owned weapons.[11] Advocates of this view also frequently urge that the Militia Clause should be read as an amplifying, rather than a qualifying, clause. They argue that, while maintaining a "well-regulated militia"[12] was the predominant reason for including the Second Amendment in the Bill of Rights, it should not be viewed as the sole or limiting reason. They argue that the Framers also contemplated a right to individual and community protection.[13] This view embodies the individual rights theory.

This debate has raised often profound questions, but questions generally treated hastily, if at all, by the community of constitutional scholars.[14] For example, if one accepts the collective rights view of the amendment, serious questions arise concerning whether the federal government's integration of the National Guard into the Army and, later, the Air Force have not in all but name destroyed the very institutional independence of the militia that is at the heart of what the collective rights theorists see as the Framers' intentions.[15] Even the gun control debate is not completely resolved by an acceptance of the collective rights theory. If the Second Amendment was designed to ensure the existence of somewhat independent state militias immune from federal encroachment, then the question arises to what extent states are free to define militia membership. Could a state include as members of its militia all adult citizens, thus permitting them an exemption from federal firearms restrictions? If, instead, the federal government has plenary power to define militia membership and chooses to confine such membership to the federally controlled National Guard, does the Second Amendment become a dead letter under the collective rights theory?

995, 1000 (1975) (Second Amendment was designed solely to protect the states against the federal government, using an historical analysis of the relationship between citizens and their sovereign as evidence).

[11] See, e.g., Halbrook, *That Every Man Be Armed*, supra note 6, pp. 55-87; Kates, *Handgun Prohibition and the Original Meaning of the Second Amendment*, supra note 6, pp. 214-18, 273.

[12] U.S. Const. amend. II.

[13] See, e.g., Kates, *Handgun Prohibition and the Original Meaning of the Second Amendment*, supra note 6.

[14] See supra note 5.

[15] See *Perpich v. Department of Defense*, 110 S. Ct. 2418, 2422-26 (1990), discussing the history of legislation governing the militia and the National Guard, and Congress's plenary authority over the National Guard.

If the collective rights theory raises difficult questions, the individual rights theory raises perhaps even more difficult, and perhaps more interesting ones. Some of these questions are obvious and frequently asked, such as where to draw the line between an individual's right to possess arms and the corollary right to self-defense on the one hand, and the community's interest in public safety and crime control on the other. Other questions are more elusive, more difficult to pose as well as to answer. At the heart of the individual rights view is the contention that the Framers of the Second Amendment intended to protect the right to bear arms for two related purposes. The first of these was to ensure popular participation in the security of the community, an outgrowth of the English and early American reliance on posses and militias made up of the general citizenry to provide police and military forces.[16] The second purpose was to ensure an armed citizenry in order to prevent potential tyranny by a government empowered and perhaps emboldened by a monopoly of force.[17]

The second argument, that an armed populace might serve as a basis for resistance to tyranny, raises questions of its own. The Framers had firsthand experience with such a phenomenon, but they lived in an age when the weapon likely to be found in private hands, the single shot musket or pistol, did not differ considerably from its military counterpart. Although the armies of the day possessed heavier weapons rarely found in private hands, battles were fought predominately by infantry or cavalry with weapons not considerably different from those employed by private citizens for personal protection or hunting.[18] Battles in which privately armed citizens vanquished regular troops, or at least gave "a good account of themselves," were not only conceivable—they happened.[19]

---

[16] See Malcolm, supra note 9, pp. 290-95.

[17] See Stephen Halbrook's exploration of that idea within the context of classical political philosophy in *That Every Man Be Armed*, supra note 6, pp. 7-35; see also Gardiner, supra note 6, pp. 73-82 (the history of the Second Amendment indicates that one of its purposes was to ensure the existence of an armed citizenry as a defense against domestic tyranny); Lund, supra note 6, at 111-16 (Second Amendment protects an individual's right to bear arms in order to secure his political freedom); Shalhope, supra note 9, pp. 610-13 (Framers of the Second Amendment, motivated by their distrust of government, intended to protect the right of individuals to bear arms).

[18] The American civilian of the mid-18th century was typically armed with the "Pennsylvania" rifle, later to be known as the "Kentucky" rifle. See Daniel Boorstin's discussion of the relative merits of the Pennsylvania rifle and the muskets that British soldiers were equipped with in Daniel J. Boorstin, *The Americans: The Colonial Experience*, pp. 350-51 (1958).

[19] For one account of the battles of Lexington and Concord, see David Hawke, *The Colonial Experience*, pp. 573-78 (1966).

Modern warfare has, of course, introduced an array of weapons that no government is likely to permit ownership by the public at large[20] and that few advocates of the individual rights view would claim as part of the public domain.[21] The balance of power has shifted considerably and largely to the side of governments and their standing armies. For individual rights theorists, this shift immediately raises the question of whether, given the tremendous changes that have occurred in weapons technology, the Framers' presumed intention of enabling the population to resist tyranny remains viable in the modern world.[22] Although partly a question of military tactics, and thus beyond the scope of this discussion,[23] it is also a constitutional question. If private ownership of firearms

---

[20] It should not be necessary to detail such obvious examples as stinger missiles and nuclear weapons, but even more ordinary military weapons are also unlikely to be permitted to the public at large. For example, the U.S. Army expects every soldier, regardless of military specialty, to be proficient with the M203 grenade launcher (a shoulder-fired light mortar capable of firing a 40 millimeter high explosive round 400 meters), the M72A2 light anti-tank weapon (LAW) (a hand-held disposable anti-tank weapon capable of penetrating an armored vehicle at 300 meters), the M67 fragmentation grenade, and the M18A1 Claymore anti-personnel mine. See Department of the Army, *Soldier's Manual of Common Tasks: Skill Level 1* (1985).

[21] For one of the better efforts to reconcile modern weaponry with the type of weapons the Framers intended to protect, see Kates, *Handgun Prohibition and the Original Meaning of the Second Amendment,* supra note 6, pp. 204, 261.

[22] We are putting aside for the moment the question of the utility or potential utility of an armed population as a useful auxiliary to national or local governments in maintaining either national or community security. It should be noted that during the Second World War, when the National Guard had been mobilized into the Army, impromptu home defense forces—some organized by state governments, some privately organized—patrolled beach areas and likely sabotage sites. The individuals who performed this service were usually equipped with their own weapons. And while this American version of "Dad's Army" encountered no significant enemy activity—doubtless to the relief of all concerned, particularly the participants—the utility of these patrols should be noted. If such patrols were necessary, and some undoubtedly were, from the military point of view, it was probably better to have civilian auxiliaries performing this function, freeing regular military units for more pressing duties. See *ibid.,* p. 272 n. 284. It should also be noted that, immediately after the attack on Pearl Harbor, the Hawaiian territorial governor ordered citizens to report with their own firearms for defense of the Islands in anticipation of a Japanese invasion. Ironically, given the later treatment of Japanese Americans on the mainland, a good percentage of the men who made up the citizens' home guard in Hawaii were of Japanese descent. See *ibid.*

In light of our later discussion of whether or not, given the racial restriction in the Uniform Militia Act of 1792, free Negroes were considered part of the militia, see *infra* Part I.c.2, it should be noted that many of the individuals who served in these home guard organizations probably did not meet the statutory definition of militia members. By statute, membership in the militia is defined as men from 18-45. Most men in that age group were in the armed forces during the Second World War so that those performing home guard duties were probably older and younger than the statutory age limits. See Kates, *Handgun Prohibition and the Original Meaning of the Second Amendment, supra* note 6, p. 272 n. 284 (research indicates that men between the ages of 16 and 65 served in home guard units). It is also probable that a fair number of women performed those tasks. For our purposes, what is interesting about this history is that it indicates that militia membership is even broader than the statutory definition. Perhaps the best way of viewing the issue is to regard statutory militia provisions as defining those who may be compelled to perform militia service, but to realize that the whole population might be permitted to volunteer for militia service.

[23] Despite modern technological advances, the impotence of privately armed civilians against organized armies is by no means obvious. Afghan guerrillas, to cite a recent example, were quite successful in resisting the Soviet Army largely with small arms. Harry Summers, retired Army

is constitutionally protected, should this right be protected with the original military and political purposes in mind, or should the protection of firearms now be viewed as protecting only those weapons used for personal protection or recreation?[24] Or, given that all firearms are potentially multi-purpose, and that all firearms potentially may be used for military, recreational or personal defense as well as for criminal purposes, what effect should legislatures and courts give to the Framers' original military rationale? Where should the proper lines be drawn with respect to modern firearms, all of which employ technologies largely unimagined by the Framers?[25]

Colonel and Professor at the Army War College, indicated in a recent column that he believed an armed population could resist a tyrannical government or at least do so better than an unarmed one. See Harry Summers, *Gun Collecting and Lithuania, Wash. Times,* March 29, 1990, p. F4 (public should protect its right to bear arms as a protection against government).

There are at least three ways to approach the question of an armed population resisting the government. The first is to look at what happens when actual armed conflict breaks out between a nation's military forces and the population or a segment of the population. Although modern technology weights the odds heavily in the government's favor, other considerations, including whether or not military forces are overextended, the skill of the population in general with arms (which might be influenced by the number of military veterans in the population or the number of people who regularly practice with firearms), the terrain, and the morale of military forces called upon to suppress the population, might tend to redress the technological imbalance.

The second way of viewing this question is to look at it as a question of deterrence. From this perspective, one might argue that, even if a government would ultimately win a confrontation with an armed population, the cost to the government is higher. It will endure substantially larger casualties and may have to endure large scale destruction of economically valuable infrastructure in order to achieve its objectives. This higher cost might cause a government to seek compromise, or cause a reluctance on the part of many in the military to participate, even if ultimate victory was assured. In the Soviet Union, press reports indicated great resistance on the part of citizens to sending reservists to the Azerbaijan region, in part because the population was armed and willing to resist. See Bill Keller, *Gorbachev Issues Emergency Decree Over Azerbaijan, N.Y. Times,* Jan. 16, 1990, at A1 (Azerbaijani leader threatens armed resistance against military); Bill Keller, *Moscow Dispatches 11,000 Troops to Azerbaijan, N.Y. Times,* Jan. 17, 1990, at A1 (Gorbachev hesitated in sending troops partly from fear of wide-scale popular resistance); Bill Keller, *Troops Seek to Calm Azerbaijan: Soviets Debate Cause of Violence, N.Y. Times,* Jan. 18, 1990, at A1 (one reason for hesitation before sending troops was fear of popular disapproval of sending troops to dangerous area); Esther B. Rein, *Gorbachev Is Backed on Azerbaijan Combat, N.Y. Times,* Jan. 18, 1990, at A8 (Gorbachev criticized in the past for sending troops to control civil unrest); Bill Keller, *Soviet Troops Bogged Down by Azerbaijanis Blockades of Railroads and Airfields, N.Y. Times,* Jan. 19, 1990, at A1 (many young Soviets not eager to be mobilized); Frances X. Clines, *Soviet Force Said to Battle With Azerbaijani Militants: Call Up of Reserves Halted, N.Y. Times,* Jan. 20, 1990, at A1 (Moscow ends mobilization of reservists after wide protest); Bill Keller, *Cry of Won't Give Up My Son! And Soviets End the Call-Up, N.Y. Times,* Jan. 20, 1990, at A6 (same).

The third consideration is the one most relevant to the Afro-American experience. Governmental oppression can occur when the state actively oppresses the population or a segment of the population. It can also occur when the state displays an active indifference to the denial of one segment of the population's rights by another. This occurred most vividly for blacks during the Jim Crow era. See infra Part IV.

[24] The latter appears to be the view taken by former Chief Justice Burger. See *Burger,* supra note 7, p. 4.

[25] In the 18th century, when the Second Amendment was adopted, firearms were single shot devices that were reloaded very slowly. Firearms were loaded by pouring black gunpowder down the muzzle of the firearm, followed by a separate bullet (usually a lead ball); the load was then rammed

Societal, as well as technological, changes raise questions for advocates of the individual rights view of the Second Amendment. In the eighteenth century, the chief vehicle for law enforcement was the *posse comitatus*, and the major American military force was the militia of the whole. While these institutions are still recognized by modern law,[26] they lie dormant in late twentieth century America. Professional police forces and a standing military establishment assisted by semi-professional auxiliaries—the reserves and the National Guard—have largely assumed the roles of public protection and national security. It is possible that the concept of a militia of the armed citizenry has been largely mooted by social change.

Yet, the effect of social change on the question of the Second Amendment is a two-edged sword. If one of the motivating purposes behind the Second Amendment was to provide a popular check against potential governmental excess, then does the professionalization of national and community security make the right to keep and bear arms even more important in the modern context? Furthermore, the question remains whether the concept of a militia of the whole is worth re-examining: Did the Framers, by adopting the Second Amendment, embrace a republican vision of the rights and responsibilities of free citizens that, despite the difficulties, should somehow be made to work today?

Finally, the Second Amendment debate raises important questions concerning constitutional interpretation, questions that need to be more fully addressed by legal historians and constitutional commentators. It poses important questions about notions of the living Constitution, and to what extent that doctrine can be used to limit as well as extend rights. It also poses important questions about social stratification, cultural bias and

---

down with a ramrod. By way of contrast, modern firearms are usually loaded with self-contained cartridges—cartridges where the bullet and the powder are contained in one single capsule. Almost all modern firearms, with the exception of a few firearms designed almost exclusively for target shooting or training children in the use of firearms, are repeaters: they can fire more than one bullet before the shooter has to reload. Among the types of repeating firearms that exist today are revolvers (pistols with between five and nine rotating cylinders), manually operated rifles and shotguns, firearms that require the operation of a lever or bolt between pulls of the trigger in order to make a new round of ammunition ready to fire, semi-automatic firearms (pistols, rifles and shotguns capable of firing a new round with each pull of the trigger), and automatic firearms (weapons that will fire a new round as long as the shooter depresses the trigger). These new developments make all modern firearms much more rapid fire than those employed in the 18th century. For books that illustrate the history of firearms technology, see Robert Held, *The Age of Firearms, A Pictorial History* (1957); Basil P. Hughes, *Firepower: Weapons Effectiveness on the Battle Field, 1630-1850* (1975); Harold L. Peterson, *The Treasury of the Gun* (1962).

[26] See, e.g., 10 U.S.C. § 311 (1988) (unorganized militia consists of all men between the ages 18 and 45, and females who are commissioned National Guard officers); *Williams v. State*, 490 S.W.2d 117, 121 (Ark. 1973) (recognizing the continued validity of the *posse comitatus* power).

constitutional interpretation. Do courts really protect rights explicit or implicit in the Constitution, or is the courts' interpretation of rights largely a dialogue with the elite, articulate sectors of society, with the courts enforcing those rights favored by dominant elites and ignoring those not so favored?

Many of the issues surrounding the Second Amendment debate are raised in particularly sharp relief from the perspective of African-American history. With the exception of Native Americans, no people in American history have been more influenced by violence than blacks. Private and public violence maintained slavery.[27] The nation's most destructive conflict ended the "peculiar institution."[28] That all too brief experiment in racial egalitarianism, Reconstruction, was ended by private violence[29] and abetted by Supreme Court sanction.[30] Jim Crow was sustained by private violence, often with public assistance.[31]

If today the memories of past interracial violence are beginning to fade, they are being quickly replaced by the frightening phenomenon of black-on-black violence, making life all too precarious for poor blacks in inner city neighborhoods.[32] Questions raised by the Second Amendment, particularly those concerning self-defense, crime, participation in the security of the community, and the wisdom or utility of relying exclusively on the state for protection, thus take on a peculiar urgency in light of the modern Afro-American experience.

This article explores Second Amendment issues in light of the Afro-American experience, concluding that the individual rights theory comports better with the history of the right to bear arms in England and Colonial and post-Revolutionary America. The article also suggests that

---

[27] See Kenneth M. Stampp, *The Peculiar Institution: Slavery in the Antebellum South*, pp. 141-91 (1956).

[28] The Civil War cost the Union and Confederate armies a combined casualty total of 498,332 deaths. By way of contrast, World War II, the nation's second bloodiest conflict, cost the United States 407,316 fatalities. See *The World Almanac & Book of Facts*, 793 (Mark S. Hoffman, ed., 1991).

[29] See generally Eric Foner, *Reconstruction: America's Unfinished Revolution, 1863-1877*, pp. 564-600 (1988); George C. Rable, *But There Was No Peace: The Role of Violence in the Politics of Reconstruction* (1984).

[30] See, e.g., *United States v. Harris*, 106 U.S. 629 (1882) (holding unconstitutional a federal criminal statute designed to protect equal privileges and immunities for blacks from invasion by private persons); *United States v. Cruikshank*, 92 U.S. 542 (1876) (holding unconstitutional a federal criminal statute designed to prevent whites from conspiring to prevent blacks from exercising their constitutional rights).

[31] See infra Part IV.

[32] See infra Part V.

Second Amendment issues need to be explored, not only with respect to how the right to keep and bear arms has affected American society as a whole, but also with an eye toward subcultures in American society who have been less able to rely on state protection.

The remainder of this article is divided into five parts. Part I examines the historical tension between the belief in the individual's right to bear arms and the desire to keep weapons out of the hands of "socially undesirable" groups. The English distrust of the lower classes, and then certain religious groups, was replaced in America by a distrust of two racial minorities: Native Americans and blacks. Part II examines antebellum regulations restricting black firearms ownership and participation in the militia. Part III examines the intentions of the Framers of the Fourteenth Amendment with respect to the Second Amendment and how nineteenth-century Supreme Court cases limiting the scope of the Second Amendment were part of the general tendency of the courts to limit the scope of the Fourteenth Amendment. This Part also examines restrictions on firearms ownership aimed at blacks in the postbellum South and the role of private violence in reclaiming white domination in the South. Part IV examines black resistance to the violence that accompanied Jim Crow. In Part V, the article suggests directions of further inquiry regarding political access, the current specter of black-on-black crime, and the question of gun control today.

I. Armed Citizens, Freemen and Well-Regulated Militias: The Beginnings of an Afro-American Experience with an Anglo-American Right

Any discussion of the Second Amendment should begin with the commonplace observation that the Framers of the Bill of Rights did not believe they were creating new rights.[33] Instead, they believed that they were simply recognizing rights already part of their English constitutional heritage and implicit in natural law.[34] In fact, many of the Framers

---

[33] Bernard Bailyn, *The Ideological Origins of the American Revolution*, pp. 184-89, 193-94 (1967).

[34] *Ibid.* Especially pertinent is John Philip Reid's reminder: "There are other dimensions that the standing-army controversy, when studied from the perspective of law, adds to our knowledge of the American Revolution. One is the degree to which eighteenth-century Americans thought seventeenth-century English thoughts." John Philip Reid, *In Defiance of the Law: The Standing-Army Controversy, the Two Constitutions, and the Coming of the American Revolution* 4 (1981) (emphasis added).

145

cautioned against a bill of rights, arguing that the suggested rights were inherent to a free people, and that a specific detailing of rights would suggest that the new constitution empowered the federal government to violate other traditional rights not enumerated.[35]

Thus, an analysis of the Framers' intentions with respect to the Second Amendment should begin with an examination of their perception of the right to bear arms as one of the traditional rights of Englishmen, a right necessary to perform the duty of militia service. Such an analysis is in part an exercise in examining the history of arms regulation and militia service in English legal history. But a simple examination of the right to own weapons at English law combined with an analysis of the history of the militia in English society is inadequate to a full understanding of the Framers' understanding of what they meant by "the right to keep and bear arms." By the time the Bill of Rights was adopted, nearly two centuries of settlement in North America had given Americans constitutional sensibilities similar to, but nonetheless distinguishable from, those of their English counterparts.[36] American settlement had created its own history with respect to the right to bear arms, a history based on English tradition, modified by the American experience, and a history that was sharply influenced by the racial climate in the American colonies.

A. English Law and Tradition

The English settlers who populated North America in the seventeenth century were heirs to a tradition over five centuries old governing both the right and duty to be armed. At English law, the idea of an armed citizenry responsible for the security of the community had long coexisted, perhaps somewhat uneasily, with regulation of the ownership of arms, particularly along class lines. The Assize of Arms of 1181[37] required the arming of all free men, and required free men to possess

---

[35] See, e.g., *The Federalist* No. 84 (Alexander Hamilton).

[36] This can be seen with reference to the right of trial by jury. A number of scholars have noted that Americans in the late 18th century regarded the right of trial by jury as including the right to have the jury decide issues of law as well as fact. This was, of course, a departure from traditional English practice. See Morton J. Horowitz, *The Transformation of American Law, 1780-1860*, pp. 28-29 (1977); William Edward Nelson, *Americanization of the Common Law: The Impact of Legal Change on Massachusetts Society, 1760-1830*, pp. 3-4, 8, 20-30 (1975).

[37] *Select Charters & Other Illustrations of English Constitutional History from the Earliest Times to the Reign of Edward the First*, pp. 181-84 (H. W. C. Davis, ed., Fred B. Cothman & Co. 1985) (1921).

armor suitable to their condition.[38] By the thirteenth century, villeins possessing sufficient property were also expected to be armed and contribute to the security of the community.[39] Lacking both professional police forces and a standing army,[40] English law and custom dictated that the citizenry as a whole, privately equipped, assist in both law enforcement and in military matters. By law, all men between sixteen and sixty were liable to be summoned into the sheriff's *posse comitatus*. All subjects were expected to participate in the hot pursuit of criminal suspects, supplying their own arms for the occasion. There were legal penalties for failure to participate.[41]

Moreover, able-bodied men were considered part of the militia, although by the sixteenth century the general practice was to rely on select groups intensively trained for militia duty rather than to rely generally on the armed male population. This move toward a selectively trained militia was an attempt to remedy the often indifferent proficiency and motivation that occurred when relying on the population as a whole.[42]

Although English law recognized a duty to be armed, it was a duty and a right highly circumscribed by English class structure. The law often regarded the common people as a dangerous class, useful perhaps in defending shire and realm, but also capable of mischief with their weapons, mischief toward each other, toward their betters, and toward their betters' game. Restrictions on the type of arms deemed suitable for common people had long been part of English law and custom. A sixteenth-century statute designed as a crime control measure prohibited the carrying of handguns and crossbows by those with incomes of less than one hundred pounds a year.[43] Catholics were also often subject to being disarmed as potential subversives after the English reformation.[44]

It took the religious and political turmoil of seventeenth-century England to bring about large scale attempts to disarm the English public

---

[38] 1 Frederick Pollock & Frederic W. Maitland, *The History of English Law Before the Time of Edward I*, pp. 421-42, 565 (1968).

[39] *Ibid.*

[40] Historian Joyce Lee Malcolm notes that England did not have a standing army until the late 17th century and did not have a professional police force until the nineteenth. See Malcolm, supra note 9, p. 391.

[41] Alan Harding, *A Social History of English Law*, 59 (1966); Malcolm, supra note 9, p. 391.

[42] Malcolm, supra note 9, p. 391-92.

[43] *Ibid.*, p. 393.

[44] *Ibid.*, pp. 393-94.

and to bring the right to keep and bear arms under English constitutional protection. Post-Restoration attempts by Charles II to disarm large portions of the population known or believed to be political opponents, and James II's efforts to disarm his Protestant opponents led, in 1689, to the adoption of the Seventh provision of the English Bill of Rights: "That the Subjects which are Protestants may have Arms for the Defence suitable to their Conditions, and as allowed by Law."[45]

By the eighteenth century, the right to possess arms, both for personal protection and as a counterbalance against state power, had come to be viewed as part of the rights of Englishmen by many on both sides of the Atlantic. Sir William Blackstone listed the right to possess arms as one of the five auxiliary rights of English subjects without which their primary rights could not be maintained.[46]

---

[45] *Ibid.*, p. 408.

[46] 1 William Blackstone, *Commentaries*, pp. 143-45. Blackstone listed three primary rights—the right of personal security, the right of personal liberty, and the right of private property—all of which he regarded as natural rights recognized and protected by the common law and statutes of England. He also argued that these would be "dead letters" without the five auxiliary rights which he listed as: (1) the constitution, powers and privileges of Parliament; (2) the limitation of the king's prerogative; (3) the right to apply to the courts of justice for redress of injuries; (4) the right of petitioning the king or either house of Parliament, and for the redress of grievances; and (5) the right of subjects to have arms for their defence. *Ibid.*, pp. 121-45.

Some commentators have argued that Blackstone's remarks and other evidence of English common law and statutory rights to possess arms should be viewed in the light of the extensive regulation of firearms that traditionally existed in England and also in light of English strict gun control in the 20th century. See, e.g., Subcommittee Report, supra note 8, p. 26; Franklin E. Zimring and Gordon Hawkins, *The Citizen's Guide to Gun Control*, pp. 142-43 (1987); Ehrman and Henigan, supra note 6, pp. 9-10. Two points should be made in that regard. First, much of English firearms regulation had an explicit class base largely inapplicable in the American context. Second, neither a common law right to keep and bear arms nor a similar statutory right such as existed in the English Bill of Rights of 1689 would, in the light of Parliamentary supremacy, be a bar to subsequent statutes repealing or modifying that right. Blackstone is cited here not as evidence that the English right, in precise form and content, became the American right; instead it is evidence that the idea of an individual right to keep and bear arms existed on both sides of the Atlantic in the 18th century.

Blackstone's importance to this discussion is twofold. His writings on the right to possess arms can be taken as partial evidence of what the Framers of the Second Amendment regarded as among the rights of Englishmen that they sought to preserve. Blackstone's views greatly influenced late 18th-century American legal thought. Blackstone also greatly influenced 19th-century American legal thinking. One influential antebellum American jurist, Justice Joseph Story, was significantly influenced by his readings of Blackstone. See, Kent Newmeyer, *Justice Joseph Story: Statesman of the Old Republic*, pp. 40-45, 137, 246 (1985). Story viewed the Second Amendment as vitally important in maintaining a free republic. In his *Commentaries on the Constitution*, he wrote: "The right of the citizens to keep, and bear arms has justly been considered, as the palladium of the liberties of a republic; since it offers a strong moral check against the usurpation and arbitrary power of rulers; and will generally, even if they are successful in the first instance, enable the people to resist, and triumph over them." Joseph Story, *Commentaries on the Constitution of the United States*, 708 (Carolina Academic Press, 1987) (1833).

While it would be inaccurate to attribute Story's Second Amendment views solely to his reading of Blackstone, Blackstone doubtless helped influence Story and other early 19th-century lawyers and jurists to regard the right to keep and bear arms as an important prerogative of free citizens. All of this is important for our discussion, not only with regard to antebellum opinion concerning the Second Amendment, but also in considering the cultural and legal climate that informed the Framers of the Fourteenth Amendment who intended to extend what were commonly regarded as the rights

He discussed the right in traditional English terms:

> The fifth and last auxiliary right of the subject, that I shall at present mention, is that of having arms for their defence, suitable to their condition and degree, and such as are allowed by law, which is also declared by the same statute 1 W. & M. st. 2 c. 2 and is indeed a public allowance, under due restrictions, of the natural right of resistance and self-preservation, when the sanctions of society and laws are found insufficient to restrain the violence of oppression.[47]

B. Arms and Race in Colonial America

If the English tradition involved a right and duty to bear arms qualified by class and later religion, both the right and the duty were strengthened in the earliest American settlements. From the beginning, English settlement in North America had a quasi-military character, an obvious response to harsh frontier conditions. Governors of settlements often also held the title of militia captain, reflecting both the civil and military nature of their office. Special effort was made to ensure that white men, capable of bearing arms, were imported into the colonies.[48] Far from the security of Britain, often bordering on the colonies of other frequently hostile European powers, colonial governments viewed the arming of able-bodied white men and the requirement that they perform militia service as essential to a colony's survival.

There was another reason for the renewed emphasis on the right and duty to be armed in America: race. Britain's American colonies were home to three often antagonistic races: red, white and black. For the settlers of British North America, an armed and universally deputized white population was necessary not only to ward off dangers from the armies of other European powers, but also to ward off attacks from the indigenous population which feared the encroachment of English settlers on their lands. An armed white population was also essential to maintain

---

of free men to the freedmen, and who also intended to extend the Bill of Rights to the states. See infra Part III.

[47] Blackstone, supra note 46, pp. 143-44.

[48] Abbott E. Smith, *Colonists in Bondage: White Servitude and Convict Labor in America, 1607-1776*, pp. 30-34 (Norton, 1971) (1947).

social control over blacks and Indians who toiled unwillingly as slaves and servants in English settlements.[49]

This need for racial control helped transform the traditional English right into a much broader American one. If English law had qualified the right to possess arms by class and religion, American law was much less concerned with such distinctions.[50] Initially all Englishmen, and later all white men, were expected to possess and bear arms to defend their commonwealths, both from external threats and from the internal ones posed by blacks and Indians. The statutes of many colonies specified that white men be armed at public expense.[51] In most colonies, all white men between the ages of sixteen and sixty, usually with the exception of clergy and religious objectors, were considered part of the militia and required to be armed.[52] Not only were white men required to perform traditional militia and posse duties, they were also required to serve as patrollers, a specialized posse dedicated to keeping order among the slave population, in those colonies with large slave populations.[53] This broadening of the right to keep and bear arms reflected a more general lessening of class, religious and ethnic distinctions among whites in colonial America. The right to possess arms was, therefore, extended to classes traditionally viewed with suspicion in England, including the class of indentured servants.[54]

If there were virtually universal agreement concerning the need to arm the white population,[55] the law was much more ambivalent with respect to blacks. The progress of slavery in colonial America reflected English

---

[49] Boorstin, supra note 18, pp. 355-56.

[50] *Ibid.*, p. 353.

[51] See A. Leon Higginbotham, Jr., *In the Matter of Color: Race and the American Legal Process: The Colonial Period*, 32 (1978). It should also be added that the abundant game found in North America during the colonial period eliminated the need for the kind of game laws that had traditionally disarmed the lower classes in England. Malcolm, supra note 9, pp. 393-94.

[52] See, e.g., *Laws of the Royal Colony of New Jersey*, pp. 15-21, 49, 96, 133, 289 (Bernard Bush, ed., 1977).

[53] Higginbotham, supra note 51, pp. 260-62.

[54] For a good discussion of the elevation of the rights of white indentured servants as a means of maintaining social control over the black population, see generally Edmund S. Morgan, *American Slavery, American Freedom: The Ordeal of Colonial Virginia* (1975).

[55] Stephen Halbrook notes that Virginia's royal government in the late 17th century became very concerned that the widespread practice of carrying arms would tend to foment rebellions, and that, as a result, statutes were enacted to prevent groups of men from gathering with arms. See, Halbrook, *That Every Man Be Armed*, supra note 6, pp. 56-57. The sharpening of racial distinctions and the need for greater social control over slaves that occurred toward the end of the 17th and beginning of the 18th century lessened the concern authorities had over the armed white population; See Morgan, supra note 54, pp. 354-55.

lack of familiarity with the institution, in both law and custom.[56] In some colonies, kidnapped Africans initially were treated like other indentured servants, held for a term of years and then released from forced labor and allowed to live as free people.[57] In some colonies, the social control of slaves was one of the law's major concerns; in others, the issue was largely of private concern to the slave owner.[58]

These differences were reflected in statutes concerned with the right to possess arms and the duty to perform militia service. One colony—Virginia—provides a striking example of how social changes were reflected, over time, in restrictions concerning the right to be armed. A Virginia statute enacted in 1639 required the arming of white men at public expense.[59] The statute did not specify the arming of black men, but it also did not prohibit black men from arming themselves.[60] By 1680 a Virginia statute prohibited Negroes, slave and free, from carrying weapons, including clubs.[61] Yet, by the early eighteenth century, free Negroes who were house owners were permitted to keep one gun in their house, while blacks, slave and free, who lived on frontier plantations were able to keep guns.[62] Virginia's experience reflected three sets of concerns: the greater need to maintain social control over the black population as caste lines sharpened;[63] the need to use slaves and free blacks to help defend frontier plantations against attacks by hostile Indians; and the recognition on the part of Virginia authorities of the necessity for gun ownership for those living alone.

These concerns were mirrored in the legislation of other colonies. Massachusetts did not have general legislation prohibiting blacks from

---

[56] See Raymond T. Diamond, *No Call to Glory: Thurgood Marshall's Thesis on the Intent of a Pro-Slavery Constitution*, 42 *Vand. L. Rev.*, pp. 93, 101-102 (1989) (colonies dealt with slavery in an unsystematic and piecemeal fashion). See generally Winthrop D. Jordan, *White Over Black: American Attitudes Towards the Negro, 1550-1812*, pp. 48-52 (1968).

[57] Higginbotham, supra note 51, pp. 21-22.

[58] See Herbert Aptheker, *American Negro Slave Revolts*, (5th ed., 1983); Diamond, supra note 56, pp. 101-102, 104; Robert J. Cottrol and Raymond T. Diamond, Book Review, 56 *Tulane L. Rev.* pp. 1107, 1110-12 (1982) (reviewing A. Leon Higginbotham, Jr., *In the Matter of Color: Race and the American Legal Process: The Colonial Period* [1978]).

[59] William W. Hening, *Statutes at Large of Virginia*, 226 (New York: R. & W. & G. Bartow, 1823); see Higginbotham, supra note 51, p. 32.

[60] Hening, supra note 59, p. 226; see Higginbotham, supra note 51, p. 32.

[61] Higginbotham, supra note 51, p. 39.

[62] *Ibid.*, p. 58.

[63] *Ibid.*, pp. 38-40.

carrying arms,[64] but free Negroes in that colony were not permitted to participate in militia drills; instead they were required to perform substitute service on public works projects.[65] New Jersey exempted blacks and Indians from militia service, though the colony permitted free Negroes to possess firearms.[66] Ironically, South Carolina, which had the harshest slave codes of this period, may have been the colony most enthusiastic about extending the right to bear arms to free Negroes. With its majority black population, that state's need to control the slave population was especially acute.[67] To secure free black assistance in controlling the slave population, South Carolina in the early eighteenth century permitted free blacks the right of suffrage, the right to keep firearms, and the right to undertake militia service.[68] As the eighteenth century unfolded, those rights were curtailed.[69]

Overall, these laws reflected the desire to maintain white supremacy and control. With respect to the right to possess arms, the colonial experience had largely eliminated class, religious and ethnic distinctions among the white population. Those who had been part of the suspect classes in England—the poor, religious dissenters and others who had traditionally only enjoyed a qualified right to possess arms—found the

---

[64] Higginbotham informs us that the Boston selectmen passed such an ordinance after some slaves had allegedly committed arson in 1724. See *ibid.*, p. 76.

[65] See Lorenzo J. Greene, *The Negro in Colonial New England,* 127 (1968). Greene notes that blacks probably served in New England militias until the latter part of the 17th century. *Ibid.* It is interesting to note that, despite this prohibition on militia service, blacks served with New England forces during the French and Indian Wars. *Ibid.*, pp. 188-89. Winthrop Jordan notes that in 1652 the Massachusetts General Court ordered Scotsmen, Indians and Negroes to train with the militia, but that, in 1656, Massachusetts and, in 1660, Connecticut excluded blacks from militia service. See Jordan, supra note 56, p. 71.

[66] See 2 *Laws of the Royal Colony of New Jersey,* supra note 52, pp. 49, 96, 289.

[67] For a good discussion of black life in colonial South Carolina, see generally Peter H. Wood, *Black Majority: Negroes in Colonial South Carolina from 1670 through the Stono Rebellion* (1974).
South Carolina in 1739 was the scene of the Stono Rebellion, one of the largest slave rebellions in North America. A recent study of the rebellion suggests that the presence of large numbers of African born men from the Kingdom of the Kongo played a critical role. The Kingdom, including parts of modern Zaire, Congo-Brazzaville, Gabon and Angola, had been heavily influenced by Portuguese traders and missionaries in such areas as language, religion and contemporary European military tactics including the use of firearms. The Stono Rebellion illustrated both the internal and external threats faced by many colonies. First, the presence of large numbers of African slaves, familiar with European military tactics and technology, posed a threat to slave society in South Carolina. Second, this threat was further enhanced by the fact that South Carolina bordered on the Spanish colony of Florida. Historical accounts of the rebellion indicate that Portuguese-speaking Catholic slaves acted in concert with Spanish agents. See generally John K. Thornton, *African Dimensions of the Stono Rebellion,* 96 *Am. Hist. Rev.,* p. 1101 (1991).

[68] See Higginbotham, supra note 51, pp. 201-15.

[69] *Ibid.*

right to be considerably more robust in the American context. But blacks had come to occupy the social and legal space of the suspect classes in England. Their right to possess arms was highly dependent on white opinion of black loyalty and reliability. Their inclusion in the militia of freemen was frequently confined to times of crisis. Often, there were significant differences between the way northern and southern colonies approached this question, a reflection of the very different roles that slavery played in the two regions. These differences would become sharper after the Revolution, when the northern states began to move toward the abolition of slavery and the southern states, some of which had also considered abolition,[70] began to strengthen the institution.

Ironically, while the black presence in colonial America introduced a new set of restrictions concerning the English law of arms and the militia, it helped strengthen the view that the security of the state was best achieved through the arming of all free citizens. It was this new view that was part of the cultural heritage Americans brought to the framing of the Constitution.

C. The Right of WHICH People?

1. Revolutionary Ideals

The colonial experience helped strengthen the appreciation of early Americans for the merits of an armed citizenry. That appreciation was strengthened yet further by the American Revolution. If necessity forced the early colonists to arm, the Revolution and the friction with Britain's standing army that preceded it—and in many ways precipitated it—served to revitalize Whiggish notions that standing armies were dangerous to liberty, and that militias, composed of the whole of the people, best protected both liberty and security.[71]

These notions soon found their way into the debates over the new constitution, debates which help place the language and meaning of the Second Amendment in context. Like other provisions of the proposed constitution, the clause that gave Congress the power to provide for the organizing, arming and disciplining of the militia[72] excited fears among

---

[70] See Robert J. Cottrol, *Liberalization and Paternalism: Ideology, Economic Interest and the Business Law of Slavery*, 31 *Am. J. Legal Hist.*, pp. 359, 363-64 (1987).

[71] See generally Reid, supra note 34.

[72] That clause is now found in U.S. Const. art. I, § 8, cl. 15.

those who believed that the new constitution could be used to destroy both state power and individual rights.[73]

Indeed, it was the very universality of the militia that was the source of some of the objections. A number of critics of the proposed constitution feared that the proposed congressional power could subject the whole population to military discipline and a clear threat to individual liberty.[74] Others complained that the Militia Clause provided no exemptions for those with religious scruples against bearing arms.[75]

But others feared that the Militia Clause could be used to disarm the population as well as do away with the states' control of the militia. Some critics expressed fear that Congress would use its power to establish a select militia, a group of men specially trained and armed for militia duty, similar to the earlier English experience.[76] Richard Henry Lee of Virginia argued that that select militia might be used to disarm the population and that, in any event, it would pose more of a danger to individual liberty than a militia composed of the whole population. He charged that a select militia "commits the many to the mercy and the prudence of the few."[77] A number of critics objected to giving Congress the power to withhold arms from the militia.[78] At the constitutional convention, Massachusetts

---

[73] Elbridge Gerry of Massachusetts thought a national government which controlled the militia would be potentially despotic. James Madison's *Notes on the Constitutional Convention of 1787* (Aug. 21, 1787), in 1 *1787 Drafting the U.S. Constitution*, 916 (Wilbowin E. Benton, Ed., 1986). With this power, national government "may enslave the States." *Ibid.*, p. 846. Oliver Ellsworth of Connecticut suggested that "[t]he whole authority over the Militia ought by no means to be taken away from the States whose consequence would pine away to nothing after such a sacrifice of power." *Ibid.*, p. 909.

It is interesting, in light of the current debate, that both advocates and opponents of this increase in federal power assumed that the militia they were discussing would be one that enrolled almost all of the white male population between the ages of 16 and 60, and that population would supply their own arms. George Mason of Virginia proposed "the idea of a select militia," but withdrew it. *Ibid.*, p. 909.

[74] This was a view argued by Luther Martin before the Maryland House of Representatives. "Luther Martin Before the Maryland House of Representatives" (1787), in 3 *The Records of the Federal Convention of 1787*, p. 157 (Max Farrand, ed., 1966) [hereinafter *The Records of the Federal Convention*]. Samuel Bryan, a Pennsylvania pamphleteer who argued against the proposed constitution, argued that it could subject the whole population to military discipline. Samuel Bryan, "Letter to the People of Pennsylvania," *Independent Gazetteer*, Oct. 5, 1787, reprinted in *The Anti-Federalists*, pp. 22-23, 27 (Cecelia M. Kenyon, ed., 1966). A number of critics argued that the provision was a threat to the liberty of every man from 16 to 60. *Ibid.*, p. 57. Thus, the language of the Fifth Amendment requiring grand jury proceedings for cases arising in the militia, except when in actual service during time of war or public danger, may have been in response to this fear.

[75] *The Anti-Federalists*, supra note 74, p. 57. This concern was the reason for the original language of the Second Amendment. See supra note 4.

[76] See supra text accompanying note 43.

[77] *The Anti-Federalists*, supra note 74, p. 228.

[78] 2 *The Records of the Federal Convention*, supra note 74, pp. 385-87; 3 *ibid.*, pp. 208-209, 272, 295.

delegate Elbridge Gerry saw such potential danger in giving the new government power over the militia, that he declared:

> This power in the United States as explained is making the states drill sergeants. He had as lief let the citizens of Massachusetts be disarmed, as to take the command from the states, and subject them to the General Legislature. It would be regarded as a system of Despotism.[79]

The fear that this new congressional authority could be used to both destroy state power over the militia and to disarm the people led delegates to state ratifying conventions to urge measures that would preserve the traditional right. The Virginia convention proposed language that would provide protection for the right to keep and bear arms in the federal constitution.[80]

In their efforts to defend the proposed constitution, Alexander Hamilton and James Madison addressed these charges. Hamilton's responses are interesting because he wrote as someone openly skeptical of the value of the militia of the whole. The former Revolutionary War artillery officer[81] expressed the view that, while the militia fought bravely during the Revolution, it had proven to be no match when pitted against regular troops. Hamilton, who Madison claimed initially wanted to forbid the states from controlling any land or naval forces,[82] called for uniformity in organizing and disciplining of the militia under national authority. He also urged the creation of a select militia that would be more amenable to the training and discipline he saw as necessary.[83] In what was perhaps a concession to sentiment favoring the militia of the

---

[79] 2 *The Records of the Federal Convention,* supra note 74, p. 385.

[80] The Virginia convention urged the adoption of the following language: "That the people have a right to keep and bear arms; that a well-regulated militia, composed of the body of the people trained to arms, is the proper, natural, and safe defence for a free state; that standing armies, in time of peace, are dangerous to liberty, and therefore ought to be avoided, as far as the circumstances and protection of the community will admit; and that in all cases, the military should be under strict subordination to, and governed by, the civil power." 3 "The Debates in the Several State Conventions on the Adoption of the Federal Constitution, as Recommended by the General Convention at Philadelphia, in 1787 Together With the Journal of the Federal Convention," pp. 657-59 (Jonathan Elliot, ed., Ayer Co., (1987) (1907) [hereinafter "Elliot's Debates"].

[81] Richard B. Morris, *Seven Who Shaped Our Destiny: The Founding Fathers as Revolutionaries,* pp. 228, 237-49 (1973).

[82] 1 *The Records of the Federal Convention,* supra note 74, p. 293.

[83] *The Federalist* No. 25, p. 161 (Alexander Hamilton) (The Heritage Press, 1945). For a modern study that supports Hamilton's views concerning the military ineffectiveness of the militia, see Boorstin, supra note 18, pp. 352-72.

whole, Hamilton stated: "Little more can be reasonably aimed at, with respect to the people at large, than to have them properly armed and equipped; and in order to see that this not be neglected, it will be necessary to assemble them once or twice in the course of a year."[84]

If Hamilton gave only grudging support to the concept of the militia of the whole, Madison, author of the Second Amendment, was a much more vigorous defender of the concept. He answered critics of the Militia Clause provision allowing Congress to arm the militia by stating that the term "arming" meant only that Congress' authority to arm extended only to prescribing the type of arms the militia would use, not to furnishing them.[85] But Madison's views went further. He envisioned a militia consisting of virtually the entire white male population, writing that a militia of 500,000 citizens[86] could prevent any excesses that might be perpetrated by the national government and its regular army. Madison left little doubt that he envisioned the militia of the whole as a potential counterweight to tyrannical excess on the part of the government:

> Let a regular army, fully equal to the resources of the country, be formed; and let it be entirely at the devotion of the federal government: still it would not be going too far to say, that the State governments with the people on their side, would be able to repel the danger. The highest number to which, according to the best computation, a standing army can be carried in any country does not exceed one hundredth part of the whole number of souls; or one twenty-fifth part of the number able to bear arms. This proportion would not yield, in the United States, an army more than twenty-five or thirty thousand men. To these would be opposed a militia amounting to near half a million citizens with arms in their hands, officered by men chosen among themselves, fighting for their common liberties and united and conducted by governments possessing their affections and confidence. It may well be doubted whether a militia thus circumstanced could ever be conquered by

---

[84] *The Federalist* No. 29, p. 183 (Alexander Hamilton) (The Heritage Press, 1945). Interestingly enough, Hamilton's views anticipated the state of modern law on this subject; the National Guard has, in effect, become a select militia with a much larger reserve militia existing in the citizenry at large.

[85] 5 *Elliot's Debates,* supra note 80, pp. 464-65.

[86] *The Federalist* No. 46, at 319 (James Madison) (The Heritage Press, 1945). The census of 1790 listed the white male population over age 16 as 813,298. See Bureau of the Census, U.S. Dept. of Commerce, Statistical History of the United States from Colonial Times to the Present, p. 16 (1976). The census did not list the number over 60 that would have been exempt from militia duty.

such a proportion of regular troops. Those who are best acquainted with the last successful resistance of this country against the British arms will be most inclined to deny the possibility of it. Besides the advantage of being armed, which the Americans possess over the people of almost every other nation, the existence of subordinate governments, to which the people are attached, and by which the militia officers are appointed, forms a barrier against the enterprises of ambition, more insurmountable than any which a simple government of any form can admit of. Notwithstanding the military establishments in the several kingdoms of Europe, which are carried as far as the public resources will bear, the . . . governments are afraid to trust the people with arms. . . .[87]

It is against this background that the meaning of the Second Amendment must be considered. For the revolutionary generation, the idea of the militia and an armed population were related. The principal reason for preferring a militia of the whole over either a standing army or a select militia was rooted in the idea that, whatever the inefficiency of the militia of the whole, the institution would better protect the newly won freedoms than a reliance on security provided by some more select body.

2. Racial Limitations

One year after the ratification of the Second Amendment and the Bill of Rights, Congress passed legislation that reaffirmed the notion of the militia of the whole and explicitly introduced a racial component into the national deliberations on the subject of the militia. The Uniform Militia Act[88] called for the enrollment of every free, able-bodied *white* male citizen between the ages of eighteen and forty-five into the militia. The act further specified that every militia member was to provide himself with a musket or firelock, a bayonet, and ammunition.

This specification of a racial qualification for militia membership was somewhat at odds with general practice in the late eighteenth century. Despite its recognition and sanctioning of slavery,[89] the Constitution had

---

[87] *Ibid.*

[88] 1 Stat. 271.

[89] See U.S. Const. art. I, § 2, cl. 3 (three-fifths of slave population counted for apportionment purposes); U.S. Const. art. I, § 9, cl. 1 (importation of slaves allowed until 1808); U.S. Const. art. IV, § 2, cl. 3 (escaped slaves must be "delivered up" to their masters).

no racial definition of citizenship.[90] Free Negroes voted in a majority of states.[91] A number of states had militia provisions that allowed free Negroes to participate.[92] Particularly in the northern states, many were well aware that free Negroes and former slaves had served with their state forces during the Revolution.[93] Despite the prejudices of the day, lawmakers in late eighteenth century America were significantly less willing to write racial restrictions into constitutions and other laws guaranteeing fundamental rights than were their counterparts a generation or so later in the nineteenth century.[94] The 1792 statute restricting militia enrollment to white men was one of the earliest federal statutes to make a racial distinction.

The significance of this restriction is not altogether clear. For the South, there was a clear desire to have a militia that was reliable and could be used to suppress potential slave insurrections. But despite the fear that free Negroes might make common cause with slaves, and despite federal law, some southern states in the antebellum period enrolled free blacks as militia members.[95] Northern states at various times also enrolled free Negroes in the militia despite federal law and often strident prejudice.[96] States North and South employed free Negroes in state forces during times of invasion.[97] While southern states often prohibited slaves from carrying weapons and strictly regulated access to firearms by free

---

[90] U.S. Const. art. I, § 2, cl. 3 (specifying congressional representation) is often cited for the proposition that blacks were not citizens because of the three-fifths clause. It should be noted that, under this clause, free Negroes were counted as whole persons for purposes of representation. The original wording of this provision specifically mentioned "white and other citizens," but that language was deleted by the committee on style as redundant. See 5 *Elliot's Debates*, supra note 78, p. 451.

[91] See infra Part II; see also Robert J. Cottrol, *A Tale of Two Cultures: Or Making the Proper Connections Between Law, Social History and The Political Economy of Despair,* 25 San Diego L. Rev., 989, 1004 & nn. 86-88 (1988).

[92] Jordan, supra note 56, pp. 125-26, 411-12.

[93] Robert J. Cottrol, *Law, Politics and Race in Urban America: Towards a New Synthesis.* 17 *Rutgers L.J.*, pp. 483, 503 & n. 129 (1986).

[94] Robert J. Cottrol, *The Thirteenth Amendment and the North's Overlooked Egalitarian Heritage,* 11 National Black L.J., pp. 198, 202-203 (1989) (discussing racism in early 19th-century America).

[95] See Jordan supra note 56, pp. 125-26, 411-12 (in varying degrees, North Carolina, South Carolina and Georgia); Bernard C. Nalty, *Strength for the Fight: A History of Black Americans in the Military* 20 (1986) (same).

[96] See Jordan, supra note 56, pp. 125-26 ("Although [the exclusion of Negroes from the militia] lay on the statute books of all four New England colonies, Negroes served in New England forces in every colonial war." Additionally, and in varying degrees, New York, New Jersey, Pennsylvania, and Delaware included Negroes).

[97] This was particularly true during the War of 1812. See Robert J. Cottrol, *The Afro-Yankees: Providence's Black Community in the Antebellum Era* 63 (1982); Eugene D. Genovese, *Roll, Jordan Roll: The World the Slaves Made* 155 (1976); Nalty, supra note 95, pp. 24-28.

Negroes,[98] northern states generally made no racial distinction with respect to the right to own firearms,[99] and federal law was silent on the subject.

The racial restriction in the 1792 statute indicates the unrest the revolutionary generation felt toward arming blacks and perhaps the recognition that one of the functions of the militia would indeed be to put down slave revolts. Yet, the widespread use of blacks as soldiers in time of crisis and the absence of restrictions concerning the arming of blacks in the northern states may provide another clue concerning how to read the Second Amendment. The 1792 act specified militia enrollment for white men between the ages of eighteen and forty-five.[100] Yet, while it specifically included only this limited portion of the population, *the statute excluded no one from militia service.*

The authors of the statute had experience, in the Revolution, with a militia and Continental Army considerably broad in membership. Older and younger men had served with the Revolutionary forces. Blacks had served, though their service had been an object of considerable controversy.[101] Even women had served, though, given the attitudes of the day, this was far more controversial than black service. Given this experience and the fact that the constitutional debates over the militia had constantly assumed an enrollment of the male population between sixteen and sixty, it is likely that the Framers of the 1792 statute envisioned a militia even broader than the one they specified. This suggests to us how broad the term "people" in the Second Amendment was meant to be.

The 1792 statute also suggests to us how crucial race has been in our history. If the racial distinction made in that statute was somewhat anomalous in the late eighteenth century, it was the kind of distinction that would become more common in the nineteenth. The story of blacks and arms would continue in the nineteenth century as racial distinctions became sharper and the defense of slavery more militant.

---

[98] See infra Part II, A; see also Stampp, supra note 27, pp. 208-28.

[99] Paul Finkelman, *Prelude to the Fourteenth Amendment: Black Legal Rights in the Antebellum North,* 17 Rutgers L.J., pp. 415, 476 (1986).

[100] See supra note 88.

[101] Nalty, supra note 95, pp. 10-18. See generally Benjamin Quarles, *The Negro in the American Revolution* (1961).

II. Arms and the Antebellum Experience

If, as presaged by the Uniform Militia Act of 1792,[102] racial distinctions became sharper in the nineteenth century, that development was at odds with the rhetoric of the Revolution and with developments of the immediate post-revolutionary era.[103] Flush with the precepts of egalitarian democracy, America had entered a time of recognition and expansion of rights. Eleven of the thirteen original states, as well as Vermont, passed new constitutions in the period between 1776 and 1777.[104] Five of these states rewrote their constitutions by the time of the ratification of the Bill of Rights in 1791.[105] A twelfth original state, Massachusetts, passed a new constitution in 1780.[106] Many of the new constitutions recognized the status of citizens as "free and equal" or "free and independent."[107] In Massachusetts and Vermont, these clauses were interpreted as outlawing the institution of slavery.[108] Many of the new constitutions guaranteed the right to vote regardless of race to all men who otherwise qualified,[109] and guaranteed many of the rights that would later be recognized in the Bill

---

[102] 1 Stat. 271; see supra note 88.

[103] See Raymond T. Diamond & Robert J. Cottrol, *Codifying Caste: Louisiana's Racial Classification Scheme and the Fourteenth Amendment*, 29 Loy. L. Rev., pp. 255, 260-63 (1983).

[104] See *Federal and State Constitutions, Colonial Charters, and Other Organic Laws of the United States* (Benjamin P. Poore, ed., 2d ed., Washington, D.C.: Government Printing Office, (1878) [hereinafter *Federal and State Constitutions*]. Massachusetts passed a new constitution in 1780. 1 *ibid.*, p. 956. Rhode Island would not do so until 1842. 2 *ibid.*, p. 1603.

[105] These states were: Georgia in 1789, see 1 *ibid.*, p. 384; New Hampshire in 1784, see 2 *ibid.*, p. 1280; Pennsylvania in 1790, see 2 *ibid.*, p. 1548; South Carolina in 1778 and 1780, see 2 *ibid.*, p. 1620, 1628; and Vermont in 1786, see 2 *ibid.*, p. 1866.

[106] 1 *ibid.*, p. 956.

[107] See N.H. Const. of 1784, pt. I, art. I, 2 *Federal and State Constitutions*, supra note 104, p. 1280; Conn. Const. of 1776, pmbl., 1 *Federal and State Constitutions*, supra note 104, p. 257; Mass. Const. of 1780, pt. I, art. I, 1 *Federal and State Constitutions*, supra note 104, p. 957; Pa. Const. of 1776, declaration of rights, art. I., 1 *Federal and State Constitutions*, supra note 104, p. 1541; Pa. Const. of 1790, art. IX, § 1, 2 *Federal and State Constitutions*, supra note 104, p. 1554; Vt. Const. of 1776, bill of rights, § 1, 2 *Federal and State Constitutions*, supra note 104, p. 1908.

[108] See Diamond, supra note 56, p. 103 nn. 59-61.

[109] See, e.g., Ga. Const. of 1779, art. IV, § 1, 1 *Federal and State Constitutions*, supra note 104, p. 386; Md. Const. of 1776, art. II, 1 *Federal and State Constitutions*, supra note 104, p. 821; Mass. Const. of 1776, pt. I, declaration of rights, art. IX, 1 *Federal and State Constitutions*, supra note 104, p. 958; N.H. Const. of 1784, pt. I, bill of rights, art. XI, 2 *Federal and State Constitutions*, supra note 104, p. 1281; N.J. Const. of 1776, art. IV, 2 *Federal and State Constitutions*, supra note 104, p. 1311; N.C. Const. of 1776, constitution or frame of government, art. IX, 2 *Federal and State Constitutions*, supra note 104, pp. 1411-12; Pa. Const. of 1776, declaration of rights, art. VII, 2 *Federal and State Constitutions*, supra note 104, p. 1541; Vt. Const. of 1777, ch. 1, declaration of rights, art. VIII, 2 *Federal and State Constitutions*, supra note 104, p. 1859.
Only Georgia, under its 1776 constitution, and South Carolina, in its 1790 constitution, provided explicit racial restrictions on the right to vote. See Ga. Const. of 1776, art. IX, 1 *Federal and State Constitutions*, supra note 104, p. 379; S.C. Const. of 1790, art. I § 4, 2 *Federal and State Constitutions*, supra note 104, p. 1628.

of Rights.[110] In no instance were any of these rights limited only to the white population; several states explicitly extended rights to the entire population irrespective of race.[111]

The right to vote, perhaps the most fundamental of rights, was limited in almost all instances to men who met property restrictions, but in most states was not limited according to race.[112] Ironically, only in the nineteenth century would black voting rights be curtailed, as Jacksonian democracy expanded voting rights for whites.[113] In its constitution of 1821, New York eliminated a one hundred dollar property requirement for white males, and concomitantly increased the requirement to two hundred fifty dollars for blacks.[114] Other states would eliminate black voting rights altogether.[115] Other than Maine, no state admitted to the union in the nineteenth century's antebellum period allowed blacks to vote.[116]

---

[110] See, e.g. Ga. Const. of 1776, art. LXI, 1 *Federal and State Constitutions,* supra note 104, p. 283 (freedom of the press); Mass. Const. of 1780, pt. 1, declaration of rights, art. XVIII, 1 *Federal and State Constitutions,* supra note 104, p. 959 (freedom of assembly); Md. Const. of 1776, declaration of rights, art. XXVII, 2 *Federal and State Constitutions,* supra note 104, p. 819 (prohibiting quartering of troops in homes); N.H. Const. of 1776, declaration of rights, art. XXIII, 1 *Federal and State Constitutions,* supra note 104, p. 959 (limits on searches and seizures and on general warrants); Pa. Const. of 1776, declaration of rights, art. XII, 2 *Federal and State Constitutions,* supra note 104, p. 1542 (freedom of speech); S.C. Const. of 1778, art. XLI, 2 *Federal and State Constitutions,* supra note 104, p. 1627 (due process of law); Va. Const. of 1776, bill of rights, § 16, 2 *Federal and State Constitutions,* supra note 104, p. 1909 (freedom of religion); Vt. Const. of 1786, ch. 1, declaration of rights, art. XVIII, 2 *Federal and State Constitutions,* supra note 104, p. 1869 (right to bear arms).

[111] See Ga. Const. of 1776, art. LVI, 1 *Federal and State Constitutions,* supra note 104, p. 283; Ga. Const. of 1789, art. IV, § 5, 1 *Federal and State constitutions,* supra note 104, pp. 819-20 (freedom of religion for "all persons"); N.C. Const. of 1776, art. VIII (rights in criminal proceedings to be informed of charges, to confront witnesses, and to remain silent for "every man," and freedom of religion for "all men"), 2 *Federal and State Constitutions,* supra note 104, p. 1409; N.Y. Const. of 1777, art. XIII (due process to be denied "no member of this state"), art. XXXVIII (freedom of religion "to all mankind"); Pa. Const. of 1776, art. II (freedom of religion for "all men"), art. VIII (due process for "every member of society"), 2 *Federal and State Constitutions,* supra note 104, p. 1541; Pa. Const. of 1790, art. XI, § 3 freedom of religion to be denied to "no person"), art. XI, § 7 (freedom of the press for "every person" and freedom of speech for "every citizen"), art. XI, § 10 (due process to be denied to "no person"), 2 *Federal and State Constitutions,* supra note 104, pp. 1626-27; S.C. Const. of 1790, art. VIII (freedom of religion "to all mankind"), 2 *Federal and State Constitutions,* § supra note 104, p. 1632.

[112] See Cottrol, supra note 97, pp. 42-43.

[113] See Cottrol, supra note 93, pp. 508-509. This is not to say that voting limitations were the sole measure of the failure of Jacksonian democracy to include blacks. *Ibid.,* pp. 508-13.

[114] N.Y. Const. of 1821, art. II, *superseding* N.Y. Const. of 1777, art. VII; See also Dixon R. Fox, *The Negro Vote in Old New York,* in Free Blacks in America, 1800-1860, pp. 95, 97-112 (John H. Bracey, Jr., *et al.,* eds., 1970).

[115] See Cottrol, supra note 97, pp. 42-43.

[116] Leon F. Litwack, *North of Slavery: The Negro in the Free States, 1790-1860,* p. 79 (1961).

This curtailment of black voting rights was part and parcel of a certain hostility toward free blacks, a hostility that ran throughout the union of states. In northern states, where slavery had been abandoned or was not a serious factor in social or economic relations, such hostility was the result of simple racism.[117] In southern states, where slavery was an integral part of the social and economic framework, this hostility was occasioned by the threat that free blacks posed to the system of Negro slavery.[118]

A. The Southern Antebellum Experience: Control of Arms as a Means of Racial Oppression

The threat that free blacks posed to southern slavery was twofold. First, free blacks were a bad example to slaves. For a slave to see free blacks enjoy the trappings of white persons—freedom of movement, expression and association, relative freedom from fear for one's person and one's family, and freedom to own the fruits of one's labor—was to offer hope and raise desire for that which the system could not produce. A slave with horizons limited only to a continued existence in slavery was a slave who did not threaten the system,[119] whereas a slave with visions of freedom threatened rebellion.

This threat of rebellion is intimately related to the second threat that free blacks posed to the system of Negro slavery, the threat that free blacks might instigate or participate in a rebellion by their slave brethren. To forestall this threat of rebellion, southern legislatures undertook to limit the freedom of movement and decision of free blacks.[120] States

---

[117] It is to be questioned whether racism is ever "simple." Winthrop Jordan has theorized that the English and their cultural descendants were culturally predisposed to racism. Jordan, supra note 56, pp. 3-43. Carl Jung has suggested that for white Americans the Negro represents the part of the unconscious that requires repression. Alexander Thomas & Samuel Sillen, *Racism and Psychiatry* pp. 13-14 (1972); *America Facing Its Most Tragic Moment*—Dr. Carl Jung, *N.Y. Times*, Sept. 29, 1912, § 5, p. 3. Whatever accounts for racism, it is clear that racism is capable of actuating the lawmaking process. See generally Higginbotham, supra note p. 51.

[118] See Stampp, supra note 27, pp. 215-17.

[119] Compare "Sambo," the idealized exposition of the slave psyche hypothesized by Stanley Elkins. Elkins viewed slaves as having internalized their circumstances to the point at which they became not only incapable of resisting the white masters but also actively cooperated in maintaining their own degradation. See Stanley M. Elkins, *Slavery: A Problem in American Institutional and Intellectual Life*, pp. 81-139 (3rd ed., 1976).

[120] Genovese, supra note 97, pp. 51, 399; Stampp, supra note 27, p. 215-17; Eugene D. Genovese, *The Slave States of North America*, in "Neither Slave nor Free: The Freedmen of African Descent in the Slave Societies of the New World," pp. 251, 261-62 (David W. Cohen and Jack P. Greene, eds., 1972).

162

limited the number of free blacks who might congregate at one time;[121] they curtailed the ability of free blacks to choose their own employment,[122] and to trade and socialize with slaves.[123] Free blacks were subject to question, to search, and to summary punishment by patrols established to keep the black population, slave and free, in order.[124] To forestall the possibility that free blacks would rebel either on their own or with slaves, the southern states limited not only the right of slaves, but also the right of free blacks, to bear arms.[125]

The idea was to restrict the availability of arms to blacks, both slave and free, to the extent consistent with local conceptions of safety. At one extreme was Texas, which, between 1842 and 1850, prohibited slaves from using firearms altogether.[126] Also at this extreme was Mississippi, which forbade firearms to both free blacks and slaves after 1852.[127] At the other extreme was Kentucky, which merely provided that, should slaves or free blacks "wilfully and maliciously" shoot at a white person, or otherwise wound a free white person while attempting to kill another person, the slave or free black would suffer the death penalty.[128]

More often than not, slave state statutes restricting black access to firearms were aimed primarily at free blacks, as opposed to slaves, perhaps because the vigilant master was presumed capable of denying arms to all but the most trustworthy slaves, and would give proper

---

[121] John H. Franklin, *From Slavery to Freedom: A History of Negro Americans*, pp. 139-40 (6th ed., 1988).

[122] *Ibid.*, p. 140.

[123] *Ibid.*, pp. 140-41.

[124] Stampp, supra note 27, pp. 214-16.

[125] See infra text accompanying notes 126-46.

[126] An Act Concerning Slaves, § 6, 1840 Laws of Tex. 171, 172. Chapter 58 of the Texas Acts of 1850, provided penalties for violators of the 1840 statute. Act of Dec. 3, 1850, ch. 58, § 1, 1850, Laws of Tex. 42-44 (amending § 6 of An Act Concerning Slaves). Masters, overseers, or employers were to be fined between $25 and $100, and the slave was to receive not less than 39 nor more than 50 lashes. But also under the 1850 Act, slaves were allowed to carry firearms on the premises of the master, overseer, or employer, where they presumably would receive proper supervision.

[127] Act of Mar. 15, 1852, ch. 206, 1852 Laws of Miss. 328 (prohibiting magistrates from issuing licenses for blacks to carry and use firearms). This act repealed Chapter 73, sections 10 and 12 of the Mississippi Acts of 1822, allowing slaves and free blacks respectively to obtain a license to carry firearms. See Act of June 18, 1822, ch. 73 §§ 10, 12, 1822 Laws of Miss. 179, 181-82.

[128] Chapter 448, § 1, of Kentucky Acts of 1818 was limited solely to slave offenders. Act of Feb. 10, 1819, ch. 448, § 1, 1819 Acts of Key. 787. The Kentucky Acts of 1850 extended these provisions to free blacks as well. Act of Mar. 24, 1851, ch. 617, art. VII, § 7, 1850 Acts of Key. 291, 300-301.

supervision to the latter.[129] Thus, Louisiana provided that a slave was denied the use of firearms and all other offensive weapons,[130] unless the slave carried written permission to hunt within the boundaries of the owner's plantation.[131] South Carolina prohibited slaves outside the company of whites or without written permission from their master from using or carrying firearms unless they were hunting or guarding the master's plantation.[132] Georgia, Maryland and Virginia did not statutorily address the question of slaves' access to firearms, perhaps because controls inherent to the system made such laws unnecessary in these states' eyes.

By contrast, free blacks, not under the close scrutiny of whites, were generally subject to tight regulation with respect to firearms. The State of Florida, which had in 1824 provided for a weekly renewable license for slaves to use firearms to hunt and for "any other necessary and lawful purpose,"[133] turned its attention to the question of free blacks in 1825. Section 8 of "An Act to Govern Patrols"[134] provided that white citizen patrols "shall enter into all negro houses and suspected places, and search for arms and other offensive or improper weapons, and may lawfully seize and take away all such arms, weapons, and ammunition. . . ." By contrast, the following section of that same statute expanded the conditions under which a slave might carry a firearm, a slave might do so

---

[129] This presumption was not dispositive of all regulation on this subject. Sale or other delivery of firearms to slaves was forbidden by several states, among them Florida, Georgia, Louisiana and North Carolina. Act of Feb. 25, 1840, no. 20, § 1, 1840 Acts of Fla. 22-23; Act of Dec. 19, 1860, no. 64, § 1860 Acts of Ga. 561; Act of Apr. 8, 1811, ch. 14, 1811 Laws of La. 50, 53-54; Act of Jan. 1, 1845, ch. 87, § 1, 2, 1845 Acts of N.C. 124. Moreover, slave states often provided for patrols manned by local men who would be authorized to search out and confiscate firearms in the possession of free blacks as well as slaves. See infra text accompanying notes 133-46.

[130] Black Code, ch. 33, § 19, Laws of La. 150, 160 (1806).

[131] *Ibid.*, § 20. Moreover, in 1811, Louisiana forbade peddlers from selling arms to slaves, upon a fine of $500 or one year in prison. Act of Apr. 8, 1811, ch. 14, 1811 Laws of La. 50, 53-54 (supplementing act relative to peddlers and hawkers).

[132] Act of Dec. 18, 1819, 1819 Acts of S.C. 28, 31 (providing more effective performance of patrol duty).

[133] An Act Concerning Slaves, § 11, Acts of Fla. 289, 291 (1824). In 1825, Florida had provided a penalty for slaves using firelight to hunt at night, but this seems to have been a police measure intended to preserve wooded land, for whites were also penalized for this offense, albeit a lesser penalty. Act of Dec. 10, 1825, § 5, 1825 Laws of Fla. 78-80. Penalties for "firehunting" were reenacted in 1827, Act of Jan. 1, 1828, 1828 Laws of Fla. 24-25, and the penalties for a slave firehunting were reenacted in 1828, Act of Nov. 21, 1828, § 46, 1828 Laws of Fla. 174, 185.

[134] 1825 Acts of Fla. 52, 55.

under this statute either by means of the weekly renewable license or if "in the presence of some white person."[135]

Florida went back and forth on the question of licenses for free blacks[136] but, in February 1831 repealed all provision for firearms licenses for free blacks.[137] This development predated by six months the Nat Turner slave revolt in Virginia, which was responsible for the deaths of at least fifty-seven white people[138] and which caused the legislatures of the Southern states to reinvigorate their repression of free blacks.[139]

Among the measures that slave states took was to further restrict the right to carry and use firearms. In its December 1831 legislative session, Delaware for the first time required free blacks desiring to carry firearms to obtain a license from a justice of the peace.[140] In their December 1831 legislative sessions, both Maryland[141] and Virginia[142] entirely prohibited free blacks from carrying arms; Georgia followed suit in 1833, declaring that "it shall not be lawful for any free person of colour in this state, to own, use, or carry fire arms of any description whatever."[143]

Perhaps as a response to the Nat Turner rebellion, Florida in 1833 enacted another statute authorizing white citizen patrols to seize arms found in the homes of slaves and free blacks, and provided that blacks without a proper explanation for the presence of the firearms be summarily punished, without benefit of a judicial tribunal.[144] In 1846 and 1861, the Florida legislature provided once again that white citizen patrols

---

[135] *Ibid.*, § 9.

[136] In 1828, Florida twice enacted provisions providing for free blacks to carry and use firearms upon obtaining a license from a justice of the peace. Act of Nov. 17, 1828, § 9, 1828 Fla. Laws 174, 177; Act of Jan. 12, 1828, § 9, 1827 Fla. Laws, 97, 100.

[137] Act of Jan. 31, 1831, 1831 Fla. Laws 30.

[138] Aptheker, supra note 58, p. 298. For a full account of the revolt, the bloodiest in United States history, see *ibid.*, pp. 293-324. For a compilation of documentary sources on the revolt, see also Henry I. Tragle, *The Southampton Slave Revolt of Eighteen Thirty-One: A Compilation of Source Material* (1971). An account of the revolt novelized from Turner's confession can be found in William Styron, *The Confessions of Nat Turner* (1967). Styron's novel has been criticized as failing to capture the power of religion to the 19th century black, and thus failing to tell the truth of the revolt. See, e.g., William F. Cheek, *Black Resistance Before the Civil War*, pp. 116-17 (1970).

[139] See Herbert Aptheker, *Nat Turner's Slave Rebellion*, pp. 74-94 (1966).

[140] *Ibid.*, pp. 74-75.

[141] *Ibid.*, p. 75.

[142] *Ibid.*, p. 81.

[143] Act of Dec. 23, 1833, § 7, 1833 Ga. Laws 226, 228.

[144] Act of Feb. 17, 1833, ch. 671, § § 15, 17, 1833 Fla. Laws 26, 29. The black person offending the statute was to be "severely punished," incongruously enough "by moderate whipping," not to exceed thirty-nine strokes on the bare back. *Ibid.*, § 17.

165

might search the homes of blacks, both free and slave, and confiscate arms held therein.[145] Yet, searching out arms was not the only role of the white citizen patrols: These patrols were intended to enforce pass systems for both slaves and free blacks, to be sure that blacks did not possess liquor and other contraband items, and generally to terrorize blacks into accepting their subordination.[146] The patrols would meet no resistance from those who were simply unable to offer any.

B. The Northern Antebellum Experience: Use of Firearms to Combat Racially Motivated Deprivations of Liberty

Even as northern racism defined itself in part by the curtailment of black voting rights,[147] it cumulatively amounted to what some have called a widespread "Negrophobia."[148] With notable exceptions, public schooling, if available to blacks at all, was segregated.[149] Statutory and constitutional limitations on the freedom of blacks to emigrate into northern states were a further measure of northern racism.[150] While the level of enforcement

---

[145] Act of Jan. 6, 1847, § 11, 1846 Fla. Laws 42, 44; Act of Dec. 17, 1861, ch. 1291, § 11, 1861 Fla. Laws 38, 40.

[146] Stampp, supra note 27, pp. 214-15.

[147] See supra text accompanying notes 112-16.

[148] See, e.g., Raoul Berger, *Government by Judiciary: The Transformation of the Fourteenth Amendment* 10 (1977).

[149] After *Roberts v. Boston*, 59 Mass. (5 Cush.) 198 (1849), upheld the provision of segregated public education in the City of Boston, the Massachusetts legislature outlaws segregated education. Act of Mar. 24, 1885 Mass. Acts 256; see Finkelman, supra note 99, pp. 465-67. In Connecticut, most schools were integrated before 1830; only in response to a request from the Hartford black community was a separate system established in that year. *Ibid.*, p. 468. The Iowa constitution provided for integration in public schools. See *Clark v. Board of Directors* 24 Iowa 266 (1868) (construing Iowa Const. of 1857, art. IX, § 12).

In Ohio, blacks were excluded entirely from public schools until 1834 when the state Supreme Court ruled that children of mixed black ancestry who were more than half white might attend; not until 1848 did the legislature provide for public education of any sort for other black children. *Williams v. Directors of Sch. Dist.*, Ohio 578 (1834); see also *Lane v. Baker*, 12 Ohio 237 (1843). In 1848, the state legislature allowed blacks to be serviced by the public schools unless whites in the community were opposed; in the alternative, the legislature provided for segregated education. Act of Feb. 24, 1848, 1848 Ohio Laws 81. The following year, the legislature provided that the choice of segregated or integrated public education lie at the option of local school districts. Act of Feb. 10, 1849, 1849 Ohio Laws 17. Cincinnati refused to comply with the mandate to educate blacks until forced to do so by a combination of statutory and judicial persuasion. Act of Mar. 14, 1853, § 31, 1853 Ohio Laws 429; Act of Apr. 18, 1854, 1854 Ohio Laws 48; Act of Apr. 8, 1856, 1856 Ohio Laws 117; State *ex rel. Directors of the E. & W. Sch. Dist. v. City of Cincinnati*, 19 Ohio 178 (1850); see Finkelman, supra note 99, pp. 468-70. See generally United States Office of Education, History of Schools for the Colored Population (1969). In Philadelphia, public education was provided for whites in 1818, and separate education was provided for blacks in 1822. Finkelman, supra note 111, p. 90. Rural schools in Rhode Island, however, were integrated. *Ibid.* In New York, some school districts were segregated, among them that of New York City. Finkelman, supra note 99, pp. 463, 467-68.

[150] From 1807 to 1849, Ohio required blacks entering the state to post a bond. Act of Jan. 25, 1807, ch. VIII, 1807 Ohio Gen. Assem. Laws 53, *repealed* by Act of Feb. 10, 1849, 1849 Ohio Laws

and the ultimate effect of these constitutional and statutory provisions may not have been great,[151] the very existence of these laws speaks to the level of hostility northern whites had for blacks during this period. It is against this background—if not poisonous, racist and hostile—that the black antebellum experience with the right to bear arms must be measured.

Perhaps nothing makes this point better than the race riots and mob violence against blacks that occurred in many northern cities in the antebellum period. These episodes also illustrate the uses to which firearms might be put in pursuit of self-defense and individual liberty.

A good deal of racial tension was generated by economic competition between whites and blacks during this period, and this tension accounts in part for violent attacks against blacks.[152] Moreover, whites were able to focus their attacks because blacks were segregated into distinct neighborhoods in northern states, rendering it easy for white mobs to find the objects of their hostility.[153]

Quite often, racial violence made for bloody, destructive confrontations. In July 1834, mobs in New York attacked churches, homes and businesses of white abolitionists and blacks. These mobs were estimated at upwards of twenty thousand people and required the intervention of the militia to suppress.[154] In Boston in August of 1843, after a handful of white sailors verbally and physically assaulted four blacks who defended themselves, a mob of several hundred whites attacked and severely beat

---

17. Michigan Territory passed a similar law in 1827, though there was only one recorded attempt to enforce it. Act of Apr. 13, 1827, 1827 Mich. Rev. Laws 1-10 (1st & 2d Councils). David M. Katzman, *Before the Ghetto: Black Detroit in the Nineteenth Century* 7 n. 6 (1973). Indiana required a bond from 1831 until 1851, when a new constitution forbade black immigration entirely. Act of Feb. 10, 1831, 1831 Ind. Rev. Laws 375 *superseded by* Ind. Const. of 1851, art. XIII, § 1 (amended 1881). Illinois went the same route by coupling the repeal of its 1829 bond provisions with a prohibition on black immigration in its 1848 constitution. Ill. Const. of 1848, art. XIV; Act of Jan. 17, 1832-33, Ill. Rev. Laws 463 *amended by* Act of Feb. 1, 1831, 1832-33 Ill. Rev. Laws 462, *repealed by* Act of Feb. 12,1853, 1853 Ill. Laws 57. Oregon's 1859 constitution forbade blacks to enter the state, Or. Const. of 1859, art. XVIII (repealed 1926), and Iowa provided for a fine of two dollars a day for any black remaining in the state for more than three days. Act of Feb. 5, 1851, 1851 Iowa Laws 172.

[151] From 1833 to 1838, Connecticut prohibited the establishment of schools for nonresident blacks. Act of May 24,1833, ch. IX, 1833 Conn. Pub. Acts 425, *repealed by* Act of May 31, 1838, ch. XXXIV, 1838 Conn. Pub. Acts 30; see also *Crandall v. State*, 10 Conn. 339 (1834) (attempted prosecution under this statute failed due to insufficient information). See Finkelman, supra note 99, pp. 430-43 (discussing the lack of enforcement of statutes regulating black immigration).

[152] See Litwack, supra note 116, pp. 159, 165 (in fields where blacks were allowed to compete with whites, who were often the new Irish immigrants, violence often erupted).

[153] *Ibid.*, p. 153; see also Leonard P. Curry, *The Free Black in Urban America 1800-1850: The Shadow of the Dream*, pp. 96-111 (1981).

[154] Curry, supra note 153, p. 101.

every black they could find, dispersed only by the combined efforts of police and fire personnel.[155]

The Providence Snowtown Riot of 1831 was precipitated by a fight between whites and blacks at "some houses of ill fame"[156] located in the black ghetto of Snowtown. After a mob of one hundred or so whites descended on Snowtown, and after warning shots had been fired, a black man fired into the crowd, killing a white. The mob then descended on Snowtown in earnest, destroying no fewer than seventeen black occupied dwellings across a period of four days. The mobs did not disperse until the militia fired into the crowd, killing four men and wounding fourteen others.[157]

Similarly, the militia in Philadelphia put down an October 1849 race riot that resulted in three deaths, injuries, and the destruction of property.[158] By contrast, in the Providence Hardscrabble Riot of October 1824, militia were not called out and the police did nothing to stop a crowd of fifty or so whites from destroying every house in the black Hardscrabble area and looting household goods.[159]

Awareness of racial hostility generally, and of incidents like these, made blacks desirous of forming militia units. The firing of the weapon in Providence in 1831 that sparked the mob to violence illustrated that blacks were willing to take up arms to protect themselves, but also illustrated the potentially counterproductive nature of individual action. The actions of the white militia in Providence and Philadelphia, as well as those of the police and fire units in Boston, proved the strength of collective armed action against mob violence. Moreover, the failure of police to take action in Providence in 1824 illustrated the vulnerability of the black community to mob violence, absent protection.

Though the Uniform Militia Act of 1792 had not specifically barred blacks from participation in the state organized militia,[160] the northern states had treated the act as such, and so the state organized militia was not an option.[161] Blacks could nonetheless form private militia groups that

---

[155] *Ibid.*, p. 100.

[156] *Ibid.*, p. 102.

[157] *Ibid.*, pp. 102-103.

[158] *Ibid.*, p. 104.

[159] *Ibid.*, p. 102.

[160] See supra Part I.c.2.

[161] Jack D. Foner, *Blacks and the Military in American History: A New Perspective*, pp. 20-21 (1974).

might serve to protect against racial violence, and did so. Free blacks in Providence formed the African Greys in 1821.[162] Oscar Handlin writes of an attempt by black Bostonians in the 1850s to form a private militia company.[163] Black members of the Pittsburgh community had no private militia but nonetheless took action against a mob expected to riot in April 1839. Instead of taking action on their own, they joined an interracial peacekeeping force proposed by the city's mayor, and were able to put a stop to the riot.[164]

It is not clear whether private black militia groups ever marched on a white mob. But that they may never have been called on to do so may be a measure of their success. The story of the July 1835 Philadelphia riot is illustrative. Precipitated when a young black man assaulted a white one, the two-day riot ended without resort to military intervention when a rumor reached the streets that "fifty to sixty armed and determined black men had barricaded themselves in a building beyond the police lines."[165]

Undoubtedly, the most striking examples of the salutary use of firearms by blacks in defense of their liberty, and concurrently the disastrous results from the denial of the right to carry firearms in self-defense, lie in the same incident. In Cincinnati, in September 1841, racial hostility erupted in two nights of assaults by white mobs of up to 1,500 people. On the first evening, after destroying property owned by blacks in the business district, mobs descended upon the black residential section, there to be repulsed by blacks who fired into the crowd, forcing it out of the area. The crowd returned, however, bringing with it a six-pound cannon, and the battle ensued. Two whites and two blacks were killed, and more than a dozen of both races were wounded. Eventually, the militia took control, but on the next day the blacks were disarmed at the insistence of whites, and all adult black males were taken into protective custody. On the second evening, white rioters again assaulted the black residential district, resulting in more personal injury and property damage.[166]

---

[162] See Cottrol, supra note 97, p. 63.

[163] Oscar Handlin, *Boston's Immigrants: A Study in Acculturation*, p. 175 and n.110 (1959).

[164] Curry, supra note 153, p. 100; Victor Ullman, Martin R. Delany, *The Beginnings of Black Nationalism*, pp. 29-31 (1971).

[165] Curry, supra note 153, pp. 105-106.

[166] *Ibid.*, pp. 107-108; Wendell P. Dabney, *Cincinnati's Colored Citizens: Historical, Sociological and Biographical*, pp. 48-55 (Dabney Publishing Co., 1970) (1926); *Cincinnati Riot*, Niles' Nat'l. Reg. (Baltimore), Sept. 11, 1841, p. 32.

This history shows that if racism in the antebellum period was not limited to the southern states, neither was racial violence. Competition with and hostility toward blacks accounted for this violence in northern states, whereas the need to maintain slavery and maintain security for the white population accounted for racial violence in southern states. Another difference between the two regions is that in the southern states blacks did not have the means to protect themselves, while in northern states, blacks by and large had access to firearms and were willing to use them.

The 1841 Cincinnati riot represents the tragic, misguided irony of the city's authorities who, concerned with the safety of the black population, chose to disarm and imprison them—chose, in effect, to leave the black population of Cincinnati as southern authorities left the black population in slave states, naked to whatever indignities private parties might heap upon them, and dependent on a government either unable or unwilling to protect their rights. As a symbol for the experience of northern blacks protecting themselves against deprivations of liberty, the 1841 riot holds a vital lesson for those who would shape the content and meaning of the Fourteenth Amendment.

III. Arms and the Postbellum Southern States

The end of the Civil War did more than simply bring about the end of slavery; it brought about a sharpened conflict between two contrasting constitutional visions. One vision, largely held by northern Republicans, saw the former slaves as citizens[167] entitled to those rights long deemed as natural rights in Anglo-American society. Their's was a vision of national citizenship and national rights, rights that the federal government had the responsibility to secure for the freedmen and, indeed, for all citizens. This vision, developed during the anti-slavery struggle and heightened by the Civil War, caused Republicans of the Civil War and

---

[167] Even during the Civil War, the Lincoln administration and Congress acted on the legal assumption that free blacks were citizens. Despite Chief Justice Taney's opinion in *Dred Scott* that neither free blacks nor slaves could be citizens, *Dred Scott v. Sanford*, 60 U.S. (15 How.) 393, 417 (1856), Lincoln's Attorney General Edward Bates issued an opinion in 1862 declaring that free blacks were citizens and entitled to be masters of an American vessel. See 10 Op. Atty. Gen. 382, 413 (1862). That same year, Congress amended the 1792 militia statute, striking out the restriction of militia membership to white men. See Act of July 17, 1862, ch. 36, § 12, 12 Stat. 597, 599. While it could be argued that these measures were in part motivated by military needs, it should be noted that the United States and various states had previously enlisted black troops during time of crisis despite the restrictions in the 1792 Act. See supra Part I.c.2. Thus, these measures reflected long standing Republican and anti-slavery beliefs concerning the citizenship of free Negroes. See generally Cottrol, supra note 91. For a good discussion of black citizenship rights in the antebellum North, see generally Finkelman, supra note 99.

postwar generation to view the question of federalism and individual rights in a way that was significantly different from that of the original Framers of the Constitution and Bill of Rights. If many who debated the original Constitution feared that the newly created national government could violate long-established rights, those who changed the Constitution in the aftermath of war and slavery had firsthand experience with states violating fundamental rights. The history of the right to bear arms is, thus, inextricably linked with the efforts to reconstruct the nation and bring about a new racial order.

If the northern Republican vision was to bring the former slaves into the ranks of citizens, the concern of the defeated white South was to preserve as much of the antebellum social order as could survive northern victory and national law. The Emancipation Proclamation and the Thirteenth Amendment[168] abolished slavery; chattel slavery as it existed before the war could not survive these developments. Still, in the immediate aftermath of the war, the South was not prepared to accord the general liberties to the newly emancipated black population that northern states had allowed their free black populations.[169] Instead, while recognizing emancipation, southern states imposed on the freedmen the legal disabilities of the antebellum free Negro population. As one North Carolina statute indicated:

> All persons of color who are now inhabitants of this state shall be entitled to the same privileges, and are subject to the same burdens and disabilities, as by the laws of the state were conferred on, or were attached to, free persons of color, prior to the ordinance of emancipation, except as the same may be changed by law.[170]

In 1865 and 1866, southern states passed a series of statutes known as the black codes. These statutes, which one historian described as "a twilight zone between slavery and freedom,"[171] were an expression of the

---

[168] Section 1. Neither slavery nor involuntary servitude, except as a punishment for crime whereof the party shall have been duly convicted, shall exist within the United States, or any place subject to their jurisdiction. Section 2. Congress shall have the power to enforce this article by appropriate legislation (U.S. Constitution, amendment XIII).

[169] See generally Finkelman, supra note 99.

[170] North Carolina Black Code, ch. 40, 1866 N.C. Sess. Laws 99, reprinted in "1 Documentary History of Reconstruction: Political, Military, Social, Religious, Educational and Industrial, 1865 to the Present Time," 291 (Walter L. Fleming, ed., 1960) [hereinafter *Documentary History of Reconstruction*].

[171] Kenneth Stampp, *The Era of Reconstruction, 1865-1877*, p. 80 (1965).

South's determination to maintain control over the former slaves. Designed in part to ensure that traditional southern labor arrangements would be preserved, these codes attempted " 'to put the state much in the place of the former master,' "[172] The codes often required blacks to sign labor contracts binding black agricultural workers to their employers for a year.[173] Blacks were forbidden from serving on juries, and could not testify or act as parties against whites.[174] Vagrancy laws were used to force blacks into labor contracts and to limit freedom of movement.[175]

As further indication that the former slaves had not yet joined the ranks of free citizens, southern states passed legislation prohibiting blacks from carrying firearms without licenses, a requirement to which whites were not subjected. Louisiana[176] and Mississippi[177] statutes were typical of the restrictions found in the codes. Alabama's[178] were more harsh.

---

[172] Foner, supra note 29, p. 198 (1988) (quoting letter from William H. Trescot to James L. Orr, Dec. 13, 1865, South Carolina's Governor's Papers). Eugene Genovese has quoted an antebellum observer who described the free Negro as "a sort of inmate on parole." Genovese, supra note 97, p. 399.

[173] Foner, supra note 29, p. 200.

[174] Stampp, supra note 171, p. 80.

[175] *Ibid.*

[176] No Negro who is not in the military service shall be allowed to carry firearms, or any kind of weapons, within the parish, without the special permission of his employers, approved and endorsed by the nearest and most convenient chief of patrol. Any one violating the provision of this section shall forfeit his weapons and pay a fine of five dollars, or in default of the payment of said fine, shall be forced to work five days on the public road, or suffer corporal punishment as hereinafter provided.

[177] [N]o freedman, free negro or mulatto, not in the military service of the United States government, and not licensed so to do by the board of police of his or her county, shall keep or carry firearms of any kind, or any ammunition, dirk or bowie knife, and on conviction thereof in the county court shall be punished by fine, not exceeding ten dollars, and pay the cost of such proceedings, and all such arms or ammunition shall be forfeited to the informer; and it shall be the duty of every civil and military officer to arrest any freedman, free negro, or mulatto found with any such arms or ammunition, and cause him or her to be committed to trial in default of bail (Mississippi Statute of 1865, reprinted in *Documentary of Reconstruction*, supra note 170, p. 290).

[178] 1.) That it shall not be lawful for any freedman, mulatto, or free person of color in this State, to own firearms, or carry about his person a pistol or other deadly weapon. 2.) That after the 20th day of January, 1866, any person thus offending may be arrested upon the warrant of any acting justice of the peace, and upon conviction fined any sum not exceeding $100 or imprisoned in the county jail, or put to labor on the public works of any county, incorporated town, city, or village, for any term not exceeding three months. 3.) That if any gun, pistol or other deadly weapon be found in the possession of any freedman, mulatto or free person of color, the same may by any justice of the peace, sheriff, or constable be taken from such freedman, mulatto, or free person of color; and if such person is proved to be the owner thereof, the same shall, upon an order of any justice of the peace, be sold, and the proceeds thereof paid over to such freedman, mulatto, or person of color owning the same. 4.) That it shall not be lawful for any person to sell, give, or lend firearms or ammunition of any description whatever, to any freedman, free negro or mulatto; and any person so violating the provisions of this act shall be guilty of a misdemeanor, and upon conviction thereof, shall be fined in the sum of not less than fifty nor more than one hundred dollars, at the discretion of the jury trying the case. See *The Reconstruction Amendments' Debates*, p. 209 (Alfred Avins, ed., 1967).

The restrictions in the black codes caused strong concerns among northern Republicans. The charge that the South was trying to reinstitute slavery was frequently made, both in and out of Congress.[179] The news that the freedmen were being deprived of the right to bear arms was of particular concern to the champions of Negro citizenship. For them, the right of the black population to possess weapons was not merely of symbolic and theoretical importance; it was vital both as a means of maintaining the recently reunited Union and a means of preventing virtual re-enslavement of those formerly held in bondage.

Faced with a hostile and recalcitrant white South determined to preserve the antebellum social order by legal and extra-legal means,[180] northern Republicans were particularly alarmed at provisions of the black codes that effectively preserved the right to keep and bear arms for former Confederates while disarming blacks, the one group in the South with clear unionist sympathies.[181] This fed the determination of northern Republicans to provide national enforcement of the Bill of Rights.[182]

---

[179] See Foner, supra note 29, pp. 225-227; Stampp, supra note 171, pp. 80-81.

[180] The Ku Klux Klan was formed in 1866 and immediately launched its campaign of terror against blacks and southern white unionists. See Foner, supra note 29, p. 342; infra text at notes 217-23.

[181] During the debates over the civil Rights Act of 1866, Republican Representative Sidney Clarke of Kansas expressed the fears of many northern Republicans who saw the clear military implications of allowing the newly formed white militias in Southern states to disarm blacks:
"Who, sir, were those men? Not the present militia; but the brave black soldiers of the Union, disarmed and robbed by this wicked and despotic order. Nearly every white man in [Mississippi] that could bear arms was in the rebel ranks. Nearly all of their able-bodied colored men who could reach our lines enlisted under the old flag. Many of these brave defenders of the nation paid for their arms with which they went to battle. And I regret, sir, that justice compels me to say, to the disgrace of the Federal Government, that the 'reconstructed' state authorities of Mississippi were allowed to rob and disarm our veteran soldiers and arm the rebels fresh from the field of treasonable strife. Sir, the disarmed loyalists of Alabama, Mississippi, and Louisiana are powerless today, and oppressed by the pardoned and encouraged rebels of those States."—*The Reconstruction Amendments' Debates*, supra note 178, p. 209.

[182] Representative Roswell Hart, Republican from New York, captured those sentiments during the debates over the Civil Rights Act of 1866:
"The Constitution clearly describes that to be a republican form of government for which it was expressly framed. A government which shall 'establish justice, insure domestic tranquility, provide for the common defense, promote the general welfare, and secure the blessings of liberty'; a government whose 'citizens shall be entitled to all privileges and immunities of other citizens'; where 'no law shall be made prohibiting the free exercise of religion'; where 'the right of the people to keep and bear arms shall not be infringed'; where 'the right of the people to be secure in their persons, houses, papers and effects, against unreasonable searches and seizures, shall not be violated,' and where 'no person shall be deprived of life, liberty, or property without due process of law.' Have these rebellious States such a form of government? If they have not, it is the duty of the United States to guaranty that they have it speedily."—*The Reconstruction Amendments' Debates*, supra note 178, p. 193.

173

The efforts to disarm the freedmen were in the background when the 39th Congress debated the Fourteenth Amendment, and played an important part in convincing the 39th Congress that traditional notions concerning federalism and individual rights needed to change. While a full exploration of the incorporation controversy[183] is beyond the scope of this article, it should be noted that Jonathan Bingham, author of the Fourteenth Amendment's Privileges or Immunities Clause,[184] clearly stated that it applied the Bill of Rights to the states.[185] Others shared that same understanding.[186]

Although the history of the black codes persuaded the 39th Congress that Congress and the federal courts must be given the authority to protect citizens against state deprivations of the Bill of Rights, the Supreme Court in its earliest decisions on the Fourteenth Amendment moved to maintain much of the structure of prewar federalism. A good deal of the Court's decision-making that weakened the effectiveness of the Second Amendment was part of the Court's overall process of eviscerating the Fourteenth Amendment soon after its enactment.

That process began with the *Slaughterhouse Cases*,[187] which dealt a severe blow to the Fourteenth Amendment's Privileges or Immunities Clause, a blow from which it has yet to recover. It was also within its early examination of the Fourteenth Amendment that the Supreme Court first heard a claim directly based on the Second Amendment. Ironically, the party first bringing an allegation before the Court concerning a Second Amendment violation was the federal government. In *United States v. Cruikshank*,[188] federal officials brought charges against William Cruikshank and others under the Enforcement Act of 1870.[189] Cruikshank

---

[183] For a good general discussion of the incorporation question, see Michael K. Curtis, *No State Shall Abridge: The Fourteenth Amendment and the Bill of Rights* (1986). For a good discussion of the 39th Congress's views concerning the Second Amendment and its incorporation via the Fourteenth, see Halbrook, supra note 6, pp. 107-23.

[184] "No state shall make or enforce any law which shall abridge the privileges or immunities of citizens of the United States; . . ." U.S. Const. amend. XIV, § 1.

[185] *The Reconstruction Amendments' Debates,* supra note 178, pp. 156-60, 217-18.

[186] *Ibid.,* p. 219 (remarks by Republican Senator Jacob Howard of Michigan on privileges and immunities of citizens).

[187] *Butchers Benevolent Ass'n. v. Crescent City Live Stock Landing & Slaughterhouse Co.*, 83 U.S. (16 Wall.) 36 (1872).

[188] 92 U.S. 542 (1876).

[189] 16 Stat. 140 (1870) (codified as amended at 18 U.S.C. §§ 241-42, 1988). The relevant passage reads: "That if two or more persons shall band or conspire together, or go in disguise upon the public highway, or upon the premises of another, with intent to violate any provision of this act, or to injure, oppress, threaten, or intimidate any citizen with intent to prevent or hinder his free exercise and enjoyment of any right or privilege granted or secured to him by the Constitution or

had been charged with violating the rights of two black men to peaceably assemble and to bear arms. The Supreme Court held that the federal government had no power to protect citizens against private action that deprived them of their constitutional rights. The Court held that the First and Second Amendments were limitations on Congress, not on private individuals and that, for protection against private criminal action, the individual was required to look to state governments.[190]

The *Cruikshank* decision, which dealt a serious blow to Congress's ability to enforce the Fourteenth Amendment, was part of a larger campaign of the Court to ignore the original purpose of the Fourteenth Amendment—to bring about a revolution in federalism, as well as race relations.[191] While the Court in the late 1870s and 1880s was reasonably willing to strike down instances of state-sponsored racial discrimination,[192] it also showed a strong concern for maintaining state prerogative and a disclination to carry out the intent of the Framers of the Fourteenth Amendment to make states respect national rights.

This trend was demonstrated in *Presser v. Illinois*,[193] the second case in which the Court examined the Second Amendment. *Presser* involved an Illinois statute which prohibited individuals who were not members of the militia from parading with arms.[194] Although Justice William Woods, author of the majority opinion, noted that the Illinois statute did not infringe upon the right to keep and bear arms,[195] he nonetheless went on to declare that the Second Amendment was a limitation on the federal and not the state governments. Curiously enough, Woods' opinion also contended that, despite the nonapplicability of the Second Amendment to state action, states were forbidden from disarming their populations because such action would interfere with the federal government's ability

---

laws of the United States or because of his having exercised the same, such persons shall be held guilty of a felony. . . ."—*Ibid.*, p. 141.

[190] 92 U.S., pp. 548-59.

[191] This can also be seen in the Court's reaction to the federal government's first public accommodations statute, the Civil Rights Act of 1875. With much the same reasoning, the Court held that Congress had no power to prohibit discrimination in public accommodations within states. See The Civil Rights Cases, 109 U.S. 3 (1883).

[192] See, e.g., *Yick Wo v. Hopkins*, 118 U.S. 356, 373 (1886) (declaring the administration of a municipal ordinance discriminatory); *Strauder v. West Virginia*, 100 U.S. 303, 308 (1879) (striking down a statute prohibiting blacks from serving as jurors).

[193] 116 U.S. 252 (1886).

[194] *Ibid.*, p. 253.

[195] *Ibid.*, p. 265.

to maintain the sedentary militia.[196] With its view that the statute restricting armed parading did not interfere with the right to keep and bear arms, and its view that Congress's militia power prevented the states from disarming their citizens, the *Presser* Court had gone out of its way in dicta to reaffirm the old federalism and to reject the Framers' view of the Fourteenth Amendment that the Bill of Rights applied to the states.

The rest of the story is all too well known. The Court's denial of an expanded role for the federal government in enforcing civil rights played a crucial role in redeeming white rule. The doctrine in *Cruikshank*, that blacks would have to look to state government for protection against criminal conspiracies, gave the green light to private forces, often with the assistance of state and local governments, that sought to subjugate the former slaves and their descendants. Private violence was instrumental in driving blacks from the ranks of voters.[197] It helped force many blacks into peonage, a virtual return to slavery,[198] and was used to force many blacks into a state of ritualized subservience.[199] With the protective arm of the federal government withdrawn, protection of black lives and property was left to largely hostile state governments. In the Jim Crow era that would follow, the right to possess arms would take on critical importance for many blacks. This right, seen in the eighteenth century as a mechanism that enabled a majority to check the excesses of a potentially tyrannical national government, would for many blacks in the twentieth century become a means of survival in the face of private violence and state indifference.

IV. Arms and Afro-American Self-Defense in The Twentieth Century: A History Ignored

For much of the twentieth century, the black experience in this country has been one of repression. This repression has not been limited to the southern part of the country, nor is it a development divorced from the

---

[196] *Ibid.*

[197] Rable, supra note 29, pp. 88-90; Stampp, supra note 171, pp. 199-204.

[198] Benno C. Schmidt, Jr., *Principle and Prejudice: The Supreme Court and Race in the Progressive Era. Part 2: The Peonage Cases,* 82 Colum. L. Rev., pp. 646, 653-55 (1982).

[199] George M. Frederickson, *White Supremacy: A Comparative Study in American and South African History,* pp. 251-52 (1981); Charles E. Silberman, *Criminal Violence, Criminal Justice,* p. 32 (1978); Joel Williamson, *A Rage for Order: Black/White Relations in the American South Since Emancipation,* p. 124 (1986).

past. Born perhaps of cultural predisposition against blacks,[200] and nurtured by economic competition between blacks and whites, particularly immigrant groups and those whites at the lower rungs of the economic scale,[201] racism in the North continued after the Civil War, abated but not eliminated in its effects.[202] In the South, defeat in the Civil War and the loss of slaves as property confirmed white Southerners in their determination to degrade and dominate their black brethren.[203]

Immediately after the Civil War and the emancipation it brought, white Southerners adopted measures to keep the black population in its place.[204] Southerners saw how Northerners had utilized segregation as a means to avoid the black presence in their lives,[205] and they already had experience with segregation in southern cities before the war.[206] Southerners extended this experience of segregation to the whole of southern life through the mechanism of "Jim Crow."[207] Jim Crow was established both by the operation of law, including the black codes and other legislation, and by an elaborate etiquette of racially restrictive social practices. The *Civil Rights Cases*[208] and *Plessy v. Ferguson*[209] gave the South freedom to pursue the task of separating black from white. The *Civil Rights Cases* went beyond *Cruikshank*, even more severely restricting congressional power to provide for the equality of blacks under Section 5 of the

---

[200] See generally Jordan, supra note 56, pp. 3-43.

[201] Litwack, supra note 116, pp. 153-86.

[202] Cottrol, supra note 91, pp. 1007-19.

[203] C. Vann Woodward, *The Strange Career of Jim Crow*, pp. 22-23 (3rd ed. 1974).

[204] See infra text accompanying notes 169-78. See generally Woodward, supra note 203, pp. 22-29.

[205] See *ibid.*, pp. 18-21 (the Jim Crow system was born in the North where systematic segregation, with the backing of legal and extralegal codes, permeated black life in the free states by 1860); see also Litwack, supra note 116, pp. 97-99 (in addition to statutes and customs that limited the political and judicial rights of blacks, extralegal codes enforced by public opinion perpetuated the North's systematic segregation of blacks from whites).

[206] See Richard C. Wade, *Slavery in the Cities: The South 1820-1860*, pp. 180-208 (1964) (although more contact between blacks and white occurred in urban areas of the South, both social standards and a legal blueprint continued the subjugation of blacks to whites).

[207] See generally Woodward, supra note 204. Jim Crow was said to have established " . . . an etiquette of discrimination. It was not enough for blacks to be second class citizens, denied the franchise and consigned to inferior schools. Black subordination was reinforced by a racist punctilio dictating separate seating on public accommodations, separate water fountains and restrooms, separate seats in courthouses, and separate Bibles to swear in black witnesses about to give testimony before the law. The list of separations was ingenious and endless. Blacks became like a group of American untouchables, ritually separated from the rest of the population."—Diamond and Cottrol, supra note 103, pp. 264-65 (footnote omitted).

[208] 109 U.S. 3 1883.

[209] 163 U.S. 537 (1896).

Fourteenth Amendment,[210] and *Plessy v. Ferguson* declared separate facilities for blacks and whites to be consonant with the Fourteenth Amendment's mandate of "equal protection of the laws."[211] In effect, states and individuals were given full freedom to effect their "social prejudices"[212] and "racial instincts"[213] to the detriment of blacks throughout the South and elsewhere.[214]

These laws and customs were given support and gruesome effect by violence. In northern cities, violence continued to threaten blacks after Reconstruction and after the turn of the century. For instance, in New York, hostility between blacks and immigrant whites ran high.[215] Negro strike-breakers were often used to break strikes of union workers.[216] Regular clashes occurred between blacks and the Irish during the nineteenth century,[217] until finally a major race riot broke out in 1900 that lasted four days.[218] And in 1919, after a Chicago race riot, 38 deaths and 537 injuries were reported as a result of attacks on the black population.[219]

---

[210] 109 U.S. 3.

[211] 163 U.S., p. 548.

[212] *Ibid.*, p. 551.

[213] *Ibid.*

[214] Jim Crow was not exclusively a southern experience after the Civil War. For example, at one point or another, antimiscegenation laws have been enacted by forty-one of the fifty states. Harvey M. Applebaum, *Miscegenation Statutes: A Constitutional and Social Problem*, 53 Geo. L.J. pp. 49, 50-51 and 50 n.9 (1964). The *Adams* case, in which the federal government challenged separate university facilities throughout the union, involved the State of Pennsylvania. See *Adams v. Richardson*, 356 F. Supp. 92, 100 (D.D.C. 1973); *Adams v. Richardson*, 351 F. Supp. 636, 637 (D.D.C. 1972). *Hansberry v. Lee*, 311 U.S. 32 (1940), involved a covenant restricting the sale of property in Illinois to blacks. The set of consolidated cases that outlawed the separate but equal doctrine would later be known as *Brown v. Board of Education*, 347 U.S. 483 (1954), the defendant board of education was located in Kansas, a Northern state.

[215] Gilbert Osofsky, *Harlem: The Making of a Ghetto: Negro New York 1890-1930*, pp. 46-52 (1963).

[216] *Ibid.*, p. 42.

[217] *Ibid.*, pp. 45-46.

[218] *Ibid.*, pp. 46-52. "After the riot ended, the situation nevertheless remained tense. Negroes began to arm. Revolvers and other weapons were easily purchased at local pawnshops and hardware stores. In a survey made of [the area where the riot took place], just one day after the riot, it was found that 145 revolvers and a substantial amount of ammunition had been sold—'all had gone to negroes.' Lloyd Williams, a Negro bartender, was seen leaving one store with an arsenal of weapons. When asked what he was going to do with them, he replied, 'I understand they're knocking down negroes 'round here. The first man tries it on me gets this. . . .' Other Negroes warned that no white men were going to bother them. As policemen patrolled the Negro blocks they were showered with bricks, bottles, and garbage, thrown from rooftops and tenement windows. They fired back with revolvers. It seems miraculous that no one was killed."—*Ibid.*, pp. 49-50.

[219] Chicago Commission of Race Relations, *The Negro in Chicago: A Study of Race Relations and a Race Riot (1922)*, pp. 595-98, 602, 640-49, reprinted in *The Negro and the City*, 126-33

178

In the South, racism found expression, not only through the power of unorganized mobs, but also under the auspices of organized groups like the Ku Klux Klan. The Klan started in 1866 as a social organization of white Civil War veterans in Pulaski, Tennessee,[220] complete with pageantry, ritual, and opportunity for plain and innocent amusement.[221] But the group soon expanded and turned its attention to more sinister activities. The Klan's activities, primarily in the South, expanded to playing tricks on blacks and then to terroristic nightriding against them.[222] The Ku Klux Klan in this first incarnation was disbanded, possibly as early as January 1868, and no later than May 1870.[223] By that time, the Klan's activities had come to include assaults, murder, lynchings, and political repression against blacks,[224] and Klan-like activities would continue and contribute to the outcome of the federal election of 1876 that ended Reconstruction.[225] As one author has put it, "The Invisible Empire faded away, not because it had been defeated, but because it had won."[226]

The Klan would be revived in 1915 after the release of D. W. Griffith's film *Birth of a Nation*,[227] but, both pre- and post-dating the Klan's revival, Klan tactics would play a familiar role in the lives of black people in the South; for up to the time of the modern civil rights movement, lynching would be virtually an everyday occurrence. Between 1882 and 1968, 4,743 persons were lynched, the overwhelming number of these in the South;[228] 3,446 of these persons were black,[229] killed for

---

(Richard B. Sherman, ed., 1970). After World War I, an outbreak of racial violence against blacks was recorded from 1917 to 1921. Riots occurred in Chicago, Omaha, Washington, D.C., and East St. Louis, Illinois. *Ibid.*, p. 126.

[220] Wyn Craig Wade, *The Fiery Cross: The Ku Klux Klan in America*, p. 33 (1987).

[221] *Ibid.*, pp. 33-35.

[222] *Ibid.*, p. 37.

[223] Stanley F. Horn, *Invisible Empire: The Story of the Ku Klux Klan 1866-1871*, pp. 356-59 (1969).

[224] See generally William L. Katz, *The Invisible Empire: The Ku Klux Klan Impact on History,* pp. 19-59 (1986).

[225] See Wade, supra note 220, pp. 57, 110-11. Through the intimidation of black voters, the Democratic party in the South, with which most Klansmen were affiliated, recovered, and Republican strength waned. The Democrats captured the House of Representatives in 1874, and with the controversial compromise between Democrats and Republicans that elevated Rutherford B. Hayes to the Presidency in 1877, the end of Reconstruction was marked. *Ibid.*

[226] Katz, supra note 224, p. 58.

[227] Wade, supra note 220, p. 120.

[228] Stephen J. Whitfield, *A Death in the Delta: The Story of Emmett Till* 5 (1988).

the most part for being accused in one respect or another of not knowing their place.[230] These accusations were as widely disparate as arson,[231] theft,[232] sexual contact or even being too familiar with a white woman,[233] murdering or assaulting a white person,[234] hindering a lynch mob,[235] protecting one's legal rights,[236] not showing proper respect,[237] or simply

---

[229] *Ibid.*

[230] National Assn. for the Advancement of Colored People, *Thirty Years of Lynching in the United States: 1889-1918* (1919) reported as follows: "Among colored victims [of lynching], 35.8 percent were accused of murder; 28.4 percent of rape and 'attacks upon women' (19 percent of rape and 9.4 percent of 'attacks upon women'); 17.8 percent of crimes against the person (other than those already mentioned) and against property; 12 percent were charged with miscellaneous crimes and in 5.6 percent no crime was charged. The 5.6 percent [sic] classified under 'Absence of Crime' does not include a number of cases in which crime was alleged but in which it was afterwards shown conclusively that no crime had been committed."—*Ibid.*, p. 10.

[231] See, e.g., Negro and Wife Hanged, Suspected of Barn-Burning, St. Paul Pioneer Press, Nov. 26, 1914, reprinted in Ralph Ginzburg, *100 Years of Lynchings*, p. 92 (1988).

[232] See, e.g., *Negro Hanged as Mule Thief, Atlanta Constitution*, July 15, 1914, reprinted in Ginzburg, supra note 231, p. 92; *Would Be Chicken Thief, N.Y. Herald*, Dec. 6, 1914, reprinted in Ginzburg, supra note 231, p. 93 (reporting a black man having been lynched "[f]or the crime of crawling under the house of a white citizen, with the intention of stealing chickens").

[233] See, e.g., Whitfield, supra note 228 (Emmett Till was killed in 1955 because he was thought to have whistled at a white woman). Other major works describing individual lynchings are James R. McGovern, *Anatomy of a Lynching: The Killing of Claude Neal* (1982) (describing a lynching in 1934 occasioned by the rape of a white woman); Howard Smead, *Blood Justice: The Lynching of Mack Charles Parker* (1986) (describing another lynching of a black man for the rape of a white woman). See also "Blacks Lynched for Remark Which May Have Been 'Hello,' " *Phila. Inquirer*, Jan. 3, 1916, reprinted in Ginzburg, supra note 231, p. 98; "Inter-Racial Love Affair Ended by Lynching of Man," *Memphis Com. Appeal*, Jan. 14, 1922, reprinted in Ginzburg, supra note 231, p. 158; "Negro Ambushed, Lynched for Writing White Girl," *Memphis Com. Appeal*, Nov. 26, 1921, reprinted in Ginzburg, supra note 231, p. 156; "Negro Insults White Women; Is Shot and Strung Up," *Montgomery Advertiser*, Oct. 10, 1916, reprinted in Ginzburg, supra note 231, p. 111; "Negro Shot Dead for Kissing His White Girlfriend," *Chi. Defender*, Feb. 13, 1915, reprinted in Ginzburg, supra note 231, p. 95; "Negro Youth Mutilated for Kissing White Girl," *Boston Guardian*, Apr. 30, 1914, reprinted in Ginzburg, supra note 231, p. 90; "White Girl Is Jailed, Negro Friend Is Lynched," *Galveston Trib.* (Texas), June 21, 1934, reprinted in Ginzburg, supra note 231, p. 217.

[234] See, e.g. "Hoosiers Hang Negro Killer," *Chi. Rec.*, Feb. 27, 1901, reprinted in Ginzburg, supra note 231, p. 37; "Negro and White Scuffle, Negro Is Jailed, Lynched," *Atlanta Const.* July 6, 1933, reprinted in Ginzburg, supra note 231, p. 197; "Negro Shot After Striking Merchant Who Dirtied Him," *Montgomery Advertiser*, Aug. 28, 1913, reprinted in Ginzburg, supra note 231, p. 88; "Negro Suspected of Slaying Bartender Is Hung by Mob," *Kansas City Star*, Oct. 31, 1899, reprinted in Ginzburg, supra note 231, p. 23.

[235] See, e.g., "Negro Father Is Lynched; Aided Son to Escape Mob," *Balt. Afro-Am.*, July 6, 1923, reprinted in Ginzburg, supra note 231, p. 170.

[236] See, e.g., "Miss. Minister Lynched," *N.Y. Amsterdam News*, Aug. 26, 1944, reprinted in Ginzburg, supra note 231, p. 236 (reporting the lynching of a black man for having hired a lawyer in a property dispute).

[237] See e.g., "Impertinent Question," *Birmingham News*, Sept. 23, 1913, reprinted in Ginzburg, supra note 231, p. 88 (relating that a black man was lynched after he asked whether a white woman's husband was home); "Insulting Remark," *Montgomery Advertiser*, Oct. 23, 1913, reprinted in Ginzburg, supra note 231, p. 89 (relating that a black man was lynched for having made an insulting remark to a white woman); "Negro Half-Wit Is Lynched; Threatened to Lynch Whites," *Montgomery Advertiser*, Aug. 25, 1913, reprinted in Ginzburg, supra note 231, p. 87; "Negro Insults White Women; Is Shot and Strung Up," *Montgomery Advertiser*, Oct. 10, 1916, reprinted in Ginzburg, supra

being in the wrong place at the wrong time.[238] This is not to say that blacks went quietly or tearfully to their deaths. Oftentimes they were able to use firearms to defend themselves, though usually not with success: Jim McIlherron was lynched in Estell Springs, Tennessee, after having exchanged over one thousand rounds with his pursuers.[239] The attitude of individuals such as McIlherron is summed up by Ida B. Wells-Barnett, a black anti-lynching activist who wrote of her decision to carry a pistol:

> I had been warned repeatedly by my own people that some-thing would happen if I did not cease harping on the lynching of three months before. . . . I had bought a pistol the first thing after [the lynching], because I expected some cowardly retaliation from the lynchers. I felt that one had better die fighting against injustice than to die like a dog or a rat in a trap. I had already determined to sell my life as dearly as possible if attacked. I felt if I could take one lyncher with me, this would even up the score a little bit.[240]

When blacks used firearms to protect their rights, they were often partially successful but were ultimately doomed. In 1920, two black men in Texas fired on and killed two whites in self-defense. The black men were arrested and soon lynched.[241] When the sheriff of Aiken, South Carolina, came with three deputies to a black household to attempt a warrantless search and struck one female family member, three other

---

note 231, p. 111; "Train Porter Lynched After Insult to Woman," *Atlanta Const.*, May 9, 1920, reprinted in Ginzburg, supra note 231, p. 130.

[238] See, e.g., "An Innocent Man Lynched," *N.Y. Times*, June 11, 1900, reprinted in Ginzburg, supra note 231, p. 31; "Boy Lynched at McGhee for No Special Cause," *St. Louis Argus*, May 27, 1921, reprinted in Ginzburg, supra note 231, p. 150; "Negro Suspect Eludes Mob; Sister Lynched Instead," *N.Y. Trib.*, Mar. 17, 1901, reprinted in Ginzburg, supra note 231, p. 38; "Posse Lynches Innocent Man When Thwarted in Its Hunt," *Wilmington Advoc.*, Dec. 16, 1922, reprinted in Ginzburg, supra note 231, p. 166; "Texans Lynch Wrong Negro," *Chi. Trib.*, Nov. 22, 1895, reprinted in Ginzburg, supra note 231, p. 9; "Thwarted Mob Lynches Brother of Intended Victim," *Montgomery Advertiser*, Aug. 5, 1911, reprinted in Ginzburg, supra note 231, p. 73.

[239] "Blood-Curdling Lynching Witnessed by 2,000 Persons," *Chattanooga Times*, Feb. 13, 1918, reprinted in Ginzburg, supra note 231, pp. 114-16.

[240] Ida B. Wells-Barnett, *Crusade for Justice: The Autobiography of Ida B. Wells*, 62 (Alfreda M. Duster, ed., 1970). Wells-Barnett's fears for her safety, fortunately, were never realized. Born a slave in 1862, she died of natural causes in 1931. *Ibid.*, pp. xxx-xxxi, 7. Eli Cooper of Caldwell, Georgia, was not so lucky, however. Cooper was alleged to have said that the "Negro has been run over for fifty years, but it must stop now, and pistols and shotguns are the only weapons to stop a mob." Cooper was dragged from his home by a mob of 20 men and killed as his wife looked on. "Church Burnings Follow Negro Agitator's Lynching," *Chi. Defender*, Sept. 6, 1919, reprinted in Ginzburg, supra note 231, p. 124.

[241] "Letter from Texas Reveals Lynching's Ironic Facts," *N.Y. Negro World*, Aug. 22, 1920, reprinted in Ginzburg, supra note 231, pp. 139-140.

family members used a hatchet and firearms in self-defense, killing the sheriff. The three wounded survivors were taken into custody, and after one was acquitted of murdering the sheriff, with indications of a similar verdict for the other two, all three were lynched.[242]

Although individual efforts of blacks to halt violence to their persons or property were largely unsuccessful, there were times that blacks succeeded through concerted or group activity in halting lynchings. In her autobiography, Ida Wells-Barnett reported an incident in Memphis in 1891 in which a black militia unit for two or three nights guarded approximately 100 jailed blacks who were deemed at risk of mob violence. When it seemed the crisis had passed, the militia unit ceased its work. It was only after the militia unit left that a white mob stormed the jail and lynched three black inmates.[243]

A. Philip Randolph, the long-time head of the Brotherhood of Sleeping Car Porters, and Walter White, one-time executive secretary of the National Association for the Advancement of Colored People, vividly recalled incidents in which their fathers had participated in collective efforts to use firearms to successfully forestall lynchings and other mob violence. As a thirteen-year-old, White participated in his father's experiences,[244] which, he reported, left him "gripped by the knowledge of my own identity, and in the depths of my soul, I was vaguely aware that I was glad of it."[245] After his father stood armed at a jail all night to ward off lynchers,[246] Randolph was left with a vision, not "of powerlessness, but of the 'possibilities of salvation,' which resided in unity and organization."[247]

The willingness of blacks to use firearms to protect their rights, their lives, and their property, alongside their ability to do so successfully when acting collectively, renders many gun control statutes, particularly of Southern origin, all the more worthy of condemnation. This is

---

[242] "Lone Survivor of Atrocity Recounts Events of Lynching," *N.Y. Amsterdam News*, June 1, 1927, reprinted in Ginzburg, supra note 231, pp. 175-78.

[243] Wells-Barnett, supra note 240, p. 50. To forestall the occurrence of future incidents of the same nature, a Tennessee court ordered the local sheriff to take charge of the arms of the black militia unit. *Ibid.*

[244] Walter White, *A Man Called White*, 4-12 (1948), reprinted in "The Negro and the City," supra note 219, pp. 121-26.

[245] *Ibid.*, p. 126.

[246] Jervis Anderson, *A. Phillip Randolph: A Biographical Portrait*, pp. 41-42 (1973).

[247] *Ibid.*, p. 42.

especially so in view of the purpose of these statutes, which, like that of the gun control statutes of the black codes, was to disarm blacks.

This purpose has been recognized by some state judges. The Florida Supreme Court in 1941 refused to extend a statute forbidding the carrying of a pistol on one's person to a situation in which the pistol was found in an automobile glove compartment.[248] In a concurrence, one judge spoke of the purpose of the statute:

> I know something of the history of this legislation. The original Act of 1893 was passed when there was a great influx of negro laborers in this State drawn here for the purpose of working in the turpentine and lumber camps. The same condition existed when the Act was amended in 1901 and the Act was passed for the purpose of disarming the negro laborers and to thereby reduce the unlawful homicides that were prevalent in turpentine and saw-mill camps and to give the white citizens in sparsely settled areas a better feeling of security. The statute was never intended to be applied to the white population and in practice has never been so applied.[249]

The Ohio Supreme Court in 1920 construed the state's constitutional right of the people "to bear arms for their defense and security" not to forbid a statute outlawing the carrying of a concealed weapon.[250] In so doing, the court followed the lead of sister courts in Alabama,[251] Arkansas,[252] Georgia,[253] and Kentucky,[254] over the objections of a dissenting judge who recognized that "the race issue [in Southern states] has intensified a decisive purpose to entirely disarm the negro, and this policy is evident upon reading the opinions."[255]

That the Southern states did not prohibit firearms ownership outright is fortuitous. During the 1960s, while many blacks and white civil rights workers were threatened and even murdered by whites with guns,

---

[248] *Watson v. Stone*, 4 So. 2d 700 (Fla. 1941).

[249] *Ibid.*, p. 703 (Buford, J., concurring).

[250] *State v. Nieto*, 130 N.E. 663 (Ohio 1920).

[251] *Dunston v. State*, 27 So. 333 (Ala. 1900).

[252] *Carrol v. State*, 28 Ark. 99 (1872).

[253] *Brown v. State*, 39 S.E. 873 (Ga. 1901).

[254] *Commonwealth v. Walker*, 7 Ky. L. Rptr. 219 (1885) (abstract).

[255] *Nieto*, 130 N.E. at 669 (Wanamaker, J., dissenting).

firearms in the hands of blacks served a useful purpose, to protect civil rights workers and blacks from white mob and terrorist activity.[256]

While the rate of lynchings in the South had slowed somewhat,[257] it was still clear by 1960 that Southerners were capable of murderous violence in pursuit of the Southern way of life. The 1955 murder of Emmett Till, a fourteen-year-old boy killed in Money, Mississippi, for wolf-whistling at a white woman, sent shock waves throughout the nation.[258] Two years later, the nation again would be shocked, this time by a riotous crowd outside Little Rock's Central High School bent on preventing nine black children from integrating the school under federal court order; President Eisenhower ordered federal troops to effectuate the court order.[259] News of yet another prominent lynching in Mississippi reached the public in 1959.[260]

In the early 1960s, Freedom Riders and protesters at sit-ins were attacked, and some suffered permanent damage at the hands of white supremacists.[261] In 1963, Medgar Evers, Mississippi secretary of the NAACP was killed.[262] Three college students were killed in Mississippi during the 1964 "Freedom Summer"; this killing would render their names—Andrew Goodman, James Chaney, and Michael Schwerner—and their sacrifice part of the public domain.[263] A church bombing in Birmingham that killed four small black children,[264] the killing of a young white housewife helping with the march from Montgomery to Selma,[265]

---

[256] See, e.g., John R. Salter, Jr. and Donald B. Kates, Jr., "The Necessity of Access to Firearms by Dissenters and Minorities Whom Government Is Unwilling or Unable to Protect," in *Restricting Handguns: The Liberal Skeptics Speak Out*, pp. 185, 189-93 (Donald B. Kates, Jr., ed., 1979).

[257] According to records kept by the Tuskeegee Institute, 4,733 lynchings occurred between 1882 and 1959. "4,733 Mob Action Victims Since '82, Tuskeegee Reports," *Montgomery Advertiser*, April 26, 1959, reprinted in Ginzburg, supra note 231, p. 244. Tuskeegee Institute's records show only ten more lynchings to have occurred by 1968. Whitfield, supra note 228, p. 5.

[258] See Whitfield, supra note 228, p. 23-108; see also "Eyes on the Prize: America's Civil Rights Years, 1954-1965: Awakenings (1954-56)" (PBS television broadcast, January 21, 1986).

[259] See *Cooper v. Aaron*, 358 U.S. 1 (1958); see also Tony A. Freyer, *The Little Rock Crisis: A Constitutional Interpretation* (1984); Raymond T. Diamond, *Confrontation as Rejoinder to Compromise: Reflections on the Little Rock Desegregation Crisis*, 11 Nat'l Black L.J. 151, 152-64 (1989); "Eyes on the Prize: America's Civil Rights Years, 1954-65: Fighting Back (1957-62)" (PBS television broadcast, Jan. 28, 1986).

[260] See generally Smead, supra note 233.

[261] Rhonda Blumberg, *Civil Rights: The 1960s Freedom Struggle*, pp. 65-81 (1984).

[262] *Civil Rights: 1960-66*, pp. 190-91 (Lester A. Sobel, ed., 1967).

[263] *Ibid.*, pp. 244-46.

[264] *Ibid.*, pp. 187-88.

[265] *Ibid.*, pp. 303-305.

and the destructive riot in Oxford, Mississippi,[266] helped make clear to the nation what blacks in the South had long known: white Southerners were willing to use weapons of violence, modern equivalents of rope and faggot, to keep blacks in their place.

It struck many, then, as the height of blindness, confidence, courage, or moral certainty for the civil rights movement to adopt nonviolence as its credo, and to thus leave its adherents open to attack by terrorist elements within the white South. Yet, while nonviolence had its adherents among the mainstream civil rights organizations, many ordinary black people in the South believed in resistance and believed in the necessity of maintaining firearms for personal protection, and these people lent their assistance and their protection to the civil rights movement.[267]

Daisy Bates, the leader of the Little Rock NAACP during the desegregation crisis, wrote in her memoirs that armed volunteers stood guard over her home.[268] Moreover, there are oral histories of such assistance. David Dennis, the black Congress of Racial Equality (CORE) worker who had been targeted for the fate that actually befell Goodman, Schwerner and Chaney during the Freedom Summer,[269] has told of black Mississippi citizens with firearms who followed civil rights workers in order to keep them safe.[270]

Ad hoc efforts were not the sole means by which black Southern adherents of firearms protected workers in the civil rights movement. The Deacons for Defense and Justice were organized first in 1964 in Jonesboro, Louisiana, but received prominence in Bogalousa, Louisi-

---

[266] *Ibid.*, pp. 110-18.

[267] Donald B. Kates, Jr., recalls that: "As a civil rights worker in a Southern state during the early 1960s, I found that the possession of firearms for self-defense was almost universally endorsed by the black community, for it could not depend on police protection from the KKK. The leading civil rights lawyer in the state (then and now a nationally prominent figure) went nowhere without a revolver on his person or in his briefcase. The black lawyer for whom I worked principally did not carry a gun all the time, but he attributed the relative quiescence of the Klan to the fact that the black community was so heavily armed. Everyone remembered an incident several years before, in which the state's Klansmen attempted to break up a civil rights meeting and were routed by return gunfire. When one of our clients (a school teacher who had been fired for her leadership in the Movement) was threatened by the Klan, I joined the group that stood armed vigil outside her house nightly. No attack ever came—though the Klan certainly knew that the police would have done nothing to hinder or punish them."—*Restricting Handguns: The Liberal Skeptics Speak Out*, supra note 256, p. 186.

[268] Daisy Bates, *The Long Shadow of Little Rock, A Memoir*, p. 94 (1982).

[269] Howell Raines, *My Soul Is Rested: Movement Days in the Deep South Remembered*, pp. 275-76 (1977).

[270] Telephone interview with David Dennis (Oct. 30, 1991).

ana.[271] The Deacons organized in Jonesboro after their founder saw the Ku Klux Klan marching in the street and realized that the "fight against racial injustice include[d] not one but two foes: White reactionaries and police."[272] Jonesboro's Deacons obtained a charter and weapons, and vowed to shoot back if fired upon.[273] The word spread throughout the South, but most significantly to Bogalousa, where the Klan was rumored to have its largest per capita membership.[274] There, a local chapter of the Deacons would grow to include "about a tenth of the Negro adult male population," or approximately 900 members, although the organization was deliberately secretive about exact numbers.[275] What is known, however, is that in 1965 there were fifty to sixty chapters across Louisiana, Mississippi and Alabama.[276] In Bogalousa, as elsewhere, the Deacons' job was to protect black people from violence, and they did so by extending violence to anyone who attacked.[277] This capability and willingness to use force to protect blacks provided a deterrent to white terroristic activity.

A prime example of how the Deacons accomplished their task lies in the experience of James Farmer, then head of CORE, a frontline, mainstream civil rights group. Before Farmer left on a trip for Bogalousa, the Federal Bureau of Investigation informed him that he had received a death threat from the Klan. The FBI apparently also informed the state police, who met Farmer at the airport. But at the airport also were representatives of the Bogalousa chapter of the Deacons, who escorted

---

[271] Hamilton Bims, "Deacons for Defense," *Ebony*, Sept. 1965, pp. 25-26; see also Roy Reed, "The Deacons, Too, Ride by Night," *N.Y. Times*, Aug. 15, 1965, Magazine, p. 10.

[272] Bims, supra note 271, pp. 25-26.

[273] *Ibid.*, p. 26. Like the Deacons for Defense and Justice was the Monroe, North Carolina chapter of the NAACP, which acquired firearms and used them to deal with the Ku Klux Klan. Robert F. Williams, *Negroes with Guns*, pp. 42-49, 54-57 (1962). The Deacons for Defense and Justice are to be contrasted with the Black Panther Party for Self Defense. The Black Panther Program included the following statement: "We believe we can end police brutality in our black community by organizing black self-defense groups that are dedicated to defending our black community from racist police oppression and brutality. The Second Amendment to the Constitution of the United States gives a right to bear arms. We therefore believe that all black people should arm themselves for self-defense." "Black Panther Party—Platform and Program," reprinted in Reginald Major, *A Panther Is a Black Cat*, 286 (1971). Yet, the Black Panthers deteriorated into an ineffective group of revolutionaries, at times using arguably criminal means of effectuating their agenda. See generally Gene Marine, *The Black Panthers* (1969); Bobby Seale, *Seize the Time: The Story of the Black Panther Party and Huey P. Newton* (1968).

[274] James Farmer, *Lay Bare the Heart: An Autobiography of the Civil Rights Movement*, p. 287 (1985).

[275] See Bims, supra note 271, p. 26; see also Reed, supra note 268, p. 10.

[276] See Reed, supra note 271, p. 10; see also Bims, supra note 268, p. 26.

[277] Raines, supra note 269, p. 417 (interview with Charles R. Sims, leader of the Bogalousa Deacons); see Bims, supra note 271, p. 26; Reed, supra note 271, pp. 10-11.

Farmer to the town. Farmer stayed with the local head of the Deacons, and the Deacons provided close security throughout the rest of his stay and Farmer's next. Farmer later wrote in his autobiography that he was secure with the Deacons, "in the knowledge that unless a bomb were tossed . . . the Klan could only reach me if they were prepared to swap their lives for mine."[278]

Blacks in the South found the Deacons helpful because they were unable to rely upon police or other legal entities for racial justice. This provided a practical reason for a right to bear arms: In a world in which the legal system was not to be trusted, perhaps the ability of the system's victims to resist might convince the system to restrain itself.

Conclusion: Self-Defense and the Gun Control Question Today

There are interesting parallels between the history of African-Americans and discussion of the Second Amendment. For most of this century, the historiography of the black experience was at the periphery of the historical profession's consciousness, an area of scholarly endeavor populated by those who were either ignored or regarded with suspicion by the mainstream of the academy.[279] Not until after World War II did the insights that could be learned from the history of American race relations begin to have a major influence on the works of constitutional policymakers in courts, legislatures, and administrative bodies. Moreover, it should be stressed that, for a good portion of the twentieth century, the courts found ways to ignore the constitutional demands imposed by the reconstruction amendments.[280]

While discussion of the Second Amendment has been relegated to the margin of academic and judicial constitutional discourse, the realization that there is a racial dimension to the question, and that the right may have had greater and different significance for blacks and others less able

---

[278] Farmer, supra note 274, p. 288.

[279] August Meir & Elliot Rudwick, *J. Franklin Jameson, Carter G. Woodson, and the Foundation of Black Historiography*, 89 Am. Hist. Rev. 1005 (1984).

[280] See, e.g., Schmidt, supra note 198, p. 647 (describing the way in which the Supreme Court failed to uphold the Fifteenth Amendment in the late 19th and early 20th centuries); see also Randall L. Kennedy, *Racial Critiques of Legal Academia*, 102 Harv. L. Rev., pp. 1745, 1753-54 (1989) (discussing the legal academia's willingness to ignore the Reconstruction Amendments in the early 20th century).

to rely on the government's protection, has been even further on the periphery. The history of blacks and the right to bear arms, and the failure of most constitutional scholars and policymakers to seriously examine that history, is in part another instance of the difficulty of integrating the study of the black experience into larger questions of legal and social policy.[281]

Throughout American history, black and white Americans have had radically different experiences with respect to violence and state protection. Perhaps another reason the Second Amendment has not been taken very seriously by the courts and the academy is that for many of those who shape or critique constitutional policy, the state's power and inclination to protect them is a given. But for all too many black Americans, that protection historically has not been available. Nor, for many, is it readily available today. If in the past the state refused to protect black people from the horrors of white lynch mobs, today the state seems powerless in the face of the tragic black-on-black violence that plagues the mean streets of our inner cities, and at times seems blind to instances of unnecessary police brutality visited upon minority populations.[282]

Admittedly, the racial atmosphere in this nation today is better than at any time prior to the passage of the Voting Rights Act of 1965.[283] It must also be stressed, however, that many fear a decline in the quality of that atmosphere.

One cause for concern is the Supreme Court's assault in its 1989 Term on gains of the civil rights movements that had stood for decades.[284]

---

[281] One scholar has criticized the failure of legal scholars with a left perspective "to incorporate the authentic experience of minority communities in America." Jose Bracamonte, *Foreword to Symposium, Minority Critiques of the Critical Legal Studies Movement*, 22 Harv. C.R.-C.L. L. Rev., pp. 297-98 (1982).

[282] The beating of Rodney King on March 3, 1991, by members of the Los Angeles Police Department, captured on tape by a serendipitous amateur photographer, focused attention on the problem of police brutality, though the problem predates and presumably continues beyond the incident. See Tracey Wood and Faye Fiore, "Beating Victim Says He Obeyed Police," *L.A. Times,* Mar. 7, 1991, p. A1.

[283] Pub. L. No. 89-110, 79 Stat. 437 (codified as amended at 42 U.S.C. § 1973 [1988]).

[284] See, e.g., *Patterson v. McLean Credit Union*, 491 U.S. 164 (1989) (urging, sua sponte, not only reconsideration of *Runyon v. McCracy*, 427 U.S. 160 [1976], on the issue of whether the right to contract on a basis equal with whites under Civil Rights Act of 1866 includes the right to be free from discriminatory working conditions, but also overruling Runyon); *Martin v. Wilkes* 490, U.S 755 (1989) (conferring on whites claiming reverse discrimination a continuing right to challenge consent decrees involving affirmative action); *Wards Cove Packing Co. v. Atonio* 490 U.S. 642 (1989) (essentially shifting the burden of proof in employment discrimination cases, such that an employee must go beyond the showing of a disparate impact on a group protected by the statute; also allowing an employer to establish a legitimate business justification as a defense, replacing the standard established in *Griggs v. Duke Power Co.*, 401 U.S. 424 [1971] which required an employer to show

Another is the prominence of former Ku Klux Klan leader David Duke, a member of the Louisiana state legislature and a defeated, but nonetheless major, candidate for the Senate in 1990.[285] In the last several years, two blacks who had entered the "wrong" neighborhood in New York City have been "lynched."[286] Is this a sign of more to come? The answer is not clear, but the question is.

Twice in this nation's history—once following the Revolution, and again after the Civil War—America has held out to blacks the promise of a nation that would live up to its ideology of equality and freedom. Twice the nation has reneged on that promise. The ending of separate but equal under *Brown v. Board* in 1954,[287]—the civil rights movement of the 1960s, culminating in the Civil Rights Act of 1964,[288] the Voting Rights Act of 1965,[289] and the judicial triumphs of the 1960s and early 1970s—all these have held out to blacks in this century that same promise. Yet, given this history, it is not unreasonable to fear that law, politics, and societal mores will swing the pendulum of social progress in a different direction, to the potential detriment of blacks and their rights, property and safety.

The history of blacks, firearms regulations, and the right to bear arms should cause us to ask new questions regarding the Second Amendment. These questions will pose problems both for advocates of stricter gun controls and for those who argue against them. Much of the contemporary

---

that a discriminatory practice was indispensable or essential); *City of Richmond v. J. A. Croson*, 48 U.S. 469 (1989) (subjecting remedial measures involving affirmative action to the same standard of strict scrutiny as in cases of invidious racial discrimination).

[285] See, e.g., Peter Applebome, "Louisiana Tally Is Seen as a Sign of Voter Unrest," *N.Y. Times*, Oct. 8, 1990, p. A1; David Maraniss, "Duke Emerges from Loss Stronger Than Ever," *Wash. Post*, Oct. 8, 1990, p. A1; James M. Perry, "Duke's Strong Run in Louisiana Sends National Politicians a Shocking Message," *Wall St. J.*, Oct. 9, 1990, p. A5. Moreover, as of the time of final editing, Duke had emerged from a field of four major candidates, including a member of Congress and the incumbent governor, to face a former governor in a runoff election. See "Ex Klan Leader in Louisiana Runoff; Primary: David Duke Will Face Former Governor Edwin Edwards, Who Led in Balloting," *L.A. Times*, Oct. 20, 1991, p. A1.

[286] Michael Griffith, "a 23-year-old black man[,] was struck and killed by a car on a Queens highway . . . after being severely beaten twice by 9 to 12 white men who chased him and other black men through the streets of Howard Beach in what the police called a racial attack." Robert D. McFadden, "Black Man Dies After Beating by Whites in Queens," *N.Y. Times*, Dec. 21, 1986, § 1, p. 1. Yesef Hawkins, "[a] 16-year-old black youth[,] was shot to death . . . in an attack by 10 to 30 white teenagers in the Bensonhurst section of Brooklyn. . . ." Ralph Blumenthal, "Black Youth Is Killed by Whites; Brooklyn Attack Is Called Racial," *N.Y. Times*, Aug. 25, 1989, p. A1.

[287] 347 U.S. 483 (1954).

[288] Pub. L. No. 88-352, 78 Stat. 241 (codified as amended at 32 U.S.C. § 2000 [1988]).

[289] Pub. L. No. 89-110, 79 Stat. 437 (codified as amended at 42 U.S.C. § 1973 [1988]).

crime that concerns Americans is in poor black neighborhoods[290] and a case can be made that greater firearms restrictions might alleviate this tragedy. But another, perhaps stronger case can be made that a society with a dismal record of protecting a people has a dubious claim on the right to disarm them. Perhaps a re-examination of this history can lead us to a modern realization of what the Framers of the Second Amendment understood: that it is unwise to place the means of protection totally in the hands of the state, and that self-defense is also a civil right.

---

[290] See, e.g., Silberman, supra note 199, pp. 160-61; Randall L. Kennedy, *McCloskey v. Kemp: Race, Capital Punishment, and the Supreme Court*, 101 Harv. L. Rev. 1388 (1988); Howard A. Palley & Dana A. Robinson, "Black on Black Crime," *Society*, July/Aug. 1988, pp. 5, 59.

Bearing Arms for Self-Defense:
A Human and Civil Right

Roy Innis

The most fundamental of human rights is the right to self-defense. In fact, in nature, self-defense seems to be a sine qua non for any form of life, plant or animal. One of the critical reasons for government is to aid and coordinate the mutual self-defense of the individual and other members of the society. This is the understanding of Hobbes, Locke and Rousseau, the founding fathers of the American Revolution, and numerous other great students of government, before and after them. The role of government in aiding and coordinating mutual self-defense of individuals in society was never intended to be a substitute for the individual's right (and obligation) of self-defense, nor was government constituted to abolish that right of freemen.

The key word in this discussion is freeman, for historically a freeman's right to self-defense has never been abridged. His right to obtain and maintain the implements of self-defense has always been sacred. The mark of a freeman was the wearing of arms; the right was restricted or prohibited for serfs, peasant and slaves.

Young America—before, during and long after the revolutionary war—offers an excellent model for study of the role of the individual and the government in self-defense. In time of peace and tranquility, while the people had delegated to law enforcement officials certain day-to-day responsibilities for law and order, they did not give up their rights nor weapons of self-defense. In time of disorder and crisis, armed ordinary decent citizens actively participated in maintaining law and order—augmenting governmental officials usually charged with those chores. In many parts of the country armed citizens still actively help law enforcement officials bring criminals to justice.

Gun control was never an issue in America until after the Civil War, when black slaves were freed. It was this change in status of the black man, from slave to freeman, that caused racist elements in the country

---

Mr. Innis is national chairman of the New York-based Congress of Racial Equality.

North and South, to agitate for restrictions on guns—ignoring long-standing customs and understanding of the Second Amendment of the U.S. Constitution.

What irony. Most black leaders (as distinct from rank-and-file blacks) are supporters, at least in public, of the gun control—really, prohibition—movement. Do they realize that America's gun control movement sprouted from the soil of Roger B. Taney, the racist chief justice who wrote the infamous *Dred Scott* decision of 1857?

In the early part of the 19th century, Dred Scott, a black slave, had been taken by his owner from Missouri, a slave state, to Illinois, a free state. From there he was taken into the Wisconsin territory, free territory above the 36° 30' latitude of the Missouri Compromise. After living in free territory for a while, he returned with his owner to Missouri.

When his owner died in 1846, Scott sued in the state courts of Missouri for his freedom, on the ground that he had lived in free territory. He won his case, but it was reversed in the Missouri Supreme Court. Scott appealed to the federal courts, since the person he was actually suing, John Sanford, the executor of the estate that owned Scott, lived in New York.

It was in that setting that Chief Justice Taney made his infamous rulings:

1. That black people, whether free or slave, were not citizens of the U.S.; therefore, they had no standing in court.
2. Scott was denied freedom.
3. The Missouri Compromise was ruled unconstitutional.

Well known to most students of race relations is the former attorney general and secretary of the Treasury's pre-civil war dictum that black people "being of an inferior order" had "no right which any white man was bound to respect." Much less known are his equally racist pronouncements denying black people, whether slave or free, specific constitutional protections enjoyed by whites.

In *Dred Scott*, Chief Justice Taney, writing for the court's majority, stated that if blacks were "entitled to the privileges and immunities of citizens. . . . [i]t would give persons of the Negro race, who were recognized as citizens in any one state of the union, the right . . . to keep and carry arms wherever they went. And all of this would be done in the face of the subject race of the same color, both free and slaves, and incvitably producing discontent and insubordination among them, and endangering the peace and safety of the state. . . ."

Although much of Justice Taney's overtly racist legal reasoning was repudiated by events that followed—such as the Civil War and Reconstruction—the subliminal effects were felt throughout that era. In the post-Reconstruction period, when the pendulum swung back to overt racism, Justice Taney's philosophy resurfaced. It was during this period that racial paranoia about black men with guns intensified. It was potent enough to cause the infringement on the Second Amendment to the Constitution's "right . . . to keep and bear arms."

Under natural law, a freeman's right to obtain and maintain the implements of self-defense has always been sacred. This right was restricted or prohibited for serfs, peasants and slaves. Gun control was never an issue in America until after the Civil War when black slaves were freed.

It was this change in the status of the black man, from slave to freeman, that caused racist elements in the country (North and South) to agitate for restrictions on guns—ignoring long-established customs and understanding of the Second Amendment. The specter of a black man with rights of a freeman, bearing arms, was too much for the early heirs of Roger Taney to bear.

The 14th and 15th Amendments to the Constitution, along with the various Reconstruction civil rights acts, prevented gun prohibitionists from making laws that were explicitly racist and that would overtly deny black people the right to bear arms. The end of Reconstruction signaled the return of Taneyism—overtly among the masses and covertly on the Supreme Court. Gun-control legislation of the late 19th and early 20th centuries, enacted at the state and local levels, were implicitly racist in conception. And in operation, those laws invidiously targeted blacks.

With the influx of large numbers of Irish, Italian and Jewish immigrants into the country, gun laws now also targeted whites from the underprivileged classes of immigrants. Eventually these oppressive gun laws were extended to affect all but a privileged few. Throughout the history of New York state's Sullivan law, enacted at the start of the 20th century, mainly the rich and powerful have had easy access to licenses to carry handguns. Some of the notables who have received that privilege include Eleanor Roosevelt, John Lindsay, Donald Trump, Arthur Sulzberger, Joan Rivers and disc jockey Howard Stern.

Of the 27,000 handgun carry permits in New York City, fewer than two percent are issued to blacks—who live and work in high-crime areas and really are in need of protection.

And what of the origins of the National Rifle Association, which is wrongly viewed as a racist organization by the black supporters of gun prohibition? It was inspired and organized by Union Army officers after the Civil War.

Aside from the possible constitutional impermissibility of most restrictive gun laws, let us consider their pragmatic effects on society. In general, those areas in our country with the most strict anti-gun laws have this in common:

1. They are the most crime ridden.
2. They have the highest murder rate.
3. They have the largest number of illegal guns on the streets in the hands of criminals.
4. The widest variety of illegal weapons are available in the black market.
5. The cost of a weapon in that area is more than the cost for the same weapon in areas without rigid gun laws.
6. Criminals, especially those involved in drugs, are able to afford better guns than ordinary people, even better than the police.
7. Criminals are more bold; they ply their trade in an environment that is safer for criminals but unsafe for the unarmed citizens.

The community profile that I have just described fits two cities with the toughest anti-gun laws in America: New York City and Washington, D.C.

Let us now consider the effects of overly restrictive gun legislation on ordinary people—the little people from the middle class and the poorer class. They are the real victims of these laws. Decent people cannot obtain legal gun permits under existing tough anti-gun laws—that allow only the rich, the powerful, the well-connected, and the influential to do so. These law-abiding citizens from the middle and poorer classes live, work, or obtain services in or on the periphery of extremely high crime areas. Many of them are senior citizens, handicapped, women who work at night and come home to single parent households, small business people, and professionals dispensing services critical to the community. These people are the prime victims of the armed criminals that, as a practical matter, cannot be disarmed and if so, cannot be disarmed as easily as the decent law-abiding citizen. Consider the plight of the following group of victims of crime who fought back and were defended by the Congress of Racial Equality:

1. James Bowman, 80 years old, who with a small pistol, confronted two young criminals who had robbed him three months earlier;

2. James Grimes, the subway clerk, who, after many robberies and a gasoline bomb attack on his change booth, armed himself and was able to save his own life while working, by killing one of two armed robbers;

3. Annie Ryan, 82-year-old widow, who saved her own life by shooting a criminal and chasing him out of her house with a pistol—on the same day that her unarmed friend, also an old widow, living less than 15 miles away, was brutally murdered by an intruder;

4. Yvonne Bureau, the so-called "Lady Goetz," who with her girl friend, while driving in Crown Heights, Brooklyn, was set upon by an armed, drug-crazed criminal—who, after being shot by one of the ladies survived, rejoined an accomplice, pursued them, and killed the girl friend;

5. Raphael Lora, the courageous Gypsy cab driver, who, after an epidemic of murders of drivers, armed himself and saved his own life, fighting back against the psychopathic killer who stalked the industry—an action that has so far stopped the slaughter of Gypsy cab drivers, since the criminal was probably wounded.

All of the above ordinary, decent, law-abiding citizens had to arm themselves illegally because they were not from a privileged social class or profession. They were placed on the horns of an immoral dilemma: go to the grave or go to jail. Courageous judges and understanding juries (grand and trial juries) have resolved that dilemma for most of these double victims of unfair, unworkable anti-gun laws and of the criminals who benefit from those laws. Judges and juries acting in the interest of justice and as the conscience of the community have absolved most of them.

Many other good citizens have suffered multi-victimization from criminals, anti-gun laws, and the criminal justice system that sometimes unwittingly aid and abet those criminals. The most celebrated of these is Bernhard Goetz. Although Goetz was absolved of the most serious charges by a trial jury, he was convicted for an illegal gun, and he served many months in jail. Ironically, Austin Weekes, the so-called "Black Bernie Goetz," a misnomer since the Weekes case was first—Goetz should be known as the "white Austin Weekes"—killed a white criminal in the subway with an illegal gun under conditions very similar to Goetz's. Weekes was absolved of all charges (including the illegal gun charge) in the interest of justice.

195

So we have gone full circle. Gun control laws originally designed to disarm blacks evolved into gun control laws that disarmed almost everybody—blacks, whites, Hispanics, and Asians—from the middle and poorer classes. And gun laws that used to be applied racially against blacks are now being applied in a reverse racist way to whites.

Another irony of oppressive gun control laws is that as decent citizens are forced to arm themselves illegally, they are less likely to practice and gain proficiency with their weapon.

The final irony of the gun control issue is the hypocrisy of many anti-gunners. Some of the most vociferous advocates of strict gun control, that strips most decent citizens of the right to bear arms in self-defense, are themselves gun owners—some of them enjoy the privilege of legal "full carry permits." This unabashed selfishness is not as unusual as one might think; some even use illegal guns—à la journalist Carl Rowan.

Gun control laws have not worked to control crime; in fact, they have served to give the criminals an advantage over the unarmed citizen. Anti-gun laws are forcing the law-abiding citizen to risk becoming criminals in order to stay alive. More and more one hears ordinary decent people say "rather tried by 12 than carried by 6." That is an immoral choice forced upon the individual; a violation of one's human and civil rights.

In order to exercise the right of self-defense, one must have the right to legally obtain and use the instruments to do so.

Bearing arms for self-defense *is* a human and a civil right.

The Swiss Report

George S. Patton and Lewis W. Walt

Switzerland epitomizes the concept of a nation of armed citizens. This concept dovetails nicely with the Swiss tradition of neutrality in the many conflicts that have raged in Europe since the Congress of Vienna in 1815 guaranteed Swiss neutrality.

It would be a mistake, however, to assume this neutrality is based on the principle of pacifism. It is, instead, based upon the principle of preparedness. The success of this policy is astounding when one considers the Swiss have no standing army. What it does have though is one of the most highly developed systems of a defensive militia found anywhere in the world.

The following study was written by two of America's premier military veterans, Major General George S. Patton, USA (Ret.) and the late General Lewis W. Walt, USMC (Ret.). First published in March 1983, it is reproduced here with the permission of the Western Goals Foundation.

Switzerland lies landlocked in Western Europe, a small densely populated nation of nearly seven million people. To the west lies France, to the south Italy and to the north and east, Germany and Austria. By modern jet fighter, it is ten minutes from the Warsaw Pact nations of Eastern Europe. Since 1815 Switzerland has remained an inviolate island of peace in the midst of war. Even Adolph Hitler's Wehrmacht, which conquered all of Europe in the early months of World War II, chose not to attack Switzerland despite the face that the small country was in the crossroads of Western Europe.

Switzerland is, of course, neutral, but it was not mere respect for its neutrality which kept the Nazi armies and others before it out of the tiny country. It was the determination of the Swiss people to defend their neutrality and the credibility of their means to do so. That determination remains alive today in the face of weapons of mass destruction. So, too, does the credibility of the means. Within 48 hours, the Swiss can field an army of more than 600,000 men, 100,000 more than the present army of West Germany. Today, it can provide shelter space for 85 percent of its civilian population and as the decade of the 1990s begins will be capable of providing shelter space for the entire population. War supplies, medical

197

supplies and food supplies are meticulously stored in more than 100 kilometers of tunnels. About 4,000 permanent obstacles and barriers and more than 2,000 demolition devices are in place, ready to hamper and block an aggressor's progress. In short, Switzerland is an armed bunker.

Yet, there is *no* standing army, *no* bunker mentality, *no* enormous drain on the Swiss economy, *no* militaristic threat to Europe's oldest and most fiercely independent democracy.

How the Swiss have achieved this credible deterrent to invasion is the subject of this report. The Swiss security system is unique as well as an example of what a democratic nation can accomplish by applying reason and logic to problems which have been realistically and carefully analyzed.

History

Niccolò Machiavelli, the 15th century Italian student of power, remarked of the Swiss, "They are the most armed—and most free people in Europe." Indeed, Switzerland was born in the 13th century out of a desire to be free of domination by the Habsburg family. In 1291 three Swiss cantons signed the Perpetual Covenant which marked the beginning of the Swiss Confederation. In the 1300s, the Swiss fought several wars for independence with Austria and in 1499 Switzerland won its independence from the Holy Roman Empire.

The policy of neutrality originated in 1515 when the Swiss suffered a stunning defeat by the French, but that early neutrality did not save it from an invasion and occupation by the French under Napoleon in 1798. The Congress of Vienna of 1815 restored Swiss independence and guaranteed its neutrality.

Switzerland adopted a new constitution in 1848, modeled somewhat after the American constitution and this was amended in 1874 to increase the federal government's powers in military and court matters, although the cantons (equivalent to American states) generally retain considerably more power than American states.

The Swiss economy today is built around precision manufacturing, chemicals, banking and tourism. It has one of the highest standards of living in the world and the land is crisscrossed by a 3,150-mile railroad network and 30,000 miles of hard-surfaced roads. Three major rivers have their origin in Switzerland—the Rhine, the Rhone and the Po. Most of the population and most of the agriculture are located in the plateau region between the Jura and the Alps. Swiss agriculture can produce only three-fifths of the nation's food supply, a factor carefully weighed in the Swiss security system planning. The nation is greatly dependent on imports for food and most raw materials for its industry, including oil, natural gas and coal.

Since 1815 the Swiss have not fought in a foreign war, yet they have maintained the tradition of a citizen army and rifle and pistol shooting are among the nation's most popular sports with almost every village having a shooting range, over 3,000 ranges in all.

Today Switzerland maintains its neutrality, but practices what it calls solidarity—participating in international humanitarian projects, offering its good offices for the resolution of disputes, and providing technical assistance to Third World countries. The Swiss participate in those international activities and organizations which do not require it to violate its policy of neutrality. Neutrality is central to Swiss thinking and, in fact, is the determining factor in the Swiss security system.

Swiss Strategic Thinking

Divisionnaire Major General Edmund Muller, deputy chief of staff, logistics, summarized Swiss strategic thinking this way:

> Historical experience shows that if a nation is not able to defend itself and to protect its spiritual and material values, it will become, sooner or later, the target of power politics and force. Efforts to defend ourselves against force are therefore still necessary. These efforts must be integrated within a comprehensive security policy expressed in the form of clear guidelines. Our government is convinced that we can successfully undertake peace-keeping efforts in the future only if we can ensure at the same time our own security in a credible way. The security policy of a country is only credible if a realistic evaluation of the threats and a sober estimation of its own possibilities lead to the implementation of a concept capable of inspiring confidence at home and respect abroad.

The words "credible," "respect," "realistic," and "planning" occur over and over in Swiss defense documents and briefings. To a remarkable degree, the Swiss government has approached its problems in a supremely logical manner, setting out basic premises and drawing the correct inferences.

The objectives of the security policy are set forth as follows: (1) preservation of peace in independence; (2) preservation of freedom of action; (3) protection of the population; and (4) defense of the territory.

Each of these objectives has been carefully analyzed and the choice of words is not careless. What the Swiss mean by "peace in independence" is made clear in the following excerpt from a report of the Federal Council to the Federal Assembly:

> The preservation of peace—no matter how much we are interested in it—is not an end in itself. It can neither be separated from the preservation of self-determination nor can one be played off against the other. Our goal is peace in independence; both aspects are therefore of equal importance.

In defining preservation of freedom of action, the Swiss make clear they mean freedom from foreign pressures, which can be achieved only by having available a powerful means of resisting them and freedom from internal pressure generated by illegal means or the use of force.

Having defined their security policy objectives, the Swiss then proceed to examine the threat. In doing so, they include the "state of relative peace" along with indirect war, conventional war, war with weapons of mass destruction, and blackmail.

The following quotations from the same Federal Council report reveal not only the Swiss view of the present threats but also provide an insight in their thinking processes:

> Today, peace does not correspond to the ideal and conditions usually associated with it. The general situation is characterized by continuous confrontations, also in those cases where there is no open employment of force.
>
> The danger of a breach of international agreement is always present. The collective security system envisioned by the Charter of the United Nations has not been allowed to become effective, particularly because of the lack of unanimity among the permanent members of the security council . . . today's state of relative peace is to a great extent due to the fact that the two superpowers neutralize each other. The balance of fear, maintained only by the mutual threat of annihilation, is not stable. It can be jeopardized by

the excessive armaments efforts of one side, by technological breakthroughs as well as by irrational actions . . . under the protection of this relative balance of forces, powers and groups of powers attempt to enlarge their spheres of influence through political, economical, propagandistic and psychological pressures.

Conflicts are increasingly being waged by indirect means, with the goal of influencing, weakening and finally overcoming the opponent through political, psychological and terrorist means . . . this type of warfare takes advantage of the increasing vulnerability of the modern state with its numerous vital facilities (such as power utilities, communication, transportation and information facilities). Those who resort to this kind of warfare, whether they act in the interest of a foreign power, a foreign ideology or out of anarchistic motives, take advantage of the frictions existing within a society, as well as of all forms of political and social malaise of certain population groups. By attempting to break up the existing liberal order through the paralysis of the public institutions, facilities and the democratic processes by way of defamation, intimidation and the employment of force, they hope to be able to achieve their goals.

The possibility of blackmail exists at each level of conflict, taking advantage of the opponent's fear of the threatened actions. Blackmail acquires a particular dimension if it is exercised by nuclear powers. The authorities of the state against which the blackmail is directed could be put under intense public pressure and be forced to make decisions of such a magnitude as to be without historical parallel . . . the four levels of conflict are characterized by those methods and means which would, at each level, be predominantly employed. During large confrontations, the parties to the conflict will try to combine these methods and means acting simultaneously in a direct and indirect manner.

Thus, the Swiss take a hard look at the world and indulge in no escapist thinking. They recognize that they could become the victim of blackmail, of subversion, of a conventional or a nuclear attack. Yet they also realize that because of their small size, they are not likely to be a primary target and therefore cannot justify a continued state of mobilization.

The Swiss see the military as only one component of a spectrum of strategic means to achieve their security objectives. Their foreign policy initiatives are a strategic means to defend their policy of armed neutrality, to provide access to raw materials and markets to exports. Social policy is a strategic means to provide the stability necessary to withstand threats. Economic policy is a strategic means of insuring that in times of crisis or war, the Swiss people can continue to exist. The Swiss government has actually formed what it calls a war economy organization with the specific goals of planning for self-sufficiency in time of war. In this regard, Swiss citizens are required to maintain in their homes a two-months' supply of food; industrialists and importers are required to maintain war stocks of raw materials and food. Civil defense is seen as the strategic means of insuring survival of the population. In short, the Swiss approach the problem of security with a totally integrated methodology that involves the entire nation.

The Militia System

The purpose of the military forces of Switzerland are two-fold: (1) to deter war by the principle of dissuasion; and (2) if deterrence fails, to defend the territory and the population.

"Dissuasion is a strategic posture which should persuade a potential aggressor to avoid an armed conflict, by convincing him of the disproportion existing between the advantages gained from an attack on the country and the risks entailed. The risks which a potential aggressor must be made to perceive consist in the loss of prestige, military forces, war-potential and time, as well as in running counter to his ideological, political and economic interests."

The Swiss have no illusions about their ability to defeat a major military power. They could not have defeated the Nazi army which for a time considered invading Switzerland. They mobilized, however, and made it clear beyond a shadow of a doubt that if the Nazi army invaded, it would be fiercely resisted and that the tunnels and passes into Italy would be destroyed. In a classic example of dissuasion at work, Hitler's general staff recommended against an invasion on the grounds that the costs would be disproportionate to the gains.

The Swiss military forces are composed almost entirely of the militia. Only 800 out of 50,000 officers are professionals. They, and the recruits which happen to be training at any given time, are the only people in Switzerland on "active duty."

The Swiss militia system is unique and is not comparable to the present Reserve and Guard forces in the United States. The basis for conscription is the constitution, which mandates military service for every Swiss male from age 20 to 50 (55 in the case of officers). There are no exceptions. Conscientious objectors are given a choice between army non-combat units and jail. Those physically unfit for military duty but employable are required to pay a tax. Women are not included in the compulsory military service system, but small numbers of them are accepted on a volunteer basis for non-combatant positions.

The universality of the Swiss system provides several advantages. It is fair and therefore enjoys popular support. In the 1970s a national referendum was held on the question of providing alternative service to conscientious objectors. The Swiss people defeated it by an overwhelming majority.

A second advantage is that the Swiss army does not have to operate a vocational school system, training unqualified people in special skills which they take, as soon as their enlistment is completed, into the civilian market. The Swiss system operates in reverse. The Swiss army, because everyone is obligated, can choose those people trained in their civilian roles for the military jobs which match their specialty. In the Swiss system, the burden of specialized training is on the civilian sector.

A third advantage is that every male, age 20 to 50, who is an elected official or civil servant in the government at all levels is also a member of the Swiss army. This helps prevent the jealousy and hostility that armies sometimes confront in competing with other government services for their share of the public resources. The lack of separation between the army, the people, and the government is one of the unique and valuable characteristics of the Swiss system.

A fourth advantage is that Switzerland does not have a high proportion of its defense dollars going to personnel costs. There are no military retirement systems (the 800 full-time officers are included in the civil service pension system), no veterans benefits, no massive payroll of a large standing army. There is a medical insurance program to take care of injuries or death while serving on active duty. Consequently, 50 percent of all Swiss defense appropriations can be directed toward the acquisition of weapons and equipment.

At the age of 19, young men are given physical and mental tests in preparation for military service. By this age, most young men in Switzerland have already chosen their career paths and having done so permit the army to channel them into the proper slots. Some consideration is given to the recruit's preference and to his locale, but the army makes the final decision according to its own needs.

At age 20, recruits report for 17 weeks of training. The Swiss do not operate separate training facilities for recruits and then others for military specialties. Each training camp handles both the recruit's basic training and his military specialty. In other words, a young man destined for the medics report directly to a medical training company; an infantryman to an infantry training camp.

At the end of the training cycle, the recruit, now a member of a militia unit with which he will stay in most cases for the duration of his obligation, returns home. He carries with him his rifle, an allotment of ammunition, uniforms, military pack, and CBR mask. He is responsible for the maintenance of this equipment and is inspected annually. Once a year he is also required to qualify with his personal weapon on a rifle range or face an additional three days of training. Once a year, he will report for three weeks of military training in a rugged field exercise set up as a problem the type of which his particular unit would face.

The Swiss army is organized into four army corps. Each corps controls three divisions. The Field Army Corps are composed of two Infantry Divisions and one Mechanized Division. The Mountain Corps has three Mountain Divisions. In addition, each Field Army Corps has some separate Border Defense Brigades and the Mountain Corps, separate Fortress Brigades.

These 12 divisions plus the Air Defense Command constitute the elite. Young men aged 20 to 32 serve in these divisions. Men of the "Landwehr," 33 to 42 years old, are found in the separate brigades. Those in the "Landsturm," 43 to 50 years old, serve in the Territorial Forces. Thus, the duties of the militiaman are adjusted as his physical capabilities change with age.

These elite field forces with the eight youngest classes of soldiers plus all Commissioned Officers and Non-Commissioned Officers are mobilized for three weeks of training each year. "Landwehr" forces train for two weeks every two years, and "Landsturm" units for one week every four years.

All officers are chosen from the ranks. A young man chosen to become an officer while he was a private must attend a one-month non-commissioned officers school. If he is successful, the soldier is promoted to corporal and, to pay off his new rank, he must serve as a group leader for a period of 17 weeks immediately following recruit school.

The requisite number of corporals to meet requirements are sent to officer training schools for four months. After successful completion of this school, he is promoted to lieutenant. This is followed by service as a platoon leader with another recruit training unit. After five years in grade, he will be promoted to first lieutenant.

After two years as a first lieutenant, he is eligible for promotion to captain. To be promoted to captain, a first lieutenant has to attend a three-week weapons school, a four-week tactical school and serve as company commander in a recruit training cycle. As a captain, he will command and administer a company.

After eight years, a captain can get promoted to major, and then, if he completes special training successfully, he may become a battalion commander. Subsequent promotions to lieutenant colonel after seven years as major and to colonel two years later depends upon individual ability and vacancies. The highest rank a militia officer may attain is that of brigade commander. Divisions and Army Corps are commanded by professional officers.

A first lieutenant or captain who desires to become a career officer has to attend a series of branch schools and then attend a one-year course at the Military Division of the Federal Institute of Technology in Zurich. To be eligible for selection as a member of the Corps of Instructors, an officer must have a civilian profession.

In peace time, the Swiss army has no supreme commander. The Federal Council leads the army. The general chief of staff is the "primus inter pares" of the army staff. In case of war mobilization, the Parliament would select a four-star general as supreme commander.

The Swiss Air Force is composed of one Air Force, one Airbase and one Anti-Aircraft Brigade. All combat aircraft are ready for use and are stored in underground bases containing fuel, ammunition, spare parts and repair shops. There is an automatic surveillance and guidance system to help engage the air defense and ground attack armaments.

The number of main weapons in the Swiss army is as follows:

350 aircraft
800 tanks
1,200 armored personnel carriers
900 artillery guns (self-propelled or mobile)
300 artillery tubes in fortresses
2,000 mobile anti-tank guns
300 anti-tank guns in bunkers

2,000 anti-aircraft guns
3,000 anti-tank guided missile systems
20,000 bazookas

Thousands of grenade launchers and millions of mines are also on hand as well as 30,000 army-owned special vehicles and 50,000 civilian-owned vehicles tagged for mobilization. Each owner knows precisely where to bring his vehicle in case of mobilization.

These and other war supplies are stored in arsenals and underground facilities all over the country. They are stored by unit. A military unit, for example, will draw the same equipment from the same arsenal each year for its annual training exercise so that it becomes familiar with it, with its location, and can assist the civilian maintenance personnel in spotting problems.

The Swiss logistics system is a work of genius and is tailored to the requirements of a militia army in a neutral country which, if it fights, cannot count on allies for re-supply or assistance.

Of 17,000 civil servants in the Ministry of Defense, 10,500 are in logistics. In 1981 the budget was 800 million Swiss francs and it maintains 5,500 buildings and installations, 600 war bases, 170 maintenance facilities, and more than 100 kilometers of underground facilities.

These underground facilities not only contain stores of ammunition and other war supplies, but also underground repair facilities for tanks, artillery pieces, electronics equipment and vehicles. The value of the Swiss army inventory is 12.8 billion Swiss francs.

The Swiss army maintains 40 military hospitals, ten of them underground—completely equipped, spotless and ready. They are used only for training purposes. When the Swiss purchase a weapons system from abroad, they purchase enough spare parts for both the life of the system and for war reserves. This is to insure continuity of use in war even though Switzerland is cut off from the original source of supply.

They also practice the principle of commonality so that military, civil defense, and civil police equipment are the same. An example of Swiss ingenuity applied to logistics is the storage of perishable medical supplies for war-time use. These supplies are obtained from pharmaceutical companies, stored, and then at the appropriate time, returned to the pharmaceuticals for sale in exchange for fresh supplies for storage. By arrangement, the Swiss government would actually pay for the supplies only in the event of their consumption during a war.

206

Military Doctrine

Once mobilized, the Swiss army would fight as a conventional force. Swiss military doctrine calls for meeting the aggressor at the borders and waging total war. This is a departure from earlier doctrine which in World War II called for abandoning the plateau area for the mountain fortresses.

In the event of mobilization, the 4,000 permanent obstacles and barriers would be activated and the more than 2,000 demolition devices already built into key bridges and tunnels would be set off. Industrial machines would be disabled; water levels in the more than 900 dams lowered; fuel tanks burned.

The Swiss terrain—a hilly plateau region between two mountain ranges—would necessarily channelize the aggressor's attacks. These obvious avenues of approach are heavily fortified and would be defended from built-in positions and by mobile forces of the three Army Corps backed up by the Air Force. The Swiss plan is to make every inch gained by the enemy a bloody and costly gain. In the event main units of the army are destroyed, Swiss doctrine calls for continued passive and active resistance by means of guerrilla warfare.

This combination of powerful resistance by conventional forces, continued resistance by guerrillas, and the self-destruction of Switzerland's industrial, communications and transportation networks constitutes the strategy of dissuasion. The message to the potential aggressor is clear: after a bloody, expensive, time-consuming war, he will have gained nothing of value. He will be faced with occupation of a hostile area, denuded of economic or transportation value, and continued resistance by a determined and armed population.

The armed population is no bluff. Swiss militiamen are not required to turn in their weapons upon completion of their obligation. It is said that every Swiss home contains at least three weapons, for not only is there the militia system, but there is a long tradition of civilian ownership of firearms and, as pointed out before, rifle and pistol shooting are virtually the national sports of Switzerland. There are few restrictions on the Swiss purchase, ownership or carrying, of firearms. An armed occupation force would indeed be literally faced with the prospect of a Swiss rifleman behind every tree.

The Territorial Service

A unique component of the Swiss army is the Territorial Service. It has no equivalent in the United States and so deserves special attention in this report.

Within the army itself, the Territorial Service operates as logistical units, but it does much more and is the main link between the army and the civilian sector. It is composed of those men in the "Landsturm" who are 43 to 50 years of age as well as some younger men assigned to it for Air Raid Rescue Battalions.

The duties of the Territorial Service can be summarized as follows: (1) It has the mission of providing warning services to both the army and the civilian population in case of danger from air, atomic, biological and chemical weapons as well as dam bursts; (2) It is responsible for coordinating the lowering of the water level of hydroelectric reservoirs and for other measures concerning the electrical supply system; (3) It has the mission of caring for internees, prisoners of war and refugees; (4) It provides military police to assist civilian authorities when necessary; (5) It is responsible for the military economy service—to supply all the goods needed by the army from the civilian sector and to handle the dismantling or destruction of civilian economic assets that could be used by the enemy; and (6) It is charged with protecting important and vital installations.

This Territorial Service is designed for war, but portions of it can be mobilized in peacetime to assist civilian authorities with non-military catastrophes.

Structurally, the Territorial Service is designed to parallel the Swiss civil government structure. The basic civilian unit of the Swiss Confederation is the canton. Some of the lager cantons are divided into districts. Cantons are grouped together to form Territorial Zones.

At the level of a district (a portion of a canton) there is a District Civil Staff and a Territorial Regional Staff; the Territorial Service equivalent of the canton is called a Territorial Circle. Here again, the military staff works with the civil staff. At the Territorial Zone level (groups of cantons), there are also parallel civilian and military staffs.

To make this relationship clearer, we might imagine a United States military service which had a command structure at the level of the federal government, at the level of federal regions, at the state levels, and at the district levels within the states with the missions of providing domestic intelligence, security for key installations, control of the economy in time of war, and assistance to civilian authorities in handling disasters and civil disturbances. There is, of course, no such organization in the United States.

The Swiss have not only clearly defined the missions of the Territorial Service but also the rules under which it operates. For example, the needs of the army take precedence over the needs of the civil sector. The Territorial Service can assist the civil sector only on the request of civilian authorities and, even then, authority and responsibility for civilians remain with the civil authorities. In other words, in the event of a catastrophe, the Territorial Service is not authorized to step in and take over operations, but only to provide assistance to civil authorities under their direction.

On the other hand, in the event of war, the Territorial Service's first obligation is to the army and under those circumstances it would override, if necessary, the civil authorities in the event of a conflict of interests. It is also the Territorial Service which provides the manpower earmarked for use by civil defense.

Civil Defense

Some critics of the Swiss system have expressed the belief that the possession of nuclear weapons has made the strategy of dissuasion obsolete. These are, to be sure, those critics who view nuclear war as an offense for which there is no defense.

The Swiss do not agree. Recalling one of their strategic objectives as protection of the civilian population, the Swiss government has realistically assessed that objective in light of nuclear, chemical and biological warfare. Their answer was to embark on an extensive civil defense program with the idea of accomplishing two of their strategic objectives—protection of the population and maintaining freedom of action. They reason that an extensive and useable civil defense program will give the Swiss government the means to withstand nuclear blackmail, thus preserving freedom of action.

Hans Mumenthaler, director of the Federal Office of Civil Defense, put it this way:

Lack of protection (for the civilian population) means an impairment of our freedom of decision and lacking freedom of decision is rightly felt as an unfree condition.

The latest Swiss laws pertaining to civil defense were revised in 1978 and they have made remarkable progress. To date, the Swiss have shelter space for 85 percent of the population and by 1990 planned to have 100 percent of the population covered. In many cases, there are two shelter spaces per person—one at the place of work and one at home.

Swiss law requires compulsory participation in civil defense for all males aged 20 to 60 with exemption only for military service. Consequently, most of the civil defense personnel are over 50. There is a mandatory five-day introductory course and two days of annual training. Swiss officials believe this is not sufficient and, even though supervisors train more extensively, they would like to see the training schedule expanded for everyone.

The law requires that communities have full responsibility for enforcing federal and cantonal civil defense regulations. Each family is required to provide a shelter at home and all new construction, even of commercial buildings, must provide shelters built to federal specifications. The confederation subsidizes the construction of public shelters, but not private ones.

Private shelters are required to withstand one atmosphere of overpressure while public shelters are built to withstand three atmospheres (one atmosphere equals ten tons per square meter). In other words, the Swiss opted for blast shelters that are rather simply shelters adequate for protection against fallout. A shelter built to withstand three atmospheres of overpressure could theoretically provide protection for people within nine-tenths of a mile from ground zero with a one-megaton explosion.

Public shelters are equipped with independent water, air filtration, communications, food and medical supplies and private citizens are required to stock food for two week's duration.

The Swiss have spent, since 1970, five billion Swiss francs on civil defense and are currently spending at the rate of 210 million Swiss francs annually. Mumenthaler says this is a ratio of about $1 for every $8 spent on defense. He estimates that for the United States to have reached the same level of protection would have required the expenditure of $85 billion.

Public support for civil defense is widespread. Mumenthaler explains, "We are mountain people and we are used to living with danger—but we are also used to preparing for it."

Several key decisions were made in approaching the problem of civil defense. One was to discard the idea of evacuation. Not only are warning times for Switzerland practically nil, but Swiss authorities reasoned the

210

country is too small for evacuation to be feasible. Evacuees would hinder other military operations and would likely be no safer. Therefore, the Swiss opted for "vertical as opposed to horizontal protection." This dictated the construction of blast-proof shelters.

Another was the adoption of the principle that every inhabitant must have an equal chance of survival. The Swiss seem to be meticulous about the principle of equal sharing of both responsibilities and privileges. The first obligation of every Swiss citizen is to their country.

Because of the proximity to likely opponents, the Swiss have adopted the strategy of ordering people into the shelters as soon as political or military tension reaches a critical level. From that point on, only key workers would leave the shelters until such time as there was an actual attack or the situation became less tense.

Finally, the Swiss made a basic decision to separate civil defense from the military operations. The office of civil defense operates under the Minister of Justice and Federal Police. While some 30,000 troops from the Territorial Service would be made available to civil defense, primarily for fire-fighting and rescue work, it is not a fighting organization nor does it replace normal civilian rescue and emergency aid organizations during peacetime. It can be mobilized for peacetime rescue work, but this is clearly a secondary mission.

Summary

Switzerland, a small country with limited resources, has conceptualized, planned and implemented a rational security policy which provides maximum effect with minimum expenditures. The militia system, being both universal and a part of the constitution, has wide public acceptance. It allows mobilization of a large army without the draining costs of a large professional army. The personnel savings have been invested in redoubts, barriers, equipment, storage facilities, hospitals and weapons.

To a remarkable degree, the Swiss require private sector participation in the defense effort. These private contributions are estimated to equal the annual government expenditures. By integrating their security policy to include foreign policy, social policy, defense, civil defense and economic measures, the Swiss have, in effect, oriented their entire public effort toward the end of security for their nation and their people.

The Swiss General Defense system provides a high dissuasive value and credibility to this small, neutral country in the heart of Europe. In case of war, Switzerland would not attract the more powerful nations who might consider Switzerland to be a military vacuum. On the contrary, Switzerland can activate the densest defense system—on the ground and in the air on short notice—in Western Europe.

Thanks to Civil Defense as well as intricate economic preparedness, there is a high degree of survivability even in a modern war of long duration. The most important factor remains that the overwhelming majority of the Swiss has a strong will to defend the country against any aggressor. They are prepared to fight and will fight whenever and whomever necessary.

The Dutch-American Guerrillas
Of the American Revolution

William Marina

Guerrilla warfare is thought by many to be a circumstance of the latter half of the twentieth century.

This is an erroneous conception. The art and strategy of guerrilla warfare have been with mankind for a large portion of its history. Ancient Egypt and China both have recorded techniques of guerrilla warfare. Guerrilla techniques are recorded in the Bible and are described, sometimes at length, by many ancient historians such as Polybius, Appius, Plutarch, Flavius Josephus, Herodotus and Tacitus.

Guerrilla warfare played an important role in our own revolutionary war with England. Countless small encounters between American colonists, using their own personal arms, and bands of English soldiers or Tories occurred throughout our War of Independence.

These brought home the point to King George and his soldiers that his rebellious colonists were armed to the teeth, and made the job of quelling the rebellion highly costly and very unlikely to succeed.

Professor William Marina, Florida Atlantic University, Boca Raton, Florida, is a leading advocate of the school of thought that considers the American Revolution as a classic example of a successful guerrilla war. He has written an insightful essay on part of the guerrilla struggle against the British here in colonial America.

This work was first published in Christianity & Civilization, *Vol. 2, The Theology of Christian Resistance, Geneva Divinity School Press, Tyler, Texas, 1983. Reprinted with permission.*

Until recently, few historians had analyzed the American Revolution from the perspective of what in the twentieth century has come to be known as "revolutionary warfare." The military history of the Revolution was usually separated from the political, social, or economic history of the War, and dealt mostly with battles between traditionally organized armies. John Shy, whose essay "The American Revolution: The Military

213

Conflict Considered As a Revolutionary War"[1] is recognized as a path-breaking study in this area, later acknowledged that the piece emerged out of some contract work which he did for the Pentagon in 1965 during the Vietnam War, having to do with "Isolating the Guerrilla" from his civilian support. "Skeptical of the project as a whole," he confessed, "I justified taking its modest stipend by thinking that the American Revolutionary War had a few lessons for our own time."[2]

In terms of revolutionary warfare, however, much of his study had to do with what is usually considered "partisan," or "irregular," warfare, rather than what is often described as "guerrilla war." In contrast to regular armies fighting each other from essentially fixed lines, irregular warfare involves skirmishes, sometimes behind enemy lines, by small army or militia units. Continued operations by such formally organized regular units indicate that the country is far from under the control of, or pacified by, the invader. On the other hand, in a technical sense guerrilla warfare is revolutionary war at its most basic level. The occupying forces are enough in control of the area that local guerrillas fight as, in effect, part-time soldiers, usually attacking by surprise at night, and then resuming their civilian occupations during the day.

In a sense, therefore, theories of revolutionary war, or counter-insurgency, are really the opposite sides of the same coin. Once a country has been occupied and its regular forces defeated, an insurgency begins with the initiation of guerrilla warfare. While this may continue in some areas, as the enemy is weakened in others, a shift to irregular warfare may be undertaken, with, finally the emergence of a regular army to face the occupying forces in the field. Militarily, counter-insurgency means smashing the regular army, mopping up any attempts at irregular warfare by small units, and the restoration of order by eliminating the local guerrillas through isolating them from the rest of the population.

If this rough scenario, outlined in numerous books on revolutionary warfare, has any validity, then despite the many traditional military books to the contrary, *the British were never anywhere near "victory" in the American Revolution.* The main American Army—there were at times several others also—under George Washington was never smashed. After his defeats in New York during 1776, "the Old Fox" withdrew into the hills in New Jersey from which in any emergency he could have thrown

---

[1] In Stephen G. Kurtz and John H. Hutson, eds., Essays on the American Revolution, 1973.
[2] John Shy, A People Numerous and Armed, 1976, p. 193.

his limited forces along a perimeter stretching from Boston to Philadelphia.[3] Far from being overly cautious, with even the slightest hint of advantage, Washington repeatedly engaged the British forces. When the British tried a strategy of extending a line of garrisons into the interior, much as the United States tried in Vietnam, he beat them so badly with a surprise attack on Trenton that they were dissuaded from any further pursuit of that tactic.[4]

Every time the British ventured into the interior, as Tom Paine predicted, they lost an army.[5] This was true at Saratoga, where militia units, coming from as far away as New England, attacked as irregulars, and then meshed together into an army which resulted in the surrender of General Burgoyne. Certainly the French fleet offshore and the American and French forces surrounding him were significant factors in Lord Cornwallis's decision to surrender, but we must not forget that his army had been severely weakened from numerous encounters with regular army and partisan forces. Far from liberating the interior of the Carolinas, he found himself losing men, and leaving behind war materials, as he drove to reach the coast for an attempted evacuation. Even in the case of Philadelphia, the British had abandoned it because, despite the use of considerable manpower, it was simply too difficult to keep it supplied in the face of constant harassment by militia.

In short, *the British were simply never in control of very much of North America.* During the period when their fleet was transferring the army from Boston to New York, in the face of Washington's artillery on the heights above the former, there were *no* British in the colonies. Except for relatively short periods, from 1776 until 1781, the British, on any continuing basis, controlled little more than the city of New York.

Given these circumstances, there was really very little opportunity, or need, for the Americans to organize, or attempt to sustain, a classic guerrilla insurgency. On the other hand, after the failure at a negotiated peace during early 1778, the British began to develop the outlines of a pacification plan.

One way to examine the course of the war and the effectiveness of British strategy, especially with respect to pacification, is to study its effect in a small area. That is, after all, what the English and Hessian

---

[3] Dave R. Palmer, *The Way of the Fox: American Strategy in the War for America 1775-1783*, 1974.

[4] Page Smith, *A People's History of the American Revolution*, 1976.

[5] Cited in James W. Pohl, "The American Revolution and the Vietnamese War: Pertinent Military Analogies," *The History Teacher* 7 (February 1974).

215

commanders seemed to be asking for, a single county that could be pacified, and from which, like a row of dominoes, they could work out in various directions, until a whole state, and then others, were secured.

New Jersey: "The Middle Ground"

The British never entertained much hope that New England would be an initial area for pacification. Connecticut, for example, had only six percent Loyalists, and no British army ventured into the New England countryside after the losses at Lexington and Concord. Late in the war, it was in the South that the British sought to establish the pacification program, but there, too, the image of a vast reservoir of Loyalists in the interior, waiting to be liberated, proved illusory. We noted above the partisan attacks on Cornwallis, so incessant that the British soldiers labelled the area around Charlotte, North Carolina, "the hornet's nest."

The middle area, however, was always supposedly the most vulnerable. Inhabited by more minority groups, General Burgoyne's planned march and occupation of this area would have split the New England states off from the South. Even if this notion had not been held by the British, they had to start somewhere, if the pacification program was ever to get underway. Since they held New York City from mid-1776 until the end of the war, what better place to begin, working out from that secure area, not toward Connecticut, but to the west and south?

New Jersey, which has been called "the cockpit of the Revolution," was the natural place to begin. In this "neutral ground" the two sides contended for the duration of the war. The struggle to control this area was evident in 1776, long before any formal British commitment to a pacification program.

If ever there was a location where the British had "time," that precious commodity for which the counter-insurgency expert is always asking, it was in New Jersey. In those areas close to New York City, it would be difficult for American partisan units to operate, if at all. Instead, for five years, the major theme would be the classic confrontation of American guerrilla forces opposing whatever British and Loyalist units invaded the area. Finally, any pacification program would apparently be aided by the fact that the area contained numerous Dutch settlers, one of those minorities which, as William Nelson has noted, was constituted of certain segments susceptible to Toryism.[6]

Unfortunately, we lack detailed studies of local areas during the years of the Revolution. Fortunately, however, what Shy has called "the only intensive study made of a single community during this period," is of Bergen County, New Jersey, the area around Paramus, on the Jersey side of where the George Washington Bridge now crosses the Hudson River. Thus, the only area of which we have an "intensive study," turns out to be one of the few areas with any potential for examining the American Revolution for examples of classical guerrilla warfare, with the British in virtual control of the area for an extended period of time.

Curiously, Shy made no real use of this study in his own essay, remarking that from its data, "it is apparent that the local and bloody battles between rebel and Loyal militia were related to the prewar animosities between ethnic groups, political rivals, churches, and even neighbors."[7] The work in question is Adrian C. Leiby's *The Revolutionary War in the Hackensack Valley: The Jersey Dutch and the Neutral Ground, 1775-1783*,[8] which Shy in both versions of his essay mistakenly cites as *The Hackensack Valley in the American Revolutionary War*.[9]

In what follows, we hope to demonstrate, contrary to Shy's implication, that there is an enormous amount of data in Leiby's work relevant to the study of revolutionary warfare and how that whole process develops over time. This is true in a strictly military sense, but, even if that were not the case, Shy's comment suggests that internal struggles between the local population involving ethnicity, politics, religion, and neighbors, is somehow not related to revolutionary warfare. But, if anything, the opposite is true! The struggle in Vietnam, for example, involved the Vietnamese divided against each other around such issues as ethnicity, politics, and religion, long before the Americans made the scene.

What this really suggests is how truly difficult a task the American revolutionary forces in this area faced. Divided by various issues, and with a considerable Loyalist population, the revolutionaries were also confronted by large British and Hessian forces. Any effective operations

---

[6] William Nelson, *The American Tory*, 1967.

[7] Shy, *People*, p. 206.

[8] 1962.

[9] See, for example, Shy, *People*, p. 286.

against the British and their Loyalist allies could only be mounted after the revolutionaries had consolidated their own forces. This brings us to an area which most theorists of the sociology of revolution have regarded as crucial: the winning over and commitment, or at the very least acquiescence, of those who would, in many respects, wish to remain neutral. Often they may want the program of the revolutionists, but as classic examples of what economists call "the free rider," they do not wish to involve themselves needlessly in a risk to achieve that goal.

The purpose of this essay is not a critique of Shy's work, but it is clear that military historians have tended to ignore, or touch lightly, upon the fact that *revolutionary warfare is primarily a question of psychology and politics, often including ideology.* But all great theoreticians of revolutionary war have recognized that it is a *struggle over legitimacy.* One of us has dealt with this question in some detail elsewhere,[10] and, as we shall see, that theme underlies much of the activities of the Americans in Leiby's description of the war in the Hackensack Valley. With these preliminary comments about revolutionary warfare in mind, let us examine Leiby's study for any illumination it might offer toward understanding this phenomenon as one aspect of the American Revolution.

The Patriot Militiaman

Leiby's characterization of "the patriot militiaman" who "farmed during the day and did sentinel duty at night" is almost a classic description of the guerrilla. In the "middle" actually, rather than "neutral," ground the battle raged back and forth, and if the British came often to forage among the inhabitants of that rich farm area, so too at times did the Americans.[11]

To understand what was to occur there during the Revolution we must go back a few years earlier. The Dutch communities in that whole area had been deeply split by a schism, and greatly affected by the Great Awakening of the 1740s, which had taken place up and down the colonies, also influencing other denominations in a similar fashion. On one side was the smaller "conferentie" which still held to a strong link

---

[10] *William Marina, "The American Revolution and the Minority Myth," Modern Age* 20 (Summer 1976), and Marina, "Revolution and Social Change: The American Revolution As a People's War," *Literature of Liberty* 1 (Summer 1978).

[11] Leiby, *War*, p. viii.

back to Amsterdam, and had a "violent hatred for all things American." From this group were to come the *Dutch Tories*. The other, and much larger group was the "coetus," which sought much lesser ties with Amsterdam, and much influenced by the Great Awakening, hoped to institute a more personal religion on a more than Sunday basis, along with a more democratic church polity. It has been called "the American party," and from it came the *Dutch Whigs* who were to bear the brunt of the militia struggle for the area.[12]

The Dutch who formed the backbone of the patriotic cause were members of the Dutch Reformed Church, sharing the democratic church polity, essentially congregational, of the Presbyterians, who so angered the British, and whose churches as rebel meeting houses bore the brunt of many of their raids. Of the New York Dutch, the Loyalist historian Thomas Jones wrote, "The Presbyterian party was in possession [of the Reformed church] and . . . their leaders were nearly all on the American side, [so the British] took possession of their edifices as rebel property." One British policymaker sent to America put the matter succinctly: "When the war is over, there must be a great reform established, . . . for, . . . Presbyterianism is really at the bottom of this whole conspiracy, has supplied it with vigor, and will never rest till something is decided upon it."[13]

These prosperous Dutch farmers were hardly radicals, but a few of them were from the beginning quite militant in defense of American rights. Early in 1775 New Jersey was one of those states that made the transition from Royal to revolutionary government "without the firing of a gun," as the Provincial Congress replaced the Provincial Assembly, the Bergen County delegates to the meeting of May 23, 1775, having been selected by the local Committee of Correspondence. The Bergen County resolutions of May 12 were typical of those throughout the colonies in the aftermath of Lexington and Concord. They called for a union of the inhabitants and freeholders to insure safety and prevent a "State of Anarchy and Confusion" which might accompany the "present Struggle for our Liberty, unless the proper Steps are taken to preserve Regularity and Unanimity among us," and were circulated in both English and Dutch. The Provincial Congress took over the functions of government, including taxation, and established a number of militia companies.

---

[12] *Ibid.*, p. 20.
[13] *Idem.*

But the fluid attitudes during this interim period before the first real battles of the war were obvious in the elections in late September 1775. A more moderate group of men was elected which still included some of the earlier selectees of the patriot committees from some sections of New Jersey, more cautious moderates, and even a few who would later become Loyalists. Leiby attributes this to a decline of peak enthusiasm after Concord, but it more likely represents the differences between a cautious electorate and a more committed Committee of Correspondence. Bergen County was one of those areas where the moderates scored most heavily. But what this demonstrated, more than anything else, was *the American commitment to legal and representative procedures*, for we find no "rump" trying to manipulate the population.[14]

As American defense measures got underway, Leiby tells us that one "Robert Erskine had evidently enlisted a company of soldiers for the Jersey Line [of the Continental army] from the workers at the ironworks, and outfitted them at his own expense." On the other hand, "Few Jersey Dutchmen in the Hackensack Valley enlisted in the Continental army, and of the few who did, most enlisted late in the war." A few of these men, who came from among the laborers or artisans, fought with the army in the South. But, speculates Leiby, "Perhaps most Jersey Dutchmen were too well settled and prosperous to be professional soldiers; perhaps they were not sufficiently exercised about the war when it began. As it turned out, they may well have been more useful as militiamen in the neutral ground than they would have been in the regular army."[15] The most accurate appraisal is that *the Jersey Dutch Whig majority was solidly in favor of defending American rights.* As an organized militia they had no intention of attacking the British, but hoped that the problems separating the two parties could be worked out short of war.

The battles in and around New York City in the last part of 1776 were indicative of the recognition that war was reality. We might recall, it was the election of the new delegation from New Jersey arriving in Philadelphia late in June, that turned the tide for independence. The American defeat of late 1776 made Bergen County a refuge for many patriots. Washington had hoped to set up a hospital in Orange County, New York, just north of Bergen, but his chief medical officer reported that no homes were available because of all the refugees, and it would be impossible

---

[14] *Ibid.*, p. 83.
[15] *Ibid.*, pp. 28-29.

short of evicting some other persons. What is glimpsed here is the patriot concern for the inhabitants, which was not to be demonstrated by the British.

The New Tactic: Foraging

As the British advanced, Washington this time ordered the potential forage supplies destroyed, as had not been done in New York, so that "not a blade should remain" for British use. Nathanael Greene was sent to convince the people to do so, or do so himself, but in the end there was insufficient time to destroy the crops and cattle, which would have denied them to the British. Even in a hurried retreat the Americans themselves did take considerable cattle. Thereupon began the foraging expeditions in New Jersey by British troops described earlier.

Leiby points out that "Between one-third and one-half of the people of the Hackensack Valley appear to have been Tories and Tory-minded neutrals" at this point in the war.[16] As the British moved into the area, they began to take vengeance on the population including destruction of some of the parsonages of ministers sympathetic to the American cause. American patriot groups struck back at the Tories, especially when British troops vacated an area, but on the whole lacked the forces to halt the continued foraging by British soldiers. While, as others have pointed out, one might under such circumstances take a Loyalist or neutral position out of self-interest, "No one was a patriot of convenience in the Hackensack Valley in December 1776."[17]

It was during this period that Charles Lee tried to rally American forces to fight a continuing partisan war in New Jersey. Then Howe, at the insistence of the Loyalists, spread his troops at Trenton, which caused the British to abandon the strategy and spelled the end of plans to be in Philadelphia that winter. Henry Muhlenberg, a captured German officer, complained that he could not understand the American people: "When the Hessians entered Trenton and occupied the region, the inhabitants swore their allegiance to the King of Britain. But as soon as the American troops attacked on Christmas, the inhabitants shot at the Hessians from their houses. In fact, even a woman fired out of a window and mortally

---

[16] *Ibid.*, p. 83.
[17] *Ibid.*, p. 69.

221

wounded a Captain."[18] That the same people who had sold the Hessians food should do this is not difficult to understand. *They did not consider binding an oath that had been inflicted upon them by force,* and when they had the chance to retaliate on the conqueror they did so.

It was at that point that Bergen County truly began to take on the appearance of a middle ground between the two sides, as the British moved back to New York. But it was now the Loyalists who were the more exposed, as attacks and plundering raged on both sides. Given all of the foraging that took place, it was "amazing" that the people in the area not only found enough food and fuel to carry them through the winter, but that a thriving business in hard currency sprang up with the British in New York.

A Guerrilla Civil War

Faced with the reality of perpetual warfare in their area, the majority in Bergen County in 1777 began to establish a militia that would function on a permanent basis. The nature of the American militia in the area began to change during that year. *From a passive force trying to organize defensive measures against an aggressor, it became a highly mobile force that could strike back at the invader.* The dynamics of how this came about are important.

During this same period, the "farmer-soldier" of the militia came under the usual criticism of regular army officers such as Colonel Aaron Burr and General Alexander McDougall, though, as Leiby notes, "neither of them had any real reason to regard himself as a professional military man. Burr complained that 'not a man of the militia are with me. Some joined last night but are gone.'"[19] Even as they began to learn the ways of the guerrilla warfare, the militia, as one would expect, chose to follow their elected leaders, whom they knew and in whom they had confidence, rather than simply any officer sent by the Continental army.

And, as Leiby further observes, "McDougall, for his part, was entirely unembarrassed by the thought that the militia could hardly be expected to do what his nine hundred troops could not do, seeing no irony whatever in complaining that the untrained Jersey Dutch militia, less than

---

[18] *Ibid.*, pp. 99-102.
[19] *Ibid.*, p. 138.

222

one hundred in number, would not venture near the Regulars, at the same time that he reported that he could not even attack Clinton's pickets because, as he put it, it was 'too hazardous an experiment, considering our strength and theirs, by the lowest computation.'" Because the Continental army has had so many defenders with respect to their problems, and the militia so few, Leiby's comments are worth citing: "Since it was the Continental officer and not the militiaman who left his journals and letters for the historian, over the years the militiaman's faults have been multiplied and his virtues forgotten. There are few Jersey Dutch militiamen's writings to tell how seldom any Continentals ventured down into the really dangerous part of the neutral ground when the British were near; none to note that, while the Bergen County militia daily risked brushes with Sir Henry's raiders from New York, all too many Continentals did not hear a gun fired in battle from one year to the next."[20]

Sir Henry Clinton's move into New Jersey with four thousand troops in the fall of 1777 was not an attempt to bring the area under British control, but to take all of the forage possible for the winter ahead, and there was little the militia or the American army could do to prevent such a force from doing that, and returning to New York. With the large British force gone, the battle in the middle ground settled down to *a guerrilla civil war*.

On the whole, the American troops who foraged among the population that supported the Revolution did not do so on a massive scale, and they sought, in many cases, to leave scrip for what was taken. The most committed Loyalists had revealed themselves, during the period when British soldiers had been in the area. Their farms were now recommended as the preferred places to forage. But the most important distinction was the way in which the two populations, Whig and Loyalist, reacted and interacted with each other and with the British, American, and external Loyalist forces that entered the area. Thus, the American majority did exercise a kind of "coercive persuasion" on the minority of Loyalists, and this could and did involve violence at times. But such violence tended to be directed at specific Loyalists and the actions which they had taken against patriots when they had the protection of British troops behind them.

---

[20] *Ibid.*, p. 139.

On the other hand, the actions of the British and Loyalists were of two kinds. Neither the British nor the Hessians were familiar with the area or the people. While their foraging might to some extent be directed at known and conspicuous patriots, it could also fall on those who were neutral in attitude (of which there were few by this time), on those who were neutral in the sense of not having become an active and mobilized patriot, and even upon those who were secret Loyalists, or known Loyalists, but unknown to the soldiers on that foraging patrol. Beyond such actions of the regular soldiers, were those of the Loyalist units, made up of militants, but also comprising men with established reputations as thieves and malcontents. As a conscious minority in their own community, *local Loyalist raids against patriots* tended to be directed, not toward bringing them into line with the views of the majority, as was a dominant patriot motive for such activities, but in *violent retaliation against a majority which they had no hopes of changing*, and toward which they consequently harbored a passionate hatred. On the other hand, Loyalist bands of brigands not familiar with the local population were simply indiscriminate in their license to pillage and would attack families from the staunchest patriot to the most dedicated Loyalist. Whether in vindictiveness or in pillaging, it was among the Loyalist raiders that violence tended toward *atrocities*, not directed at any political goal. Clinton was but touching the tip of the iceberg when he wrote, "I could not but view with concern the very afflicting damage [the raids] had already been productive of to private property, it never having been my intention to extend the destruction to homes of individuals, much less to those of public worship."[21] He was able to stop most of those in Long Island, but not in Bergen County.

The net effect of this indiscriminate British raiding seems to have been to drive the neutrals, whether in thought or in action, toward some participation in the American cause. *The only real protection could come from involvement in the Bergen County militia.* "Free riding" grew expensive. The militia not only grew with the need to organize for constant patrol and skirmishing with raiders, but with the passage of time, changed from a hastily called and inexperienced defensive group into a hardened band of guerrilla fighters. About this organization Leiby comments, "As the winter of 1777-78 set in, it must have been hard for Jersey Dutchmen to realize that but a single year had passed since the

---

[21] *Ibid.*, p. 212.

dread days of the British occupation; . . . a year since Bergen County had been a conquered land, helpless in the hands of its enemies. The improvement in patriots' affairs during the past twelve months was little short of miraculous, . . . A year earlier patriotic Jerseymen had been the hapless victims of a cruel invader; in the fall and winter of 1777, though by no means beyond the reach of British power, they were again actors in the war, not mere sufferers from its cruelty."[22]

1777: A Revitalized Militia

The leader in this change was Major John Mauritius Goetschius, a graduate of the college of New Jersey, who had studied for the ministry but had been urged to do more work before application. Leiby suggests that his "spelling and grammar" were not that of an intellectual, but, as we shall see, his skill as a guerrilla tactician and leader of men was unsurpassed. In reading of his exploits and that of his militia, it is difficult to disagree with Leiby's assessment that "as the war progressed it would have been hard to find any more active and spirited officer on the continent."[23] One may venture the guess, however, that as American historians finally begin to explore the deeds of the local American militia, where records exist to do so, they will find numbers of men who functioned much as did this heroic Dutchman.

In late 1776, the militia had marched out to the sound of fife and drum, but "had flown apart before it could fire a shot." The militia scrapped the silly foot drills that were featured in drill manuals of the time, and only much later did the musical instruments reappear. Goetschius was not the only guerrilla who was a hunted man. One of his officers, Samuel Demarest, had seen some action with Washington's army in New York. Leiby quotes the pension records on Demarest: "He was unable to attend to his business or even to remain at home except by stealth on account of his exposure to capture by the enemy . . . they having made repeated attempts to effect his capture from his own house." Unable to farm during this period, Demarest later had to sell his farm to pay off debts contracted to maintain his family.[24]

---

[22] *Ibid.*, p. 144.
[23] *Ibid.*, pp. 116ff.
[24] *Idem.*

The way in which the "farmer-soldiers" organized themselves is best told in their own words. One of them, Cornelius Board, described their preparations: "It was necessary to keep up a constant guard each night in order to protect our families and ourselves from the depredations of the Cow Boys [British-Loyalist raiders]." His group "would assemble according to orders . . . just after sundown upon the heights and keeping themselves and their station concealed as much as possible would remain under arms through the night, those not engaged on sentry or on patrols sleeping on their arms until it came their turn to relieve those on guard and keeping out sentinels and patrols through the night, then returning to our ordinary business in the morning."[25]

A further account is added by Cornelius Blauvelt: The companies "were divided into classes of four men in a class, and the arrangement was made that one man in a class should guard one week and be relieved by another, and so continue until each had served his week, that a continued guard might be kept and their necessary labor at home might be done in which manner the militia served until the end of the war from early in the spring until winter and often in the winter." Each class served one month in four.[26]

Such militia service was difficult, but slowly the men became a fighting unit in constant contact with British and Loyalist elements. That kind of defense was extremely hard, for the British could strike at any point in a radius of twenty-five miles, and the Americans never knew where they might hit next. When the British treated the captured American militia badly, the patriots threatened to reciprocate on captured British soldiers. Clinton's acceptance of the American argument simply angered the Tories, who felt a hard policy should be pursued at all times. The most important result of the British raids and the American organization was to mobilize any persons who were left in the middle, if they wished to protect their property, and to push the American militia into the formation of a fighting organization undreamed of in 1776. For men thus committed, the British idea of pacification in 1778 was irrelevant. Though few, if any, would have recognized it at the time, even in the middle ground, *the war had essentially been decided by the end of 1777.* Though the Continental army in the area did not grow much stronger, the militia continued to do so. As Leiby notes, "To the patriots

---

[25] *Idem.*
[26] *Ibid.*, pp. 129ff.

the Revolution was no mere nationalistic revolt against legitimate government, it was a rebellion against Toryism in politics, economics, and religion, a Toryism that bred poverty, ignorance, and despair in Europe and would, given a free hand, do the same in America. . . . To patriots far more than allegiance to Britain was at stake; Tory success would have meant a far different England and a far different world."[27] The Jersey Dutch were no provincials, but understood the larger context of the war.

The Militia Becomes Dominant

Very slowly the militia began to assert American control of the area. Two of the more important American victories of 1779 were in the area; General Anthony Wayne's surprise bayonet and sword night attack on Stony Point, and the raid on Paulus Hook, which, while not major engagements, threw off Clinton's plans for the year. Wayne's large foraging expedition was also a success, though the farmers probably were not happy about losing their produce and animals to the American army either. Thus, "it was plain for anyone to see that it was" the Americans, not the British "who dominated the neutral ground in 1779; and the land that had filled the storehouses of the British during 1776, 1777, and 1778 now supplied" the American forces.[28]

Late in 1779 a "remarkable indication" of how "the British cause had lost ground in the past three years" occurred, "for which there must be few parallels indeed in the history of war and Revolution." In 1776 dozens of young men from families in the valley who were of Loyalist sympathies had enlisted for three years in the British forces. As their enlistments expired, these men sought to return to their homes and begin farming again, almost as if there had been no war. The American patriot militia began arresting them to be put on trial for high treason, but the men claimed to be deserters from the British army.[29]

General Wayne ordered them released on the basis that such desertion ought to be encouraged, and that prosecution "would inevitably deter all others under similar circumstances from coming over . . . and shutting the

---

[27] *Ibid.*, p. 215.
[28] *Ibid.*, p. 225.
[29] *Ibid.*, pp. 226-27.

door of mercy against poor deluded wretches who wish to return to the bosom of their country." Though the Americans did not know of it, and no formal effort was ever made to implement it, the British were at this very time considering planting deserters among the Americans to serve as spies.[30]

The winter of 1779-80 was a very bad one, made worse by a drought. In late March, the British, with six hundred men, launched a raid into New Jersey from two directions. In the ensuing skirmishes, it appears that the American militia was less prone to retreat than the regular forces. The British burned many of the homes of patriots in Hackensack, and carried off all of the adult males they could find, but the American harassment was so fierce they could take little or no plunder with them. As Leiby concludes, "The time was long past when the British could attack Bergen County as a refreshment for their troops."[31] The prisoners were later exchanged, but the British acts only increased the enmity of the Americans. It was hardly the kind of "pacification" that would win over the inhabitants. In fairness to Clinton, it appears that the idea for such reprisals had come from the Loyalist refugees in New York, who, in the absence of Sir Henry in the South, had convinced the Hessians that such raids were a good policy. On his return Clinton was "furious," and later wrote that the raid was "ill-timed . . . malapropos," and based upon "the ill-founded suggestions of . . . over-sanguine Refugees."[32] In April the British staged a raid on Paramus, much less interested in retaliation than foraging. While some of the regular army units were surprised by the action, it was the militia which "again turned out like veterans, hanging on the flanks and rear of the withdrawing troops in the best tradition of the embattled farmer, firing from behind every stone fence and tree from Paramus to Fort Lee, inflicting heavy casualties on the British columns and finally forcing them to slow their march and throw out flanking parties to protect their main force from the galling fire, with the result that a great many prisoners escaped and a good deal of booty had to be abandoned." Pursuing the British right to the edge of the Hudson, the Americans recaptured four wagons and sixteen horses.

---

[30] *Ibid.*, p. 219.
[31] *Ibid.*, p. 244.
[32] *Ibid.*, p. 303.

The Problem of Paper Money

Leiby's information about the regular army in the area tends to confirm other data about it. Washington continued to have supply problems, the lack of anything but inflated paper money being a prime factor. As William Pennington, a Jersey soldier stationed at Tappan, reported: "We are encamped near a pleasant little village about two miles from the Hudson. The inhabitants are principally low Dutch, though there are some refugees from New York. I am told that there are some very good Whigs here. Silver and gold is the only established currency in the country as the Dutch have substantial wealth. We are in the heart of a delightful and plentiful country but for the want of specie cannot reap much advantage from it."[33] Others in the regular army had far less scruples, for they foraged and plundered among the farms of Orange County while the militia in that area was away fighting Loyalists and Indian raiders farther west. A major reason for such actions was the composition of the American army, for one could not "fail to see that the troops of the line were no longer farm boys with muskets. The Continentals at Tappan were campaign-hardened professional soldiers, a good number of them captives and deserters from the redcoats, men who knew very well how to live on the country when the commissaries failed them, and plundering was only a part of the story." British intelligence files are filled with reports and information from the men who *re-deserted* after the British issued a proclamation of pardon to all such deserters. (Since many of those in the British army were foreigners, the deserters help, in part, to explain the high proportion of foreigners in the American army.) The militia was active in pursuing these men as they re-deserted and tried to make their way to the British lines in New York.[34]

The "middle ground" was thus the locale for an incredible number of different levels of fighting during the war. It was near here that the most serious mutiny, that of the Pennsylvania Line, took place late in 1780. The plight of these men during the war, many of them foreign-born, was no doubt severe, they having received little or no pay for months. Some were deserting, but a larger number simply were tired of fighting without pay, and went on a rampage of plundering. Major Goetschius reported to Washington that "the wicked and inconsiderate soldiery" were "entirely

[33] *Ibid.*, pp. 253ff.
[34] *Ibid.*, p. 265.

destroying the Schraalenburgh neighborhood," having taken all sorts of farm animals and produce, "and in a violent manner abuse the well-affected in this place, running about with clubs and bayonets upon pikes by whole companies as bad as our enemies ever have done." General Nathanael Greene wrote, "There have been committed some of the most horrid acts of plunder by some of the Pennsylvania Line that has disgraced the American army during the war. . . . Two soldiers were taken that were out upon the business, both of which fired upon the inhabitants to prevent their giving intelligence. A party plundered a house yesterday in sight of a number of officers, and even threatened the officers if they offered to interfere." Greene recommended that such offenders be hanged without trial, while Goetschius and the militia sought to halt any deserters from reaching New York.[35]

Washington also found the plundering outrageous. "Without a speedy change in circumstances . . . either the army must disband, or what is if possible worse, subsist upon the plunder of the people." The army had at this point been without any meat for over a week, and foraging raids had raised only a supply for several days. "Military coercion is no longer to any avail, as nothing further can possibly be collected from the country in which we are obliged to take a position without depriving the inhabitants of the last morsel. This mode of subsisting, supposing the desired end could be answered by it, besides being in the highest degree distressing to individuals, is attended with ruin to the morals and discipline of the army; during the few days which we have been obliged to send out small parties to procure provisions for themselves, the most enormous excesses have been committed." As an American officer, Major Samuel Shaw, put it: "The country between us and the enemy, and below him, has been pretty thoroughly gleaned by us of the little the enemy left there. We call this foraging, but it is only a gentle name for plundering."[36]

Goals of Guerrilla Troops

It was, of course, in this area that the treason of Benedict Arnold was uncovered, and Major John Andre was captured and hanged as a spy. As the foraging began to run short, Washington moved his army to the north

---

[35] *Ibid.*, p. 277.
[36] *Idem.*

and west. His orders to Goetschius as he did so are revealing of the different way in which the commander of the army perceived the war in contrast to a leader of the local militia. Washington ordered Goetschius to detach about twenty men for duty around Dobbs Ferry in New York "to protect and cover the country below as far as possible." The Dutch leader did so, but he wrote, "It makes a great uneasiness among the inhabitants at the lines of this country. My detachment is particular enlisted for a guard at the frontiers of this country. To complete the number, the inhabitants at the lines paid a large sum of money to the soldiery particular to have rest themselves and to follow their employ. . . . Garrisoning the blockhouse at Dobbs Ferry which lays in York State is little or no guard to this country . . . [which] lays now open [and] horse thieves and robbers slip through to ruin of the inhabitants."[37]

Goetschius understood that *such warfare involves people, not places, and that protecting the patriot population was more important than anything else.* He might also have added that only a few months before Loyalist raiders had burned his own home and barn and carried away all he owned. But perhaps even more important than his theory of warfare is his information that the militia was a paid defense force. It helps to explain the way in which Americans chose to support the war effort, and how reluctant inhabitants were to pay for the regular army, after having contributed toward the local militia.

Away from his home base, Goetschius and his militia were faced with the same provision problem that plagued the regular army. Thus, he wrote to the governor of New Jersey that the militia had served some weeks "whilst the army laid here, [under] about fifteen different commanders as picket to the whole army," having to take orders from all these officers while receiving rations from none. He had applied to Washington, to the state, and to the several surrounding counties, but had received nothing. On Washington's advice, his men had also foraged, but there was little left about, and "it must be taken by force of arms. The inhabitants will not sell any longer for certificates." With all these problems, nonetheless, the militia continued to patrol the dangerous territory between the two armies, in which occurred most of the fighting. Leiby's comment is worth noting: The militia "would have been more than human, however, if they had not observed the Continental's contempt for all militiamen and if they had not observed, even more clearly, how

---

[37] *Ibid.*, p. 290.

often Continentals marched and countermarched during a whole campaign without seeing a redcoat, how seldom any Continental ventured down as close to the British as the militia headquarters posts.

"After the war, when Goetschius's old militia men stood outside the South Church at Schraalenbugh on Sunday mornings waiting for the service to begin and boasting quietly about their exploits in low Dutch, if some of them were a little scornful of Continental officers who never saw a British gun, it was perhaps natural jealousy over their own unsung feats. No Continental need have troubled himself for a moment about their mild grumbling, there were none but Jersey Dutchmen to hear them, there was to be no Bancroft or Longfellow to tell of their deeds."[38]

1781: The End of the War

By the middle of 1781 things were little changed in the Hackensack Valley. Cornwallis was in Virginia, but the British force remained in New York, able to raid into New Jersey. Washington kept his army nearby, but was unable to mount an assault on the British base. "The neutral ground continued to be the stage for probing raids, espionage, and partisan warfare." In March the British made a large raid, but the militia drove them back before any Continental units had time to get organized to meet the threat. In these closing months of the war occurred some of the worst retributions of all. Early in 1781, the government in London agreed with the demands of the Loyalists to charter an organization, the Associated Loyalists, "to wage a private war-within-a-war, to take their own prisoners, and to treat military booty as their own; in a word to wage war without let or hindrance from British headquarters."[39] Though Clinton opposed it, the Loyalists were, in effect, given a license to pillage and plunder, taking out their frustrations on the population.

In May some Loyalist forces occupied old Fort Lee, and Goetschius and the militia moved to dislodge them. In the meantime, Washington heard about the Loyalists and ordered several regular army units "and any Jersey militia that you may find . . . but . . . trust no officer among them . . ." to attack the fort. Before the army could make such preparations, the word arrived that the militia had taken the fort. Leiby notes that "The British command was fortunate that the Bergen and Orange County

---

[38] *Ibid.*, pp. 291ff.
[39] *Ibid.*, p. 303.

militiamen [who had quickly assembled, two hundred strong, for the joint attack] were not thrown against a more important objective."[40]

If there is any weakness in Leiby's study, it is his account of the last months of the fighting, and the year and a half from the British surrender at Yorktown late in 1781 until the signing of the peace agreement early in 1783. It would appear that *many Loyalists and some neutrals, who had done little in the war effort, did reintegrate themselves back into the society*, much to the consternation of many of the more committed Whigs. This upset Washington also, but we can close this account of Leiby's with a comment by Governor William Livingston: "I have seen Tory members of Congress, Judges upon tribunals, Tory representatives in our Legislative councils, Tory members of our Assemblies . . . I have seen self-interest predominating and patriotism languishing."[41]

It is not clear from Leiby's account how willingly the patriots accepted the reintegration of these Loyalists back into their society. That they did so at all seems to disturb him somewhat. There is no research on this question, but the suggestion offered by Leonard Liggio seems the most likely explanation. That the Jersey Dutch did have a number of Loyalists would tend to confirm Nelson's views about the prime source of that outlook among minority groups. At the end of the conflict, the patriot Dutch would have been caught in a quandary: whether to punish their deviant fellow ethnics, or very quickly to re-assimilate them back, thus affirming the idea that the Dutch were solidly part of the patriot movement, and thus good Americans. Such an interpretation certainly fits into later patterns of American ethnic behavior. Thus, the ethnic factor may have played a part in the apparently light reaction to the Loyalist reintegration into Dutch society.[42]

Some Observations About Revolutionary Warfare

It is impossible, in this brief summary of a few of Leiby's points about the Revolution in the Hackensack Valley, to do justice to what must be regarded as a magnificent, detailed account of local history and the

---

[40] *Ibid.*, pp. 297-98.

[41] *Ibid.*, pp. 305-307.

[42] Various conversations with Leonard Liggio during the Summer of 1976, when we (Marina) were both Liberty Fund Research Fellows at the Institute for Humane Studies in Menlo Park, California. Liggio had done considerable research with Murray N. Rothbard on the Revolution, much of which is contained in the latter's five-volume study of early American history entitled, *Conceived in Liberty*.

interaction of military events with socio-economic developments. Anyone at all familiar with the basic concepts of revolutionary warfare, and the process by which a community organizes itself to fight a guerrilla war virtually under the gun of the invader, must acknowledge that Shy was incorrect when he suggested that Leiby's study was simply an example of "local" history dealing with "bloody battles" growing out of "prewar animosities."

It is a microcosmic account of what most areas have experienced as they became involved in the process of revolutionary change, but unique in the American Revolution because the area was dominated by British forces for most of the war, and thus forced the Americans into fighting a true guerrilla war. Commitment from those in the middle came less because of ideology, than from the realization that *there would be no free riders*, and that those who did not participate in the militia would not be offered protection against British incursions. Indiscriminate British, and especially Loyalist, plundering and retaliations further polarized the population toward the American cause.

As the war progressed, the militia became, in many ways, a more effective fighting force than the regular army, which contained a large segment of some of the less desirable elements in American society. In Major John M. Goetschius we glimpse an American military officer whose grasp of the principles of people's guerrilla warfare was equal to any of the great historical theorists of those concepts. Complaints about the militia by officers such as General George Washington reflected an unwillingness to recognize these concepts of warfare, and how such a force could most effectively be used.

Unlike the inflated scrip used to pay sporadically the regular army, *the Bergen County militia was paid, apparently, in gold.* Their commitment was to attacking the British and Loyalists whenever they chose to attack that county, and the militia leaders felt less effective when told to encamp in other, distant areas. This attitude toward the militia of some army officers is indicative of one of the major "fault lines" within the revolutionary coalition.[43] Some leaders had always desired *imperial territorial gains* from the war, as well as independence. This desire ran so deep that they had launched an attack on Canada early in the war, greatly over-extending American resources. Such leaders were not interested in securing peace in 1778 unless it also included Canada and Florida. *Local*

---

[43] See Marina, "People's War," for a more detailed account.

farmer militia self-defense forces, as those in Bergen County, were simply not excited by such imperial adventures. A good example of this was evident late in the war, in 1781, when Washington sent General Lafayette north to attempt to mount an assault. The leaders of the Vermont militia replied that they would not enlist unless they were promised "double pay, double rations and plunder," a clever way of aborting the whole idea.[44]

For many Americans who have spent years reading back on the origins of the Republic, it must have become apparent how much yet needs to be learned about the history of this period. Even such a perceptive historian as Shy, for example, repeats the myth about John Adams's statement that it was a minority Revolution. What is apparent from some of the very careful local studies such as Leiby's, drawn from a variety of obscure, and long-forgotten records, is that perhaps the American Revolution has more than "a few lessons for our own time."

[44] Quoted in Smith, *People's History.*

The Israelite Militia in the Old Testament

James B. Jordan

The purpose of this essay is to outline the structure and principles of the local Israelite militia, as we see it functioning in the Old Testament. While Christians living under the New Covenant are not bound to every particular form and structure seen in the Old Testament, Christians are obliged to consider the whole Bible as wisdom for a godly civilization. To this end, let us look first of all at key Biblical principles of war, and then more closely at the organization of the Israelite militia.

The Biblical Theology of Warfare

War began when Adam joined Satan in revolting against God. God had promised that Adam would die if he rebelled, a death which Jesus revealed would take the form of everlasting torment in the fires of hell and outer darkness. While Scripture reveals God as the God of love and compassion, it also reveals Him as the God of wrath and vengeance—indeed, vengeance is one of His exclusive personal prerogatives (Romans 12:19). The Christian does not hope in a God who somehow overlooks and excuses sin and rebellion; rather the Christian trusts in the God who punished his sin once and for all in the person of His Son. Jesus Christ took the wrath and vengeance deserved by His people, and on the basis of that substitutionary transaction, Christians are freed from judgment. At the outset, though, we need to realize that the ferocity and horror of God's war against man is nowhere more dramatically seen than on Golgotha.

James B. Jordan served in the United States Air Force as a military historian, before studying for the ministry. A graduate of the University of Georgia with a Bachelor's degree in Comparative Literature, Mr. Jordan did graduate work at Reformed Theological Seminary, and completed his M.A. and Th.M. degrees at Westminster Theological Seminary. He is presently Director of Biblical Horizons Ministries. He is author of numerous essays and several books. He can be contacted at P.O. Box 10, Niceville, Florida, 32588.

Man deserves the undying fires of hell. As a foretaste, God gives him war. The presence of wars and rumors of war, then, is part of God's continual warning to humanity, a gracious warning that gives men time to reconsider their ways. "There Will Be War," as a recent series of books edited by J. E. Pournelle reminds us, and Christians cannot avoid coming to grips practically with what this means.

"Blessed are the peacemakers," we are told by our Lord in the Sermon on the Mount, and in all the liturgies of the historic churches we are constantly reminded of God's peace. All the same, the mere absence of conflict is not the highest of all Christian virtues. There are principles of right and justice that qualify our commitment to peace in the external sense. We have a proper right of self-defense, and we have a neighborly duty to do what we can to prevent harm from coming to others. There is, thus, a proper and holy violence, a just defense and a just war, grounded in the Biblical and catholic Christian principle of the wrath of God.

The orthodox and Biblical Christian churches have sought to restrain war by use of the principle of "just war," but no orthodox Christian church has ever been pacifistic. Pacifism is an arch-heresy, from the point of view of Biblical, catholic, and Reformational Christianity, because pacifism rejects the fundamental opposition of righteousness and sin, and substitutes for it as an ultimate principle the opposition of violence and non-violence, and the ultimate vice is violence, not sin or rebellion against God. Ultimately, then, all pacifists must reject the Biblical revelation of the wrath and vengeance of God, which is what makes them heretics. Ultimately, also, the pacifist undermines all of human society, since without a principle of proper holy wrath and justice, there is no restraint on evil.[1]

Scripture reveals God as one who punishes wickedness and rewards faithfulness. God does not make war against the righteous but against the wicked. When sin has developed to a certain point, God will not permit it to go farther, and acts to destroy it. This happened at the Flood, and also at the conquest of Canaan. Human beings were not called upon to act as God's agents in the first of these, but were enlisted for the second.

How shall we understand this? The Bible teaches that God created Adam naked (Gen. 2:25). This has occasioned considerable speculation,

---

[1] I have discussed several recent attempts to prove pacifism from the Old Testament in a review essay, "Pacifism and the Old Testament," in Gary North, ed., *The Theology of Christian Resistance* (Tyler, TX; Geneva Ministries, 1983). This essay deals generally with the heresy of pacifism.

but the reason for it is fairly obvious: Adam and Eve were naked because they were *newborn*. God Himself is always revealed as enrobed in a cloud of glory, and man, as His image, was to mature and become similarly enrobed. Man was not to seize the robe for himself, but to await God's time of investiture. The robe, in Scripture, signifies the authority of God. It conveys the right to pass judgments concerning good and evil, to dispense blessings and curses. The robe is the sign of the office of judge.

Now, judgments are not rendered before acts are committed, but come afterward. Theologians say that judgment is "eschatological," that is, it comes at the end of a given period of time. In Genesis 1, God created things, and then at the end of each day, God *saw* what He made, and *pronounced judgment on it* ("saw that it was good"). Man, as the image and copy of God, was to mature to the point of doing the same thing.

When Cain killed Abel, God said that no man would put him to death. This was because the robe of judicial authority had not yet been committed to the human race. After the Flood, however, God told Noah that the power to dispense capital punishment had now been committed to human magistrates (Gen. 9:5, 6). The sign of this power was Noah's robe. When Ham tried to enlist his brothers to help him steal the robe, Noah came out and passed judgment. In the Garden, God had passed judgment on Adam and Eve, but now a godly human elder is seen passing judgment, dispensing curses and blessings (Gen. 9:20-27). This is a sign of the maturing of the human race, by grace, and in spite of sin.[2]

Having given human beings the right to exercise holy violence on His behalf, God worked with His children to train them in the proper exercise of it. Thus, as we read the Old Testament, we see God progressively relinquishing more and more of the reins to His maturing children (though always reserving final judgment to Himself). God struck the definitive blow against Egypt without human aid. God enlisted Israel to help Him destroy Canaan, but worked miracles to make it possible, and gave explicit guidance for the battlefield.[3] By the time of David, however, we have far less direct Divine guidance; men are to make their decisions

---

[2] For a much more detailed study of the nakedness of Adam and the robe as a sign of God-bestowed office, see James B. Jordan, "Rebellion, Tyranny, and Dominion in the Book of Genesis," in Gary North, ed., *Tactics of Christian Resistance* (Tyler, TX: Geneva Ministries, 1983).

[3] For a study of the battles in the book of Judges, see James B. Jordan, *Judges: God's War Against Humanism* (Tyler, TX: Geneva Ministries, 1985).

based on wisdom. With the New Covenant, we are told that we are now come of age, and by implication, we are not to expect our Father to bail us out of every situation we get ourselves into (Gal. 4:1ff.). This does not eliminate the reality of the miraculous, but it does show a general trend in Biblical revelation, one which we need to bear in mind as we consider the Biblical teaching on war.

Though He permitted His people to join with Him in exterminating the Canaanites and Amalekites, God did not permit Israel to launch wars of aggression.[4] There is, thus, a distinction to be drawn between God's special holy wars, and the general defensive actions that Israel had to take from time to time. Examining the rules for defensive warfare, we can come up with Biblical principles for a "just war." To start with, then, a just war is a defensive war, an application of what God told Noah: "Whoever sheds man's blood, by man shall his blood be shed." Wherever possible, aggression is to be met with resistance, and bloodshed is to be avenged. God has committed this charge to His people, and we are obliged to carry it out, though always according to the rules He has laid down.

So concerned is God with vengeance, that He set out an elaborate system of blood vengeance for His people of old. If a man killed another man, deliberately or accidentally, he could run to a place of sanctuary, one of the cities of refuge. The Levites of the sanctuary would form a defense attorney, and argue the case with the blood avenger, who was the nearest of kin of the slain man. The blood avenger was required to track down his brother's killer, and either kill him or chase him to sanctuary for trial. The avenger did not have the option of overlooking the matter.[5] Indeed, if a dead body were found in a field, vengeance was still required even if the killer could not be found (Deut. 21:1-9).

The avenger/sanctuary system of the Old Covenant was linked to the curse on the ground. Blood defiled the ground, and called up the avenger, who was in this sense an agent for the land. In the New Covenant, the ground has been cleansed once and for all by the blood of Jesus Christ.

---

[4] Deut. 17:16 forbad the king to have horses. Since horses were used exclusively for chariot warfare, which was exclusively offensive in character, this was understood to prohibit aggression. For a picture of this, see Ezekiel 38:10ff. See the discussion in Yigael Yadin, *The Art of Warfare in Biblical Lands* (New York: McGraw-Hill Book Co., 1963) I:86-90; and also R. J. Rushdoony, *The Institutes of Biblical Law* (Phillipsburg, N.J.: Presbyterian and Reformed Publishing Co., 1973), p. 279.

[5] I have discussed this system in some detail in my book, *The Law of the Covenant: An Exposition of Exodus 21-23* (Tyler, TX: Institute for Christian Economics, 1984).

The ground no longer cries for vengeance when a murder is committed. The New Testament tells us that God has committed the duty of vengeance to the state, to the civil magistrate (Romans 12:17–13:17). Thus, the principle of blood vengeance is still in force, even though it is applied somewhat differently.[6]

The avenger in the Old Covenant was not a vigilante, but an officer appointed by God to carry out a specific task of prosecution in cooperation with the authorities in church (Levites) and state (elders). Since every Israelite was potentially an avenger, however, he had to be armed.

Wrongs must be avenged, we noted above, and also aggression resisted. We come, thus, to the fundamental right of self-defense. Exodus 22:2 says that if a thief "is discovered while he is breaking in, and he is struck, and he dies, there is no bloodguiltiness for him." Since we don't know the intention of the person breaking into our house, we have the right to shoot first and ask questions later. This law also presupposes the right to bear arms.[7]

The notion of defensive warfare presupposes the validity of boundaries. God established the principle of boundary when He set a distinction between the land of Eden and the rest of the world, and within Eden, between the Garden therein and the rest of it. The separate lands of Havilah, Cush, and Assyria are also mentioned. This is all found in the creation passage (Genesis 2), and thus boundaries are not an aspect of the world under sin, but part of God's desired diversification of the flowering of humanity. The Bible everywhere presumes the validity of such boundaries, drawn along ethnic and linguistic lines (unlike many modern national boundaries). Invading armies may properly be repulsed.

Now, these two principles, the principle of avenging bloodshed and the principle of self-defense, form the foundation for the Biblical conception of a just war. When Israel was attacked, she had the right to defend herself. And, when horrible acts were committed in a city, God's people had a duty to set things right by making war. The foremost illustration of this latter duty is found in Judges 19–21. A group of

---

[6] The reason for this is a bit complicated. Man was made of the ground, and the killing of a man was an offense against the ground from which he was made. Thus, the ground cried for vengeance. In the New Covenant, Jesus is the new ground or soil of the New Creation and He calls upon the magistrate to be agenger of blood. With an understanding of this principle, we can study the Old Testament laws of vengeance and sort out between what applies to us today and what does not.

[7] I have discussed this law at some length in my book, *The Law of the Covenant*, p. 136f.

241

homosexuals raped and murdered a woman in Gibeah. The Israelite confederacy demanded that the city of Gibeah turn these men over to justice. Gibeah refused to do so, and their entire tribe of Benjamin stood with them. Thus, Israel made war on Benjamin, and under explicit Divine guidance, virtually wiped out the whole tribe.[8]

Principles of Warfare

Having established the conditions of warfare, let us briefly survey some of the most important Biblical principles of warfare. I wish to mention five.

The first is the principle of crushing the head. The Bible holds the leaders of society primarily responsible for social decisions. Thus, the most important matter in victory over an invading army is the destruction of its leadership. Assassination of the heads of the enemy state is a foremost Biblical principle of war. This is seen particularly in the book of Judges, where in each case it is the heads of state that are the primary target of the battle, for when the leader dies, the army scatters. Thus, Ehud assassinated Eglon; Jael killed Sisera; Gideon slew Zebah, Zalmunna, Oreb and Zeeb; and Samson killed all five of the lords of the Philistines. When Saul sought to spare Agag, who after all was "fellow royalty," his sin was so great that it cost him the crown (1 Sam. 15:8-9, 20-33). Not only is the principle of assassinating the heads of aggressor states more just, in that it punishes those who are responsible, it is also simpler and less costly.

The second principle is the offer of peace. This is seen in Deuteronomy 20:10ff. The law commences, "when you approach a city to fight against it, you shall call to it for peace," but this applies only to cities that are far away. No peace was to be offered to Canaanite cities. Under what conditions would Israel ever be involved in fighting against a city far away? Since only defensive wars were permitted, we have to fill in a context here. We must assume that this city or nation has launched an attack against Israel. Defeated in battle, the invaders have been beaten back to the walls of their city. At this point, the offer of peace by Israel

---

[8] I mention this passage because I think it stands against a certain kind of isolationism which says we have no responsibility to try and deal with the Hitlers, Stalins, and Idi Amins of this world. There is, I believe, a place for wars of punishment and vengeance, though there are many factors involved in making a determination whether to get into one or not. On the war against Benjamin, see my book on *Judges* mentioned above.

is credible, for Israel has already shown herself to be militarily superior on the battlefield. If the city surrenders, it must make reparations and serve Israel. If the city refuses peace, then all the men of the city are to be killed. This may sound excessive, but the threat of such a horrible vengeance was designed to provoke an early peace. What we learn from this is that total war and absolute surrender are not Biblical principles. The carrot of a negotiated peace is to be offered right up to the end, with the stick of cultural annihilation as the alternative.[9]

The third principle is that the land is not to be wasted in warfare (Deut. 20:19-20). What this means in principle is that war is to be made against warmongers, not against everything and everyone residing in the enemy nation. The law is phrased in terms of trees; fruit trees are not to be cut down and used in siegeworks. Since, however, trees are a standard symbol for men (as in Psalm 1, for instance, and Judges 9), the law is intended to apply to men. Civilians (fruit-bearing trees) are not to be attacked. We are not to bomb cities.

The fourth principle is the principle of universal participation. When capital punishment was administered in Israel, every citizen of the place was required to cast a stone (Lev. 24:14; Deut. 13:9; 17-7). This does not mean that the man was killed by being struck by stones. Apparently, the man was usually thrown down from a high place, and a large stone cast down upon him to kill him instantly (compare Luke 4:29). Then, each man in the place would walk by and cast a rock on the pile, creating a memorial heap. The point is that nobody was permitted to disagree with the justice administered. Even if he disagreed in his heart, he was still required to perform the public ritual of affirming the *system* of justice.

This same principle applied to warfare. When Israel made war on Benjamin, the city of Jabesh-Gilead refused to supply any troops, and that city was destroyed (Judges 21).[10] Similarly, Succoth and Penuel were

---

[9] I question whether some modification in just war strategy is implied by the coming of the New Covenant. The vanquished nation in the Old Testament was incorporated into Israel, either by enslavement or by the elimination of the men and the simple incorporation of the women. In the Gospel age, however, the integrity of each and every language and people seems emphasized by the multiplication of tongues at Pentecost (Acts 2) and by assurances of worldwide conversion (Rev. 21:24; 22:2). Additionally, warfare today is not conducted against small city-states, but against vast national areas. Thus, I should like to propose that in a Christian just war there would be no aggrandizement of the defending nation at the expense of the aggressor. Reparations might be exacted in the form of war debt, but no colonization, nor the elimination of the entire male citizenry. Certain guarantees might be exacted, such as free trade and safe passage for Christian missionaries, but no more. This is also predicated on the Christian view that "national" boundaries should be drawn along ethnic and lingual lines, not along lines of conquest. Notice also that when Jerusalem resisted Nebuchadnezzar, that king, though advised by the prophet Daniel, did not kill all the men of Israel (2 Kings 25).

[10] This may seem extreme. For an explanation of it, see my commentary on *Judges*, mentioned above.

punished for not supporting Gideon (Judges 8:4-17). Meroz was cursed into oblivion for refusing to heed the call of war (Judges 5:23). During the same war, several of the tribes failed to send any support. They, however, were punished only by the public ridicule of having the Song of Deborah sung against them at every watering place in Israel (Judges 5:11, 16-17).

Why the difference in degree? Because of a fifth principle: localism. Those near the battle were expected to send more men and support the war more heavily than those farther away. Some token of support, however, was expected from every tribe. How much was expected also depended on the seriousness of the situation. At any rate, the principle is that local men defend their local situation. The militia was not a national army.

How the Militia Functioned

With this, we have arrived at a consideration of the Israelite militia, how it was organized, and how it operated.

When Israel marched out of Egypt, she marched five in a rank. The term translated "battle array" (or some equivalent) in English versions of Exodus 13:18 actually means "five in a rank," and the same term with the same meaning is found in Numbers 32:17; Joshua 1:14; 4-12; and Judges 7:11. According to Exodus 18, this army was to be organized as a nation with elders over 10s, 50s, 100s, and so forth. Now, five squads of 10 men, marching in ranks, form a platoon of 50 men, and this would have been the fundamental marching unit of the Israelite host. Two platoons of 50 men form a company of 100 men. And so forth.

This was the ordinary arrangement of the Israelite militia, in peacetime. In time of war, men who had shown particular military skills would temporarily assume the positions normally held by the elders or judges of Israel, as heads of hundreds and thousands.

All laymen were numbered in the muster of the militia. We see this in Numbers 2:2, 3, "Take a sum of all the congregation of the sons of Israel . . . every male, head by head from twenty years old and upward, whoever can go out to war in Israel. You [Moses] and Aaron shall muster them by their armies." Throughout this chapter, the word translated "number" is actually "muster," and so the Book of Numbers might better be called the Book of the Mustering of God's Army. At any rate, we see from this that the Israelite militia was not a purely voluntary army.

Everybody had to show up. The Levites were not, however, mustered (Num. 1:48-49), though they not infrequently joined in battle voluntarily. This establishes the principle that the clergy are exempt from military service. Men below the age of 20 and men too old to fight were not mustered.

Once all the men had arrived for the muster, several things happened. First, as they were counted, each man contributed a half-shekel of silver for the upkeep of the church. This money was collected because the army camp of Israel was especially holy to the Lord, and the nearness of the Lord was a threat to sinful Israel. The money atoned, or protected, them from the Lord (Exodus 30:1-10).[11] This is not needed in the New Covenant.

Second, once mustered, two categories of men were permitted to go home. They had shown their support for the Lord and the nation, but they were not required to stay and fight. According to Deuteronomy 20:5-8 and 24:5, those who were to go home in the first category were:

1. A man who was in the process of building a new house and had not yet lived in it for any period of time.
2. A man who had planted a vineyard and had not begun to enjoy its produce.
3. A man who was engaged to be married, or who had not been married for at least a year.

The unifying principle in these three cases is that a man had not yet experienced the joys of covenant life. Salvation restores men to the Garden of Eden, so to speak, and God grants them time to enjoy the Garden (house, wine, wife) before sending them off to war. Practically speaking, the army would be the stronger without these men, for they would be thinking of their homes and brides, and not be singleminded about the battle. Thus, this provision is not only gracious and kind, it is also commonsensical.

The other group allowed to go home were the fearful and faint-hearted. The reason for this was so that "he might not make his brothers' hearts melt like his heart" (Deut. 20:8). In other words, though all men were drafted, yet men might excuse themselves if they were willing to admit being afraid (and see Judges 7:3). Theologically speaking, this was

---

[11] See my essay on this entitled, "State Financing in the Bible," in *The Law of the Covenant*, mentioned above.

because all the wars of the Lord were to be fought by faith, with confidence. Practically, it sorted out most potential deserters up front.

Third, a decision was made as to how many men were actually needed for the battle, and the rest of the men were assigned as reserves or put to work as support (Judges 7:4-8; 20:10). At the same time, decisions were made regarding how the army would be organized, and who would be in charge of various military units (Deut. 20:9; Num. 31:14). Sometimes these decisions were made in advance, and each tribe was required to select a certain number of men to send to the muster (Num. 31:4).

The militia was provisioned in various ways at various times. Normally, each man provided his own weapon (1 Sam. 25:13; Num. 31:3; 32:20). Israel was an armed nation, as we have seen. So much was this the case that the various tribes tended to specialize in various weapons (Judges 20:16; 1 Chron. 12:33-37). Men brought their weapons from home. In general, men were provisioned from home (1 Sam. 17:17), or by friends (2 Sam. 17:2ff.). Sometimes, however, supply lines were set up (Judges 20:10). And later, under the monarchy, the state supplied weapons and provisions when necessary (2 Chron. 26:14; in context this refers to the militia). Thus, for instance, it would be proper for a local government to assist a poor man in obtaining his own weapon, if he cannot afford it.

A study can be made of the shifting conditions of the Israelite armaments. The Israelites initially were able to arm themselves from the carcasses of the Egyptian army washed up on the shore of the Red Sea (Ex. 14:30). During the period of the judges, the population was disarmed by oppressing invaders (Judges 5:8), though the defeat of the invaders enabled the citizenry to rearm itself each time. The Philistines eventually came to hold a more sustained grip upon the nation, and maintained a very strict iron monopoly, as it says in 1 Samuel 13:19-22, for the purpose of preventing Israel from arming herself. Thus, during this period such weapons as slings (David) and arrows (Jonathan) came to the forefront.[12] Two things emerge from all this: First, godly people always sought to be armed and trained in weaponry, and sought out obscure weapons when normal ones were forbidden them. Second, a central goal of any tyrannical or oppressive state is to disarm the population, and an attempt to disarm the people is fundamentally satanic.

---

[12] For an excellent study of this whole period, and the meaning of various weapons, see James Hoyle, "The Weapons of God in Samuel," in *This World* 7 (Winter, 1984):118-134.

How was the militia paid? They were paid by booty from the war. We see this in Numbers 31:27-47. The booty was divided in half. Half was distributed evenly among the men who fought, and the other half was distributed evenly among the men who had come to muster but who had not been selected to fight (and see 1 Samuel 31:21-25). A percentage of the spoils was given to the church (Numbers 31:28, 47). Such booty was a form of war reparations paid by the aggressors to the victorious defenders (Israel).

It should be noted that no booty went to the coffers of the state, and no special amount to the leaders of the state or to the military commanders. Gideon, as commander and as civil ruler of Israel, had to request extra booty from his men, who were only too happy to give it voluntarily (Judges 8:25).[13] The fact that the state gains nothing from war is one more great restraint on wars of aggression.

Thus, the Israelite militia was a genuine citizen army. Even though the state had the right to summon the militia, the citizenry could refuse to fight (2 Sam. 20:1; 1 Kings 12:16). For this reason, the kings of Israel were motivated to cripple the militia.

The Crippling of the Militia

There was nothing wrong with Israel's request for a king, because a true king would be a viceroy to the Lord. When, however, they demanded that they be given a king "like all the nations," they were rejecting the Lord as king, and opting for statism (1 Sam. 8).[14] Samuel promised that such a king would form a professional army, and draft the sons of Israel into it: "He will take your sons and place them for himself in his chariots and among his horsemen and they will run before his chariots" (1 Sam. 8:11). Here is a different kind of draft. Instead of a simple call in time of invasion, to which each man had to respond, we now have a professional army, oriented toward conquest (chariots, horses), with men ripped from their homes for seasons of military duty.

Initially, the kings were satisfied with a small corps of professional soldiers as a bodyguard and an active force ready for emergencies. Saul had his 3,000 (1 Sam. 13:2; 14:52; 24:2), and David his 600 (1 Sam.

---

[13] It is interesting to note the sequel. On this one occasion when the ruler was given lots of extra spoil, he used it to create an idol! See further the discussion of this passage in my book on *Judges*.

[14] For an extended treatment of this, see my book on *Judges*, particularly the last chapter.

23:13; 25:13; 2 Sam. 15:18; 20:7). There was nothing wrong with this. It was David who committed the great sin predicted by Samuel.

David determined to hold a peacetime muster, to incorporate the militia into a national army under the leadership of the professional army. The militia was only to have been mustered in the event of war, and so God visited Israel with a plague to punish David.[15] Joab, the captain of the professional army, opposed this. We are not told why, but the most likely reason is that Joab was suspicious of the militia. (Joab was not known for his sensitivity to the law of God, so we look for a reason closer to his personal interests.) David, however, wanted to control the militia.

Generally this event is studied from 2 Samuel 24, but there is more information on it in the book of 1 Chronicles. David's sinful muster, and the resultant plague, is discussed in 1 Chronicles 21. In 1 Chronicles 27, we see the result of this mustering. Israel was divided into 12 administrative districts, apparently not along tribal lines (thus breaking down local loyalties). Each district had 24,000 militia men who were enrolled as army reserves. These went on maneuver one month at a time, so that the army was always in a state of readiness. The remainder of the militia was still tribally organized (1 Chron. 27:16ff.).

It is interesting to note that this action on David's part cost him the honor of building the Temple for God. Ordinarily, the money collected from muster, and a percentage of the spoils of war, went to the upkeep of the church. Thus, the fact that David had fought a lot of wars, and laid up a lot of booty and muster money, would naturally lead to the supposition that he would build the Temple. God, however, stated that David was a man of excessive blood, and forbad him to do so. God's condemnation is rehearsed in two places in Scripture, the first immediately after David numbers the people (1 Chron. 22:8), and the second right after the chapter detailing the structure of the nationalized militia (1 Chron. 28:3). In this way, Scripture makes it plain that God was most displeased with this nationalizing tendency.

Given the fact that David's action was wrong, why did God not order him to undo it? The answer is because the people had demanded just this kind of king. God gave them what they wanted, and in the process brought them under judgment. (This is why though 1 Chronicles 21:1 says Satan moved David to muster the people, 2 Samuel 24:1 says that "the anger of the Lord burned against Israel, and He incited David against

---

[15] See my discussion of this in "State Financing in the Bible," referred to above.

them," showing that Satan acted with God's permission.) Once David had created a national army reserves, things did not go back to the way they had been. In the time of Uzziah, centuries later, this arrangement was still in force (2 Chron. 26:11-15).

The kings did not succeed in crippling the militia, at least not right away. Thus, when they were displeased with Rehoboam's increasingly statist measures, the militia exercised its constitutional right to refuse service, and departed from him (1 Kings 12:16). We see here the right of resistance, under the leadership of local magistrates (the context of 1 Kings 12 indicates that the elders of the people were leading them).[16]

We can summarize the relationship between local militia and professional army under the following points:

1. Scripture plainly teaches the right, and the importance, of an armed local militia consisting of every able-bodied man over 20 years of age.

2. It is entirely proper for a developed nation-state to maintain a small professional army, ready at all times to bear the brunt of attack while the militia is being organized.

3. It is proper for the professional army to organize the militia in times of war, and act as its captains.

4. It is not permitted, however, to turn the entire nation into an armed camp by drafting the militia into the professional army on a permanent, continuing basis.

5. The armed local militia has an extremely important role to play in the balance of power within a nation-state, which is why the tendency to nationalize the militia must be resisted.

The Importance of a Local Militia

In conclusion, I should like to comment briefly on the theological importance of the militia as a check on statist power. God is three and one, and thus in the Christian faith, the oneness of human society (made in His image) is not more important than the manyness of human society. What this has meant historically is that Christian nations operate in terms of balances of power. In the United States, for instance, there is supposed

---

[16] On the Christian doctrine of resistance to tyranny, see the two books edited by Gary North, *The Theology of Christian Resistance* and *Tactics of Christian Resistance* (Tyler, TX: Geneva Ministries, 1983).

to be a balance of power among the executive, legislative and judicial branches of government. There was originally a balance of power between the states and the national government. There was also originally a balance of power between the states and their citizens, seen in the fact that federal senators were appointed by state governments while federal representatives were elected by the people directly.

In terms of this conception of balance of power, the presence of an armed populace, trained in the use of weapons, and loosely organized into local militia, is a tremendous check on the power of any national government and its professional army.[17] This is true in two ways, as we have seen. First, it enables the citizenry to resist tyrannical moves on the part of the state. Second, it enables the citizenry to refuse being drafted to fight in unjust or pointless wars. Biblically speaking, all men are commanded to come when summoned to the muster, but this can be a very dangerous thing for the state to do. The assembled host might decide to refuse the demands of the king (as the Puritan parliament refused the demands of Charles I). Thus, the king is constrained to be wise and circumspect in any attempt to use the militia. (Indeed, in my opinion the fact that David got away with his move to incorporate the citizenry into the army reserves shows how popular he must have been with the people. God had to intervene personally to punish David.)

Our American forefathers imitated ancient Israel in providing for an armed militia. We would do well to return to their principles.

---

[17] R. J. Rushdoony provides an excellent study of the local character of police forces in the United States, as opposed to the nationalized police of most other nations. See "Localism and the Police Power" in *The Nature of the American System* (Tyler, TX: Thorburn Press, 1965 [1978]).

What Does the Bible Say About Gun Control?

Larry Pratt

The underlying argument for gun control seems to be that the availability of guns causes crime. By extension, the availability of any weapon would have to be viewed as a cause of crime. What does the Bible say about such a view?

Perhaps we should start at the beginning, or at least very close to the beginning—in Genesis 4. In this chapter we read about the first murder. Cain had offered an unacceptable sacrifice, and Cain was upset that God insisted that he do the right thing. In other words, Cain was peeved that he could not do his own thing.

Cain decided to kill his brother rather than get right with God. There were no guns available, although there may well have been a knife. Whether it was a knife or a rock, the Bible does not say. The point is, the evil in Cain's heart was the cause of the murder, not the availability of the murder weapon.

God's response was not to ban rocks or knives, or whatever, but to banish the murderer. Later (see Genesis 9:5-6) God instituted capital punishment, but said not a word about banning weapons.

Did Christ Teach Pacifism?

Many people, Christians included, assume that Christ taught pacifism. They cite Matthew 5:38-39 for their proof. In these verses Christ said: "You have heard that it was said, 'An eye for an eye and a tooth for a tooth.' But I tell you not to resist an evil person. But whoever slaps you on your right cheek, turn the other to him also."

The Sermon on the Mount from which this passage is taken deals with righteous personal conduct. In our passage, Christ is clearing up a

Parts of this article first appeared in Plymouth Rock Foundation's FAC-SHEET #62, "The Right To Bear Arms." Plymouth Rock Foundation can be contacted by writing to P.O. Box 577, Marlborough, NH 03455.

confusion that had led people to think conduct proper for the civil government—that is, taking vengeance—was also proper for an individual.

Even the choice of words used by Christ indicates that He was addressing a confusion, or a distortion, that was commonplace. Several times, in the rest of the Sermon on the Mount, Christ used this same "you have heard it said" figure of speech to straighten out misunderstandings or falsehoods being taught by the religious leaders of the times.

Contrast this to Christ's use of the phrase "it is written" when He was appealing to the Scriptures for authority (for example, see Matthew 4, where on three occasions during His temptation by the devil, Christ answered each one of the devil's lies or misquotes from Scripture with the words: "it is written").

To further underscore the point that Christ was correcting the religious leaders on their teaching that "an eye for an eye" applies to private revenge, consider that in the same Sermon, Christ strongly condemned false teaching: "Whoever therefore breaks one of the commandments, and teaches men so, shall be called least in the kingdom of heaven . . ." (Matthew 5:19). Clearly, then, Christ was not teaching something different about self-defense than is taught elsewhere in the Bible. Otherwise, He would be contradicting Himself for He would now be teaching men to break one of the commandments.

The Bible distinguishes clearly between the duties of the civil magistrate (the government) and the duties of an individual. Namely, God has delegated to the civil magistrate the administration of justice. Individuals have the responsibility of protecting their lives from attackers. Christ was referring to this distinction in the Matthew 5 passage. Let us now examine in some detail what the Scriptures say about the roles of government and of individuals.

Both the Old and New Testaments teach individual self-defense, even if it means taking the assailant's life in certain circumstances.

Self-Defense in the Old Testament

Exodus 22:2-3 tells us "If the thief is found breaking in, and he is struck so that he dies, there shall be no guilt for his bloodshed. If the sun has risen on him, there shall be guilt for his bloodshed. He should make full restitution; if he has nothing, then he shall be sold for his theft."

One conclusion which can be drawn from this is that a threat to our life is to be met with lethal force. During the day, presumably because we can recognize and later apprehend the thief if he escapes, we are not to kill him in non-life-threatening circumstances.

In Proverbs 25:26 we read that "A righteous man who falters before the wicked is like a murky spring and a polluted well." Certainly, we would be faltering before the wicked if we chose to be unarmed and unable to resist an assailant who might be threatening our life.

Trusting God

Another question asked by Christians is "Doesn't having a gun imply a lack of trust that God will take care of us?"

Indeed, God will take care of us. He has also told us that if we love Him, we will keep His commandments (John 14:15).

Those who trust God work for a living, knowing that 1 Timothy 5:8 tells us "But if anyone does not provide for his own, and especially for those of his household, he has denied the faith and is worse than an unbeliever." For a man not to work, yet expect to eat because he was "trusting God" would actually be to defy God.

King David wrote in Psalm 46:1 that God is our refuge and strength, a very present help in trouble. This did not conflict with praising the God "Who trains my hands for war and my fingers for battle" (Psalm 144:1).

The doctrine of Scripture is that we prepare and work, but we trust the outcome to God.

Those who trust God should also make adequate provision for their own defense even as we are instructed in the passages cited above. For a man to refuse to provide adequately for his and his family's defense would be to defy God.

The Role of Government

Resisting an attack is not to be confused with taking vengeance which is the exclusive domain of God (Romans 12:19). This has been delegated to the civil magistrate, who, as we read in Romans 13:4, "is God's minister to you for good. But if you do evil, be afraid; for he does not bear the sword in vain; for he is God's minister, an avenger to execute wrath on him who practices evil."

Private vengeance means one would stalk down a criminal *after* one's life is no longer in danger as opposed to defending oneself *during* an attack. It is this very point that has been confused by Christian pacifists who would take the passage in the Sermon on the Mount about turning the other cheek (which prohibits private vengeance) as a command to falter before the wicked.

Let us consider also that the Sixth Commandment tells us "Thou shall not murder." In the chapters following, God gave Moses many of the situations which require a death penalty. God clearly has not told us never to kill. He has told us not to murder, which means we are not to take an innocent life.

Consider also that the civil magistrate is to be a terror to those who *practice* evil. This passage does not in any way imply that the role of law enforcement is to prevent crimes or to protect individuals from criminals. The magistrate is a minister to serve as "an avenger to execute wrath on him who practices evil" (Romans 13:4).

This point is reflected in the legal doctrine of the United States. Repeatedly, courts have held that the government has no responsibility to provide individual security. One case (*Bowers v. DeVito*) put it this way: "There is no constitutional right to be protected by the state against being murdered."

Self-Defense in the New Testament

The Christian pacifist may try to argue that God has changed His mind from the time that He gave Moses the Ten Commandments on Mount Sinai. Perhaps they would want us to think that Christ canceled out the Ten Commandments in Exodus 20 or the provision for justifiably killing in thief in Exodus 22. But the writer of Hebrews makes it clear that this cannot be, because "Jesus Christ is the same yesterday, today and forever" (Hebrews 13:8). In the Old Testament, the prophet Malachi records God's words this way: "For I am the Lord, I do not change" (Malachi 3:6).

Paul was referring to the unchangeability of God's Word when he wrote to Timothy that "All Scripture is given by inspiration of God, and is profitable for doctrine, for reproof, for correction, for instruction in righteousness, that the man of God may be complete, thoroughly equipped for every good work" (2 Timothy 3:16-17). Clearly, Paul viewed *all Scripture*, including the Old Testament, as useful for training Christians in every area of life.

We must also consider what Christ told his disciples in his last hours with them: ". . . But now, he who has a money bag, let him take it, and likewise a sack; and *he who has no sword, let him sell his garment and buy one*" (Luke 22:36, emphasis added). Keep in mind that the sword was the finest offensive weapon available to an individual soldier—the equivalent then of a military rifle today.

The Christian pacifist will likely object at this point that only a few hours later, Christ rebuked Peter who used a sword to cut off the ear of Malchus, a servant of the high priest in the company of a detachment of troops. Let us read what Christ said to Peter in Matthew 26:52-54:

> Put your sword in its place, for all who take the sword will perish by the sword. Or do you think that I cannot now pray to My Father, and He will provide Me with more than twelve legions of angels? How then could the Scriptures be fulfilled, that it must happen thus?

It was not the first time that Christ had to explain to the disciples why He had come to earth. To fulfill the Scriptures, the Son of God had to die for the sin of man since man was incapable of paying for his own sin apart from going to hell. Christ could have saved His life, but then believers would have lost their lives forever in hell. These things only became clear to the disciples after Christ had died and been raised from the dead and the Spirit had come into the world at Pentecost (see John 14:26).

While Christ told Peter to "put your sword in its place," He clearly did not say get rid of it forever. That would have contradicted what he had told the disciples only hours before. Peter's sword was to protect his own mortal life from danger. His sword was not needed to protect the Creator of the universe and the King of kings.

Years after Pentecost, Paul wrote in a letter to Timothy "But if anyone does not provide for his own, and especially for those of his household, he has denied the faith and is worse than an unbeliever" (1 Timothy 5:8). This passage applies to our subject because it would be absurd to buy a house, furnish it with food and facilities for one's family, and then refuse to install locks and provide the means to protect the family and the property. Likewise it would be absurd not to take, if necessary, the life of a night-time thief to protect the members of the family (Exodus 22:2-3).

255

A related, and even broader concept, is found in the parable of the Good Samaritan. Christ had referred to the Old Testament summary of all the laws of the Bible into two great commandments: " 'You shall love the Lord your God with all your heart, with all your soul, with all your strength, and with all your mind,' and 'your neighbor as yourself' " (Luke 10:27). When asked who was a neighbor, Christ related the parable of the Good Samaritan (Luke 10:30-37). It was the Good Samaritan who took care of the mugging victim who was a neighbor to the victim. The others who walked by and ignored the victim's plight were not acting as neighbors to him.

In the light of all we have seen the Scriptures teach to this point, can we argue that if we were able to save another's life from an attacker by shooting the attacker with our gun that we should "turn the other cheek instead"? The Bible speaks of no such right. It only speaks of our responsibilities in the face of an attack—as individual creatures made by God, as householders or neighbors.

National Blessings and Cursings

The Old Testament also tells us a great deal about the positive relationship between righteousness, which exalts a nation, and self-defense.[1]

It makes clear that in times of national rebellion against the Lord God, the rulers of the nation will reflect the spiritual degradation of the

---

[1] "When our forefathers wrote the Constitution of the United States, consciously or unconsciously, they followed the Israel system of the right of every man to keep and bear arms. [The Second Amendment] was patterned after the Israel method: when every able-bodied man capable of bearing arms and who might be called upon by the nation for military duties to defend his country, his life, liberty and freedom was thus able and prepared to take his place in the ranks of the army.

"Tyranny, as a rule, arises from within a nation when the government has been captured by men who would use their acquired power to oppress the people. *These facts were known to the Framers of the Constitution, hence they recognized the need and right of citizens to keep and bear arms in order to insure real liberty. God in His wisdom . . . made it a fundamental law in the land that every man should be a part of the military forces of the nation—keeping his arms and equipment in his own possession.*

"Now the right of citizens to keep and bear arms is fundamental in preserving true freedom, so much so that subversive forces in sundry and subtle ways first move to disarm the citizens of a nation which they later plan to dominate. We have witnessed such moves in the past while states which have already passed laws violating Article II of our Constitution did so under the pretext of disarming the criminal. *The states which have violated this fundamental principle of the protection of its citizens against armed violence have not only failed to reduce crime but have also contributed to the increase in violence and crime. The criminal, who never disarms, knows he is dealing with law-abiding unarmed citizens. Honest men and leaders never fear an armed, law-abiding civilian population.*"

Howard B. Rand, LL.B., *Digest of the Divine Law* (Destiny Publishers: Merrimac, Mass., 1943), pp. 163-64.

people and the result is a denial of God's commandments, an arrogance of officialdom, disarmament, and oppression.

For example, the people of Israel were oppressed during the time of the rule of the Judges. This occurred every time the people apostatized. Judges 5:8 tells us that, "They chose new gods; then there was war in the gates; not a shield or spear was seen among forty thousand in Israel."

Consider Israel under Saul: The first book of Samuel tells of the turning away of Israel from God. The people did not want to be governed by God; they wanted to be ruled by a king like the pagan, God-hating nations around them. Samuel warned the people what they were getting into—the curses that would be upon them—if they persisted in raising up a king over themselves and their families. Included in those curses was the raising up of a standing, professional army which would take their sons and their daughters for aggressive wars (I Samuel 8:11).

This curse is not unknown in the United States. Saul carried out all the judgments that Samuel had warned the people about. His build up of a standing army has been repeated in the United States, and not just in terms of the military, but also the 650,000 full-time police officers from all levels of government.

Saul was the king the Israelites wanted and got. He was beautiful in the eyes of the world but a disaster in the eyes of the Lord. Saul did not trust God. He rebelled against His form of sacrifice unto the Lord. Saul put himself above God. He was impatient. He refused to wait for Samuel because God's way was taking too long. Saul went ahead and performed the sacrifice himself, thus violating God's commandment (and, incidentally, also violating the God-ordained separation of duties of church and state).

Thus was the kingdom lost to Saul. And, it was under him that the Philistines were able to defeat the Jews and put them into bondage. So great was the bondage exerted by the Philistines that "Now there was no blacksmith to be found throughout all the land of Israel: for the Philistines said, 'Lest the Hebrews make them swords or spears.' But all the Israelites went down to the Philistines to sharpen each man's plowshare, his mattock, his ax, and his sickle; . . . So it came about, on the day of battle, that there was neither sword nor spear found in the hand of any of the people who were with Saul and Jonathan . . ." (Samuel 13:19-20, 22-23).

Today, the same goals of the Philistines would be carried out by an oppressor who would ban gunsmiths from the land. The sword of today is the handgun, rifle or shotgun. The sword control of the Philistine's is today's gun control of those governments that do not trust their people with guns.

It is important to understand that what happened to the Jews at the time of Saul was not unexpected according to the sanctions spelled out by God in Leviticus 26 and Deuteronomy 28. In the first verses of those chapters, blessings are promised to a nation that keeps God's laws. In the long second parts of those chapters, the curses are spelled out for a nation that comes under judgment for its rebellion against God. Deuteronomy 28:47-48 helps us understand the reason for Israel's oppression by the Philistines during Saul's reign:

> Because you did not serve the Lord your God with joy and gladness of heart, for the abundance of all things, therefore you shall serve your enemies, whom the Lord will send against you, in hunger, in thirst, in nakedness, and in need of all things; and He will put a yoke of iron on your neck until He has destroyed you.

The Bible provides examples of God's blessing upon Israel for its faithfulness. These blessings included a strong national defense coupled with peace. A clear example occurred during the reign of Jehoshaphat. 2 Chronicles 17 tells of how Jehoshaphat led Israel back to faithfulness to God which included a strong national defense. The result: "And the fear of the Lord fell on all the kingdoms of the lands that were around Judah, so that they did not make war against Jehoshaphat" (2 Chronicles 17:10).

The Israelite army was a militia army which came to battle with each man bearing his own weapons—from the time of Moses, through the Judges, and beyond. When threatened by the Midianites, for example: "So Moses spoke to the people, saying, 'Arm some of yourselves for the war, and let them go against the Midianites to take vengeance for the Lord on Midian' " (Numbers 31:3). Again, to demonstrate the Biblical heritage of individuals bearing and keeping arms, during David's time in the wilderness avoiding capture by Saul: "David said to his men, 'Every man gird on his sword.' So every man girded on his sword, and David also girded on his sword" (1 Samuel 25:13).

Finally, consider Nehemiah and those who rebuilt the gates and walls of Jerusalem. They were both builders and defenders, each man—each servant—armed with his own weapon:

Those who built on the wall, and those who carried burdens loaded themselves so that with one hand they worked at construction, and with the other held a weapon. Every one of the builders had his sword girded at his side as he built (Nehemiah 4:17-18).

Conclusion

The wisdom of the Framers of the Constitution is consistent with the lessons of the Bible. Instruments of defense should be dispersed throughout the nation, not concentrated in the hands of the central government. In a godly country, righteousness governs each man through the Holy Spirit working within. The government has no cause to want a monopoly of force; the government that desires such a monopoly is a threat to the lives, liberty and property of its citizens.

The assumption that only danger can result from people carrying guns is used to justify government monopoly of force. The notion that the people cannot be trusted to keep and bear their own arms informs us that our time, like Solomon's, may be one of great riches, but is also a time of peril to free people. If Christ is not our King, we shall have a dictator to rule over us, just as Samuel warned.

For those who think that God treated Israel differently from the way He will treat us today, please consider what God told the prophet Malachi: "For I am the Lord, I do not change . . ." (Malachi 3:6).

259

Trust the People:
The Case Against Gun Control

David B. Kopel

*Men by their constitutions are naturally divided into two parties: 1)
Those who fear and distrust the people. . . . 2) Those who identify
themselves with the people, have confidence in them, cherish and
consider them as the most honest and safe . . . depository of the public
interest.*

Thomas Jefferson

Few public policy debates have been as dominated by emotion and
misinformation as the one on gun control. Perhaps this debate is so highly
charged because it involves such fundamental issues. The calls for more
gun restrictions or for bans on some or all guns are calls for significant
change in our social and constitutional systems.

Gun control is based on the faulty notion that ordinary American
citizens are too clumsy and ill-tempered to be trusted with weapons. Only
through the blatant abrogation of explicit constitutional rights is gun
control even possible. It must be enforced with such violations of
individual rights as intrusive search and seizure. It most severely
victimizes those who most need weapons for self-defense, such as blacks
and women.

The various gun control proposals on today's agenda—including
licensing, waiting periods, and bans on so-called Saturday night
specials—are of little, if any, value as crime-fighting measures. Banning
guns to reduce crime makes as little sense as banning alcohol to reduce
drunk driving. Indeed, persuasive evidence shows that civilian gun
ownership can be a powerful deterrent to crime.

The gun control debate poses the basic question: Who is more trustworthy, the government or the people?

David B. Kopel, formerly an assistant district attorney in Manhattan, is an attorney in Denver,
and a research associate with the Independence Institute in Golden, Colorado.

Guns and Crime

Guns as a Cause of Crime

Gun control advocates—those who favor additional legal restrictions on the availability of guns or who want to outlaw certain types of guns—argue that the more guns there are, the more crime there will be. As a Detroit narcotics officer put it, "Drugs are X; the number of guns in our society is Y; the number of kids in possession of drugs is Z. X plus Y plus Z equals an increase in murders."[2] But there is no simple statistical correlation between gun ownership and homicide or other violent crimes. In the first 30 years of this century, U.S. per capita handgun ownership remained stable, but the homicide rate rose ten-fold.[3] Subsequently, between 1937 and 1963, handgun ownership rose by 250 percent, but the homicide rate fell by 35.7 percent.[4]

Switzerland, through its militia system, distributes both pistols and fully automatic assault rifles to all adult males and requires them to store their weapons at home. Further, civilian long-gun purchases are essentially unregulated, and handguns are available to any adult without a criminal record or mental defect. Nevertheless, Switzerland suffers far less crime per capita than the United States and almost no gun crime.

Allowing for important differences between Switzerland and the United States, it seems clear that there is no direct link between the level of citizen gun ownership and the level of gun misuse. Instead of simplistically assuming that the fewer guns there are, the safer society will be, one should analyze the particular costs and benefits of gun ownership and gun control and consider which groups gain and lose from particular policies.

---

[2] "Urban Murders on the Rise," *Newsweek*, February 9, 1987, p. 30. The officer's formula does not consider the possibility that gun ownership might be a deterrent to rising crime rates. For gun ownership as a response to crime rate increases, see B. Benson, "Private Sector Responses to Rising Crime," in *Firearms and Violence: Issues of Public Policy*, ed. Donald B. Kates (Cambridge, Mass.: Ballinger, 1984), pp. 329-56.

[3] D. Lunde, *Murder and Madness* (San Francisco: San Francisco Book Co., 1976), p. 1.

[4] Donald B. Kates, *Why Handgun Bans Can't Work* (Bellevue, Wash.: Second Amendment Foundation, 1982), p. 23. One study of various Illinois counties found no relation between gun ownership and crime, except that female gun ownership appeared to rise in response to a rising crime rate. See David Bordua, "Firearms Ownership and Violent Crime: A Comparison of Illinois Counties," in *The Social Ecology of Crime* (New York: Springer-Verlag, 1986).

Guns as a Tool Against Crime

Several years ago the National Institute of Justice offered a grant to the former president of the American Sociological Association to survey the field of research on gun control. Peter Rossi began his work convinced of the need for strict national gun control. After looking at the data, however, Rossi and his University of Massachusetts colleagues James Wright and Kathleen Daly concluded that there was no convincing proof that gun control curbs crime.[5] A follow-up study by Wright and Rossi of serious felons in American prisons provided further evidence that gun control would not impede determined criminals.[6] It also indicated that civilian gun ownership does deter some crime. Three-fifths of the prisoners studied said that a criminal would not attack a potential victim who was known to be armed. Two-fifths of them had decided not to commit a crime because they thought the victim might have a gun. Criminals in states with higher civilian gun ownership rates worried the most about armed victims.

Real-world experiences are not inconsistent with the sociologists' findings. In 1966 the police in Orlando, Florida, responded to a rape epidemic by embarking on a highly publicized program to train 2,500 women in firearm use. The next year rape fell by 88 percent in Orlando (the only major city to experience a decrease that year); burglary fell by 25 percent. Not one of the 2,500 women actually ended up firing her weapon; the deterrent effect of the publicity sufficed. Five years later Orlando's rape rate was still 13 percent below the pre-program level, whereas the surrounding standard metropolitan area had suffered a 308 percent increase.[7] During a 1974 police strike in Albuquerque armed citizens patrolled their neighborhoods and shop owners publicly armed themselves; felonies dropped significantly.[8] In March 1982, Kennesaw, Georgia, enacted a law requiring householders to keep a gun at home; house burglaries fell from 65 per year to 26, and to 11 the following year.[9] Similar publicized training programs for gun-toting merchants

---

[5] James Wright, Peter Rossi, and Kathleen Daly, *Under the Gun: Weapons, Crime and Violence in America* (Hawthorne, N.Y.: Aldine, 1983).

[6] James Wright and Peter Rossi, *Armed and Considered Dangerous: A Survey of Felons and Their Firearms* (Hawthorne, N.Y.: Aldine, 1986), pp. 141, 145, 151.

[7] Gary Kleck, "Policy Lessons from Recent Gun Control Research," *Journal of Law and Contemporary Problems* 49 (Winter 1986): 35-47.

[8] Carol Ruth Silver and Donald B. Kates, "Self-Defense, Handgun Ownership, and the Independence of Women in a Violent, Sexist Society," in *Restricting Handguns: The Liberal Skeptics Speak Out*, ed. Donald B. Kates (Croton-on-Hudson, N.Y.: North River Press, 1979), p. 152.

[9] "Town to Celebrate Mandatory Arms," *New York Times*, April 11, 1987, p. 6.

sharply reduced robberies in stores in Highland Park, Michigan, and in New Orleans; a grocers organization's gun clinics produced the same result in Detroit.[10]

Gun control advocates note that only two burglars in 1,000 are driven off by armed homeowners. However, since a huge preponderance of burglaries take place when no one is home, the statistical citation is misleading. Several criminologists attribute the prevalence of daytime burglary to burglars' fear of confronting an armed occupant.[11] Indeed, a burglar's chance of being sent to jail is about the same as his chance of being shot by a victim if the burglar breaks into an occupied residence (one to two percent in each case).[12]

Can Gun Laws Be Enforced?

As Stanford law professor John Kaplan has observed, "When guns are outlawed, all those who have guns will be outlaws."[13] Kaplan argued that when a law criminalizes behavior that its practitioners do not believe improper, the new outlaws lose respect for society and the law. Kaplan found the problem especially severe in situations where the numbers of outlaws are very high, as in the case of alcohol, marijuana, or gun prohibition.

Even simple registration laws meet with massive resistance. In Illinois, for example, a 1977 study showed that compliance with handgun registration was only about 25 percent.[14] A 1979 survey of Illinois gun owners indicated that 73 percent would not comply with a gun prohibition.[15] It is evident that New York City's almost complete prohibition is not voluntarily obeyed; estimates of the number of illegal handguns in the city range from one million to two million.[16]

With more widespread American gun control, the number of new outlaws would certainly be huge. Prohibition would label as criminal the

---

[10] Gary Kleck and David Bordua, "The Factual Foundation for Certain Key Assumptions of Gun Control," *Law and Policy Quarterly* 5 (1983): 271-98.

[11] George Rengert and John Wasilchick, *Suburban Burglary: A Time and a Place for Everything* (Springfield, Ill.: Charles C. Thomas, 1985), p. 30; J. Conklin, *Robbery and the Criminal Justice System* (Philadelphia: Lippincott, 1972), p. 85.

[12] Wright, Rossi, and Daly, pp. 139-40.

[13] John Kaplan, "Controlling Firearms," *Cleveland State Law Review* 28 (1979), p. 8.

[14] Donald B. Kates, "Handgun Control: Prohibition Revisisted," *Inquiry*, December 5, 1977, p. 20, n. 1.

[15] David Bordua, Alan Lizotte, and Gary Kleck, *Patterns of Firearms Ownership, Use, and Registration in Illinois* (Springfield, Ill.: Illinois Law Enforcement Commission, 1979), p. 253.

[16] Kates, *Why Handgun Bans Can't Work*, p. 43.

millions of otherwise law-abiding citizens who believe they must possess the means to defend themselves, regardless of what legislation dictates.

In addition, strict enforcement of gun prohibition—like our current marijuana prohibition and our past alcohol prohibition—would divert enormous police and judicial resources to ferreting out and prosecuting the commission of private, consensual possessory offenses. The diversion of resources to the prosecution of such offenses would mean fewer resources available to fight other crime.

Assume half of all current handgun owners would disobey a prohibition and that 10 percent of them would be caught. Since the cost of arresting someone for a serious offense is well over $2,000, the total cost in arrests alone would amount to $5 billion a year. Assuming that the defendants plea-bargained at the normal rate (an unlikely assumption, since juries would be more sympathetic to such defendants than to most other criminals), the cost of prosecution and trial would be at least $4.5 billion a year. Putting each of the convicted defendants in jail for a three-day term would cost over $660 million in one-time prison construction costs, and over $200 million in annual maintenance, and would require a 10 percent increase in national prison capacity.[17] Given that the entire American criminal justice system has a total annual budget of only $45 billion, it is clear that effective enforcement of a handgun prohibition would simply be impossible.

Do Gun Laws Disarm Criminals?

Although gun control advocates devote much attention to the alleged evils of guns and gun owners, they devote little attention to the particulars of devising a workable, enforceable law. Disarming criminals would be nearly impossible. There are at least 100 to 140 million guns in the United States, a third of them handguns.[18] The ratio of people who commit handgun crimes each year to handguns is 1:400, that of handgun homicides to handguns is 1:3,600.[19] Because the ratio of handguns to

---

[17] David Hardy, "Critiquing the Case for Handgun Prohibition," in *Restricting Handguns*, pp. 87-88. Hardy's article was published in 1979, so it is fair to assume that the actual costs would be considerably higher than the figures quoted here. See also Raymond Kessler, "Enforcement Problems of Gun Control: A Victimless Crimes Analysis," *Criminal Law Bulletin* 16 (March/April 1980): 131-44.

[18] Wright, Rossi, and Daly, pp. 25-44. A more recent estimate by the Bureau of Alcohol, Tobacco and Firearms puts the number at 200 million.

[19] The armed crime ratio is based on an assumption that there are about 100,000 handgun criminals in the United States. About 300,000 handgun crimes are reported annually to the FBI. Since many robbers and burglars carry out several dozen crimes or more a year, it seems safe to divide the total of 300,000 by at least three, allotting three crimes per criminal. The homicide

handgun criminals is so high, the criminal supply would continue with barely an interruption. Even if 90 percent of American handguns disappeared, there would still be 40 left for every handgun criminal. In no state in the union can people with recent violent felony convictions purchase firearms. Yet the National Institute of Justice survey of prisoners, many of whom were repeat offenders, showed that 90 percent were able to obtain their last firearm within a few days. Most obtained it within a few hours. Three-quarters of the men agreed that they would have "no trouble" or "only a little trouble" obtaining a gun upon release, despite the legal barriers to such a purchase.[20]

Even if the entire American gun stock magically vanished, resupply for criminals would be easy. If small handguns were imported in the same physical volume as marijuana, 20 million would enter the country annually. (Current legal demand for new handguns is about 2.5 million a year.) Bootleg gun manufacture requires no more than the tools that most Americans have in their garages. A zip gun can be made from tubing, tape, a pin, a key, whittle wood and rubber bands. In fact, using wood fires and tools inferior to those in the Sears & Roebuck catalog, Pakistani and Afghan peasants have been making firearms capable of firing the Russian AK-47 cartridge.[21] Bootleg ammunition is no harder to make than bootleg liquor. Although modern smokeless gunpowder is too complex for backyard production, conventional black powder is simple to manufacture.[22]

Apparently, illegal gun production is already common. A 1986 federal government study found that one-fifth of the guns seized by the police in Washington, D.C., were homemade.[23] Of course, homemade guns cannot win target-shooting contests, but they suffice for robbery purposes. Furthermore, the price of bootleg guns may even be lower than

---

ratio is based on an assumption of 10,000 handgun homicides annually (and no gun being used in more than one homicide). In 1984 there were 9,819 gun homicides in the United States, of which 7,277 were committed with a handgun. See Department of Commerce (Bureau of Census), *Statistical Abstract of the United States 1986* (Washington, D.C.: Government Printing Office, 1985), p. 171.

[20] Wright and Rossi, pp. 189, 211.

[21] "Tribesmen in Pakistan Thrive," *New York Times*, November 2, 1977, p. 2; Wright, Rossi, and Daly, p. 321.

[22] Kaplan, p. 20

[23] Bureau of Alcohol, Tobacco and Firearms, *Analysis of Operation CUE (Concentrated Urban Enforcement)*, interim report (Washington, D.C.: February 15, 1977), pp. 133-34, cited in Paul Blackman and Richard Gardiner, *Flaws in the Current and Proposed Uniform Crime Reporting Programs Regarding Homicide and Weapons Use in Violent Crime*, paper presented at 38th Annual Meeting of the American Society of Criminology, Atlanta, October 29–November 1, 1986.

the price of the quality guns available now (just as, in prohibition days, bootleg gin often cost less than legal alcohol had).

Most police officers concur that gun control laws are ineffective. A 1986 questionnaire sent to every major police official in the country produced the following results: 97 percent believed that a firearms ownership ban would not reduce crime or keep criminals from using guns; 89 percent believed that gun control laws such as those in Chicago, Washington, D.C., and New York City had no effect on criminals; and 90 percent believed that if firearms ownership was banned, ordinary citizens would be more likely to be targets of armed violence.[24]

Guns and the Ordinary Citizen

Some advocates of gun prohibition concede that it will not disarm criminals, but nevertheless they favor it in the belief that disarming ordinary citizens would in itself be good. Their belief seems to rely heavily on newspaper accounts of suicidal or outlandishly careless gun owners shooting themselves or loved ones. Such advocates can reel off newspaper stories of children or adults killing themselves in foolish gun accidents (one headline: "2-Year-Old Boy Shoots Friend, 5") or shooting each other in moments of temporary frenzy.

In using argument by anecdote, the advocates are aided by the media, which sensationalize violence. The sensationalism and selectivity of the press lead readers to false conclusions. One poll showed that people believe homicide takes more lives annually than diabetes, stomach cancer,

---

[24] Gerald Arenberg, *Do the Police Support Gun Control?* (Bellevue, Wash.: Second Amendment Foundation, n.d.), p. 10. Arenberg is executive director of the National Association of Chiefs of Police.

In the past several years, Handgun Control Inc. has attempted to create the impression that the police support gun control. It is true that some police organizations, such as the Police Foundation and the International Association of Chiefs of Police, often favor gun control. It is hardly surprising that some police lobbies support a narrow view of the Second Amendment, since police organizations often take a dim view of all constitutional rights, such as search and seizure protections or suspects' right to legal counsel.

The anti-gun police lobbies, however, can hardly claim the unanimous support of rank-and-file police. The then-president of the American Federation of Police, Dennis Ray Martin, appeared in print advertisements as a Second Amendment Foundation spokesman (e.g., *Gun Week*, April 22, 1988, p. 7). After Handgun Control Inc. placed an advertisement in *Police* magazine, the magazine received mail "unrivaled by any subject in the last two years," most of the writers "saying they didn't like the contents of the ad one bit." *Police*'s editor composed an editorial condemning Handgun Control Inc., defending the NRA, and warning that "HCI is trying to erode" the Second Amendment, F. McKeen Thompson, "Readers Respond to HCI . . . And We Agree," *Police (The Law Officer's Magazine)*, December 1987, p. 4.

or stroke; in fact, strokes alone take 10 times as many lives as homicides.[25]

Even in the war of anecdotes, however, it is not at all clear that the gun control advocates have the advantage. Every month the National Rifle Association's magazines feature a section called "The Armed Citizen," which collects newspaper clippings of citizens successfully defending themselves against crime. For example, one story tells of a man in a wheelchair who had been beaten and robbed during five break-ins in two months; when the man heard someone prying at his window with a hatchet, he fired a shotgun, wounding the burglar and driving him away.[26]

Anecdotes rarely settle policy disputes, though. A cool-headed review of the facts debunks the scare tactics of the gun control advocates.

Some people with firsthand experience blame guns for domestic homicides. Said the chief of the homicide section of the Chicago Police Department, "There was a domestic fight. A gun was there. And then somebody was dead. If you have described one, you have described them all."[27] Sociologist R. P. Narlock, though, believes that "the mere availability of weapons lethal enough to produce a human mortality bears no major relationship to the frequency with which this act is completed."[28]

Guns do not turn ordinary citizens into murderers. Significantly, fewer than one gun owner in 3,000 commits homicide; and that one killer is far from a typical gun owner. Studies have found two-thirds to four-fifths of homicide offenders have prior arrest records, frequently for violent felonies.[29] A study by the pro-control Police Foundation of domestic homicides in Kansas City in 1977 revealed that in 85 percent of homicides among family members, the police had been called in

---

[25] W. Allman, "Staying Alive in the 20th Century," Science 85, vol. 6, no. 8 (October 1985) p. 34, cited in Lance Stell, "Guns, Politics and Reason," Journal of American Culture 9 (Summer 1986): 71-85.

[26] "The Armed Citizen," American Hunter, February 1987, p. 6, citing Miami Herald, December 16, 1986.

[27] Quoted in Wright, Rossi, and Daly, pp. 129-30.

[28] R. P. Narlock, Criminal Homicide in California (Sacramento: California Department of Justice, Bureau of Criminal Statistics, 1967), p. 55, cited in Congressional Record, 90th Cong., 2d sess., January 30, 1968, p. 1497. Even the University of Pennsylvania's Marvin Wolfgang, who favors gun control, agrees (Marvin Wolfgang, Patterns in Criminal Homicide [Philadelphia: University of Pennsylvania Press, 1958], p. 83). The conclusion is strongly disputed by some pro-control scholars, such as the University of California's Franklin Zimring.

[29] Kates, Why Handgun Bans Can't Work, pp. 25-26. See also Kleck, "Policy Lessons," pp. 40-41, stating that 70-75 percent of domestic homicide offenders have a previous arrest, and about half have a previous conviction.

before to break up violence.[30] In half the cases, the police had been called in five or more times. Thus, the average person who kills a family member is not a non-violent solid citizen who reaches for a weapon in a moment of temporary insanity. Instead, he has a past record of illegal violence and trouble with the law. Such people on the fringes of society are unlikely to be affected by gun control laws. Indeed, since many killers already had felony convictions, it was already illegal for them to own a gun, but they found one anyway.

Of all gun homicide victims, 81 percent are relatives or acquaintances of the killer.[31] As one might expect of the wives, companions, and business associates (e.g. drug dealers and loansharks) of violent felons, the victims are no paragons of society. In a study of the victims of near-fatal domestic shootings and stabbings, 78 percent of the victims volunteered a history of hard-drug use, and 16 percent admitted using heroin the day of the incident.[32] Many of the handgun homicide victims might well have been handgun killers, had the conflict turned out a little differently.

Finally, many of the domestic killings with guns involve self-defense. In Detroit, for example, 75 percent of wives who shot and killed their husbands were not prosecuted, because the wives were legally defending themselves or their children against murderous assault.[33] When a gun is fired (or brandished) for legal self-defense in a home, the criminal attacker is much more likely to be a relative or acquaintance committing aggravated assault, rather than a total stranger committing a burglary.

It is often alleged that guns cause huge numbers of fatal accidents, far outweighing the minimal gain from whatever anti-crime effects they may have. For example, former U.S. Senate candidate Mark Green (D-NY) warned that "people with guns in their homes for protection are *six times* more likely to die of gunfire due to accidental discharge than those without them."[34] Of course, that makes sense; after all, people who own swimming pools are more likely to die in drowning accidents.

---

[30] M. Wilt, G. Marie, J. Bannon, R. K. Breedlove, J. W. Kennish, D. M. Snadker, and R. K. Satwell, *Domestic Violence and the Police: Studies in Detroit and Kansas City* (Washington, D.C.: Government Printing Office, 1977), quoted in Wright, Rossi, and Daly, p. 193, n. 3.

[31] Robert Sherrill, *The Saturday Night Special* (New York: Charterhouse, 1975), p. 29, citing "Gun Murder Profile," written by Senate Judiciary Committee's Juvenile Delinquency Subcommittee (Washington, D.C.: Government Printing Office, n.d.).

[32] Kirkpatrick and Walt, "The High Cost of Gunshot and Stab Wounds," *Journal of Surgical Research* 14 (1973): 261-62.

[33] M. Daly and M. Wilson, *Homicide* (New York: Aldine, 1988), pp. 15, 200 (table, p. 1).

[34] Mark Green, *Winning Back America* (New York: Bantam, 1982), p. 222.

The actual number of people who die in home handgun accidents, though, is quite small. Despite press headlines such as "Pregnant Woman Killed by Own Gun While Making Bed," the actual death toll is somewhat lower than implied by the press. Each year roughly 7,000 people commit suicide with handguns and 300 or fewer people die in handgun accidents.[35] People who want to commit suicide can find many alternatives, and even pro-control experts agree that gun control has little impact on the suicide rate. Japan, for example, has strict gun control and a suicide rate twice the U.S. level. Americans have a high rate of suicide by shooting for the same reason that Norwegians have a high rate of suicide by drowning: guns are an important symbol in one culture, water in the other.[36]

If a U.S. gun prohibition were actually effective, it might save the 300 or so handgun victims and 1,400 or so long-gun accident victims each year. Even one death is too many, but guns account for only two percent of accidental deaths annually.[37]

Guns are dangerous, but hardly as dangerous as gun control advocates contend. Three times as many people are accidentally killed by fire as by firearms.[38] The number of people who die in gun accidents is about one-third the number who die by drowning.[39] Although newspapers leave a contrary impression, bicycle accidents kill many more children than do gun accidents. The average motor vehicle is 12 times more likely to cause

---

[35] David Hardy, "Product Liability and Weapons Manufacture," *Wake Forest Law Review* 20 (Fall 1984), p. 551; Federal Bureau of Investigation, *Uniform Crime Report 1982* (Washington, D.C.: Government Printing Office), p. 10; National Safety Council, *Accident Facts 1986 Edition* (Washington, D.C.: Government Printing Office), p. 12. Total deaths from all firearms suicides are about 17,000 annually (*Statistical Abstract of the United States 1985*, p. 79).

[36] George Newton and Franklin Zimring, *Firearms and Violence in American Life*, report to the National Commission on the Causes and Prevention of Violence (Washington, D.C.: Government Printing Office, 1970), ch. 6. See also Bruce Danto, "Firearms and Their Role in Suicide," *Life-Threatening Behavior* 1 (1971), p. 14 (Study of foreign and American suicide; "[D]ata shows that people will find a way to commit suicide regardless of the availability of firearms."); Herbert Hendin, *Suicide in America* (New York: W. W. Norton, 1982), pp. 144-46, citing Maurice Taylor and Jerry Wicks, "The Choice of Weapons: A Study in Suicide by Sex, Race, and Religion," *Suicide and Life-Threatening Behavior* 10 (1980): 142-49; Paul Friedman, "Suicide Among the Police," in *Essays in Self-Destruction*, ed. E. Shneidman (New York: Science House, 1967), pp. 414-49.

[37] National Safety Council, *Accident Facts 1986 Edition* (Washington, D.C.: Government Printing Office), p. 12. According to the Council, in 1983 there were 92,488 accidental deaths, and 1,695 accidental firearms deaths.

[38] National Safety Council, p. 12, reporting 1,695 deaths from firearms accidents, and 5,028 deaths from flame or fire accidents.

[39] National Safety Council, p. 12, reporting 1,695 deaths from firearms accidents, and 5,254 deaths from drowning or submersion accidents (not including drowning deaths relating to water transport).

a death than the average firearm.[40] Further, people involved in gun accidents are not typical gun owners but self-destructive individuals who are also "disproportionately involved in other accidents, violent crime and heavy drinking."[41]

Moreover, there is little correlation between the number of guns and the accident rate. The per capita death rate from firearms accidents has declined by a third in the last two decades, while the firearms supply has risen over 300 percent. In part this is because handguns have replaced many long guns as home protection weapons, and handgun accidents are considerably less likely to cause death than long-gun accidents.[42] Handguns are also more difficult for a toddler to accidentally discharge than are long guns.[43]

The risks, therefore, of gun ownership by ordinary citizens are quite low. Accidents can be avoided by buying a trigger lock and not cleaning a gun while it is loaded. Unless the gun owner is already a violent thug, he is very unlikely to kill a relative in a moment of passion. If someone in the house is intent on suicide, he will kill himself by whatever means are at hand.

Gun control advocates like to cite an article in the *New England Journal of Medicine* that argues that for every intruder killed by a gun, 43 other people die as a result of gunshot wounds incurred in the home.[44] (Again, most of them are suicides; many of the rest are assaultive family members killed in legitimate self-defense.) However, counting the number of criminal deaths is a bizarre method of measuring anti-crime utility; no one evaluates police efficacy by tallying the number of criminals killed. Defensive use of a gun is far more likely to involve scaring away an attacker by brandishing the gun, or by firing it without causing death. Even if the numbers of criminal deaths were the proper measure of anti-

---

[40] Mark Benenson, "A Controlled Look at Gun Controls," *New York Law Forum* 14 (Winter 1968), p. 741.

[41] Philip Cook, "The Role of Firearms in Violent Crime: An Interpretative Review of the Literature," in M. Wolfgang and N. Weiler, eds. *Criminal Violence* (Beverly Hills, Calif.: Sage, 1982), pp. 236, 269.

[42] Colin Greenwood, "Comparative Statistics," in *Restricting Handguns*, pp. 58-59.

[43] The trigger on a rifle or shotgun is much easier to pull than is the trigger on a revolver or the slide on an automatic pistol. Rifles or shotguns are also more prone to fire if accidentally dropped. Finally, handguns can be hidden from inquisitive children more easily than long guns can.

[44] Arthur T. Kellerman and Donald T. Reay, "Protection or Peril? An Analysis of Firearm-Related Deaths in the Home," *New England Journal of Medicine* 24 (June 1986): 1557-60; discussed for example in "Sons of Guns," *The New Republic*, March 2, 1987, p. 12.

crime efficacy, citizens acting with full legal justification kill at least 30 percent more criminals than do the police.[45]

On the whole, citizens are more successful gun users than are the police. When police shoot, they are 5.5 times more likely to hit an innocent person than are civilian shooters.[46] Moreover, civilians use guns effectively against criminals. If a robbery victim does not defend himself, the robbery will succeed 88 percent of the time, and the victim will be injured 25 percent of the time. If the victim resists with a gun, the robbery "success" rate falls to 30 percent, and the victim injury rate falls to 17 percent. No other response to a robbery—from using a knife, to shouting for help, to fleeing—produces such a low rate of victim injury and robbery success.[47] In short, virtually all Americans who use guns do so responsibly and effectively, notwithstanding the anxieties of gun control advocates.

Enforcing Gun Bans

Apart from the intrinsic merit (or demerit) of banning or restricting gun possession, the mechanics of enforcement must also be considered. Illegal gun ownership is by definition a possessory offense, like possession of marijuana or bootleg alcohol. The impossibility of effective enforcement, plus the civil liberties invasions that necessarily result, are powerful arguments against gun control.

---

[45] Donald B. Kates, "Handgun Prohibition and the Original Meaning of the Second Amendment," *Michigan Law Review* 82 (1984), p. 269, n. 278, citing 1981 Federal Bureau of Investigation statistics. Sources other than the FBI put justifiable civilian killing of criminals at much higher levels. Although the Bureau estimates that civilians kill 300 criminals annually, Lawrence Sherman of the pro-control Police Foundation puts the figure at 600. Gary Kleck of Florida State University's School of Criminology estimates that 1,500–2,800 criminals are shot to death annually by citizens acting lawfully. The different statistical results may be due to the FBI's reliance exclusively on incidents reported to the police, and the fact that if a homicide is initially labelled a criminal homicide, but later determined to be self-defense, the homicide is still reported to the FBI as a criminal homicide. Gary Kleck, "Crime Control Through the Private Use of Armed Force," *Social Problems* 35 (February 1988), pp. 4-7.

[46] Silver and Kates, pp. 154-55. The problems police encounter do not necessarily imply that the police are poorer shooters, or that they possess worse judgment. Official guidelines may force the police to intervene in situations that ordinary citizens could avoid, and may prevent an officer from drawing his weapon at the most opportune time.

[47] Kleck, "Crime Control," pp. 7-9.

Search and Seizure

No civil libertarian needs to be told how the criminalization of liquor and drugs has led the police into search-and-seizure violations. Consensual possessory offenses cannot be contained any other way. Search-and-seizure violations are the inevitable result of the criminalization of gun possession. As Judge David Shields of Chicago's special firearms court observed: "Constitutional search and seizure issues are probably more regularly argued in this court than anywhere in America."[48]

The problem has existed for a long time. In 1933, for example, long before the Warren Court expanded the rights of suspects, one-quarter of all weapons arrests in Detroit were dismissed because of illegal searches.[49] According to the American Civil Liberties Union, the St. Louis police have conducted over 25,000 illegal searches under the theory that any black driving a late-model car must have a handgun.[50]

The frequency of illegal searches should not be surprising. The police are ordered to get handguns off the streets, and they attempt to do their job. It is not their fault that they are told to enforce a law whose enforcement is impossible within constitutional limits. Small wonder that the Chicago Police Department gives an officer a favorable notation in his record for confiscating a gun, even as a result of an illegal search.[51] One cannot comply with the Fourth Amendment—which requires that searches be based upon probable cause—and also effectively enforce a gun prohibition. Former D.C. Court of Appeals Judge Malcolm Wilkey thus bemoaned the fact that the exclusionary rule, which bars courtroom use of illegally seized evidence, "has made unenforceable the gun control laws we now have and will make ineffective any stricter controls which may be devised."[52] Judge Abner Mikva, usually on the opposite side of the conservative Wilkey, joined him in identifying the abolition of the exclusionary rule as the only way to enforce gun control.[53]

---

[48] David J. Shields, "Two Judges Look at Gun Control," *Chicago Bar Record* (January/February 1976), p. 182. (The second judge referred to in the title was Marvin E. Aspen, who wrote a pro-control article.)

[49] J. B. Waite, "Public Policy and the Arrest of Felons," *Michigan Law Review* 31 (April 1933), pp. 764-66.

[50] A.C.L.U. estimate cited in Kates, "Handgun Control: Prohibition Revisited," p. 23.

[51] Steven Brill, *Firearms Abuse: A Research and Policy Report* (Washington, D.C.: Police Foundation, 1977), p. 34.

[52] Malcolm Wilkey, "Why Suppress Valid Evidence?" *Wall Street Journal*, October 10, 1977. See also Mike Royko, "Magnum Force," *San Francisco Examiner*, May 14, 1982.

[53] Blackman, "Civil Liberties and Gun-Law Enforcement," p. 27.

Abolishing the exclusionary rule is not the only proposal designed to facilitate searches for illegal guns. Harvard professor James Q. Wilson, the Police Foundation and other commentators propose widespread street use of hand-held magnetometers and walk-through metal detectors to find illegal guns.[54] The city attorney of Berkeley, California, has advocated setting up "weapons checkpoints" (similar to sobriety checkpoints), where the police would search for weapons all cars passing through dangerous neighborhoods.[55] School administrators in New Jersey have begun searching student lockers and purses for guns and drugs; Bridgeport, Connecticut, is considering a similar strategy. Detroit temporarily abandoned school searches after a female student who had passed through a metal detector was given a manual pat-down by a male security officer, but the city has resumed the program.[56] New York City is also implementing metal detectors.[57]

Searching a teenager's purse or making her walk through a metal detector several times a day is hardly likely to instill much faith in the importance of civil liberties. Indeed, students conditioned to searches without probable cause in high school are unlikely to resist such searches when they become adults. Additionally, it is unjust for the state to compel a student to attend school, fail to provide a safe environment at school or on the way to school, and then prohibit the student from protecting himself or herself.[58]

---

[54] James Q. Wilson, "Again, the Gun Question," *Washington Post*, April 1, 1986; Police Foundation quoted in "Whether It Sharply Reduces Crime or Not, Is a Federal Ban Worth Trying?" *New York Times*, April 5, 1981, p. IV 3. See also, J. Fyfe, "Enforcement Workshop: Detective McFadden Goes Electronic," *Criminal Law Bulletin* 19 (March/April 1983): pp. 162-67; N. Morris and G. Hawkins, *The Honest Politician's Guide to Crime Control* (Chicago: University of Chicago Press, 1970). In 1992, the U.S. Department of Justice began funding programs to pay for hand-held metal detectors in selected cities.

[55] "Berkeley City Attorney Mulls Car Searches for Weapons," Associated Press, December 19, 1987 (available in NEXIS in Wires library).

[56] For New Jersey, see Jonathan Friendly, "Schools Ease Curbs on Drug and Weapons Checks," *New York Times*, June 17, 1986, p. B2. For Bridgeport, see Richard L. Madden, "Bridgeport Acts to Keep Guns Out of Schools," *New York Times*, March 20, 1987, p. B2 (locker searches for guns); for Detroit, see "In Detroit, Kids Kill Kids," *Newsweek*, May 11, 1987, p. 24. The Police Foundation proposal for general "perimeter control" metal detectors in schools is discussed in the National Rifle Association's letter of March 13, 1985, to Alfred Regnery, director of the Justice Department's Office of Juvenile Justice and Delinquency Prevention. The Baltimore city government considered a perimeter-control proposal in 1985.

[57] "5 Schools to Use Detectors for Guns," *New York Times*, May 5, 1988, p. B3; Mark Mooney, "Green Wants Weapon Searches in Schools," *New York Post*, March 25, 1988, p. 7.

[58] A. Mackay-Smith, "Should Schools Permit Searching Students for Weapons, Drugs?" *Wall Street Journal*, May 30, 1984. Mackay-Smith discussed policy in Detroit, where police searches looked for knives and Mace carried by girls to protect themselves from rapists.

Perhaps the most harmful effect of the metal detectors is their debilitating message that a community must rely on paid security guards and their hardware in order to be secure. It does not take much imagination to figure out how to pass a weapon past a security guard, with trickery or bribery. Once past the guard, weapons could simply be stored at school. Instead of relying on technology at the door, the better solution would be to mobilize students inside the school. Volunteer student patrols would change the balance of power in the schoolyard, ending the reign of terror of outside intruders and gangs. Further, concerted student action teaches the best lessons of democracy and community action.

The majority of people possessing illegal weapons during a gun prohibition would never carry them on the streets and would never be caught even by omnipresent metal detectors. Accordingly, a third of the people who favor a ban on private handguns want the ban enforced with house-to-house searches.[59] Eroding the Second Amendment guarantees erosion of the Fourth Amendment.

Those who propose abolishing the exclusionary rule and narrowing the Fourth Amendment apparently trust the street intuition of the police to sort out the true criminals so that ordinary citizens would not be subject to unjustified intrusions. However, one-fourth of the guns seized by the police are not associated with any criminal activity.[60] Our constitutional scheme explicitly rejects the notion that the police may be allowed to search at will.

Other Civil Liberties Problems

Although gun control advocates trust the police to know whom to arrest, the experience of gun control leads one to doubt police judgment. A Pennsylvania resident was visiting Brooklyn, New York, to help repair a local church when he spotted a man looting his truck. The Pennsylvania man fired a warning shot into the air with his legally registered Pennsylvania gun, scaring off the thief. The police arrived too late to catch the thief but arrested the Pennsylvania man for not acquiring a special permit to bring his gun into New York City.[61] In California a police chief went to a gun show and read to a machine gun dealer the

---

[59] Blackman, "Civil Liberties and Gun Law Enforcement," p. 2.
[60] Wright, Rossi, and Daly, pp. 177-78.
[61] "Deadly Weapons," *The Park Slope Paper*, October 23, 1986.

revocation of his license; the dealer was immediately arrested for possessing an unlicensed machine gun.[62]

The Bureau of Alcohol, Tobacco and Firearms has been particularly outrageous in its prosecutions. Sometimes the BATF's zeal to inflate its seizure count turns its agents into Keystone Kops. One year in Iowa, for example, the BATF hauled away an unregistered cannon from a public war memorial; in California it pried inoperable machine guns out of a museum's display.

In the early 1970s changes in the price of sugar made moonshining unprofitable. To justify its budget, the BATF had to find a new set of defendants. Small-scale gun dealers and collectors served perfectly. Often the bureau's tactics against them are petty and mean. After a defendant's acquittal, for example, agents may refuse to return his seized gun collection, even under court order. Valuable museum-quality antique arms may be damaged when in BATF custody. Part of the explanation for the refusal to return weapons after an acquittal may lie in BATF field offices using gun seizures to build their own arsenals.[63]

The BATF's disregard for fair play harms more than just gun owners. BATF searches of gun dealers need not be based on probable cause, or any cause at all. The 1972 Supreme Court decision allowing these searches, *United States v. Biswell*, has since become a watershed in the weakening of the Constitution's probable cause requirement.[64]

Lack of criminal intent does not shield a citizen from the BATF. In *United States v. Thomas*, the defendant found a 16-inch-long gun while horseback riding. Taking it to be an antique pistol, he pawned it. But it turned out to be a short-barreled rifle, which should have been registered before selling. Although the prosecutor conceded that Thomas lacked criminal intent, he was convicted of a felony anyway.[65] The Supreme Court's decision in *United States v. Freed* declared that criminal intent was not necessary for a conviction of violation of the Gun Control Act of 1968.[66]

---

[62] Kates, "Civil Liberties Obstacles," pp. 1-2.

[63] BATF abuses are chronicled in detail in David Hardy, *The B.A.T.F.'s War on Civil Liberties* (Bellevue, Wash.: Second Amendment Foundation, 1979).

[64] *United States v. Biswell*, 406 U.S. 311 (1972), discussed in Robert Batey, "Strict Construction of Firearms Offenses," *Journal of Law and Contemporary Problems* 49 (Winter 1986), pp. 184-85.

[65] Batey, p. 163. In Florida, as everywhere else, it is illegal for a felon to possess a gun. One Florida felon discovered this when he wrested a pistol away from someone who was attacking him—and was convicted of illegal possession of a weapon (*Thorpe v. State*, 377 So.2d 221 [Fla. App., 1979]).

[66] *United States v. Freed*, 401 U.S. 601 (1974).

The strict liability principle has since spread to other areas and contributed to the erosion of the *mens rea* (guilty mind) requirement of criminal culpability.[67] U.S. law prohibits the possession of unregistered fully automatic weapons (one continuous trigger squeeze causes repeat fire). Semiautomatic weapons (which eject the spent shell and load the next cartridge, but require another trigger squeeze to fire) are legal. If the sear (the catch that holds the hammer at cock) on a semiautomatic rifle wears out, the rifle may malfunction and repeat fire. Accordingly, the BATF arrested and prosecuted a small-town Tennessee police chief for possession of an automatic weapon (actually a semiautomatic with a worn-out sear), even though the BATF conceded that the police chief had not deliberately altered the weapon. In March and April of 1988, BATF pressed similar charges for a worn-out sear against a Pennsylvania state police sergeant. After a 12-day trial, the federal district judge directed a verdict of not guilty and called the prosecution "a severe miscarriage of justice."[68]

The Police Foundation has proposed that law enforcement agencies use informers to ferret out illegal gun sales and model their tactics on methods of drug law enforcement.[69] Taking this advice to heart, the BATF relies heavily on paid informants and on entrapment—techniques originated during alcohol prohibition, developed in modern drug enforcement, and honed to a chilling perfection in gun control. So that BATF agents can fulfill their quotas, they concentrate on harassing collectors and their valuable rifle collections. Undercover agents may entice or pressure a private gun collector into making a few legal sales from his personal collection. Once he has made four sales, over a long period of time, he is arrested and charged with being "engaged in the business" of gun sales without a license.[70]

To the consternation of many local police forces, the BATF is often unwilling to assist in cases involving genuine criminal activity. Police

---

[67] Batey, p. 187.

[68] For Tennessee, see J. J. Baker, "Assault on Semi-Autos," *American Rifleman*, April 1987, p. 42. For Pennsylvania, *United States v. Corcoran*, Crim. no. 88-11, (W.D. Pa., April 6, 1988) (Ziegler, J.).

[69] Brill, pp. 134ff. See also Lawrence Sherman, "Equity Against Truth: Value Choices in Deceptive Investigations," in *Police Ethics*, eds. Heffernand and Stroup (New York: John Jay Press, 1985), pp. 117-32 (Police Foundation head arguing that random selection of undercover investigation targets is fairer than probable cause selection).

[70] Hardy, *The B.A.T.F.'s War on Civil Liberties*, pp. 11-41, 75-86.

officials around the nation have complained about BATF's refusing to prosecute serious gun law violations.[71]

In 1982 the Senate Subcommittee on the Constitution investigated the BATF and concluded that the agency had habitually engaged in

> . . . conduct which borders on the criminal. . . . [E]nforcement tactics made possible by current firearms laws are constitutionally, legally and practically reprehensible. . . . [A]pproximately 75 percent of BATF gun prosecutions were aimed at ordinary citizens who had neither criminal intent nor knowledge, but were enticed by agents into unknowing technical violations.[71]

Although public pressure in recent years has made the BATF a somewhat less lawless agency, it would be a mistake to conclude that the organization has been permanently reformed.

One need not like guns to understand that gun control laws pose a threat to civil liberties. Explained Aryeh Neier, former director of the American Civil Liberties Union:

> I want the state to take away people's guns. But I don't want the state to use methods against gun owners that I deplore when used against naughty children, sexual minorities, drug users, and unsightly drinkers. Since such reprehensible police practices are probably needed to make anti-gun laws effective, my proposal to ban all guns should probably be marked a failure before it is even tried.[72]

---

[71] *Ibid.*, pp. 53-55.

[71] Senate Committee on the Judiciary, Subcommittee on the Constitution, *The Right to Keep and Bear Arms*, 97th Congress, 2d sess., Senate Doc. 2807 (February 1982): 20-23.

[72] Aryeh Neier, *Crime and Punishment: A Radical Solution* (New York: Stein & Day, 1976), p. 76.

The Fourth and Fifth Amendments are not the only parts of the Bill of Rights threatened by anti-gun sentiment. In derogation of the Sixth Amendment's right to jury trial, a Pennsylvania federal district court judge recently tried to categorically bar National Rifle Association members from serving on a jury in a gun law prosecution. The Third Circuit Court of Appeals reversed the lower court (*United States v. Salamone*, 800 F.2d 1216 [3d Cir. 1986]). If not reversed, the lower court's ruling would have provided precedent for excluding all Sierra Club members from environmental cases, or NAACP members from discrimination suits.

The First Amendment is not safe either. Attempts to censor allegedly violent entertainment are legion. For example, the National Coalition on Television Violence wants the government to ban "Photon Warrior" because the program shows "adolescents fighting 'the forces of evil' with infra-red Photon guns." The Coalition insists that "the toy industry's greed for money must not be allowed to trample the moral development of our next generation." Previous generations, which include veterans of foreign wars, might find shooting guns at evil forces like the Wehrmacht to be quite moral.

Gun Control and Social Control

Gun control cannot coexist with the Fourth Amendment (probable cause for search and seizure) and has a deleterious effect on the Fifth Amendment (due process of law). Gun control is also suspect under the equal protection clause of the Fourteenth Amendment, for it harms most those groups that have traditionally been victimized by society's inequities.

Racial Discrimination

Throughout America's history, white supremacists have insisted on the importance of prohibiting arms to blacks. In 1640 Virginia's first recorded legislation about blacks barred them from owning guns. Fear of slave revolts led other Southern colonies to enact similar laws.[73] The laws preventing blacks from bearing arms (as well as drinking liquor or traveling) were enforced by what one historian called a "system of special and general searches and night patrols of the posse comitatus."[74] In the 1857 *Dred Scott* decision, Chief Justice Roger B. Taney announced that blacks were not citizens; if they were, he warned, there would be no legal way to deny them firearms.[75]

Immediately after the Civil War, President Andrew Johnson permitted several Southern states to return to the Union without guaranteeing equality to blacks. These states enacted "black codes," which were designed to keep the ex-slaves in de facto slavery and submission. For example, in 1865 Mississippi forbade freedmen to rent farmland, requiring instead that they work under unbreakable labor contracts, or be sent to jail. White terrorist organizations attacked freedman who stepped out of line, and the black codes ensured that the freedmen could not fight back. Blacks were, in the words of *The Special Report of the Anti-Slavery Conference of 1867*, "forbidden to own or bear firearms and thus . . . rendered defenseless against assaults" by whites.[76] In response to the black codes, the Republican Congress passed the Fourteenth Amendment, guaranteeing to all citizens, freedmen included, their national constitu-

---

[73] Lee Kennett and James L. Anderson, *The Gun in America: The Origins of a National Dilemma* (New York: Westport Press, 1975), p. 50.

[74] Donald B. Kates, "Attitudes Toward Slavery in the New Republic," *Journal of Negro History* 53 (1968), p. 37.

[75] 60 U.S. (19 How.) 393, 417 (1857).

[76] Quoted in H. Hyman, *The Radical Republicans and Reconstruction* (New York: Bobbs-Merrill, 1967), p. 217. For the black codes, see Howard Zinn, *A People's History of the United States* (New York: Harper, 1980), p. 194.

tional rights, especially the right to bear arms. Said Rep. Sidney Clarke of Kansas, during the debate on the Fourteenth Amendment, "I find in the Constitution of the United States an article which declared that 'the right of the people to keep and bear arms shall not be infringed.' For myself, I shall insist that the reconstructed rebels of Mississippi respect the Constitution in their local laws."[77]

White supremacy eventually prevailed, though, and the South became the first region of the United States to institute gun control. During the Jim Crow era around 1900, when racial oppression was at its peak, several states enacted handgun registration and licensing laws. As one Florida judge explained, the laws were "passed for the purpose of disarming the Negro laborers . . . [and] never intended to be applied to the white population."[78]

For several years in the 1970s the American Civil Liberties Union lobbied for stricter gun control to forestall white terrorist attacks on minorities. (The ACLU currently does not work for or against gun control.) Concern over racist shooting was certainly justified, for during the civil rights era in the 1960s, white supremacist tactics were just as violent as they had been during Reconstruction. Over 100 civil rights workers were murdered during that era, and the Department of Justice refused to intervene to prosecute the Klan or to protect civil rights workers. Help from the local police was out of the question; Klan dues were sometimes collected at the local station.[79]

Blacks and civil rights workers armed for self-defense. John Salter, a professor at Tougaloo College and NAACP leader during the early 1960s, wrote "No one knows what kind of massive racist retaliation would have been directed against grass-roots black people had the black community not had a healthy measure of firearms within it." Salter personally had to defend his home and family several times against attacks by night riders. When Salter fired back, the night riders, cowards that they were, fled. The unburned Ku Klux Klan cross in the Smithsonian Institution was donated by a civil rights worker whose shotgun blast drove Klansmen away from her driveway.[80]

---

[77] Quoted in David Hardy, "The Constitution as a Restraint on State and Federal Firearm Restrictions," in *Restricting Handguns*, p. 181.

[78] *Watson v. Stone*, 148 Fla. 516, 450 So.2d 700, 703 (1941) (Buford, J., concurring specially).

[79] John Salter, *Social Justice Community Organizing and the Necessity for Protective Firearms*, paper presented at the 18th annual meeting of the Popular Culture Association, New Orleans, March 26, 1988, p. 2.

[80] Salter, p. 3.

Civil rights professionals and the black community generally viewed nonviolence as a useful tactic for certain situations, not as a moral injunction to let oneself be murdered on a deserted road in the middle of the night. Based in local churches, the Deacons for Defense and Justice set up armed patrol car systems in cities such as Bogalusa and Jonesboro, Louisiana, and completely succeeded in deterring Klan and other attacks on civil rights workers and black residents. Sixty chapters of the Deacons were formed throughout the South.[81] Of the more than 100 civil rights workers martyred in the 1960s, almost none were armed.[82]

Of course civil rights activists were not the only people who needed to defend themselves against racist violence. Francis Griffin, a clergyman in Farmville, Virginia, related, "Our last trouble came when some Klansmen tried to 'get' a black motorist who had hit a white child. They met blacks with guns, and that put a stop to that." Moreover, the tendency of Southern blacks to arm themselves not only deterred white racist violence, it reduced the incidence of robberies of blacks by drug addicts.[83]

Lest anyone think that blacks' need to defend themselves against racist mobs—whom the police cannot or will not control—is limited to the old South, New York City provides a few counterexamples. In 1966 a mob burned the headquarters of the Marxist W. E. B. DuBois Club while New York City police looked on. When a club member pulled his pistol to hold off the mob while he fled from the burning building, the police arrested him for illegal gun possession. No one in the mob was arrested for anything.[84]

In 1976 Ormistan Spencer, a black, moved into the white neighborhood of Rosedale, Queens. Crowds dumped garbage on his lawn, his children were abused, and a pipe bomb was thrown through his window. When he responded to a menacing crowd by brandishing a gun, the

---

[81] Richard Maxwell Brown, "The American Vigilante Tradition," in *The History of Violence in America*, eds. Hugh Davis Graham and Ted Robert Gurr (New York: Praeger, 1969), pp. 203, 217 n. 150.

[82] Donald B. Kates, "Why a Civil Libertarian Opposes Gun Control," *The Great Gun Control Debate* (Bellevue, Wash.: Second Amendment Foundation, 1976), p. 4. For more, see J. Weiss, "A Reply to Advocates of Gun Control Laws," *Journal of Urban Law* 53 (1974), p. 577. At the time, Weiss was director of the Office of Economic Opportunity's national legal services office for the elderly poor.

[83] "Decade of Change in South Gives Negroes High Hopes," *New York Times*, August 16, 1970, pp. 1, 54. See also "Panel Told Mississippi Negroes Are Prepared for Self-Defense," *New York Times*, August 13, 1970, p. 20.

[84] John Salter and Donald B. Kates, "The Necessity of Access to Firearms by Dissenters and Minorities Whom the Government Is Unwilling or Unable to Protect," in *Restricting Handguns*, p. 187.

police confiscated the gun and filed charges against him.[85] The mob attack on black pedestrians in Howard Beach, New York would not have resulted in the death of one of the victims if the black victims had been carrying a gun with which to frighten off or resist the mob.

In some ways, social conditions have not changed much since the days when Michigan enacted its handgun controls after Clarence Darrow's celebrated defense of Ossian Sweet in 1925. Sweet, a black, had moved into an all-white neighborhood; the Detroit police failed to restrain a mob threatening his house. Sweet and his family fired in self-defense, killing one of the mob. He was charged with murder and was acquitted after a lengthy trial.[86]

Racially motivated violence is not the only threat to which blacks are more vulnerable than whites. A black in America has at least a 40 percent greater chance of being burgled and a 100 percent greater chance of being robbed than a white.[87] Simply put, blacks need to use deadly force in self-defense far more often than whites. In California, in 1981, blacks committed 48 percent of justifiable homicides, whites only 22 percent.[88]

In addition, although blacks are more exposed to crime, they are given less protection by the police. In Brooklyn, New York, for example, 911 callers have allegedly been asked if they are black or white.[89] Wrote the late Senator Frank Church:

> In the inner cities, where the police cannot offer adequate protection, the people will provide their own. They will keep handguns at home for self-defense, regardless of the prohibitions

---

[85] Eleanor Blau, "Black Couple in Home Bombing Shot in Accident," *New York Times*, August 29, 1975, p. 31 (the "accident" was due to Spencer's resisting the officer's attempt to wrest the gun away); Nathaniel Shephard, "Policeman Attacked at Bombed Home," *New York Times*, January 5, 1975, p. 46; Jill Gerston, "Home of Blacks Struck by Bomb," *New York Times*, January 1, 1975, p. 21. Half a year later, the charges against Spencer were dropped. Murray Illson, "Harassed Rosedale Black Cleared of Gun Charges," *New York Times*, April 17, 1976, p. 25.

[86] Donald B. Kates, "A History of Handgun Prohibition," in *Restricting Handguns*, p. 19; Walter White, "The Sweet Trial," *Crisis* 31 (January 1926) pp. 125-29. See generally Irving Stone, *Clarence Darrow for the Defense* (New York: Doubleday, 1941), pp. 529-547.

[87] James Q. Wilson and Richard J. Hernstein, *Crime and Human Nature* (New York: Simon and Schuster, 1976), p. 463. Other statistics indicate a black is almost three times as likely to be robbed as a white. See Department of Justice (Bureau of Justice Statistics), *Report to the Nation on Crime and Justice: The Data* (Washington, D.C.: Government Printing Office, October 1983), p. 20.

[88] Benson. p. 342.

[89] "We're Mad as Hell and We're Not Going to Take It Anymore," *Brooklyn Free Press*, November 24, 1986, p. 35.

that relatively safe and smug inhabitants of the surrounding suburbs would impose upon them.[90]

Judge David Shields of the special firearms court in Chicago came to the court as an advocate of national handgun prohibition. Most of the defendants he saw, however, were people with no criminal record who carried guns because they had been robbed or raped because the police had arrived too late to protect them. Explaining why he never sent those defendants to jail, and indeed ordered their guns returned, the judge wrote that most people

> . . . would not go into ghetto areas at all except in broad daylight under the most optimum conditions—surely not at night, alone or on foot. But some people have no choice. To live or work or have some need to be on this "frontier" imposes a fear which is tempered by possession of a gun.[91]

Gun control laws are discriminatorily enforced against blacks, even more so than other laws. In Chicago the black-to-white ratio of weapons arrests one year was 7:1 (prostitution, another favorite for discriminatory enforcement, was the only other crime to have such a high race ratio).[92] Black litigants have gone to federal court in Maryland and won permits after proving that a local police department almost never issues permits to blacks.[93] General searches for guns can be a nightmare-come-true for blacks. In 1968, for example, rifles were stolen from a National Guard Armory in New Jersey; the guard ransacked 45 homes of blacks in

---

[90] Frank Church, foreword to *Restricting Handguns*, p. xiii. Consider also an item in the (New York) *Daily News*, June 17, 1977, "Where Survival Is a Crime." A crippled black middle-aged cab driver was preparing dinner in his Harlem tenement when a junkie broke in, began beating the cab driver on the head with a lead pipe, and demanded money. The cab driver having none, the junkie continued the assault until the cabbie reached for his "Saturday night special" and killed his attacker. The police arrested him for criminal possession of a weapon. Commented the writer, "Willie [the cab driver], of course had no gun permit. To get one in New York City you need to know somebody. Willie doesn't know anybody. All he knows is he had to defend himself. Our politicians don't give a damn about Willie, anymore than they give a damn about you. They ride in limos and carry guns."

[91] David Shields, p. 184.

[92] David Hardy and Kenneth Chotiner, "The Potential for Civil Liberties Violations in the Enforcement of Handgun Prohibition," in *Restricting Handguns*, p. 211.

[93] *Clark v. Gabriel*, civil action no. M-75-581 (D. Md., Dec. 13, 1976), cited in Paul Blackman, "Carrying Handguns for Personal Protection," paper presented at the 37th annual meeting of the American Society of Criminology, San Diego, November 13-16, 1985, p. 6.

warrantless searches for weapons, found none, and left the houses in shambles.[94]

Sexual Discrimination

Many of the same arguments about gun possession that apply to blacks also apply to women. Radical feminist Nikki Craft worked with an anti-rape group in Dallas. After one horror story too many, she founded WASP—Women Armed for Self Protection. Craft explained that she "was opposed to guns, so this was a huge leap. . . . I was tired of being afraid to open a window at night for fresh air, and sick of feeling safer when there was a man in bed with me." One of her posters read, "Men and Women Were Created Equal . . . And Smith & Wesson Makes Damn Sure It Stays That Way."[95] Her slogan echoed a gun manufacturer's motto from the 19th century:

> Be not afraid of any man, no matter what his size;
> When danger threatens, call on me and I will equalize.[96]

If guns somehow vanished, rapists would suffer little. A gun-armed rapist succeeds 67 percent of the time, a knife-armed rapist 51 percent. Only seven percent of rapists even use guns.[97] Thus, a fully effective gun ban would disarm only a small fraction of rapists, and even those rapists could use knives almost as effectively. In fact, a complete gun ban would make rape all the easier, with guaranteed unarmed victims.

One objection to women arming themselves for self-defense is that the rapist will take away the gun and use it against the victim. This argument (like most other arguments about why women should not resist rape) is based on stereotypes, and proponents of the argument seem unable to cite any real world examples. Instead of assuming that all women are incapable of using a weapon effectively, it would be more appropriate to leave the decision up to individual women. Certainly the cases of women, even grandmothers, using firearms to stop rapists are

[94] Sherrill, p. 274.

[95] Quoted in Tricia Lootens and Alice Henry, "Interview: Nikki Craft, Activist and Outlaw," *Off Our Backs: A Women's Newsjournal*, 15, no. 7 (July 1985), p. 3.

[96] Inscription on a Winchester rifle, quoted in Kennett and Anderson, p. 108.

[97] Philip J. Cook, "Gun Availability and Violent Crime," *Crime & Justice* 4 (1982), p. 61 n. 8, analyzing data in Joan McDermott, *Rape Victimization in Twenty-Six American Cities* (Washington, D.C.: Government Printing Office, 1979), pp. 20-21. Rate of firearms use in rape is from Department of Justice, *Report to the Nation on Crime and Justice*, p. 14.

legion.[98] If a woman is going to resist, she is far better off with a gun than with her bare hands, Mace, or a knife. Mace fires a pin-point stream, not a spray, and the challenge of using it to score a bull's-eye right on a rapist's cornea would daunt even Annie Oakley. And it is more difficult to fight a bigger person with one's hands or with a knife than with a handgun—especially a small, light handgun that can be deployed quickly, and which has a barrel that is too short for the attacker to grab.

The Second Amendment and the Sources of Political Power

Regardless of the utility or disutility of guns, laws about them are circumscribed by the Constitution. The Second Amendment means what it says: "A well-regulated Militia, being necessary to the security of a free State, the right of the people to keep and bear Arms, shall not be infringed." If we are to live by the law, our first step must be to obey the Constitution.

Attitudes of the Founding Fathers Toward Guns

The leaders of the American Revolution and the early republic were enthusiastic proponents of guns and widespread gun ownership. The Founding Fathers were unanimous about the importance of an armed citizenry able to overthrow a despotic government. Virtually all the political philosophers whose ideas were known to the Founders—such as Plato, Aristotle, Cicero, Machiavelli, Montesquieu, Beccaria, Locke and Sidney—agreed that a republic could not long endure without an armed citizenry.[99] Said Patrick Henry, "Guard with jealous attention the public liberty. Suspect every one who approaches that jewel. Unfortunately, nothing will preserve it but downright force. Whenever you give up that force, you are ruined. . . . The great object is that every man be armed.

---

[98] A feature in the National Rifle Association magazine every month, called "The Armed Citizen," collects such stories from newspapers around the nation. Only incidents that have been verified as legitimate self-defense by the police, grand jury, or other official body are included. See also Silver and Kates, "Self-Defense, Handgun Ownership" and the "Independence of Women in a Violent, Sexist Society," p. 139, citing numerous instances of women defending themselves from criminal attack.

[99] Stephen Halbrook, "The Second Amendment as a Phenomenon of Liberal Political Philosophy," in *Firearms and Violence*, pp. 363-83.

. . . Everyone who is able may have a gun."[100] Thomas Jefferson's model constitution for Virginia declared, "No freeman shall be debarred the use of arms in his own lands or tenements."[101] Jefferson's colleague John Adams spoke for "arms in the hands of citizens, to be used at individual discretion . . . in private self-defense."[102]

The Original Meaning of the Second Amendment

The only commentary available to Congress when it ratified the Second Amendment was written by Tench Coxe, one of James Madison's friends. Explained Coxe: "The people are confirmed by the next article of their right to keep and bear their private arms."[103]

Madison's original structure of the Bill of Rights did not place the amendments together at the end of the text of the Constitution (the way they were ultimately organized); rather, he proposed interpolating each amendment into the main text of the Constitution, following the provision to which it pertained. If he had intended the Second Amendment to be mainly a limit on the power of the federal government to interfere with state government militias, he would have put it after Article I, section 8, which granted Congress the power to call forth the militia to repel invasion, suppress insurrection and enforce the laws; and to provide for organizing, arming and disciplining the militia. Instead, Madison put the right to bear arms amendment (along with the freedom of speech amendment) in Article I, section 9—the section that guaranteed individual rights such as habeas corpus.[104] Finally, in ratifying the Bill of Rights, the

---

[100] Quoted in Morton Borden, ed., *The Antifederalist Papers*, vol. 3 (East Lansing: Michigan State University Press), p. 386.

[101] Thomas Jefferson, "The Virginia Constitution, Third Draft," in *The Papers of Thomas Jefferson, Vol. I, 1760-1776* (Princeton: Princeton University Press, 1950), p. 363. The limitation regarding private property was added in Jefferson's second draft.

[102] Stephen Halbrook, "What the Framers Intended," *Journal of Law and Contemporary Problems* 49 (Winter 1986), p. 155; John Adams, *A Defence of the Constitutions of the Government of the United States of America against the Attack of M. Turgot* (Philadelphia, 1788), p. 471.

[103] A Pennsylvanian (Coxe's pen name), "Remarks on the First Part of the Amendments to the Federal Constitution," *The Federal Gazette and Philadelphia Evening Post*, June 18, 1789, p. 2, quoted in Stephen Halbrook, *That Every Man Be Armed* (Albuquerque: University of New Mexico Press, 1984), p. 76.

[104] Donald B. Kates, "Second Amendment," in *Encyclopedia of the American Constitution*, Leonard Levy, ed. (New York: MacMillan, 1986), p. 1639. See also Robert Shalhope, "The Ideological Origins of the Second Amendment," *Journal of American History* 69 (December 1982), pp. 599-614; Joyce Malcolm, "The Right of the People to Keep and Bear Arms: The Common Law Tradition," *Hastings Constitutional Law Quarterly* 10 (Winter 1983), pp. 285-314.

Senate rejected a change in the Second Amendment that would have limited it to bearing arms "for the common defense."[105]

Gun control advocates argue that the Second Amendment's reference to the militia means the amendment protects only official uniformed state militias (the National Guard). It is true that the Framers of the Constitution wanted the state militias to defend the United States against foreign invasion, so that a large standing army would be unnecessary. But those militias were not uniformed state employees. Before independence was even declared, Josiah Quincy had referred to "a well-regulated militia composed of the freeholder, citizen and husbandman, who take up their arms to preserve their property as individuals, and their rights as freemen."[106] "Who are the Militia?" asked George Mason of Virginia. "They consist. now of the whole people."[107] The same Congress that passed the Bill of Rights, including the Second Amendment and its militia language, also passed the Militia Act of 1792. That act enrolled all able-bodied white males in the militia and required them to own arms.

Although the requirement to arm no longer exists, the definition of the militia has stayed the same; section 311(a) of volume 10 of the United States Code declares, "The militia of the United States consists of all able-bodied males at least 17 years of age and . . . under 45 years of age." The next section of the code distinguishes the organized militia (the National Guard) from the "unorganized militia." The modern federal National Guard was specifically raised under Congress's power to "raise and support armies," not its power to "Provide for organizing, arming and disciplining the Militia."[108]

Indeed, if words mean what they say, it is impossible to interpret the Second Amendment as embodying only a "collective" right. As one Second Amendment scholar observed, it would be odd for the Congress

---

[105] Senate Committee on the Judiciary, *The Right to Keep and Bear Arms*, p. 6. The senators in part may have wished to avoid the implication that a large standing army was acceptable for nondefensive, overseas war.

[106] Quoted in Clinton Rossiter, *The Political Thought of the American Revolution* (New York: Harcourt, Brace and World, 1953), pp. 126-27.

[107] Quoted in Borden, p. 425.

[108] House Report No. 141, 73d Congress, 1st sess. (1933), pp. 2-5. Congress did so in order that the National Guard could be sent into overseas combat. The National Guard's weapons plainly cannot be the arms protected by the Second Amendment, since Guard weapons are owned by the federal government (32 United States Code sect. 105[a] [1]).

The most thorough discussion on the political status of the National Guard is John G. Kester, "State Governors and the Federal National Guard," *Harvard Journal of Law and Public Policy* 11 (Winter 1988): 177-212. As Kester explains, there are technically two distinct National Guards. State National Guards are created by state governments under their power to raise an organized militia.

that enacted the Bill of Rights to use "right of the people" to mean an individual right in the First, Fourth and Ninth Amendments, but to mean a state's right in the Second Amendment. After all, when Congress meant to protect the states, Congress wrote "the States" in the Tenth Amendment.[109] Moreover, several states included a similar right to bear arms guarantee in their own constitutions. If the Second Amendment protected only the state uniformed militias against federal interference, a comparable article would be ridiculous in a state constitution.[110]

Modern Interpretations of the Second Amendment

For the Constitution's first century, there was no question that the Second Amendment prohibited federal interference with the individual right to bear arms. During this period the Supreme Court did not view any articles of the Bill of Rights, the Second Amendment included, as applicable to the states. Accordingly, the Second Amendment, like the First Amendment and all the others, was construed by the Supreme Court to place no limits on state interference with individual rights. (Some state courts, however, treated the Second Amendment as binding on the states.)[111]

In 1906 the Kansas Supreme Court announced in dicta that the Second Amendment did not guarantee an individual right to bear arms but only guarded official state militias against federal interference. Over the following decades, the collectivist state militia theory was accepted by many in the intellectual community but never by the American population as a whole. Today, 89 percent of Americans believe that as citizens they have a right to own a gun, and 87 percent believe the Constitution guarantees them a right to keep and bear arms.[112] Recently,

---

[109] Kates, "Handgun Prohibition and the Original Meaning of the Second Amendment," p. 218. In *United States v. Verdugo-Urguidez*, the U.S. Supreme Court affirmed that "the right of the people" refers to individual American citizens wherever the phrase appears in the Bill of Rights; 110 S. Ct. 1056, 1061 (1990).

[110] Today, 42 state constitutions guarantee a right to firearms ownership.

[111] Halbrook, *That Every Man Be Armed*. See, e.g., *Nunn v. State*, 1 Ga. 243 (1846).

[112] Wright, Rossi, and Daly, p. 229, quoting survey conducted by Decision-Making Information, Inc. Decision-Making Information is headed by conservative pollster Richard Wirthlin, and the particular survey was funded by the National Rifle Association. Despite the potential for bias, the survey is probably reliable, Wright and his coauthors concluded. Wright compared the Wirthlin data with data in a contemporaneous poll by Cambridge Research, Patrick Caddell's polling organization. The Caddell poll was sponsored by the Center for the Study and Prevention of Handgun Violence, whose then-director Pete Shields was also the head of Handgun Control Inc. Although the Wirthlin and Caddell polls both could have suffered from their sponsors' biases, "the actual empirical findings from the two surveys are remarkably similar. Results from comparable (even roughly comparable) items rarely differ between the two surveys by more than 10 percentage points. . . . [O]n virtually all points where a direct comparison is

the collectivist theory has begun to lose its standing even in the intellectual community. In the past two decades, scholarship of the individual rights view has dominated the law reviews, especially the major ones. Indeed, very few articles published in a top-50 law review argue that individual citizens are not protected by the Second Amendment.[113] The Senate Subcommittee on the Constitution investigated the historical evidence and concluded that the individual rights interpretation was unquestionably the intent of the authors of the Second Amendment, and was intended by the authors of the Fourteenth Amendment to be applied against the states.[114] Stephen Halbrook's *That Every Man Be Armed*, the first book to deal in depth with the historical background of the Second Amendment, also endorses the individual rights interpretation.

Sometimes writers in popular magazines claim that the Supreme Court has endorsed the collective theory. They are wrong. Twice in the 19th century, the Court heard cases involving state or private interference with gun use. Both times the Court took the now-discredited view that the Bill of Rights did not restrict state governments and therefore the Second Amendment offered no protection from state firearms laws.[115] The collective theory was not even invented until the early 20th century; neither of the Court's 19th century cases endorsed it.

The next (and last) time the Court squarely ruled on the Second Amendment was 1939. In *United States v. Miller* the Court held that since there was no evidence before that Court that sawed-off shotguns are militia-type, militarily useful weapons, the Court could not conclude that sawed-off shotguns were protected by the Second Amendment. As for the meaning of "a well-regulated Militia," the Court noted that to the authors of the Second Amendment, "The Militia comprised all males physically capable of acting in concert for the common defense. . . . Ordinarily when called for service these men were expected to appear bearing arms supplied by themselves and of the kind in common use at the time."[116]

---

possible, the evidence for each survey says essentially the same thing." Wright, Rossi, and Daly, p. 240.

[113] One that does so argue is Peter Feller and Karl Gotting, "The Second Amendment: A Second Look," *Northwestern University Law Review* 61 (March/April 1967), pp. 46-69. The authors did not address any of the evidence against the collective view discussed in the previous section. Surprisingly, the collective interpretation, lacking support in Supreme Court precedent, academic scholarship or popular opinion, still abounds in many lower federal courts—generally in an offhand sentence or two in cases where arms smugglers invoke frivolous Second Amendment defenses.

[114] Senate Committee on the Judiciary, *The Right to Keep and Bear Arms*, pp. 11-12.

[115] *Presser v. Illinois*, 116 U.S. 252 (1886); *United States v. Cruikshank*, 92 U.S. 542 (1875).

[116] 307 U.S. 174, 179.

Since the 1930s the Court has not had much to say about the Second Amendment. It denied a petition to review the *Morton Grove* case, in which a suburb's handgun ban was upheld. (The lower court had gotten its result by stating that the intent of the Framers of the Second Amendment was "irrelevant" to the amendment's meaning.)[117] As the Supreme Court has stated, though, a denial of review has no precedential effect.[118] Had the Court wanted the *Morton Grove* case to apply nationally, the Court could have issued a summary affirmance. More indicative of the modern Court's view of the Second Amendment is Justice Powell's opinion for the Court in *Moore v. East Cleveland*, where he listed "the freedom of speech, press, and religion; the right to keep and bear arms; the freedom from unreasonable searches and seizures" as part of the "full scope of liberty" guaranteed by the Constitution.[119]

Modern Utility

Some gun control advocates argue that the Second Amendment's goal of an armed citizenry to resist foreign invasion and domestic tyranny is no longer valid in light of advances in military technology. Former attorney general Ramsey Clark contended that "it is no longer realistic to think of an armed citizenry as a meaningful protection."[120]

But during World War II, which was fought with essentially the same types of ground combat weapons that exist today, armed citizens were considered quite important. After Pearl Harbor the unorganized militia was called into action. Nazi submarines were constantly in action off the East Coast. On the West Coast, the Japanese seized several Alaskan islands, and strategists wondered if the Japanese might follow up on their dramatic victories in the Pacific with an invasion of the Alaskan mainland, Hawaii, or California. Hawaii's governor summoned armed

---

[117] *Quilici v. Village of Morton Grove*, 532 F. Supp. 1169 (N.D. Ill.), *affd.* F.2d 261 (7th Cir., 1982), *cert. denied* 464 U.S. 863 (1983).

[118] *Hopfman v. Connolly*, 471 U.S. 459 (1985).

[119] 431 U.S. 494, 502 (1976). Justice Powell was quoting Justice Harlan's dissent in *Poe v. Ullman*, 367 U.S. 497, 542-43 (1961) (Harlan, J., dissenting.) The "liberty" that Justice Powell was referring to was the liberty protected by the Fourteenth Amendment's clause "nor shall any State deprive any person of life, liberty, or property without due process of law." That clause has been construed, in the last century, to mean that states must not violate the individual freedoms guaranteed in the Bill of Rights. (The Bill of Rights had originally been held only to limit federal power.)
   If the Second Amendment were only a limit on federal power over official state militias, it would have been preposterous for Justice Powell to list the right to bear arms as one of the rights protected by the Fourteenth Amendment's liberty clause; for that clause is explicitly a limit on state powers over individuals.

[120] Ramsey Clark, *Crime in America* (New York: Simon & Schuster, 1970), p. 88.

citizens to man checkpoints and patrol remote beach areas.[121] Maryland's governor called on "the Maryland Minute Men," consisting mainly of "members of Rod and Gun Clubs, of Trap Shooting Clubs and similar organizations," for "repelling invasion forays, parachute raids, and sabotage uprisings," as well as for patrolling beaches, water supplies, and railroads. Over 15,000 volunteers brought their own weapons to duty.[122] Gun owners in Virginia were also summoned into home service.[123] Americans everywhere armed themselves in case of invasion.[124] After the National Guard was federalized for overseas duty, "the unorganized militia proved a successful substitute for the National Guard," according to a Defense Department study. Militiamen, providing their own guns, were trained in patrolling, roadblock techniques, and guerrilla warfare.[125] The War Department distributed a manual recommending that citizens keep "weapons which a guerrilla in civilian clothes can carry without attracting attention. They must be easily portable and easily concealed. First among these is the pistol."[126] In Europe, lightly armed civilian guerrillas were even more important; the U.S. government supplied anti-Nazi partisans with a $1.75 analogue to the zip gun (a very low-quality handgun).[127]

Of course ordinary citizens are not going to grab their "Saturday night specials" and charge into incoming columns of tanks. Resistance to

---

[121] Alan Gottlieb, "Gun Ownership: A Constitutional Right," *Northern Kentucky Law Review* 10 (1982), p. 138.

[122] Governor O'Conor of Maryland delivered a radio address on March 10, 1942, at which he called for volunteers to defend the state: "[T]he volunteers, for the most part, will be expected to furnish their own weapons. For this reason, gunners (of whom there are sixty thousand licensed in Maryland), members of Rod and Gun Clubs, of Trap Shooting and similar organizations will be expected to constitute a part of this new military organization." State Papers and Addresses of Governor O'Conor, vol. III, p. 618, quoted in Bob Dowlut, "The Right to Bear Arms: Does the Constitution or the Predilection of Judges Reign?" *Oklahoma Law Review* 36 (1985), pp. 76-77n. 52. See also Kates, *Why Handgun Bans Can't Work*, p. 74, citing Baker, "I Remember 'The Army' with Men from 16 to 79," *Baltimore Sun Magazine*, November 16, 1975, p. 46.

[123] M. Schlegel, *Virginia On Guard—Civilian Defense and the State Militia in the Second World War* (Richmond: Virginia State Library, 1949), pp. 45, 129, 131. According to Schlegel, the Virginia militia "leaned heavily on sportsmen," because they could provide their own weapons. *Ibid.*, p. 129, quoted in Bob Dowlut, "State Constitutions and the Right to Keep and Bear Arms," *Oklahoma City University Law Review* 2 (1982), p. 198.

[124] "To Arms," *Time*, March 30, 1942, p. 1.

[125] Office of the Assistant Secretary of Defense, *U.S. Home Defense Forces Study* (March 1981), pp. 32, 34, 58-63, quoted in Dowlut, "State Constitutions," p. 197.

[126] Originally printed as Bert Levy, *Guerrilla Warfare* (New York: Penguin Books, 1942), p. 55, reprinted as Bert Levy, *Guerrilla Warfare* (Panther Publications, 1964), p. 56, quoted in Dowlut, "State Constitutions," p. 198 n. 91.

[127] Julian Hatcher, Frank Jury, and Joe Weller, *Firearms Investigation Identification and Evidence* (Harrisburg, Pa.: Stackpole, 1957), p. 59.

tyranny or invasion would be a guerrilla war. In the early years of such a war, before guerrillas would be strong enough to attack the occupying army head on, heavy weapons would be a detriment, impeding the guerrillas' mobility. As a war progresses, Mao Zedong explained, the guerrillas would use ordinary firearms to capture better small arms and eventually heavy equipment.[128]

The Afghan Mujahedeen were greatly helped by the belated arrival of the Stinger anti-aircraft missiles, but they had already fought the Soviets to a draw using a locally made version of the outdated Lee-Enfield rifle.[129] One clear lesson of this century is that a determined guerrilla army can wear down an occupying force until the occupiers lose spirit and depart—just what happened in Ireland in 1920 and Palestine in 1948. As one author put it: "Anyone who claims that popular struggles are inevitably doomed to defeat by the military technologies of our century must find it literally incredible that France and the United States suffered defeat in Vietnam . . . that Portugal was expelled from Angola; and France from Algeria."[130]

If guns are truly useless in a revolution, it is hard to explain why dictators as diverse as Ferdinand Marcos, Fidel Castro, Idi Amin, and the Bulgarian communists have ordered firearms confiscations upon taking power.[131]

Certainly the militia could not defend against intercontinental ballistic missiles, but it could keep order at home after a limited attack. In case of conventional war, the militia could guard against foreign invasion after the army and the National Guard were sent into overseas combat.

---

[128] Mao Zedong, *Mao-Tse Tung on Guerrilla Warfare*, translated by S. Griffith (New York: Praeger, 1961), cited in Raymond Kessler, "Gun Control and Political Power," *Law and Policy Quarterly* 5 (1983), p. 395.

[129] "One Year Later, Analysts Groping for Answers to Afghanistan," *Kansas City Times*, December 26, 1980, p. B3, cited in Kessler, p. 395.

[130] Gottlieb, p. 139. Even the pro-control *New York Times* editorial board sometimes understands the efficacy of lightly armed guerrillas; see, for example, "Who Will Hold the Guns in Rhodesia?" *New York Times*, August 31, 1977, p. 18. Nor do the guerrillas have to drive the occupier out single-handedly. At the least, guerrillas can tie down the enemy army, weakening the enemy so that he is defeated elsewhere. Although the Nazis faced critical manpower shortages on the Eastern Front against the Soviet Union, a sixth of their forces were deployed fighting Tito and his Yugoslavian partisans.

[131] For the Philippines, see Sherrill, p. 272. For Uganda, "Uganda Curbs Firearms," *New York Times*, December 22, 1969, p. 36. For Cuba, see Kessler, p. 382; Crum, "Gun Control Paved Castro's Way," *Conservative Digest*, April 1976, p. 33 (use of Batista's registration lists to facilitate confiscation); Williams, "The Rise of Castro: 'If only we hadn't given up our guns!,'" *Medina County Gazette*, October 15, 1978, p. 5. For Bulgaria, see "Gun Control Laws in Foreign Countries," rev. ed. (Washington, D.C.: Library of Congress, 1976), p. 33. (Upon coming to power, Bulgarian communists immediately confiscated all firearms.)

Especially given the absence of widespread military service, individual Americans familiar with using their private weapons provide an important defense resource. Canada already has an Eskimo militia to protect its northern territories.[132]

The United States is virtually immune from foreign invasion, but as the late vice president Hubert Humphrey explained, domestic dictatorship will always be a threat: "The right of citizens to bear arms is just one more guarantee against arbitrary government, one more safeguard against the tyranny which now appears remote in America, but which historically has proved to be always possible."[133]

The most advanced technology in the world could not keep track of guerrilla bands in the Rockies, the Appalachians, the great swamps of the South, or Alaska. The difficulty of fighting a protracted war against a determined popular guerrilla force is enough to make even the most determined potential dictator think twice.[134]

The Second Amendment debate goes to the very heart of the role of citizens and their government. By retaining arms, citizens retain the power claimed in the Declaration of Independence to "alter or abolish" a despotic government. And citizens retain the power to protect themselves from private assault. Ramsey Clark asked the question, "What kind of society depends on private action to defend life and property?"[135] The answer is a society that trusts its citizenry more than the police and the army and knows that ultimate authority must remain in the hands of the people.

Particular Forms of Gun Control

The foregoing discussion has focused on gun control in general. Many people who are skeptical about a complete ban on all guns nevertheless favor some sort of intermediate controls, which would regulate but not ban guns or ban only certain types of guns. While some

---

[132] "Far North Has Militia of Eskimos," *New York Times*, April 1, 1986, p. A14.

[133] Quoted in David Hardy, "The Second Amendment as a Restraint on State and Federal Firearm Restrictions," in *Restricting Handguns*, pp. 184-85.

[134] From Aaron Burr to Huey Long, Joseph McCarthy, Douglas MacArthur, and Richard Nixon, American history has seen its share of potential dictators. So far, our other safeguards have succeeded. But in a Constitution and political structure designed to last several hundred years, one cannot always count on the press or Congress to save things at the last minute.

[135] Clark, p. 89.

of these proposals seem plausible in the abstract, closer examination raises serious doubts about their utility.

Registration

Gun registration is essentially useless in crime detection. Tracing the history of a recovered firearm generally leads to the discovery that it was stolen from a legal owner and that its subsequent pattern of ownership is unknown.[136]

Analogies are sometimes drawn between gun registration and automobile registration. Indeed, a majority of the public seems to favor gun registration not because a reduction in crime is expected but because automobiles and guns are both intrinsically dangerous objects that the government should keep track of.[137] The analogy, though, is flawed. Gun owners, unlike drivers, do not need to leave private property and enter a public roadway. No one has ever demanded that prospective drivers prove a unique need for a car and offer compelling reasons why they cannot rely solely on public transportation. No Department of Motor Vehicles has ever adopted the policy of reducing to a minimum the number of cars in private hands. Automobile registration is not advocated or feared as a first step toward confiscation of all automobiles. However, registration lists did facilitate gun confiscation in Greece, Ireland, Jamaica, and Bermuda.[138] The Washington, D.C., city council considered (but did not enact) a proposal to use registration lists to confiscate all shotguns and handguns in the city. When reminded that the registration plan had been enacted with the explicit promise to gun owners that it would not be used for confiscation, the confiscation's sponsor retorted, "Well, I never promised them anything!"[139] The Evanston, Illinois, police department

---

[136] J. Howard Mathews, *Firearms Identification* (Springfield, Ill.: Charles C. Thomas, 1962), pp. 77, 80; Hatcher, Jury, and Weller, pp. 177, 180, 184.

[137] Wright, Rossi, and Daly, pp. 236, 241.

[138] B. Bruce-Briggs, "The Great American Gun War," *The Public Interest* (Fall 1976), p. 59. Historians disagree about whether the Nazis used registration lists to carry out confiscations in Denmark and Norway. Gun confiscation in Jamaica was part of a severe government anti-crime program, which drastically curtailed civil liberties; the program did little to stop crime in the long run but did imprison many innocent people, particularly from outcast groups such as the Rastafarians. Edward Diener and Rick Crandall, "An Evaluation of the Jamaican Anticrime Program," *Journal of Applied Social Psychology* (March 1979), pp. 137-48; Dudley Allen, in *Crime and Punishment in the Caribbean*, R. and G. Brana-Shute, eds. (Gainesville, Fl.: Center for Latin American Studies, 1980), pp. 29-57 [Allen was formerly the Jamaican Commissioner of Corrections]; Kates, *Why Handgun Bans Can't Work*, p. 16.

[139] "Wilson's Gun Proposal," *Washington Star-News*, February 15, 1975, p. A12; Lawrence Francis, "Washington Report," *Guns & Ammo*, December 1976, p. 86.

also attempted to use state registration lists to enforce a gun ban.[140] In 1990, the New York City government outlawed certain politically incorrect "semiautomatic assault rifles." The police used registration lists to enforce the ban, which applied retroactively to licensed gun owners—even though no licensed owner had ever perpetrated a crime with such a gun.

Unlike automobiles, guns are specifically protected by the Constitution, and it is improper to require that people possessing constitutionally protected objects register themselves with the government, especially when the benefits of registration are so trivial. The Supreme Court has ruled that the First Amendment prohibits the government from registering purchasers of newspapers and magazines, even of foreign communist propaganda.[141] The same principle should apply to the Second Amendment: The tools of freedom should be privately owned and unregistered.

Gun Licensing

Although opinion polls indicate that most Americans favor some form of gun licensing (for the same reasons they approve of auto licensing), 69 percent of Americans oppose laws giving the police power to decide who may or may not own a firearm.[142] That is exactly what licensing is. Permits tend to be granted not to those who are most at risk but to those with whom the police get along. In St. Louis, for example, permits have routinely been denied to homosexuals, nonvoters, and wives who lack their husbands' permission.[143] Other police departments have denied permits on the basis of race, sex, and political affiliation, or by determining that hunting or target shooting is not an adequate reason for owning a handgun.

Class discrimination pervades the process. New York City taxi drivers, who are more at risk of robbery than anyone else in the city, are denied gun permits, since they carry less than $2,000 in cash. (Of course,

---

[140] Blackman, "Civil Liberties and Gun-Law Enforcement," p. 14.

[141] *Lamont, DBA Basic Pamphlets v. Postmaster General*, 381 U.S. 301 (1965). The U.S. Post Office intercepted "foreign Communist propaganda" before delivery, and required addressees to sign a form before receiving the items. The Court's narrow holding was based on the principle that addressees should not have to go to the trouble of filling out a form to receive particular items of politically oriented mail. Since the Post Office had stopped maintaining lists of propaganda recipients before the case was heard, the Court did not specifically rule on the list-keeping practices. One may infer that the Post Office threw away its lists because it expected the Court would find them unconstitutional.

[142] Wright, Rossi, and Daly, pp. 223-35.

[143] Donald B. Kates, "On Reducing Violence or Liberty," *Civil Liberties Review* (August/September 1976), p. 56.

taxi drivers carry weapons anyway, and only rookie police officers arrest them for doing so.) As the courts have ruled, ordinary citizens and storeowners in the city may not receive so-called carry permits because they have no greater need for protection than anyone else in the city.[144] Carry permits are apparently reserved for New Yorkers such as Rockefellers, John Lindsay, the publisher of the *New York Times* (all of them gun control advocates), and the husband of Dr. Joyce Brothers.[145] Other licensees include an aide to a city councilman widely regarded as corrupt, several major slumlords, a Teamsters Union boss who is a defendant in a major racketeering suit, and a restaurateur identified with organized crime and alleged to control important segments of the hauling industry—hardly proof that licensing restricts gun ownership to upstanding citizens.[146]

The licensing process can be more than a minor imposition on the purchaser of a gun. In Illinois the automated licensing system can take 60 days to authorize a clearance.[147] Although New Jersey law requires that the authorities act on gun license applications within 30 days, delays of 90 days are routine; some applications are delayed for years, for no valid reason.[148] Licensing fees may be raised so high as to keep guns out of the hands of the poor. Until stopped by the state legislature, Dade County, Florida, which includes Miami, charged $500 for a license; nearby Monroe County charged $2,000.[149] These excessive fees on a means of self-defense are the equivalent of a poll tax. Or licensing may simply turn into prohibition. Mayor Richard Hatcher of Gary, Indiana, ordered his police department never to give anyone license application forms.[150] The police department in New York City has refused to issue legally required licenses, even when commanded by courts to do so. The department has also refused to even hand out blank application forms.[151]

---

[144] *Slatky v. Murphy, New York Law Journal*, October 14, 1971, p. 10.

[145] "Permit 29,000 to Pack Guns," (New York) *Daily News*, June 11, 1981; Susan Hall, "Nice People Who Carry Guns," *New York*, December 12, 1977; Kates and Silver, p. 153.

[146] William Bastone, "Born to Gun: 65 Big Shots With Licenses to Carry," *Village Voice*, September 29, 1987, p. 11.

[147] Pete Shields, *Guns Don't Die—People Do* (New York: Arbor House, 1981), p. 83.

[148] Statement of Robert F. Mackinnon, on behalf of the Coalition of New Jersey Sportsmen, before the House Committee on the Judiciary, on *Legislation to Modify the 1968 Gun Control Act*, part 2, serial no. 131, 99th Congress, 1st and 2d sess., February 27, 1986 (Washington, D.C.: Government Printing Office, 1987), p. 1418.

[149] Blackman, "Carrying Handguns," p. 8. The Florida state legislature enacted a statewide gun law, effective November 1987, which supplanted all local fees with a $125 state fee.

[150] *Motley v. Kellogg*, 409 N.E.2d 1207 (Ind. App. 1980).

[151] For some examples of the New York City Police Department's flagrant abuse of the statutory licensing procedure, see *Shapiro v. Cawley*, 46 A.D.2d 633, 634, 360 N.Y.S.2d 7, 8 (1st

In addition to police abuse of licensing discretion, there is also the problem of the massive data collection that would result from a comprehensive licensing scheme. For example, New York City asks a pistol permit applicant:

- Have you ever . . . Been discharged from any employment?
- Been subpoenaed to, or attended[!] a hearing or inquiry conducted by any executive, legislative, or judicial body?
- Been denied appointment in a civil service system, Federal, State, Local?
- Had any license or permit issued to you by any City, State, or Federal Agency?

Applicants for a business premises gun permit in New York City must also supply personal income tax returns, daily bank deposit slips, and bank statements. Photocopies are not acceptable. A grocer in the South Bronx may wonder what the size of his bank deposits has to do with his right to protection.

The same arguments that lead one to reject a national identity card apply to federal gun licensing. A national licensing system would require the collection of dossiers on half the households in the United States (or a quarter, for handgun-only record-keeping).

Implementing national gun licensing would make introduction of a national identity card more likely. Assuming that a large proportion of American families would become accustomed to the government collecting extensive data about them, they would probably not oppose making everyone else go through the same procedures for a national identity card.

Finally, licensing is not going to stop determined criminals. The most thorough study of the weapons behavior of felony prisoners (the Wright-

Dept. 1974) (ordering N.Y.C. Police Department to abandon illegal policy of requiring applicants for on-premises pistol license to demonstrate unique "need"); *Turner v. Codd*, 85 Misc. 2d 483, 484, 378 N.Y.S.2d 888, 889 (Special Term Part 1, N.Y. County, 1975) (ordering N.Y.C. Police Department to obey *Shapiro* decision); *Echtman v. Codd*, no. 4062-76 (N.Y. County) (class action lawsuit that finally forced Police Department to obey *Shapiro* decision.)

Also: *Bomer v. Murphy*, no. 14606-71 (N.Y. County) (to compel Department to issue blank application forms for target shooting licenses); *Klapper v. Codd*, 78 Misc.2d 377, 356 N.Y.S.2d 431 (Sup. Ct., Spec. term, N.Y. Cty.) (overturning refusal to issue license because applicant had changed job several times); *Casteli v. Cawley*, New York Law Journal, March 19, 1974, p. 2, col. 2. (Applicant suffered from post-nasal drip, and repeatedly cleared his throat during interview. His interviewer "diagnosed" a "nervous condition" and rejected the application. An appeals court overturned the decision, noting that the applicant's employment as a diamond cutter indicated "steady nerves.")

Rossi project funded by the National Institute of Justice) found that five-sixths of the felons did not buy their handguns from a retail outlet anyway. (Many of the rest used a legal, surrogate buyer, such as a girlfriend.)[152] As noted above, felons have little trouble buying stolen guns on the streets. In sum, it remains to be proven that gun licensing would significantly reduce crime. Given the very clear civil liberties problems with licensing, it cannot be said that the benefits outweigh the costs.

Waiting Periods

In the 1960s and 1970s bills to implement federal gun registration and licensing were soundly defeated in Congress, never to resurface as politically viable proposals. The broadest federal gun legislation currently under consideration is a national waiting period for gun purchases. Senator Howard Metzenbaum (D-OH) has introduced legislation to require a national seven-day (or five-business-day) waiting period for handgun transfers, which would be permitted only after police officials had an opportunity to check an applicant's background. Although the proposal applies only to retail sales, the anti-gun lobby has already announced plans to outlaw private gun transfers, thereby bringing all transactions under the waiting period.[153]

However, statistical evidence shows no correlation between waiting periods and homicide rates.[154] The image of a murderously enraged person leaving home, driving to a gun store, finding one open after 10 p.m. (when most crimes of passion occur), buying a weapon, and driving home to kill is a little silly.[155] Of course, a licensing system is bound to deny some purchasers an opportunity to buy, but only the most naive rejected purchaser would fail to eventually find a way to acquire an illegal weapon.

In addition, waiting periods can be subterfuges for more restrictive measures. Former Atlanta mayor Maynard Jackson proposed a six-month waiting period—a long time to wait for a woman who is in immediate

---

[152] Wright and Rossi, p. 185.

[153] The Attorney General's 1981 Task Force on Violent Crime also offered a waiting period proposal. Recommendation 18 of *Report of the Attorney General's Task Force on Violent Crime* (Washington, D.C.: Government Printing Office, August 17, 1981).

[154] *Report on the Federal Firearms Owners Protection Act*, S. Rep. no. 3476, 97th Cong., 2d sss. (1982), pp. 51-52; David B. Kopel, "Why Handgun Waiting Periods Threaten Public Safety," Issue Paper no. 4-91 (Golden, Colo.: Independence Institute, 1991).

[155] David Hardy, "Legal Restrictions on Firearms Ownership as an Answer to Violent Crime: What Was the Question?" *Hamlin Law Review* 6 (July 1983), p. 404.

danger of attack from her ex-boyfriend. Senator Metzenbaum's bill would give the police de facto licensing powers, even in states that have explicitly considered and rejected a police-run licensing system.

Mandatory Sentencing

Those who want to make simple gun possession a crime frequently call for a mandatory prison sentence for unlawful possession of a gun. The National Handgun Information Center demands a one-year mandatory minimum sentence for possession of a handgun during "any crime" (apparently including drunk driving or possession of a controlled substance). Detroit recently enacted a 30-day mandatory sentence for carrying an unlicensed gun.[156] None of those proposals is a step toward crime control.

Massachusetts's Bartley-Fox law, with a mandatory one-year sentence for carrying an unlicensed gun, has apparently reduced the casual carrying of firearms but has not significantly affected the gun use patterns of determined criminals.[157] Of the Massachusetts law, a Department of Justice study concluded that "the effect may be to penalize some less serious offenders, while the punishment for more serious offenses is postponed, reduced, or avoided altogether."[158] New York enacted a similar law and saw handgun homicides rise by 25 percent and handgun robberies 56 percent during the law's first full year.[159]

The effects of laws that impose mandatory sentences are sometimes brutally unfair. In New Mexico, for example, one judge resigned after being forced to send to prison a man with a clean record who had brandished a gun during a traffic dispute.[160] One of the early test cases under the Massachusetts Bartley-Fox law was the successful prosecution of a young man who had inadvertently allowed his gun license to expire. To raise money to buy his high school class ring, he was driving to a pawn shop to sell his gun. Stopping the man for a traffic violation, a policeman noticed the gun. The teenager spent the mandatory year in jail

---

[156] Isabel Wilkerson, "Urban Homicide Rates in U.S. Up Sharply in 1986," *New York Times*, January 15, 1987, p. A14.

[157] Wright, Rossi and Daly, pp. 290-94, 298, 308.

[158] Kenneth Carlson, "Mandatory Sentencing: The Experience of Two States," Department of Justice, National Institute of Justice policy brief (Washington, D.C.: Abt Associates, May 1982), p. 15. The document analyzes the Massachusetts gun law and the New York drug laws.

[159] "State's Gun Law: Impact and Intent Uncertain," *New York Times*, April 11, 1982, p. 1.

[160] "Judge Hears Conscience, Not 'Gun Law' Sentence," *American Bar Association Journal* 67 (November 1981), p. 1433.

with no parole.[161] Another Massachusetts case involved a man who had started carrying a gun after a co-worker began threatening to murder him.[162] The Civil Liberties Union of Massachusetts had opposed Bartley-Fox precisely because of the risk that innocent people would be sent to jail.[163]

The call for mandatory jail terms for unlicensed carrying is in part an admission by the gun control advocates that judges reject their values and instead base sentences on community norms. A Department of Justice survey of how citizens regard various crimes found that carrying an illegal gun ranked in between indecent exposure and cheating on taxes—hardly the stuff of a mandatory year in jail.[164] The current judicial/community attitude is appropriate. In a world where first-time muggers often receive probation, it is morally outrageous to imprison for one year everyone who carries a firearm for self-defense.

As a general matter of criminal justice, mandatory sentences are inappropriate. One of the most serious problems with any kind of mandatory sentencing program is that its proponents are rarely willing to fund the concomitant increase in prison space. It is very easy for legislators to appear tough on crime by passing draconian sentencing laws. It is much more difficult for them to raise taxes and build the prison space necessary to give those laws effect. Instead of more paper laws, a more effective crime-reduction strategy would be to build enough prisons to keep hard-core violent criminals off the streets for longer periods. If there are to be mandatory sentences for gun crimes, the mandatory term should apply only to use of a firearm in a violent crime.

[161] Hardy, "Legal Restrictions on Firearms Ownership as an Answer to Violent Crime," p. 407.

[162] *Commonwealth v. Lindsey*, (Mass. Supreme Judicial Court, March 5, 1986) (available in LEXIS library, Massachusetts file). Wrote the court, "The threat of physical harm was founded on an earlier assault by Michel with a knife and became a real and direct matter once again when Michel attacked the defendant with a knife at the MBTA station. . . . [D]efendant is a hard-working, family man, without a criminal record, who was respected by his fellow employees (Michel excepted). Michel, on the other hand, appears to have lacked the same redeeming qualities. He was a convicted felon with serious charges pending against him. . . . It is possible that defendant is alive today only because he carried the gun that day for protection. Before the days of a one-year mandatory sentence, the special circumstances involving the accused could be reflected reasonably in the sentencing or dispositional aspects of the proceeding. That option is no longer available in the judicial branch of government in a case of this sort." Eventually, the defendant was pardoned by the Governor.

[163] Brief for Civil Liberties Union of Massachusetts as *amicus curiae, Commonwealth v. Jackson*, pp. 22-26, cited in James Beha, "And *Nobody* Can Get You Out," *Boston University Law Review* 57 (1977) p. 110, n. 55. The Massachusetts legislature's black caucus had also opposed the bill, because of concern about discriminatory licensing and arrests. Beha, p. 108, n. 45.

[164] Department of Justice, "The Severity of Crime," *Bureau of Justice Statistics Bulletin* (January 1984), p. 4.

300

Handgun Bans

A total ban on the private possession of handguns is the ultimate goal of a Washington lobby, once called the National Coalition to Ban Handguns, now renamed the Coalition to Stop Gun Violence. Unlike some other gun control measures, a ban lacks popular support; only one-sixth to one-third of the citizenry favors such a measure.[165]

Handgun-ban proponents sometimes maintain that handguns have no utility except to kill people. The statement is patently wrong and typical of how little the prohibitionists understand the activities they condemn. Although self-defense is the leading reason for handgun purchases, about one-sixth of handgun owners bought their gun primarily for target shooting, and one-seventh bought the gun primarily as part of a gun collection. In addition, hunters frequently carry handguns as a sidearm to use against snakes or to hunt game.[166]

Cost-benefit analysis hardly offers a persuasive case for a ban. One recent study indicates that handguns are used in roughly 645,000 self-defensive gun uses each year—a rate of once every 48 seconds. (As noted above, most defensive uses simply involve brandishing the gun.) The number of self-defense uses is at least equal to, and probably more than, the number of times handguns are used in a crime.[167] Most homicides (between 50 and 84 percent) occur in circumstances where a long gun could easily be substituted.[168] Besides, sawing off a shotgun and secreting it under a coat is simple. Many modern submachine guns are only 11 to 13 inches long, and an M1 carbine can be modified to become completely concealable.[169] Since long guns are so much deadlier than handguns, an effective handgun ban would result in at least some criminals switching to sawed-off shotguns and rifles, perhaps increasing fatalities from gun crimes. In the Wright and Rossi prisoner survey, 75 percent of "handgun

---

[165] Wright, Rossi, and Daly, pp. 234-35. Public opinion on this issue has changed rather strongly since the late 1950s, when the Gallup Poll found a majority in favor of a handgun ban.

[166] Wright, Rossi, and Daly, pp. 57-58, citing survey conducted by Decision-Making Information, Inc.; Finn Aagard, "Handgun Hunting Today," *American Hunter*, February 1987, p. 32 ("I doubt if any branch of the shooting sports has grown more phenomenally over the last decade than hunting with a handgun.")

[167] Kleck, "Crime Control," pp. 2-4.

[168] Gary Kleck, "Handgun-Only Control," in *Firearms and Violence*, p. 193.

[169] David Hardy and Donald B. Kates, "Handgun Availability and the Social Harm of Robbery," in *Restricting Handguns*, p. 127. M1 information is from the California attorney general's 1965 appearance before the Senate Judiciary Committee's Subcommittee on Juvenile Delinquency, hearings *On Amendments of Federal Firearms Act 1965*, quoted in Sherrill, p. 63.

predators" said they would switch to sawed-off shoulder weapons if handguns were unavailable.[170]

If families had to give up handguns and replaced them with long guns, fatalities from gun accidents would likely increase. Since handguns have replaced long guns as a home defense weapon over the last 50 years, the firearm accident fatality rate has declined.[171] The overwhelming majority of accidental gun deaths are from long guns.[172]

Handguns are also much better suited for self-defense, especially in the home, than are long guns, which are more difficult to use in a confined setting. Rifle bullets may penetrate their intended target and keep on going through a wall, injuring someone in an adjacent apartment. Further, the powerful recoil of long guns makes them more difficult for women, frail people, or the elderly to shoot accurately. Lastly, a robber or assailant has a much better chance of eventual recovery if he is shot with a handgun rather than a long gun.

Banning "Saturday Night Specials"

If a "Saturday night special" is defined as any handgun with a barrel length less than three inches, a caliber of .32 or less, and a retail cost of under $100, there are roughly six million such guns in the United States. Each year, between one and six percent of them are employed in violent gun crimes, a far higher percentage of criminal misuse than for other guns.[173] Although opinion polls find the majority of Americans in favor of banning "Saturday night specials," the practical case for banning these weapons is not compelling.[174]

Criminals do prefer easily concealable weapons; roughly 75 percent of all crime handguns seized or held by the police have barrel lengths of three inches or less.[175] At least for serious felons, though, low price is a very secondary factor in choice of firearm. Experienced felons prefer powerful guns to cheap one. The Wright and Rossi survey, which focused

---

[170] Wright and Rossi, p. 220.

[171] Benenson, "A Controlled Look at Gun Controls," p. 720; John Kaplan, "The Wisdom of Gun Prohibition," *Annals of the American Academy of Political and Social Sciences* 455 (1981), p. 17.

[172] Pete Shields, the founding chairman of Handgun Control, writes, "Of the accidental deaths, again it is safe to assume that over 50 percent were by handguns." (Pete Shields, p. 28.) As noted above, handgun accidents comprise 300 of the 1,700 accidental gun fatalities yearly.

[173] Affidavit of professor of criminology Gary Kleck in *amicus curiae* memorandum of law by Congress on Racial Equality and Second Amendment Foundation in *Kelly v. R. G. Industries,* at 20-23 (Md.Ct.App. 1983).

[174] Wright, Rossi, and Daly, pp. 234-35.

[175] Wright, Rossi, and Daly, p. 17.

on hardened criminals, found that only 15 percent had used a "Saturday night special as their last gun used in a crime.[176] It should not be surprising that serious criminals prefer guns as powerful as those carried by their most important adversaries, the police.

It is often said that a "Saturday night special" is "the kind of gun that has only one purpose: to kill people."[177] Again, this is untrue. Such guns are commonly used as hunting sidearms, referred to as "trail guns" or "pack guns." One does not need long-range accuracy to kill a snake, and lightness and compactness are important. Nor can all hunters afford $200 for a quality sidearm.[178] More importantly, inexpensive handguns are used for self-defense by the poor.

There is no question that laws against "Saturday night specials" are leveled at blacks. The first such law came in 1870 when Tennessee attempted to disarm freedmen by prohibiting the sale of all but "Army and Navy" handguns. Ex-confederate soldiers already had their military handguns, but ex-slaves could not afford high-quality weapons.[179]

The situation today is not very different. As the federal district court in Washington, D.C., has noted, laws aimed at "Saturday night specials" have the effect of selectively disarming minorities, who, because of their poverty, must live in crime-ridden areas.[180] Little wonder that the Congress on Racial Equality filed an *amicus curiae* brief in a 1985 suit challenging the Maryland Court of Appeals's virtual ban on low-caliber handguns (which was later mitigated by the legislature). As the Wright and Rossi National Institute of Justice study concluded:

> The people most likely to be deterred from acquiring a handgun by exceptionally high prices or by the nonavailability of certain kinds of handguns are not felons intent on arming themselves for criminal purposes (who can, if all else fails, steal the handgun they want), but rather poor people who have decided they need a gun to protect themselves against the felons but who find that the cheapest gun in the market costs more than they can afford to pay.[181]

---

[176] Wright and Rossi, pp. 167, 233. (As noted above, the survey was part of a National Institute of Justice project.)

[177] Pete Shields, p. 46.

[178] Wright, Rossi, and Daly, p. 58.

[179] Kates, "Toward a History of Handgun Prohibition in the United States," p. 14.

[180] *Delahanty v. Hinckley* (D.D.C. July 1986) (Penn, J.).

[181] Wright and Rossi, p. 238.

Indeed, one wonders what a ban on these law-caliber guns would accomplish. Criminals who use them could easily take up higher-powered guns. Some criminals might switch to knives, but severe knife wounds are just as deadly (and almost as easy to inflict at close range, where most robberies occur).[182]

If a ban on "Saturday night specials" failed to reduce crime, is it likely that its proponents would admit defeat and repeal the law? Or would they conclude that a ban on all handguns was what was really needed? Once criminals started substituting sawed-off shotguns, would the new argument be that long guns too must be banned?[183] That is the point that gun control in Great Britain is approaching, after beginning with a seemingly innocuous registration system for handguns.

Conclusion

In 1911 state senator Timothy Sullivan of New York promised that if New York City outlawed handgun carrying, homicides would decline drastically. The year the Sullivan law took effect, however, homicides increased and the *New York Times* pronounced criminals "as well armed as ever."[184] Gun control insists that citizens rely on the authorities. Gun owners know better than to put their lives and liberty in the hands of 911 and the police. Gun control and the Bill of Rights cannot coexist. The advocates of gun control believe that government agents are more trustworthy than ordinary citizens. The authors of the Second Amendment believed just the opposite.

The original version of *Trust the People: The Case Against Gun Control* is available for two dollars (one dollar in bulk) from the Cato Institute, 224 Second St., SE, Washington, DC 20036 (202-546-0200). Other works of interest by Kopel include *The Samurai, the Mountie, and the Cowboy: Should America*

---

[182] The son of the founding chairman of Handgun Control was slain by San Francisco's "Zebra killer," an insane black man who murdered whites for no reason at all (Pete Shields, p. 12). Had the man been armed with a sawed-off shotgun, he still could have concealed it inside his jacket. Any psychopath capable of carrying out so many slayings and evading detection for so long would probably know where to buy a stolen shotgun. Even an effective prohibition on all guns would not stop such maniacs; the man committed his first homicide with a machete (*ibid.*, p. 37).

[183] Clyde Barrow, of Bonnie and Clyde fame, could "quick draw" his shotgun from a special holster in his pants. Kennett and Anderson, p. 203.

[184] *New York Times*, May 23, 1913, p. 9; Kennett and Anderson, p. 185.

Adopt the Gun Controls of Other Democracies? (Buffalo: Prometheus Books, 1992); and "The 'Assault Weapon' Panic: Political Correctness Takes Aim at the Constitution." The latter two are available for eight dollars (each) from the Independence Institute, 14142 Denver West Parkway, Suite 101, Golden, CO 80401 (303-279-6536).

Weapons Control Laws:
Gateways to Victim Oppression and Genocide

David I. Caplan

A Short History of Weapons Control Laws in Common-Law Jurisprudence

The Riot of York, England (1189)

Weapons control laws have a long history in Anglo-American jurisprudence. One of the first such documented laws, the Assize of Arms,[1] contained a stringent weapons control provision directed against all Jews. It forbade any Jew from possessing even a coat of mail or a breastplate. Eight years later, a vicious anti-Semitic mob of rioters attacked the Jews of York, England. This attack precipitated an uneven fight in which Jewish resistance collapsed because the Jews had "few weapons."[2] As a result, virtually the entire Jewish community of York was annihilated.

The impact of this very early weapons control law demonstrates a dire result to which such laws can lead. The intent and effect of weapons control laws, whether articulated or not, often is to place only certain segments of the community at a disadvantage. In this way, from earliest times weapons control laws have facilitated the oppression and devastation of the disarmed.

The Statute of Northampton (1328)

In 1328, the English Statute of Northampton[3] was enacted, flatly prohibiting everyone, except upon the king's order or in concert with the

This chapter first appeared in *To Be A Victim: Encounters with Crime and Injustice*, Diane Sank, Ph.D., and David I. Caplan, Ph.D., L.L.B., eds. (New York: Plenum Press, Insight Books, 1991).

---

[1] Statute of England (1181). *Assize of Arms*, Art. 3. Printed in W. Stubbs, *Select Charters and Other Illustrations of English Constitutional History* (8th ed.) (Oxford: Clarendon Press, 1900).

[2] Grayzel, S., *History of the Jews*. (New York: New American Library, 1968) p.307.

[3] Statute of England (1328). 2 Edward III, Chapter 3. Printed in *The Statutes at Large,* Vol. 1, p. 197 (London: Charles Eyre & Andrew Strahan, 1786).

community, from carrying any arms. Concerning this Statute of North-ampton, Jean Jules Jusserand wrote, "Manners being violent, the wearing of arms was prohibited, but honest folk alone conformed to the law, thus facilitating matters for the others."[4] This statement demonstrates another socially undesirable outcome of even well-meaning weapons control laws: more frequently than not, such laws are obeyed only by persons who are law-abiding.

Anglo-American Constitutional Approach to the Right to Keep Arms

The Glorious Revolution of 1688

Among the causes of England's Glorious Revolution of 1688 was a royal proclamation by James II ordering that the militia should "cause strict search to be made for . . . muskets or other guns and to seize and safely keep them."[5] Although this proclamation was not on its face directed against Protestants, James II, being a Catholic, enforced this disarmament proclamation selectively against only Protestants. He also quartered troops in the private homes of Protestants.[6]

Firearms control laws nondiscriminatory on their face thus often provide temptation for politically motivated and discriminatory enforce-ment. Even though weapons control laws may be worded to apply universally, in practice they have been enforced to victimize disfavored segments of the population.

English Bill of Rights of 1689

At the end of the Glorious Revolution, James II fled to France, and a Parliament was elected which enacted the English Bill of Rights of 1689. Chief among its provisions was a guarantee of the right of Protestants to "have arms for their defense, suitable to their conditions and as allowed by law."[7] It is of great importance to note that, when the English Bill of Rights was being debated in Parliament, attempts were made to limit the right of individuals to possess arms strictly for the

---

[4] Jusserand, J. J. (1896), *A Literary History of the English People* (New York: Putnam's, 1896), p. 270.

[5] Calendar of State Papers (1686). Dec. 6. *Domestic Series, James II*, 2, p. 314.

[6] *State of Oregon v. Kessler*. Oregon Supreme Court, *Oregon Reports* (Salem: State Printing, 1980), p. 289.

[7] *Ibid.*, p. 364.

purpose of "their common defense."[8] These attempts were soundly defeated. Thus, to prevent victimization of individuals, an individual right, as opposed to a collective right, to possess arms was clearly intended.

American Revolution of 1776

Although not frequently noted, the imposition by General Gage, the British military Governor of Massachusetts, of an arms confiscation scheme on the colonists in Boston, played an important role in igniting the American Revolution. As a condition for leaving Boston, the inhabitants of Boston were required to deliver up their arms, with the stipulation that these arms would be returned to them when they returned to Boston. However, the arms were not returned when their owners came back to Boston. Note that General Gage's arms confiscation program included the seizure of privately owned firearms kept at home.

Ultimately, the American Revolution resulted in the adoption in 1789 of the United States Constitution, followed in 1791 by its Bill of Rights. The Second Amendment in the Bill of Rights provides:

> A well regulated militia being necessary to the security of a free state, the right of the people to keep and bear arms shall not be infringed.[9]

It is frequently debated whether an individual right was intended by the Second Amendment. The legislative history of the amendment is crucial to deciding this question. As in the debates a hundred years earlier in the English Parliament, the First Congress of the United States decided conclusively that an individual right was intended. In 1789 an attempt was made on the floor of congress to dilute the right to keep arms by adding the qualifying words "for the common defense."[10] This attempt was soundly defeated.

---

[8] *House of Commons Journal* (1689). February 11, Vol. 10, pp. 25-26.

[9] United States Constitution, Amendment II (1791). *The Constitution of the United States.* Reprinted by Commission on the Bicentennial of the United States Constitution (Washington, D.C.: Government Printing Office, 1989).

[10] Schwartz, B., *The Bill of Rights: A Documentary History*, Vol. 2 (New York: McGraw-Hill, Chelsea House, 1971), pp. 1153-54.

Anglo-American Right of Victims to Use Arms

Right to Use Deadly Force in Defense Against Heinous Felonious Attacks

Inherent in the right to have arms for security is the right to use those arms in self-defense and with deadly force to repel, resist, or suppress violent and heinous crimes such as cold-blooded murder, robbery, arson, forcible rape, housebreaking, or mayhem.[11] When a victim resists any of these heinous felonies, at common law the victim has the right—if not the duty[12]—to use deadly force to the point of killing the criminal assailant, without demonstrating actual need for using the deadly force: the need is presumed. The traditional rationale for this approach is that the resisting victim is regarded as protecting not only himself or herself but also the next victims, and that his or her life is presumably in peril during the attack. Such resisting victims were thus regarded as "protecting the public order,"[13] that is, protecting both themselves and countless future victims. Such victims also had the duty, using deadly force if necessary, to arrest the felon to prevent his or her escape in immediate flight from the scene of the crime, but not later on.[14]

On the other hand, crimes escalating from mere quarrels or mutual combat, such as homicides occurring during barroom brawls and other fights, were regarded as being in an entirely different category. They are not included here. The rules concerning the use of deadly force in such situations were much more circumscribed and limiting, on the theory that both participants had acted wrongfully in instigating the situation or allowing it to escalate and that neither was protecting the public, whereas in cases of resistance against heinous felonies no wrongful activity on the part of the victim could be presumed[15] and the resisting victim was viewed as protecting the "public order."

The New Rules and Their Harmful Effects on Victims

During this century, in many states, new statutes and court decisions abolished the common law rules and allow the victims of heinous

---

[11] Perkins, R. M., and Boyce, R. N., *Criminal Law* (3rd ed.), Chapter 10, Section 3. (Mineola, N.Y.: Foundation Press, 1982).

[12] Bishop, J. P., *Bishop on Criminal Law* (9th ed.), Vol. 2, Section 648 (Chicago: T. H. Flood, 1923).

[13] Perkins and Boyce, *Criminal Law*, p. 1108.

[14] Bishop, *On Criminal Law.*

[15] Bacon, F. (1630). *Elements of the Common Laws of England, Regula 5* (London: I. More).

felonious attacks to use deadly force if and only if such force "reasonably seem[s] necessary to prevent the commission" of the felony.[16] Thus the law-abiding victim of a dangerous felonious attack has been placed at a severe tactical disadvantage. The use of force by the defending victim, too much or too soon, sends him or her to prison; too little or too late, to the cemetery.

In 1962 the American Law Institute, an unofficial group of jurists and law professors, promulgated its Model Penal Code.[17] Some dozen or so states have adopted this code, either by statute or by court decision. The Model Penal Code goes further than the newer statutes and decisions discussed in the preceding paragraph and forbids the victims of a heinous felonious attack from using deadly force in all cases, the only exception arising when the victim has good reason to believe that "there is a substantial risk that the [felonious attacker] will cause death or serious [bodily] harm unless the crime is prevented."[18]

A robbery victim carrying money would be privileged, under the rules established before the Model Penal Code, to use deadly force against the robbers if the victim reasonably believed such force to be necessary to prevent the success of the robbery. The victim could use such force "even if the robbers, by superior strength and numbers, would be able to take the money without causing any serious injury to him and assured him that they would not hurt him in any way."[19] Victims would not have this privilege under the Model Penal Code but would have to allow the robbers to take their property.

Restrictive deadly force rules require an innocent victim to rely on the criminals' body-language assurances that his or her life is not in peril. These rules also criminalize self-defense and the defense of the public order. Worst of all, they artificially and by legalistic sleight-of-hand transform innocent victims into criminals and criminals into so-called victims.

Restrictive Firearms Licensing and the Transformation of Crime Victims into "Criminals"

The headlines of two recent newspaper stories tell it all about restrictive firearms licensing: "A Bronx livery-cab driver was arrested on

---

[16] Perkins and Boyce, *Criminal Law*, p. 1111.

[17] American Law Institute (1985). *Model Penal Code and Commentaries*, Section 3.07, (Philadelphia: Author).

[18] Perkins and Boyce, *Criminal Law*, pp. 1111-12.

[19] *Ibid.*, p. 1112.

charges of carrying an unlicensed gun after he shot at a man who robbed him, the police said yesterday";[20] "Man Kills Robber; Murder Is Charged."[21] Moreover, restrictive deadly force and gun control laws unfairly impose Marquis of Queensberry rules on the victims of heinous felonies, while signaling to aggressive perpetrators the strategies and tactics that can be used to take unfair advantage of their legally restricted victims.

Right to Use Deadly Force to Arrest Fleeing Felons

After a heinous felonious attack—such as attempted cold-blooded murder, arson, robbery, burglary, forcible rape, or mayhem—has abated and the victim is completely out of danger, what level of force may be used to apprehend the criminal? Today, in most states, it is perfectly lawful for a private person, a victim or bystander, to use deadly force to apprehend the felon on the spot or to prevent the escape of the fleeing felon if, but only if, this degree of force is necessary for the purpose.[22] The traditional societal justification for this rule of law is that a heinous felon at large poses an immediate and dangerous threat to the entire community, and that therefore the safety and security of society require the speedy arrest and imprisonment of a felon. Police simply cannot be expected to be on the spot to make an arrest at the commission of every dangerous crime.

The Model Penal Code, however, prohibits a private person from using deadly force to arrest or prevent the escape of a fleeing felon, unless *both* (1) the felony included the use or threatened use of deadly force, *and* (2) the person effecting the arrest is "assisting" one who is "authorized to act as a peace officer." Thus, under the Model Penal Code, a fleeing armed robber, burglar, or rapist would be legally immune from being apprehended with deadly force by his victims. For example, the code would prevent the victims from using such force even if they had just been shot by the criminal and were bleeding to death, unless they were "assisting" a "peace officer" who happened to be there.

---

[20] *New York Times*, May 1, 1990, p. B2.

[21] *New York Times*, July 22, 1990, Metropolitan Section, p. 25.

[22] Dressler, J., *Understanding Criminal Law*, Section 21.03[B] (New York: Matthew Bender, 1987).

312

Utility of Private Firearms Possession to Prevent Victimization

Criminologists[23] have shown that over one-half million Americans use firearms annually—most often without firing a single shot—in defense against violent criminals. They also found that using a firearm for protection, especially in the home, where the victim is more likely to have the advantage of familiarity with the environment, reduces the likelihood that a crime will be completed by the criminal. It also reduces the likelihood of injury to the victim. Moreover, burglars seek to avoid areas where firearms are kept by many, though not necessarily all, houses.[24] Thus the anonymous keeping of home-defense arms by many householders protects the entire community.

Vigilantism Versus Legitimate Defense of Self and of Public Order

Vigilantism occurs when a person who makes an arrest or captures a heinous felon does not immediately deliver the captured miscreant to the proper authorities. A vigilante might instead deliver the captured individual to a vigilance committee, which might conduct a mock trial and/or execution.[25] By contrast, the availability of a lawful manner for an ordinary person to arrest a wrongdoer on the spot provides an important socially approved escape valve for the law-abiding victim when confronted by a criminal when the police are not available to make an immediate arrest. Under the novel restrictive rules, it is not difficult to understand the temptation of a crime victim to administer rough justice on the spot and simply to disappear, a type of event that is becoming repetitive in New York City, for example.[26]

[23] Kleck, G., "Crime Control through the Private Use of Armed Force." *Social Problems*, 35 (1988), pp. 1-21; Lizotte, A. J., "Determination of Completing Rape and Assault." *Journal of Quantitative Criminology*, 2 (1986), pp. 203-17.

[24] Kleck, "Crime Control."

[25] Friedman, L. M., *A History of American Law* (2nd ed.) (New York: Simon & Schuster, 1985).

[26] *New York Post*, " 'Death Wish' Shooter Blasts Thug." June 20, 1990, p. 7.

313

Deadly Force to Suppress Civil Disorders

The common law of England[27] and America[28]—until abolished by statute in England in 1967 and by various states in America during this century—allowed, if not commanded, private citizens to use deadly force *if necessary* to suppress or disperse a dangerous or destructive riot. Even the Model Penal Code would allow deadly force to be used by riot victims on the theory that, during a riot or civil disturbance, there is always a danger that the police "may be overwhelmed and rendered impotent by the sheer weight of numbers."[29] Such overtaxing of police resources occurred during the 1967 Newark, New Jersey, riot where there were 62 major fires, and 1,029 business establishments and 29 residences were damaged.[30]

During an April 1968 riot in New York City, a shopkeeper heeded a warning by police not to protect his business establishment with his own firearm.[31] His shop was looted and damaged. On his suing the city, the trial judge overturned a previous jury verdict in his favor. The judge opined that, because the police had been overextended during the "widespread crisis" occasioned by the riot, police protection of one person's premises "might have resulted in a neglect of the public at large." The judge added that, in such a crisis, the concept of reasonableness demanded that the allocation of police resources be left "to the discretion of the police department." The court concluded, "It is this concept of reasonableness which excuses a municipality from liability when in the exercise of high administrative judgment the overriding interest of the public requires that rioting be permitted."[32]

Aside from the foregoing ruling, even if the police had attempted in good faith to respond quickly, there is no guarantee that they would have or could have arrived in time to prevent the looting and burning of a shop or residence. By contrast, right after a July 1977 New York City blackout riot, a shopkeeper explained why his store had been neither looted nor

---

[27] Hawkins, W. (1788). *A Treatise of the Please of the Crown* (6th ed.), Chapter 28, Sections 14, 23 (Dublin: Elizabeth Lynch).

[28] Wharton, F., *Wharton's Criminal Law, 2*, Section 1878 (Rochester, N.Y.: The Lawyers Co-operative Publishing Co., 1932).

[29] American Law Institute, *Model Penal Code and Commentaries*, Section 3.07, p. 135 (Philadelphia: Author, 1985).

[30] *New Jersey Superior Court Reports, A & B Auto Stores of Jones St., Inc. v. City of Newark, 106,* 491-514 (St. Paul: West Publishing, 1969).

[31] *Bloom v. City of New York. New York Law Journal,* September 5, *174* (No. 47), 6 (New York: New York Law Publishing, 1975).

[32] *Ibid.,* p. 6.

damaged as many others had been: "This store is okay because I stayed here all night with my .32 caliber pistol and my attack dog."[33]

The aftermath of Hurricane Hugo in the Virgin Islands in September 1989 furnishes another example of the futility of victims' reliance for their safety and well-being on the constituted authorities during riots or other widespread disorders. After Hurricane Hugo had wreaked its havoc on St. Croix, widespread looting followed.[34] At first the police attempted to stop the looting by shooting in the air. When that failed, they joined in the looting. National Guardsmen were then called in to restore law and order, but they likewise joined in the looting "while gangs were moving through the streets with rifles."[35]

There are thus times when the victims of crime have no alternative but to rely on their own resources and devices. During civil disturbances in which victims are faced with hordes of criminals descending on their persons and property, threatening their lives, homes, and businesses, firearms with large-capacity magazines—so-called assault weapons—would seem to be the only practical and realistic option for the potential victims to hold mobs at bay.

Political Oppression and Genocide, and Weapons Control Laws

"Prompt defensive measures are the most effective means for the prevention of genocide," observed V. V. Stanciu,[36] Secretary of the International Society for the Prevention of Genocide, Paris, France. Mr. Stanciu unequivocally proclaimed, "The most moral violence is that used in self defense, the most sacred juridical institution."[37] He clearly appreciated and perceived the keeping and using of arms by potential victims as a most effective means for preventing genocide.

---

[33] *New York Times*, "A Game of Cat and Mouse on Tour of East Harlem." July 15, 1977, p. A1.

[34] *USA Today.* "Looting Spree: 'There's no Law and Order.' " September 21, 1989, p. 5A.

[35] *New York Times*, "Bush Dispatches Troops to Island in Storm's Wake." September 21, 1989, p. A1.

[36] Stanciu, V. V., "Reflections on the Congress for the Prevention of Genocide." *Yad Vashem Studies on the European Jewish Catastrophe*, Vol. 7, p. 185 (Jerusalem: Post Press, 1968).

[37] *Ibid.*

Weapons Control Laws and Oppression of the Masses

Historically, weapons control laws have been used to oppress the bulk of the population. For example, the kingdoms of Europe kept the masses under their domination by prohibiting them from keeping arms.[38] One of the goals of the English Game Act of 1671[39]—which prohibited any person who was below the rank of esquire or who did not have an annual income of at least 100 pounds from keeping any gun—was "prevention of popular insurrections and resistance to [oppressive] government, by disarming the bulk of the people."[40]

Disarmament and Oppression of Blacks in the South

Immediately after the Civil War in the United States, in the southern states the slave codes reappeared as the Black codes.[41] These codes restricted the access of African-Americans to firearms, typically by means of restrictive licensing provisions.[42] In this way, the white establishment in the South was able to continue to oppress African-Americans, as by using the white militia to "hang some freedman or search negro houses for arms."[43]

Disarmament and Oppression of the Sioux Indians

In 1876, the U.S. Army took from the on-reservation Sioux Indians their weapons and horses.[44] Consequently, when in 1877 Congress passed a statute offering the Sioux food rations and a very low cash payment in exchange for their favorite lands, known as Black Hills, the Sioux were faced with the "Hobson's choice of ceding the Black Hills or starving. Not surprisingly, the Sioux chiefs and head men chose the former rather than the latter."[45]

---

[38] Madison, J. (1788). *The Federalist,* No. 46. Reprinted in *The Federalist Papers* (New York: New American Library, Mentor Books, 1961).

[39] Statute of England. 1671. 22 and 23 Charles II, Chapter 25. Printed in *The Statutes at Large,* Vol. 3, pp. 349-50 (London: Charles Eyre & Andrew Strahan, 1786).

[40] Blackstone, W. (1766). *Commentaries on the Laws of England,* Vol. 2, Chapter 27 (Oxford: T. H. Flood), p. 411.

[41] Coulter, E., *The South during Reconstruction* (Baton Rouge: Louisiana State University Press, 1947); see also DuBois, W. E. B., *Black Reconstruction in America* (New York: S. A. Russell, 1935).

[42] Laws of Mississippi. (1865). Printed in W. Fleming, *Documentary History of Reconstruction,* Vol. 1 (Cleveland: A. H. Clark). pp. 289-90.

[43] Trumbull, L. (1866). *Congressional Globe,* 39th Congress, 1st Session, Part 1, p. 474 (Washington, D.C.: Globe Office for F. & J. Rives).

[44] *Sioux Nation of Indians v. United States. Federal Reporter, Second Series, 601* (St. Paul: West Publishing, 1979), p. 1166.

[45] *Ibid.*, p. 1167.

Disarmament and Massacre of Jews in Morocco (1912)

In 1912, the French military invaded Fez, Morocco. In order to consolidate their grip over the native population, the French ordered the entire community to turn in their firearms. The native Arabs did not comply, but the Jews turned in their weapons. Taking advantage of this arms imbalance, the Arabs proceeded to act out long-standing feuds and massacred the disarmed Moroccan Jewish community.[46]

Weapons Registration Laws and Genocide in the Ukraine (1932-1933)

In 1926, the Soviets imposed strict arms registrations on the Ukrainians.[47] These registrations furnished convenient lists of all Ukrainian-held firearms and their owners. Just before the Harvest of Sorrow famine in the Ukraine in 1932-33 the Soviets, greatly facilitated by the registration lists, confiscated all civilian-owned firearms. The disarmed population was then rendered helpless and unable to defend itself from Stalin's forced collectivization. This collectivization included not only forced reorganization of Ukrainian farms but also Soviet confiscation of Ukrainian food supplies from private homes, as well as huge deportations of people and "mass execution of innocents."[48]

Weapons Registration Laws in Nazi Europe

When the Nazis invaded various countries of Europe, they forced countries, like Denmark, that did not have gun registration laws to enact them.[49] The Nazis then proceeded to issue proclamations in the occupied countries ordering the submission of all privately held firearms to the authorities, and they carried out searches to enforce these proclamations. The registration lists were used to facilitate the firearms confiscation process: The authorities knew who had registered firearms, and the registered firearms owners knew that the authorities knew it, and therefore they were the targets of the confiscation process and had better hand over their firearms voluntarily.

---

[46] Videotape at Museum of the Diaspora, Israel (Tel Aviv, Israel, n.d.).

[47] Conquest, R., *Harvest of Sorrow* (New York: Oxford University Press, 1986).

[48] Gray, F. P., "The Journalist and the Dictator." *The New York Times Book Review*, June 24, 1990, Section 7, p. 3, reviewing S. J. Taylor, *Stalin's Apologist Walter Duranty, The New York Times' Man in Moscow* (New York: The New York Times Co.).

[49] Kessler, R. G., "Gun Control and Political Power." *Law and Policy Quarterly, 5 (1983),* pp. 381-400.

317

Strict Gun Control and Soviet Dissidents

In the Soviet Union, the acquisition and possession of firearms were subject to severe restrictions and limitations.[50] Private handgun ownership was banned for most of the population. Soviet dissidents were often subjected to harassment and assaults by vigilante groups, which the government acquiesced in or even encouraged. The Soviet police did nothing to stop the victimization of the dissidents by the vigilantes. If the dissidents armed themselves for protection against the violence, they were arrested for violating the gun laws; if they did not arm, they were hapless victims awaiting serious injury or death.

Recent Use of Weapons Registration Laws in the Soviet Union

In 1989, firearms registration lists were used by Soviet police to confiscate hunting rifles in the Republic of Georgia, those firearms being the only kind that previously could be legally possessed.[51] Similarly, in March 1990, the Soviet government ordered all Lithuanians to turn in their hunting rifles,[52] registration lists again acting as a strong inducement for Lithuanians to comply.[53]

Dangers of Firearms-Purchase Waiting Periods and of Firearms Licensing Laws

Laws requiring a waiting period from the time a person purchases a firearm until the time he or she is allowed to take possession of it pose dangers separate from and similar to those posed by licensing or registration lists. A waiting period can impede or delay the acquisition of arms by an entire community when it needs them most. A stark example of sudden peril to an entire community is furnished by the autumn back-to-school serial murderer of college students at the University of Florida at Gainesville, where the three-day Florida firearms-purchase waiting

---

[50] *Ibid.*

[51] *Atlanta Journal and Constitution*, May 21, 1989, p. A-42; see also *Wall Street Journal*, "Soviet Police Arrested Hundreds of People in The Republic of Georgia." April 12, 1989, p. 1.

[52] *Washington Post*, "Lithuanians Ordered to Surrender Arms; Gorbachev Asserts Power of New Office," March 22, 1990, p. A1.

[53] *Washington Times*, "Arts, Arms and Stonewalling; Farewell to Arms," March 23, 1990, p. F2.

period impaired the ability of the students to take precautions[54] or defend themselves. Likewise, an individual may be threatened with immediate deadly retaliation for having obstructed organized or unorganized crime, such as drug trafficking, as by having organized his or her neighbors into an anti-crime watch.

There is another serious danger in waiting-period legislation. Waiting periods are claimed to be necessary to give the police sufficient time to check the eligibility of each prospective firearm purchaser from the standpoint of satisfactory criminal and mental record. Retention of the records compiled by this procedure will produce, in effect, a registration list of all persons owning firearms. Even though a waiting-period law may contain a provision requiring the police to destroy the records of all checks, the police are not known for their scrupulous adherence to such destruction-of-records requirements. For example, police in New York City have ignored requirements that records of participants in political demonstrations be destroyed.[55]

Value of Unregistered Small Arms to Deter Tyranny by a Government Equipped with Modern Sophisticated Weapons

Partisan Resistance Against the Nazis

Heroic partisan guerilla movements all over Nazi-occupied Europe used pistols, shotguns, bolt-action rifles, and hand-carried submachine guns against the German war machine's sophisticated weaponry, which included tanks and warplanes. That these movements could not be vanquished by the modern mechanized Nazi war machine was in no small part attributable to the fact that the partisan resisters' firearms, not being legally "listed" with any government agency but having been illegally obtained by air drops from the allied governments, could not easily be confiscated.

Undoubtedly less well known than the partisan movements are the stories of people like Marion Pritchard, a non-Jewish student of social work who, during the Nazi occupation of the Netherlands, found hiding

---

[54] *USA Today*, "Spectre of New Bundy Stalks Fearful Florida." August 31–September 3, 1990, p. 3A.
[55] *Handschu v. Special Services Division, Federal Reporter, Second Series*, Vol. 787 (St. Paul, Minn.: West Publishing, 1985), pp. 828-34.

places for Jews, obtaining for them false identity papers, food, clothing, ration cards, and medical care.[56] One day, a Dutch Nazi policeman surprised her as she was releasing several children from a hiding place beneath the floorboards of a country house near Amsterdam. With a "small revolver" that a friend had given her, but that she had never planned to use, she shot the Nazi policeman.

The Lessons of South Vietnam and Northern Ireland

The sophisticated weaponry of the United States did not enable its forces to prevail over the conventionally small-armed guerilla fighters of North Vietnam. For one reason or another, the United States would not use nuclear weapons in Vietnam. For similar, if not more cogent reasons, the federal government would not go nuclear against pockets of small-armed resistance in New York City or Indiana farmlands. To this day, the sophisticated weaponry possessed by Great Britain has proved "almost totally beside the point,"[57] in its attempt to put down the rebels in Northern Ireland. Therefore, it is "simply silly" to argue that "small arms are irrelevant against nuclear-armed states."[58]

The decision by a government to use military force of a certain level, or military force at all, against its own people is not determined solely by whether the contemplated benefits can be successfully obtained by using such force; rather, it is determined by the attendant cost-benefit ratio.[59] Thus, at Tiananmen Square, because a military operation would be faced with little, if any, armed opposition—and hence there was little expected cost in lives or materiel—it was easy and natural for the Chinese government to decide to use military force against the unarmed students. Had the Chinese students possessed AK-47 assault rifles, for example, the decision to use military force might well have been different,[60] and some sort of serious negotiations for an accommodation might well have been achieved.

---

[56] *New York Times,* "For the Young, a Lesson in the Acts of the 'Righteous Gentiles' who Defied the Holocaust." May 12, 1990, p. 11.

[57] Levinson, S., "The Embarrassing Second Amendment." *The Yale Law Journal, 9* (1989), p. 657. (Also reprinted in this book.)

[58] *Ibid.*

[59] Lund, N., "The Second Amendment, Political Liberty, and the Right to Self-Protection." *Alabama Law Review,* 39 (1987), pp. 103-30.

[60] Levinson, supra.

Likewise, the question arises whether the Holocaust would or could have occurred if Europe's Jews had owned thousands of then-modern military Mauser bolt-action rifles.[61]

These cost-benefit ratio considerations may also explain why "governments bent on the oppression of their people almost always disarm the civilian population before undertaking more drastically oppressive measures."[62] Conversely, armed civilians serve as a potent deterrent against drastically oppressive measures, such as a unilateral governmental edict that the election booths be closed.

The Warsaw Ghetto Uprising

When the Jews in the Warsaw ghetto in 1942 finally realized that meek submission to the slaughter did not lessen the Holocaust but increased it, they decided on a plan of armed resistance. In January 1943, the first armed resistance by the Jewish resisters was carried out with only "ten pistols."[63] Nevertheless, the shock of encountering even this relatively small resistance forced the German war machine to retreat and "discontinue their work in order to make more thorough preparations."[64] For three months thereafter, the Nazi German soldiers did not dare to venture into the ghetto. During that three-month period, the Nazis decided that they would have to burn down the ghetto house by house in order to conquer it.[65] The Nazis then proceeded to do so, though not without considerable difficulty and casualties in the face of the armed Jewish resistance fighters.

Had the Germans known from the beginning that the Jewish resistance fighters initially had only those ten pistols—some of them probably so-called Saturday Night Specials—the Nazis would almost certainly "have continued the raids, [and] Jewish resistance would have been nipped in the bud as a minor, insignificant episode."[66]

The Warsaw ghetto uprising thus illustrates serious flaws and dangers in firearms registration or licensing laws. Especially in the present age of computerization, any lists or records of arms registration or licensing create an almost irresistible temptation for governmental bureaucrats to

---

[61] *Ibid.*
[62] Lund, supra, p. 115.
[63] Borzykowski, T., *Between Tumbling Walls* (Israel: Ghetto Fighters' House, 1976), p. 29.
[64] *Ibid.*, p. 72.
[65] Suhl, Y., *They Fought Back: The Story of Jewish Resistance in Nazi Europe* (New York: Crown, 1967).
[66] Borzykowski, supra, p. 720.

use these lists later on to confiscate the listed arms when perceived exigencies of government allegedly justify such an action. Armed with registration lists or waiting-period lists, rogue bureaucrats or agents of government run amok can disarm their citizens quickly and thoroughly. Disfavored segments of the population can then be more easily oppressed or subjected to genocide.

Conclusion

It is obvious that a government engaged in illegal seizures of power or in the political oppression of its citizens or in genocide would certainly hesitate to provoke armed guerilla insurrections or impose house-by-house fighting or burning on its own territory. However, using weapons registration lists to make house-by-house searches for, and confiscation of, weapons in the name of "public safety" can be made politically palatable. Such a confiscation program is, to be sure, a safe course of action for government to pursue; but it is also a course that results in a situation in which, as experience has shown, government officialdom may well be tempted to oppress its thus disarmed citizens. Therein lies the danger of weapons control or registration laws.

When government imposes restrictive deadly force rules on householders or when government outlaws the private possession in the house of the effective means of repelling or resisting criminal and wanton intrusions into people's homes—that is, when it outlaws the private possession of unregistered firearms—then it swings wide open the gates to victim degradation, oppression and genocide.

Crime Control Through the Private Use of Armed Force

Gary Kleck

Legal defensive violence by private citizens armed with firearms is a significant form of social control in the United States. Evidence indicates that private gun use against violent criminals and burglars is common and about as frequent as legal actions like arrests, is a more prompt negative consequence of crime than legal punishment and is often far more severe. In 1980 about 1,500–2,800 felons were legally killed by gun-wielding civilians, about 8,700–16,000 were nonfatally wounded and guns were used defensively about one million times. Victim resistance with guns is associated with lower rates of both victim injury and crime completion for robberies and assaults than any other victim action, including nonresistance. Survey and quasi-experimental evidence is consistent with the hypothesis that the private ownership and use of firearms deters criminal behavior.

In his 1972 Presidential Address to the American Sociological Association, William Goode argued that because sociologists share a humanistic tradition that denies the importance of physical coercion, they have failed to accurately assess the degree to which social systems rest on force. While affirming his personal dislike for the use of force, Goode urged social analysts to put aside their "kindly bias" against the effectiveness of threats and punishment and recognize the degree to which force is a crucial element in the social structure, in democracies as well as tyrannies, in peacetime as well as in war. He stated that "in any civil society . . . everyone is subject to force. All are engaged in it daily, not alone as victims but as perpetrators as well. . . . We are all potentially dangerous to one another."[1] This paper addresses the social control effects of private citizens' uses of guns in response to predatory criminal behavior, particularly violent crime and residential burglary.

The prevalence and defensive use of guns in America are important topics for many research questions, yet they have been almost entirely

---

[1] William J. Goode, "Presidential Address: The Place of Force in Human Society," *American Sociological Review*, 37:507-19 (1972).

ignored. For example, the "routine activities" approach to crime sees criminal incidents as the result of the convergence of "likely offenders and suitable targets in the absence of capable guardians."[2] While this view has broadened criminologists' interests beyond the supply of "likely offenders," it ignores the extent to which being armed with a deadly weapon would seem to be an important element of capable guardianship. Given that about half of U.S. households and a quarter of retail businesses keep firearms,[3] gun ownership must surely be considered a very routine aspect of American life and of obvious relevance to the activities of criminals.

Victimology is concerned with, among other things, the response of victims to their victimization. Yet, despite evidence that people buy guns to defend against becoming victims of crimes,[4] victimology scholars have largely ignored victim gun ownership and use. Similarly, the recent wave of interest in private crime control has been largely limited to either the "privatization" of police and corrections services and the use of commercial security services by businesses and other large institutions[5] or to nonforceful private crime control efforts like neighborhood watch activities.[6] Finally, nearly all of the considerable literature on deterrence of criminal behavior focuses on the effect of public criminal justice agencies. Conventional definitions of deterrence are often limited to the crime preventive effects of legal punishment, arrest and prosecution.[7] This precludes considering private ownership and use of firearms as a deterrent to crime. That victim gun use may be one of the most serious risks a criminal faces is only beginning to be recognized.[8]

---

[2] Lawrence E. Cohen and Marcus Felson, "Social Change and Crime Rate Trends: A Routine Activities Approach," *American Sociological Review*, 44:588-608, (1979).

[3] Royce Crocker, "Attitudes Toward Gun Control: A Survey," in *Federal Regulation of Firearms*, Harry L. Hogan, ed. (Washington, D.C.: U.S. Government Printing Office, 1982) 229-67; U.S. Small Business Administration, *Crime Against Small Business*, Senate Document No. 91-14 (Washington, D.C.: U.S. Government Printing Office, 1969).

[4] Gary Kleck, "The Relationship Between Gun Ownership Levels and Rates of Violence in the United States," in *Firearms and Violence: Issues of Public Policy*, Don B. Kates, Jr. ed. (Cambridge, Mass.: Ballinger, 1984).

[5] William C. Cunningham and Todd H. Taylor, *Crime and Protection in America: A Study of Private Security and Law Enforcement Resources and Relationships,* National Institute of Justice (Washington, D.C.: U.S. Government Printing Office, 1985).

[6] Stephanie W. Greenberg, William M. Rohe and J. R. Williams, *Informal Citizen Action and Crime Prevention at the Neighborhood Level: Synthesis and Assessment of the Research*, National Institute of Justice (Washington, D.C.: U.S. Government Printing Office, 1984).

[7] Jack P. Gibbs, *Crime, Punishment and Deterrence* (New York: Elsevier, 1975).

[8] James D. Wright and Peter H. Rossi, *The Armed Criminal in America: A Survey of Incarcerated Felons* (Hawthorne, N.Y.: Aldine, 1986).

Without denying the possible criminogenic effects of gun ownership, I want to establish as plausible and worthy of research the hypothesis that when citizens own and use guns to defend themselves, the amount of violent crime is reduced to a degree that could rival the effect of the criminal justice system. Toward that end I consider three kinds of evidence: the frequency and nature of private citizens' defensive uses of firearms against criminals, the effectiveness and risks of such actions and the potential deterrent impact on crime of defensive gun ownership and use. Finally, I discuss the implications of this evidence for crime control policy.[9]

The Frequency and Types of Defensive Gun Use

Overall Use, Including Display and Firing

At least six national and statewide surveys have asked probability samples of the adult population about defensive gun use. The most informative of the surveys is the 1981 Hart poll of 1,228 registered voters (see Table 1). It is the only survey to cover a national population, ask about defensive uses in a specific, limited time period, ask the question of all respondents, distinguish civilian use from police and military uses and distinguish uses against humans from uses against animals. Note, however, that the five other national and state surveys, while not as satisfactory as the Hart poll, yield results that are compatible with the results of that survey. These results as reported here have never been published; they were obtained privately from Peter D. Hart Research Associates, Inc.[10] (This poll was sponsored by the now defunct National Alliance Against Violence. The data cannot be analyzed further because the original data set has been lost and only a record of the marginals remains.) In this survey, 6 percent of the adults interviewed replied "yes" to the question: "Within the past five years, have you yourself or another member of your household used a handgun, even if it was not fired, for self-protection or for the protection of property at home, work, or elsewhere, excluding military service or police work?" Those who replied "yes" were then asked "Was this to protect against an animal or a

---

[9] Gary Kleck, "Guns and Self-Defense: Crime Control Through the Use of Armed Force in the Private Sector" (Unpublished manuscript, 1987).

[10] Telephone conversation with Geoffrey Garin of Peter D. Hart Research Associates, Inc., Washington, D.C., April 30, 1986.

person?" Of the total sample, 2 percent replied "animal," 3 percent "person" and 1 percent "both." Therefore, 4 percent of the sample reported gun use against a person by someone in their household.

Like crime victimization prevalence figures, the defensive gun use percentages are small. They represent, however, large numbers of actual uses. In 1980 there were 80,622,000 U.S. households.[11] Extrapolating from the 4 percent Hart figure yields an estimate of 3,224,880 households with at least one person who used a handgun defensively during the period 1976–1981. Conservatively assuming only one use per household and dividing by five (the number of years covered), I estimate there were about 645,000 defensive uses of handguns against persons per year, excluding police or military uses. (The 95 percent confidence interval estimate of the proportion of household handguns used defensively against persons over the five-year period is .0290–.0510, implying from 468,000 to 822,000 uses per year.)

The Hart sample was of registered voters, who are older and wealthier than the general public. This implies a population less frequently victimized by crime, especially by violent crime, and thus less likely to have used a gun defensively. Since gun ownership increases with income,[12] however, there should be more gun owners in a sample of registered voters. It is unclear what the net effects of these sample biases might be on the estimate of defensive uses.

The Hart survey asked only about handgun use, ignoring defensive uses of the far more numerous long guns (rifles and shotguns). And the DMI (Decision-Making-Incorporated) surveys, which did ask about all gun types, did not ask about a specific time period. The best all-guns estimate is based on an extrapolation of the Hart survey handgun results. According to the December 1978, DMIb survey (Table 1), 45 percent of respondents in handgun-owning households reported handguns were owned primarily for "self-defense and protection at home," while the corresponding figure for all gun types combined was 21 percent. It was estimated that at the end of 1978, the total private stock of handguns in the United States was about 47 million and the stock of all guns was

---

[11] U.S. Bureau of the Census, Statistical Abstract of the United States, 1982-83 (Washington, D.C.: U.S. Government Printing Office).

[12] James D. Wright, Peter H. Rossi and Kathleen Daly, *Under the Gun: Weapons, Crime, and Violence in America* (Hawthorne, N.Y.: Aldine, 1983).

Table 1 • Defensive Gun Use, Information from Six Surveys

Survey	Field Poll	Cambridge Reports	DMI[a]	DMI[a]	Hart Poll	State of Ohio
Area Covered	California	U.S.	U.S.	U.S.	U.S.	Ohio
Year of Interviews	1976	1978	1978	1978	1981	1982
Population covered	noninstitutionalized adults	noninstitutionalized adults	registered voters	registered voters	registered voters	"residents"
Gun Type Covered	handguns	handguns	all guns	all guns	handguns	handguns
Time Span of Use	ever/1,2 years	ever	ever	ever	5 years	ever
Distinguished Uses Against Persons	No	No	No	Yes	Yes	No
Excluded Military, Police Uses	Yes	No	Yes	Yes	Yes	No
"Self-defense" or "protection"?	Protection	Protection or self-defense	Protection	Protection	Protection	Self-defense
Defensive question asked of:	All Rs	Protection handgun owners	All Rs	All Rs	All Rs	Handgun owners
Defensive question refers to:	Respondent	Respondent	Household	Household	Household	Respondent
Percent Who Used Gun	8.6[b]	3	15	12/7[c]	4	6.5
Percent Who Fired Gun	2.9	2	6	n.a.[d]	d.k.[e]	2.6

Notes:

a. DMI = :Decision/Making/Information

b. 8.6 percent ever, 3 percent in past two years, 1.4 percent in past year.

c. Defensive uses against persons or animals, 12 percent. Use against persons only, 7 percent

d. n.a. = not available

e. d.k. = don't know

Sources:

Field Institute (1976); Cambridge Reports (1978); DMI (1978); Garin (1986); Ohio (1982).

about 156 million.[13] Combining these figures, there were about 21 million handguns and 33 million guns of all types, including handguns, owned primarily for protection or defense in December 1978. If among guns owned primarily for defense, we assume both types of guns are equally likely to be so used, we can multiply the handguns defenses uses figure of 645,000 by the ratio 33/21 to roughly estimate that guns of all types are used for defensive purposes about one million times a year.

The magnitude of these figures can be judged by comparison with an estimate of the total number of crimes in which guns were somehow used in 1980, based on the Uniform Crime Reports (UCR) count of homicides and National Crime Survey (NCS) victimization survey estimates of assaults, robberies and rapes. Including minor assaults in which the gun was not fired and including both crimes reported to the police and unreported crimes, the total for handguns was about 580,000, while the corresponding figure for all gun types was about 810,000.[14] Thus the best available evidence suggests that handguns may be used about as often for defensive purposes as for criminal purposes, and guns of all types are used substantially more often defensively than criminally.

Firing

Most of the surveys listed in Table 1 did not delve into the exact circumstances in which guns were used defensively or the manner in which they were used. However, most did ask whether the gun was fired. Results generally indicate the gun was fired in somewhat less than half of the defensive uses; the rest of the times the gun presumably was merely displayed or referred to in order to threaten or frighten away a criminal.

Killings and Woundings

Although shootings of criminals represent a small fraction of defensive uses of guns, Americans shoot criminals with a frequency that must be regarded as remarkable by any standard. While the FBI does not publish national statistics on all types of self-defense killings, its unpublished counts of civilian justifiable homicides (CJH) gathered through the Supplementary Homicides Reports (SHR) program provide a starting point for producing a national estimate. For a variety of reasons

---

[13] Gary Kleck, supra, p. 112.

[14] Gary Kleck, "Evidence that 'Saturday night specials' not very important for crime," *Sociology and Social Research*, 70:303-7, (1986).

the FBI SHR totals for CJHs represent only a minority of all civilian legal defensive homicides (CLDHs). First, some cases which even police label as CJHs are not reported as such to the FBI. Wilbanks[15] helps explain this by noting that some police in Dade County (Miami) were unwilling to spend much time recording homicides where prosecution of the killer was not to be pursued. Second, many homicides ultimately ruled noncriminal by prosecutors or judges are reported to the FBI as criminal homicides because that is how the initial police investigation labelled them. Third, and most significantly, in jurisdictions which follow legal distinctions between justifiable and excusable homicides fairly closely, most CLDHs will be recorded as excusable rather than justifiable, and thus will not be counted by the FBI.[16] Cases in which the killer legally defends only against an assault, i.e., purely self-defense killings, are defined by the FBI as "excusable" homicides; but those in which the killer is the victim of some other felony *in addition* to assault, e.g., cases in which a robbery, burglary or rape victim kills a criminal committing the related felony, are defined as "justifiable" homicides.

Because no national data exist distinguishing the different types of CLDHs, we must rely on data from single legal jurisdictions such as cities and counties. Table 2 summarizes information on the legal classifications of homicides in six unusually detailed local homicide studies. Although the true distribution of homicides may differ somewhat from city to city, the results suggest that there also are sharp differences from place to place in the way authorities classify homicides as noncriminal. For example, row 12 of the table indicates that the fraction of intentional civilian homicides labelled as CLDHs varies from 1.6 percent to 19.5 percent over the six studies. Because the Detroit and Dade County results are more "middling," are from two regionally distinct parts of the country and are also the most recent, they seem more likely to be representative of the contemporary United States. I use these results, in combination with the national SHR counts of civilian justifiable homicides, to roughly estimate national CLDH totals. The reader should note that because Detroit and Dade County are high crime areas, it is possible that a higher fraction of their homicides are declared justifiable, but we have no data sufficient to test this.

---

[15] William Wilbanks, *Murder in Miami* (Lanham, Md.: University Press, 1984).

[16] Gary Kleck, "Guns and Self-Defense: Crime Control Through the Use of Armed Force in the Private Sector" (Unpublished manuscript, 1987).

One way to estimate these totals is to assume that self-defense homicides grow out of criminal threats to life, as indexed by murders and nonnegligent manslaughters reported to the FBI, and that the ratio of the former to the latter will be roughly the same for the United States as it is for Detroit and Dade County. In the 1980 Uniform Crime Reports a combined total of 1,062 killings in these two local areas were counted by the FBI as murders and nonnegligent manslaughters.[17] Row 11 of Table 2 shows that 145 killings were CLDHs, giving a ratio of the latter to the former of 0.1365. Multiplying this number times the national total of 23,044 murders and nonnegligent manslaughters[18] yields an estimate of 3,146 CLDHs for the United States in 1980. Another estimation method is to use the national counts of civilian justifiable homicide reported to the FBI as a starting point and adjust for its incomplete coverage of CLDHs. In 1980 there were 145 CLDHs in our two sample jurisdictions, of which only 36 were reported to the FBI as CJHs,[19] a ratio of 4.167 CLDHs to every CJH counted in the SHR program. Multiplying this times the 1980 national SHR total of 423 CJHs yields an estimate of 1,704 CLDHs. Of the 423 CJHs, 379 or 89.6 percent involved guns, so our best estimate is that from 1,527 (.896 × 1,704) to 2,819 (.896 × 3,146) felons were legally killed by gun-wielding civilians in self-defense or some other legally justified cause in 1980.

These estimates are rough, but they support the claim that civilians use guns to legally kill a large number of felons each year. The various estimates are summarized in Table 3, along with data on justifiable homicides by police officers, included for comparative purposes. The police homicide estimates are simple totals as compiled by the vital statistics system, (Estimation Method I)[20] which were then doubled (Estimation Method II) because only about half of the killings by police are reported as such to the national vital statistics system.[21] FBI/SHR counts of police justifiable homicides are also reported here. Regardless

---

[17] U.S. Federal Bureau of Investigation (FBI), Crime in the United States (Washington, D.C.: U.S. Government Printing Office, 1981), pp. 74, 107.

[18] Ibid., p. 41.

[19] Inter-University Consortium for Political and Social Research (ICPSR), Codebook for ICPSR Study 9028, Uniform Crime Reports, 1980-1982: Supplementary Homicide Report (Ann Arbor, Mich.: ICPSR, 1984).

[20] U.S. National Center for Health Statistics (NCHS), Public Use Data Tape Documentation: Mortality Detail 1980 Data (Hyattsville, Md.: U.S. Public Health Service, 1983).

[21] Lawrence W. Sherman and Robert H. Langworth, "Measuring Homicide by Police Officers," Journal of Criminal Law and Criminology, 70:546-60 (1979).

Table 2 • Number Civilian Legal Defensive Homicides by Category in Six Local Studies

Row	Homicide Category[a]	Study, Location, Period Covered					
		Bensing and Schroeder (1960); Cuyahoga County (Cleveland), 1947-1953	Wolfgang (1958); Philadelphia, 1948-1952	Rushforth et al. (1977); Cuyahoga County (Cleveland), 1958-1974	Lundsgaarde (1977); Houston, 1969	Dietz (1983); Detroit, 1980	Wilbanks (1984); Dade County (Miami), 1980
(1)	Total sample homicides	662	625	3371	c. 312	583	569
(2)	Criminal homicides	505	588	n.a.[e]	282	493	478
(3)	Murders, nonnegligent manslaughters	505	c. 502[b]	n.a.	281	487	478
(4)	Estimated unintentional excusable homicides	d.k.[f]	23	n.a.	≤ 12	c. 4	5
(5)	Involuntary/negligent manslaughters	d.k.	c. 86[b]	d.k.	≤ 1	6	0
(6)	Justifiable police homicides	35	14	c. 110	10	13	14
(7)	Estimated intentional civilian homicides	627	502	c. 3261	c. 289	560	550
(8)	Justifiable civilian homicides (CJH)	122	8	c. 329	19	16	72
(9)	CJH reported on SHRs[d]	n.a.	n.a.	n.a.	n.a.	12	24
(10)	Other civilian legal defensive homicides	0	n.a.	d.k.	≤ 1	57	0
(11)	Total civilian legal defensive homicides (CLDH)[c]	122	8	c. 329	≤ 20	73	72
(12)	Ratio, (11)/(7)	.195	.016	.101	≤ .069	.130	.131
(13)	Ratio, (11)/(1)	.184	.013	.098	≤ .064	.125	.127
(14)	Ratio, (11)/(3)	.242	.024	n.a.	≤ .071	.150	.151

NOTES:

a. Homicides were classified according to their final legal classifications as reported in the study, whether police, coroner, or court-determined.

b. 14.7% of criminal homicide offenders prosecuted were charged with involuntary manslaughter. .147 x 588 = 86. 588 − 86 = 502.

c. Row (7)=(1)−(4)−(5)−(6); Row (11)=(8)+(10).

d. SHRs = Supplementary Homicide Reports of the FBI.

e. n.a. = not available, usually because authors did not report any frequencies for such categories.

f. d.k. = don't know

SOURCES:

Bensing and Schroeder (1960: 5,59,80); Wolfgang (1958: 24,228,301,303); Rushforth et al. (1977: 531-33); Lundsgaarde (1977: 68-69,162,219,236,237); Dietz (1983: 203); Wilbanks (1984: 29-30,57,70-72,154).

331

of which counts of homicides by police one uses, the results indicate that civilians legally kill far more felons than police officers do.

Nonfatal woundings by guns are far more frequent than fatal shootings. Cook[22] reviewed data which indicate that about 15 percent of gunshot wounds are fatal, implying a ratio of about 5.67 (85/15) nonfatal gun woundings to each fatal one. If the same applies to legal civilian defensive shootings, there were about 8,700–16,600 nonfatal, legally permissible woundings of criminals by gun-armed civilians in 1980. Therefore, the rest of the one million estimated defensive gun uses, over 98 percent, involved neither killings nor woundings but rather warning shots fired or guns pointed or referred to.

Effectiveness and Risks of Armed Resistance to Criminals

It has been argued that resistance by crime victims, especially forceful resistance, is generally useless and even dangerous to the vic-

Table 3 • *Number Reported and Estimated Police and Civilian Legal Defensive Homicides, by Homicide Type, U.S., 1980*

Homicide type	Justifiable Homicides, Reported to FBI/SHR[a]	Estimated Legal Defensive Homicides	
		Method I[b]	Method II[b]
Police, gun	368	303	606
Police, nongun	14	8	16
Police, total	382	311	622
Civilian, gun	379	2819	1527
Civilian, nongun	44	327	177
Civilian, total	423	3146	1704

Notes:
   a. SHR = Supplementary Homicide Reports.
   b. Estimation methods — see text.

Sources:
   Analysis of 1980 U.S. Supplementary Homicide Reports computer tape; U.S. NCHS (1983:35-36).

[22] Philip J. Cook, "The Case of the Missing Victims: Gunshot Woundings in the National Crime Survey," *Journal of Quantitative Criminology*, 1:91-102 (1985).

tim.[23] Evidence is moderately consistent with this problem as it applies to some forms of resistance. However, the evidence does not support the claim as it pertains to resistance with a gun.

Preventing Completion of the Crime

The figures in Table 4 are from analysis of the 1979–1985 incident-level files of the National Crime Survey (NCS) public use computer tapes.[24] They contain information on over 180,000 sample crime incidents reported by nationally representative samples of noninstitutionalized persons aged 12 and over. The surveys asked respondents if they had been victims of crimes. Those who reported crimes involving personal contact with the offender were asked if they used any form of self-protection, if they were attacked, if they suffered injury and if the crimes were completed. For assaults, "completion" means injury was inflicted; thus completion data convey nothing beyond what injury data convey. For robberies, "completion" refers to whether the robber took property from the victim. The figures in column 1 of Table 4 show that victims who resisted robbers with guns or with weapons other than guns or knives were less likely to lose their property than victims who used any other means of resistance or who did nothing.

Avoiding Injury

Attack and injury rates for each self-protection method are reported in columns 2 and 3 for robbery and columns 5 and 6 for assault. For both robbery and assault, victims who used guns for protection were less likely either to be attacked or injured than victims who responded any other way, including those who did not resist at all. Only 12 percent of gun resisters in assault and 17 percent in robberies suffered any kind of injury.

After gun resistance, the course of action least likely to be associated with injury is doing nothing at all, i.e., not resisting. However, passivity is not a completely safe course either since 25 percent of robbery victims and 27 percent of assault victims who did not resist were injured anyway.

---

[23] Richard Block, *Violent Crime* (Lexington, Mass.: Lexington, 1977); see also Matthew G. Yeager, Joseph D. Alviani and Nancy Loving, "How Well Does the Handgun Protect You and Your Family?" Handgun Control Staff Technical Report 2 (Washington, D.C.: United States Conference of Mayors, 1976).

[24] Inter-University Consortium for Political and Social Research (ICPSR), Codebook for ICPSR Study 8608. National Crime Surveys: National Sample, 1979-1985 (Revised Questionnaire), (Ann Arbor, Mich.: ICPSR, 1987).

Table 4 • *Attack, Injury and Crime Completion Rates in Robbery and Assault Incidents, by Self-Protection Method, U.S., 1979-1985*[a]

Method of Self-Protection	Robbery				Assault		
	(1) Percent Completed	(2) Percent Attacked	(3) Percent Injured	(4)[b] Number Times Used	(5) Percent Attacked	(6) Percent Injured	(7)[b] Estimated Number Times Used
Used gun	30.9%	25.2%	17.4%	89,009	23.2%	12.1%	386,083
Used knife	35.2	55.6	40.3	59,813	46.4	29.5	123,062
Used other weapon	28.9	41.5	22.0	104,700	41.4	25.1	454,570
Used physical force	50.1	75.6	50.8	1,653,880	82.8	52.1	6,638,823
Tried to get help or frighten offender	63.9	73.5	48.9	1,516,141	55.2	40.1	4,383,117
Threatened or reasoned with offender	53.7	48.1	30.7	955,398	40.0	24.7	5,743,008
Nonviolent resistance, including evasion	50.8	54.7	34.9	1,539,895	40.0	25.5	8,935,738
Other measures	48.5	47.3	26.5	284,423	36.1	20.7	1,451,103
Any self-protection	52.1	60.8	38.2	4,603,671	49.5	30.7	21,801,957
No self-protection	88.5	41.5	24.7	2,686,960	39.9	27.3	6,154,763
Total	65.4	53.7	33.2	7,290,631	47.3	29.9	27,956,719

Notes:

a. See U.S. Bureau of Justice Statistics (1982) for exact question wordings, definitions, and other details of the surveys.

b. Separate frequencies in columns (4) and (7) do add to totals in "Any self-protection" row since a single crime incident can involve more than one self-protection method.

Sources:

Analysis of incident files of 1979-1985 National Crime Survey public use computer tapes (ICPSR, 1987b).

Finally, columns 4 and 7 show that using guns for protection in robberies and assaults is considerably less common than milder, less forceful methods not requiring weapons. This presumably is at least partly due to the fact that so many crimes occur in circumstances where victims do not have effective access to their guns.

Some analysts of robbery data have assumed that where crimes involve victims who resisted and were also injured, resistance somehow caused the injury by provoking the offender into an attack.[25] Although the NCS does not yet routinely ask questions about the sequence of attack and self-protection acts by the victim, such questions were included in a special Victim Risk Supplement questionnaire administered to 14,258 households as part of the regular NCS in February of 1984. In only 9.8 percent of assaults involving both forceful self-protective actions and attack did the actions occur before the attack. For assaults involving nonforceful self-protective actions, only 5.7 percent of the actions preceded the attack. For cases involving both robbery and attack, forceful self-protective actions never preceded attack, while in only 22 percent of similar incidents involving nonforceful self-protective actions did the actions precede the attack. Thus, even among the minority of cases where forceful self-protective acts were accompanied by attacks on the victim, few incidents support the contention that the victim's defensive action provoked the attack.

Crime Control Effects of Civilian Gun Ownership and Use

When victims use guns to resist crimes, the crimes usually are disrupted and the victims are not injured. This does not necessarily imply that such resistance has any general deterrent effect on crimes. Whether criminals are deterred by the prospect of armed resistance is an issue separate from how effective defensive gun use is for victims who resist. In this section, I consider the kinds of crimes most likely to involve victim defensive gun use and the kinds of crimes most likely to be deterred by such use. I also consider evidence on the deterrent effect of civilian gun ownership and on the effects of possible confrontation by a gun-wielding citizen on burglars and burglaries in occupied homes.

---

[25] Matthew G. Yeager, Joseph D. Alviani and Nancy Loving, "How Well Does the Handgun Protect You and Your Family?" Handgun Control Staff Technical Report 2 (Washington, D.C.: United States Conference of Mayors, 1976).

Table 5 • *Crimes Associated with Defensive Uses of Guns, Frequency and Percent*

1976 Survey of California Adults[a]			1980 Dade County (Miami)[b]		
Crime	Frequency	Percent	Crime	Frequency	Percent
Assault or rape at home	40	41	Assault	46	64
Assault elsewhere	20	21	Rape	1	1
Theft at home	19	20	Burglary	6	8
Theft elsewhere	11	11	Robbery	19	26
All other reasons for use	7	7			
Total	97	100%	Total	72	100%

Notes:
    a. Handgun use only
    b. Civilian justifiable homicides
Sources:
    California survey, Field Institute (1976); Dade County justifiable homicides compiled from short narrative descriptions in Wilbanks (1984: 190-374).

Crimes Involving Defensive Gun Use

What crimes are defensive gun users defending against? Evidence from NCP surveys suggests that about 64,000 rapes, robberies and assaults involved a victim using a gun for self-protection in 1983.[26] However, this figure is unreliable since it is well established that victim surveys seriously underestimate violent crime among nonstrangers.[27] Because such crimes are especially likely to occur in the home, where guns are available to their owners, the victim surveys must also underestimate victim defensive uses of guns. Further, commercial robberies are no longer covered in these surveys, and the doubts victims may have about the legality of their gun uses may further contribute to an underreporting of defensive uses. Finally, since crimes involving victim gun use usually involve neither property loss nor victim injury, victims are especially likely to forget or otherwise fail to report them to interviewers, just as they fail to report them to police.

---

[26] U.S. Bureau of Justice Statistics, "Criminal Victimization in the United States, 1983" (Washington, D.C.: U.S. Government Printing Office, 1985), pp. 12, 69, 70.

[27] Walter R. Gove, Michael Hughes and Michael Gerrken, "Are Uniform Crime Reports a Valid Indicator of the Index Crimes? An Affirmative Answer with Minor Qualifications," *Criminology* 23:451-501 (1985).

There are no published data on the number of defensive gun uses in burglary. The best that can be done is to estimate the number of opportunities for victim gun use. NCS data indicate that about 12.7 percent of residential burglaries occur while a household member is present[28] and that there were an estimated 6,817,000 household burglaries in 1980.[29] Averaging the results of two national surveys in 1980, I estimate that about 46 percent of U.S. households have at least one gun.[30] If it is assumed that gun ownership is at least as high in burglarized homes as in homes in general, about 400,000 residential burglaries occurred in gun-owning households while a household member was present (6,817 × 0.127 × 0.46 = 398,249).

If all of the opportunities for victims to use guns during burglaries were actually taken, they would constitute about 40 percent of the estimated one million annual defensive gun uses. However, two very different sources of information suggest that burglary-related uses are less numerous than that and that assaults at home are the most common crimes involving victim gun use. Table 5 displays the results of the 1976 Field poll of California[31] and data from medical examiner records concerning civilian justifiable homicides committed in Dade County in 1980.[32] The Field poll addresses only handgun use and indicates locations of gun uses, while the medical data cover all gun types but do not usually indicate the location of homicides. Nevertheless, the results are consistent concerning the crimes with which defensive gun uses are associated.

The California survey data indicate that 62 percent of uses are connected to assault or rape. The medical examiner data indicate a figure of 65 percent for these offenses, while also showing that nearly all of these uses are connected to assault rather than rape. "Theft at home" in the California survey includes burglary, and the justifiable homicide data suggest that burglary accounts for most of the cases in this category. "Theft elsewhere" in the California survey includes retail store robberies, and the robbery category among justifiable homicides may consist largely

---

[28] U.S. Bureau of Justice Statistics, "Household Burglary," BJS Bulletin (Washington, D.C.: U.S. Government Printing Office, 1985), p. 4.

[29] U.S. Bureau of Justice Statistics, "Criminal Victimization in the United States, 1980 (Washington, D.C.: U.S. Government Printing Office, 1982), p. 22.

[30] Royce Crocker, "Attitudes Toward Gun Control: A Survey," in *Federal Regulation of Firearms*, Harry L. Hogan, ed. (Washington, D.C.: U.S. Government Printing Office, 1982), pp. 229-67.

[31] Field Institute, *Tabulations of the Findings of a Survey of Handgun Ownership and Access Among a Cross Section of the California Adult Public* (San Francisco: Field Institute, 1976).

[32] Wilbanks, supra, pp. 190-374.

of uses linked to such crimes. This interpretation is supported by information on the locations of civilian justifiable homicides in California in 1982, 86 percent of which involved guns. Police records showed that 32 percent occurred in the killer's residence, 23 percent in a business location (especially in robbery-prone businesses like liquor stores and bars, 14 percent on the street or sidewalk and 30 percent elsewhere.[33] This set of California homicides excludes pure self-defense homicides (i.e., killings not involving any other felonies besides an assault on the defender) and thus is not strictly comparable with the Dade County defensive homicides, most of which are pure self-defense killings. This at least partially accounts for the smaller share of California homicides occurring in the home, since it means that cases like those involving women defending themselves against abusive husbands or boyfriends would ordinarily be excluded. Therefore the California data do not undercut the conclusion that most defensive gun uses occur in the home and involve defense against assaults. Home defenses against burglars and retail store defenses against robbers each account for substantial minorities of the uses.

Gun Deterrable Crimes

If there is a deterrent effect of defensive gun use, it would depend on a criminal being able to realistically anticipate a potential victim using a gun to disrupt the crime. The types of crimes most likely to be influenced by this possibility are crimes occurring in homes—where victims might have access to a gun—and in the kinds of business establishments where proprietors keep guns, i.e., crimes such as residential burglary, assault in home and retail store robbery. About one in eight residential burglaries occurs while a household member is present,[34] and, by definition, all robberies, rapes, assaults and homicides involve direct contact between a victim and an offender. In many of these incidents the offender has the initiative, often taking the victim by surprise. Further, the situations often develop too quickly for victims to get to their guns. The most common single location for violent crimes, especially homicides and assaults

---

[33] *Homicide in California, 1982* (Sacramento, Calif.: Bureau of Criminal Statistics and Special Services, 1983), p. 67.

[34] U.S. Bureau of Justice Statistics, "Household Burglary," BJS Bulletin (Washington, D.C.: U.S. Government Printing Office, 1985), p. 4.

between intimates, is in or near the home of the victim or the home of both victim and offender.[35]

Strategic attributes of some crime types make them better than average candidates for disruption by armed victims. For example, violent acts between intimates are typically part of a persistent, ongoing pattern of violence.[36] While prospective victims of such violence may not ordinarily be able to predict the exact time of the next violent episode, they often are able to recognize the usual precursors of repetitive violence. Wives and girlfriends of violent men, for example, may understand well the significance of their husband/boyfriend getting drunk and verbally abusive. This implies a distinct tactical difference between violence among intimates and other crimes. Victims of intimate violence can take advantage of behavioral cues which serve as advance warning signs and ready themselves accordingly. In the most threatening situations, advance preparations could include securing a weapon.

Deterrence Effects

Demonstrating deterrent effects of criminal justice system punishment has proven difficult[37] and the same must certainly be true for the private use of force, which is even less well measured than the risk-generating activities of the criminal justice system. Therefore, the following evidence should be regarded only as suggestive. Nevertheless, while more limited in quantity, this evidence is quite diverse, consistent and in some ways as compelling as evidence cited in favor of the deterrence thesis for criminal justice system activity.

Results from deterrence research have been highly mixed and often negative. Why should we expect deterrence from the armed citizenry when the criminal justice system appears to have so little impact? The deterrence doctrine states that punishment deters as its certainty, severity and celerity (promptness) increase.[38] One obvious difference between the risk from criminal justice activity and that from civilian gun use for the

---

[35] U.S. Bureau of Justice Statistics, "Intimate Victims: A Study of Violence Among Friends and Relatives" (Washington, D.C.: U.S. Government Printing Office, 1980), p. 22; see also Lynn A. Curtis, *Criminal Violence: National Patterns and Behavior* (Lexington, Mass.: Lexington, 1974), p. 176.

[36] G. Marie Wilt, J. Bannon, Ronald K. Breedlove, John W. Kennish, Donald M. Snadker, and Robert K. Sawtell, *Domestic Violence and the Police: Studies in Detroit and Kansas City* (Washington, D.C.: U.S. Government Printing Office, 1977).

[37] Alfred Blumstein, Jacqueline Cohen, and Daniel Hagin, eds., *Deterrence and Incapacitation: Estimating the Effects of Criminal Sanctions on Crime Rates* (Washington, D.C.: National Academy of Sciences, 1978).

[38] Gibbs, supra.

criminal is that the maximum potential severity of citizen self-help is far greater than legal system responses to crime. The maximum legal penalty a burglar, robber or even a murderer is likely to face is a few years in prison; only 20 persons were legally executed, all for murders, between mid-1967 and mid-1984.[39] Since thousands of criminals are killed by gun-wielding private citizens every year, criminals following a "minimax" strategy (i.e., acting to minimize their chances of experiencing the maximum potential negative consequence of their actions) should be influenced more by the risks of civilian gun use than by risks from the legal system. How many criminals are guided by such a strategy is unknown.

The frequency of defensive gun uses roughly equals the total number of U.S. arrests for violent crime and burglary, which numbered about 988,000 in 1980.[40] Being threatened or shot at by a gun-wielding victim is about as probable as arrest and substantially more probable than conviction or incarceration. This is not surprising since there are only about 600,000 police officers in the United States, fewer than a quarter of whom are on duty at any one time.[41] There are, on the other hand, tens of millions of civilians with immediate access to firearms, obviously well motivated to deter or disrupt crimes directed at themselves, their families or their property.

Finally, victims almost always use guns defensively within minutes of the attempted crime. In contrast, when an arrest occurs, it can follow the crime by days or even weeks. At the very quickest, it comes after the minutes it takes a patrol car to respond to a citizen's call. In any case, the average celerity of even arrest is much lower than for citizen gun use, while the celerity of conviction and punishment is lower still.

Evidence from Surveys of Criminals

There is direct, albeit not conclusive, evidence on the deterrent effects of victim gun use from surveys of apprehended criminals. Wright and Rossi[42] interviewed 1,874 felons in prisons in ten states and asked about their encounters with armed victims and their attitudes toward the risks of such encounters. Among felons who reported ever committing a violent crime or a burglary, 42 percent said they had run into a victim

---

[39] U.S. Bureau of Justice Statistics, "Capital Punishment, 1983," BJS Bulletin (Washington, D.C.: U.S. Government Printing Office, 1984).

[40] U.S. Federal Bureau of Investigation, supra, 1981, p. 190.

[41] U.S. Bureau of the Census, supra, 1982, p. 184.

[42] Wright and Rossi, supra.

who was armed with a gun, 38 percent reported they had been scared off, shot at, wounded or captured by an armed victim (these were combined in the original survey question) and 43 percent said they had at some time in their lives decided not to do a crime because they knew or believed the victim was carrying a gun.[43]

Concerning the felons' attitudes toward armed victims, 56 percent agreed with the statement that "most criminals are more worried about meeting an armed victim than they are about running into the police," 58 percent agreed that "a store owner who is known to keep a gun on the premises is not going to get robbed very often," and 52 percent agreed that "a criminal is not going to mess around with a victim he knows is armed with a gun." Only 27 percent agreed that "committing a crime against an armed victim is an exciting challenge."[44] Further, 45 percent of those who had encountered an armed victim reported that they thought regularly or often about the possibility of getting shot by their victims. Even among those without such an encounter the figure was 28 percent.[45] These results agree with earlier findings from less sophisticated surveys of prisoners.[46]

Many objections to prison survey research on deterrence concern flaws the correction of which would tend to strengthen conclusions that there are deterrent effects For example, Zimring and Hawkins[47] discuss the "Warden's Survey fallacy" whereby wardens concluded that the death penalty could not deter murder since all the killers on death row to whom they spoke said the penalty had not deterred them. Clearly, prisoners are biased samples of criminals and prospective criminals since their presence in prison itself indicates that deterrence was not completely effective with them. However, prison survey results supporting a deterrence hypothesis are all the more impressive in light of this bias. Such doubts about the validity of prisoners' responses to surveys are discussed through the Wright and Rossi book.[48] Given that being "scared off" by a victim is not the sort of thing a violent criminal is likely to want to admit, incidents of

[43] ICPSR, supra 1986; author's tabulations.
[44] *Ibid.*
[45] Wright and Rossi, supra, p. 149.
[46] Gordon R. Firman, "In Prison Gun Survey the Pros Are the Cons," *The American Rifleman* 23 (Nov. 1975), p. 13; see also Mitchell Link, "No Handguns in Morton Grove—Big Deal!" *Menard Times* (prison newspaper of Menard, Ill. Federal Penitentiary, 1982), 33, p. 1.
[47] Franklin E. Zimring and Gordon J. Hawkins, *Deterrence: The Legal Threat in Crime Control* (Chicago, Ill.: University of Chicago Press, 1973), pp. 31-32.
[48] Wright and Rossi, supra, see especially pp. 32-38.

this nature may well have been underreported, if misreported at all. Even more significantly, the most deterrable prospective criminals and those deterred from crime altogether will not be included in prison samples. These results, therefore, may reflect a minimal baseline picture of the deterrent potential of victim gun use.

Quasi-Experimental Evidence

Increases in actual gun ownership are ordinarily fairly gradual, making interrupted time series analyses of such increases impractical. However, highly publicized programs to train citizens in gun use amount to "gun awareness" programs that could conceivably produce sharp changes in prospective criminals' *awareness* of gun ownership among potential victims. The impact of these programs can be assessed because they have specific times of onset and specific spans of operation which make it easier to say when they might be most likely to affect crime.

From October 1966 to March 1967 the Orlando Police Department trained more than 2,500 women to use guns.[49] Organized in response to demands from citizens worried about a recent sharp increase in rape, this was an unusually large and highly publicized program. It received several front page stories in the local daily newspaper, the *Orlando Sentinel*, a co-sponsor of the program. An interrupted time series analysis of Orlando crime trends showed that the rape rate decreased by 88 percent in 1967, compared to 1966, a decrease far larger than in any previous one-year period. The rape rate remained constant in the rest of Florida and in the United States. Interestingly, the only other crime to show a substantial drop was burglary. Thus, the crime targeted, rape, decreased, and the offense most likely to occur where victims have access to guns, burglary, also decreased.[50]

Green[51] has interpreted the results of the Orlando study as indicating a partial "spillover" or displacement of rape from the city to nearby areas, i.e., a mixture of absolute deterrence of some rapes and a shifting in location of others. Unfortunately, this possibility of displacement can never be eliminated when considering any location-specific crime control

---

[49] Alan S. Krug, "The Relationship Between Firearms Ownership and Crime Rates: A Statistical Analysis," *The Congressional Record* (January 30, 1968):H570-2.

[50] Gary Kleck and David J. Bordua, "The Factual Foundations for Certain Key Assumptions of Gun Control," *Law & Policy Quarterly* (1983), 5, pp. 271-98.

[51] Gary S. Green, "Citizen Gun Ownership and Criminal Deterrence: Theory, Research, and Policy" *Criminology* (1987), 25, p. 75.

effort, be it a local job training program, an increase in police manpower or patrol frequency or a gun training program.

Green also suggests that the apparent rape decrease might have been due to allegedly irregular crime recording practices of the Orlando city police department, without, however, presenting any evidence of police reporting changes over time beyond the sharp changes in the rape rates themselves. Although largely speculative, Green's comments point to potential problems that could affect interpretation of this sort of quasi-experimental evidence.

A much smaller training program was conducted with only 138 persons from September through November 1967 by the Kansas City Metropolitan Police in response to retail businessmen's concerns about store robberies.[52] Table 6 displays crime trends in Kansas City and its metropolitan areas, as well as robbery trends in the rest of Missouri, the West North Central (WNC) region of which Kansas City is a part, and in the United States. While the frequency of robbery increased from 1967 to 1968 by 35 percent in the rest of Missouri, by 20 percent in the WNC region and by 30 percent in the United States, it essentially levelled off in Kansas City and declined by 13 percent in surrounding areas. Robberies had been increasing in the five years prior to the training program and continued to increase again in 1968. Thus, the upward trend was distinctly interrupted in the year immediately following the gun training program. This cannot be attributed to some general improvement in the social conditions generating robbery rates in the nation, region or state, given the upward trends in robbery elsewhere. Nor can the effect be attributed to improvements in conditions producing violent crime in general in Kansas City, since robbery was the only violent crime to level off. Something occurred in the Kansas City area in the 1967–68 period which caused an upward trend in reported robberies to level off, something not generally occurring elsewhere and something not related to other violent crime categories. Interestingly, Kansas City also experienced a levelling off in its sharply upward trend in burglary, suggesting a possible "by-product" deterrent effect much like the one indicated by the Orlando data.

---

[52] U.S. Small Business Administration, supra, pp. 253-56. *Crime Against Small Business,* Senate Document No. 91-14 (Washington, D.C.: U.S. Government Printing Office, 1969).

Table 6 • *Crimes Known to the Police, Kansas City and Comparison Areas, 1961-1974*

| | Kansas City, Missouri[a] | | | | | | Kansas City SMSA[c], excluding Kansas City | | | | | | Robbery | | |
Year	Robbery	MNNM[b]	Aggravated Assault	Rape	Burglary	Auto Theft	Robbery	MNNM	Assault	Rape	Burglary	Auto Theft	Missouri excl. K.C. SMSA	West North Central	U.S.
1961	1169	49	1194	222	6020	1995	202	14	135	42	2430	622	2266	5702	106670
1962	1069	49	946	147	5337	2336	239	21	184	38	2680	840	2166	5597	110860
1963	1164	60	935	197	5600	2911	347	20	234	47	2937	958	2277	6241	116470
1964	1180	48	1126	205	6484	2701	270	26	745	83	3416	1109	2505	6594	130390
1965	1212	71	1180	209	7219	3054	261	25	770	100	4234	1148	2722	6938	138690
1966	1574	59	1315	205	7495	3689	432	27	674	124	4917	1414	2763	8022	157990
1967	2120	62	1711	231	9455	4835	644	41	760	93	6612	1925	3241	10624	202910
1968	2171	92	1995	307	10020	4929	563	33	874	170	6219	2319	4374	12724	262840
1969	2679	105	1921	375	12269	6926	559	33	879	174	6733	2810	5245	14272	298850
1970	2982	120	1805	401	11265	5570	712	38	1102	183	7554	2815	5699	16279	349860
1971	2473	103	1961	371	11550	5408	641	48	1389	173	8104	2666	5419	14582	387700
1972	2092	71	1960	344	9472	3921	742	35	1295	200	8391	2607	5513	14928	376290
1973	2333	81	2433	302	10394	3884	715	64	1288	185	10073	2554	6153	16571	384220
1974	3002	109	2575	363	13406	3719	1087	57	1856	201	12585	2761	6364	19894	442400
Percent change. 1967-68	2	48	25	33	6	2	-13	-20	15	83	-6	20	35	20	30

Notes:
a. Figures before 1961 for Kansas City are not comparable with later years (U.S. FBI, 1962: 131). The Kansas City Metropolitan Police Department firearms training program sessions were held in September through November 1967.
b. MNNM = murders and nonnegligent manslaughters.
c. SMSA = standard metropolitan statistical area.

Sources:
Annual Issues, *Uniform Crime Reports* (U.S. FBI 1962-1975).

The results of these natural quasi-experiments are not cited for the narrow purpose of demonstrating the short-term deterrent effects of gun training programs. Indeed, there is no evidence as to whether citizens used the training in any significant number of real-life defensive situations and no solid evidence that gun ownership increased in the program areas. These results, however, do support the argument that routine gun ownership and defensive use by civilians has an ongoing impact on crime, with or without such programs, an impact which is intensified at times when prospective criminals' awareness of potential victims' gun possession is dramatically increased. Gun training programs are just one source of increased awareness; publicity surrounding citizen gun use against criminals would be another, as would general stories in the news media about gun ownership and increases in gun sales. The two examples cited resemble instances of crime drops following gun training programs elsewhere, including decreases in grocery robberies in Detroit after a grocer's organization began gun clinics and decreases in retail store robberies in Highland Park, Michigan, attributed to "gun-toting merchants."[53]

After "subway vigilante" Bernhard Goetz used a handgun to wound four robbers on a New York City subway train on December 22, 1984, subway robberies decreased by 43 percent in the next week, compared to the two weeks prior to the incident, and decreased in the following two months by 19 percent, compared to the same period in the previous year, even though nonrobbery subway crime increased and subway robberies had been increasing prior to the shootings.[54] However, because New York City transit police also greatly increased manpower on the subway trains immediately after the shootings, any impact uniquely attributed to the Goetz gun use was confounded with potential effects of the manpower increase. (There were no correspondingly large increases in police manpower in Orlando in 1966–67 or in Kansas City in 1967–68.)[55]

Finally, the deterrent effect of civilian gun ownership is supported by the experience of Kennesaw, Georgia, a suburb of Atlanta with a 1980 population of 5,095.[56] To demonstrate their disapproval of a ban on

---

[53] Krug, supra.

[54] *Tallahassee Democrat*, "Subway Robberies Drop," January 25, 1985, p. A1; see also *New York Times*, "22% Drop Reported in Crime on Subways," March 22, 1985, p. B4 and "Subway Felonies Reportedly Down," April 18, 1985, p. 87.

[55] U.S. Federal Bureau of Investigation, *Crime in the United States* (Washington, D.C.: U.S. Government Printing Office, 1969).

[56] U.S. Bureau of the Census, *County and City Data Book, 1983* (Washington, D.C.: U.S. Government Printing Office, 1983), p. 832.

handgun ownership passed in Morton Grove, Illinois, the Kennesaw City Council passed a city ordinance requiring heads of households to keep at least one firearm in their homes. In the seven months following passage of the ordinance (March 15, 1982 to October 31, 1982), there were only five reported residential burglaries, compared to 45 in the same period in the previous year, an 89 percent decrease.[57] This drop was far in excess of the modest 10.4 percent decrease in the burglary rate experienced by Georgia as a whole from 1981 to 1982, the 6.8 percent decrease for South Atlantic states, the 9.6 percent decrease for the United States, and the 7.1 percent decrease for cities under 10,000 population.[58]

Guns and the Displacement of Burglars from Occupied Homes

Residential burglars devote considerable thought, time and effort to locating homes that are unoccupied. In interviews with burglars in a Pennsylvania prison, Rengert and Wasilchick[59] found that nearly all of the two hours spent on the average suburban burglary was devoted to locating an appropriate target, casing the house and making sure no one was home. There are at least two reasons why burglars make this considerable investment of time and effort: to avoid arrest and to avoid getting shot. Several burglars in this study reported that they avoided late night burglaries because it was too difficult to tell if anyone was home, explaining, "That's the way to get shot."[60] Burglars also stated they avoided neighborhoods occupied largely by persons of a different race because "you'll get shot if you're caught there."[61] Giving weight to these opinions, one of the 31 burglars admitted to having been shot on the job.[62] In the Wright-Rossi survey, 73 percent of felons who had committed a burglary or violent crime agreed that "one reason burglars avoid houses when people are at home is that they fear being shot."[63]

The nonconfrontational nature of most burglaries at least partly accounts for the infrequency of associated deaths and injuries. Don

---

[57] Mark K. Benenson. Memorandum recording telephone conversation with Kennesaw, Georgia Police Chief Ruble, November 4, 1982.

[58] U.S. Federal Bureau of Investigation, *Crime in the United States* (Washington, D.C.: U.S. Government Printing Office, 1983), pp. 45-47, 143.

[59] George Rengert and John Wasilchick, *Suburban Burglary: A Time and Place for Everything* (Springfield, Ill.: Charles Thomas, 1985).

[60] *Ibid.*, p. 30.

[61] *Ibid.*, p. 62.

[62] *Ibid.*, p. 98.

[63] Inter-University Consortium for Political and Social Research (ICPSR), Codebook for ICPSR Study 8437. Armed Criminals in America: A Survey of Incarcerated Felons (Ann Arbor, Mich.: ICPSR, 1986).

Kates[64] has argued that because victim gun ownership is partly responsible for the nonconfrontational nature of burglary, it is therefore to be credited with reducing deaths and injuries by its deterrent effects. The benefit is enjoyed by all potential burglary victims, not just those who own guns, since burglars are rarely in a position to know exactly which households have guns and thus must attempt to avoid confrontation in all their burglaries.

Under hypothetical no-guns circumstances, the worst a burglar would ordinarily have to fear is having to break off a burglary attempt if confronted by a householder who managed to call the police. A typical strong, young burglar would have little reason to fear attack or apprehension by unarmed victims, especially if the victim confronted was a woman, a smaller male or an elderly person. Further, there would be positive advantages to burglary of occupied premises since this would give the burglar a much better chance to get the cash in victims' purses or wallets.

Even under no-guns conditions, many burglars would continue to seek out unoccupied residences simply because contact with a victim would increase their chances of capture by the police. Others may have chosen to do burglaries rather than robberies because they were emotionally unable or unwilling to confront their victims and thus would avoid occupied premises for this reason. However, this certainly does not seem to be true of all burglars. Prison surveys indicate that few criminals specialize in one crime type, and most imprisoned burglars report having also committed robberies. In the Wright-Rossi survey, of those who reported ever committing a burglary, 62 percent also reported committing robberies.[65] Thus, most of these burglars are temperamentally capable of confronting victims, even though they clearly prefer to avoid them when committing a burglary.

Results from victimization surveys in at least three nations indicate that in countries with lower rates of gun ownership than the United States, residential burglars are much more likely to enter occupied homes, where confrontation with a victim is possible. In the 1982 British Crime Survey, 59 percent of attempted burglaries and 26 percent of completed burglaries were committed with someone at home.[66] A 1977 survey in the

[64] Don B. Kates, Jr., "Handgun Prohibition and the Original Meaning of the Second Amendment" (*Michigan Law Review*, 1983), 82, p. 269.

[65] ICPSR, 1986, supra (author's secondary analysis of data set).

[66] Pat Mayhew, *Residential Burglary: A Comparison of the United States, Canada and England and Wales* (Washington, D.C.: U.S. Government Printing Office, Nat'l. Institute of Justice, 1987).

Netherlands found an occupancy rate of 48 percent for all burglaries, compared to 9 percent in the United States the previous year.[67] And Waller and Okihiro[68] reported that 44 percent of burglarized Toronto residences were occupied during the burglaries, with 21 percent of the burglaries resulting in confrontations between victim and offender. The differences between the United States and Great Britain and Canada cannot be explained by differences in legal threats since the probability of arrest and imprisonment and the severity of sentences served for common crimes are at least as high in the latter nations as in the United States.[69]

Implications for Crime Control Policy

I have argued that gun use by private citizens against violent criminals and burglars is common and about as frequent as arrests, is a more prompt negative consequence of crime than legal punishment, and is more severe, at its most serious, than legal system punishments. Victim gun use in crime incidents is associated with lower rates of crime completion and of victim injury than any other defensive response, including doing nothing to resist. Serious predatory criminals say they perceive a risk from victim gun use which is roughly comparable to that of criminal justice system actions, and this perception appears to influence their criminal behavior in socially desirable ways.

The evidence presented here is, of course, subject to multiple, differing interpretations. I believe, however, that the simplest and most plausible interpretation is that the civilian ownership and defensive use of guns has a deterrent and social control effect on violent crime and burglary. None of the foregoing can establish exactly how many crimes are deterred by the civilian possession and use of firearms. We cannot precisely calculate the social control impact of gun use and ownership any more than we can do so for the operations of the legal system.

---

[67] Richard Block, "The Impact of Victimization, Rates and Patterns: A Comparison of the Netherlands and the United States," in Richard Block, ed., *Victimization and Fear of Crime: World Perspectives* (Washington, D.C.: U.S. Government Printing Office, Bureau of Justice Statistics, 1984), pp. 23-28.

[68] Irvin Waller and Norman Okihiro, *Burglary: The Victim and the Public* (Toronto: University of Toronto Press, 1978), p. 31

[69] James Q. Wilson, "Crime and Punishment in England," *The Public Interest* (1976), 43, pp. 3-26, see also U.S. Bureau of Justice Statistics, "Imprisonment in Four Countries," BJS Special Report (Washington, D.C.: U.S. Government Printing Office, 1987).

However, available evidence is compatible with the hypothesis that gun ownership among potential crime victims may exert as much effect on violent crime and burglary as do criminal justice system activities.

The paucity of scholarly attention to civilian use of guns for defense may be partially due to the very limited visibility of such acts. No criminology text reports estimates of the frequency of defensive uses of guns. Published police-based crime statistics like those found in the Uniform Crime Reports do not cover the subject, and such incidents are rarely reported in the national news media, the Bernhard Goetz case notwithstanding. It is also possible that scholars feel shooting or threatening to shoot another person, even in self-defense, is so morally wrong that it is preferable not to address the subject at all.[70] It could be argued that to study the matter seriously might imply some endorsement and encourage the indiscriminant spread of the behavior.

Nevertheless, much social order in America may precariously depend on the fact that millions of people are armed and dangerous to each other. The availability of deadly weapons to the violence-prone probably contributes to violence by increasing the probability of a fatal outcome of combat.[71] However, it may also be that this very fact raises the stakes in disputes to the point where only the most incensed or intoxicated disputants resort to physical conflict, the risks of armed retaliation deterring attack and coercing minimal courtesy among otherwise hostile parties. Likewise, rates of commercial robbery and residential burglary might be far higher than their already high levels were it not for the dangerousness of the prospective victims. Gun ownership among prospective victims may even have as large a crime-*inhibiting* effect as the crime-*generating* effects of gun possession among prospective criminals. This would account for the failure of researchers to find a significant net relationship between rates of crime like homicide and robbery and those measures of gun ownership which do not distinguish between gun availability among criminals and availability in the largely

---

[70] William J. Goode, "Presidential Address: The Place of Force in Human Society," *American Sociological Review* (1972), 37, pp. 507-19; See also William R. Tonso, "Social Problems and Sagecraft: Gun Control as a Case in Point," in Don B. Kates, Jr., ed., *Firearms and Violence: Issues of Public Policy* (Cambridge, Mass.: Ballinger, 1984).

[71] Wright, et al., supra, pp. 189-212.

noncriminal general public.[72] The two effects may roughly cancel each other out.[73]

Guns are potentially lethal weapons whether wielded by criminals or crime victims. They are frightening and intimidating to those they are pointed at, whether these be predators or the preyed-upon. Guns thereby empower both those who would use them to victimize and those who would use them to prevent their victimization. Consequently, they are a source of both social order and disorder, depending on who uses them, just as is true of the use of force in general. The failure to fully recognize this can lead to grave errors in devising public policy to minimize violence through gun control.

Some gun laws are intended to reduce gun possession only among relatively limited "high-risk" groups such as convicted felons, e.g., laws licensing gun owners or requiring permits to purchase guns. However, other laws are aimed at reducing gun possession in all segments of the civilian population, both criminal and noncriminal. Examples would be the aforementioned Morton Grove handgun possession ban, near approximations of such bans (as in New York City), prohibitions of handgun sales (such as those in Chicago and Washington, D.C.) and most laws restricting the carrying of concealed weapons. By definition, laws are most likely to be obeyed by the law-abiding, and gun laws are no different. Therefore, measures applying equally to criminals and noncriminals are almost certain to reduce gun possession more among the latter than the former. Because very little serious violent crime is committed by persons without previous records of violence,[74] there would be little direct crime control benefit to be gained by reductions in gun possession among noncriminals, although even marginal reductions in gun possession among criminals could have crime-reducing effects. Consequently, one has to take seriously the possibility that "across-the-board" gun control measures could decrease the crime-control effects of noncriminal gun ownership more than they decreased the crime-causing effects of criminal gun ownership. For this reason, more narrowly

---

[72] Philip Cook, "The Effect of Gun Availability on Robbery and Murder," in Robert Haveman and B. Bruce Zellner, eds., *Policy Studies Review Annual*, Vol. 3 (Beverly Hills, Calif.: Sage, 1979); see also Kleck, supra, 1984.

[73] David J. Bordua, "Firearms Ownership and Violent Crime: A Study Comparing Illinois Counties," *Working Papers in Criminology*, CR8501, Department of Sociology (Urbana, Ill.: University of Illinois, 1986).

[74] Kleck and Bordua, supra, 1983.

targeted gun control measures like gun owner licensing and purchase-to-permit systems seem advisable.[75]

Having an armed victim population is obviously not without risks. Some victims are also offenders, and their possession of guns may embolden them to commit assaults and other crimes they otherwise would not have attempted. And the use of guns in assaults instead of likely substitutes such as knives or fists probably increases the fraction of assaults which result in death. However, evidence gathered to date on these questions has been very mixed and is no more conclusive than the evidence presented here concerning defensive effects of guns.[76] Similarly ambiguous conclusions apply to evidence concerning gun involvement in suicides and accidental deaths. The number of gun suicides which would not have occurred in the absence of guns appears to be fairly small.[77] And gun accidents appear to be less a by-product of routine gun ownership and use by ordinary citizens than the result of unusually hazardous activities with guns by a small, extremely reckless minority of gun owners. For example, insurance company studies indicate that many gun accidents occur when the shooter handles a gun while intoxicated, "plays" Russian roulette with a revolver or points a loaded gun at another person "in fun." And examination of police and traffic records indicates that accidental shooters have histories of arrests for violent acts, alcohol-related arrests, traffic citations and highway crashes far in excess of those matched controls.[78]

---

[75] Kleck, "Policy Lessons from Recent Gun Control Research," *Law and Contemporary Problems 49*, pp. 35-62.

[76] Wright, et al., pp. 129-38, 189-212; see also Kleck, "Suicide, Firearms and Gun Control," unpublished manuscript, 1986.

[77] Kleck, "Firearms Accidents," unpublished manuscript, 1986.

[78] *Ibid.*

Appendix
Militia Act of 1792

SECOND CONGRESS, FIRST SESSION, CH. 33, 1792

Chapter 33. — Approved May 8, 1792, vol. 1, p. 272.

An Act more effectually to provide for the national defence, by establishing an uniform militia throughout the United States.

1. Every able bodied white male citizen, of the age 18, and under 45 years, to be enrolled, &c. Duty of captains with respect to enrolling, &c. Citizens enrolled, to provide themselves with arms and accoutrements in six months after enrollment, &c. Militiamen to appear armed, &c., when called out to exercise, &c., except &c. Muskets to carry balls eighteen to the pound. Arms, &c., free from distress, executions, &c.

2. Enumeration of officers and persons, who are exempt from militia duty under this act.

3. Militia in each state to be arranged into divisions, brigades, &c., as the legislature thereof may direct. Organization of brigades, regiments, &c. To be officered by the states in the manner here prescribed.

4. One company of grenadiers, light-infantry or riflemen, to each battalion. A company of artillery and troop of horse to each division. Officers of the dragoons, their horses, arms. &c. Dragoons, their horses, arms, &c. Company of artillery and troop of horse to be formed of volunteers, &c.

5. Colors to battalions and regiments, and by whom provided.

6. An adjutant-general in each state. His duties.

8. Commissioned officers to take rank according to date, &c.

9. Militiamen wounded and disabled in public service, to be provided for, &c.

10. Duties of brigade inspectors.

Sec. 1. That each and every free able bodied white male citizen of the respective states, resident therein, who is or shall be of the age of eighteen years, and under the age of forty-five years, (except as hereinafter excepted), shall, severally and respectively, be enrolled in the militia by the captain or commanding officer of the company, within whose bounds such citizen shall reside, and that within twelve months after the passing of this act. And it shall, at all times hereafter, be the duty of every such captain or commanding officer of a company, to enroll every such citizen, as aforesaid, and also those who shall, from time to time, arrive at the age of eighteen years, or, being of the age of eighteen years and under the age of forty-five years, (except as before excepted,) shall come to reside within his bounds; and shall, without delay, notify such citizen of the said enrollment, by a proper non-commissioned officer of the company, by whom such notice may be proved. That every citizen so enrolled and notified, shall, within six months thereafter, provide himself with a good musket, or firelock, a sufficient bayonet and belt, two spare flints, and a knapsack, a pouch, with a box therein to contain not less than twenty-four cartridges, suited to the bore of his musket or firelock, each cartridge to contain a proper quantity of powder and ball; or, with a good rifle, knapsack, shot pouch and powder horn, twenty balls, suited to the bore of his rifle, and a quarter of a pound of powder; and shall appear, so armed, accoutred, and provided, when called out to exercise, or into service; except, that when called out on company days to exercise only, he may appear without a knapsack. That the commissioned officers shall, severally, be armed with a sword or hanger, and espontoon; and that, from and after five years from the passing of this act, all muskets for arming the militia, as herein required, shall be of bores sufficient for balls of the eighteenth part of a pound. And every citizen so enrolled, and providing himself with the arms, ammunition, and accoutrements, required as afore said, shall hold the same exempted from all suits, distresses, executions, or sales, for debt, or for the payment of taxes.

Sec. 2. That the Vice-President of the United States; the officers, judicial and executive, of the government of the United States; the members of both houses of Congress and their respective officers; all custom-house officers, with their clerks; all post officers, and stage drivers, who are employed in the care and conveyance of the mail of the post office of the United States; all ferrymen employed at any ferry on the post road; all inspectors of exports; all pilots; all mariners, actually employed in the sea service of any citizen or merchant within the United

States; and all persons who now are, or may hereafter be, exempted by the laws of the respective states, shall be, and are hereby, exempted from militia duty, notwithstanding their being above the age of eighteen and under the age of forty-five years.

Sec. 3. That within one year after the passing of this act, the militia of the respective states shall be arranged into divisions, brigades, regiments, battalions, and companies, as the legislature of each state shall direct; and each division, brigade, and regiment, shall be numbered at the formation thereof; and a record made of such numbers in the adjutant-general's office in the state; and when in the field, or in service in the state, each division, brigade, and regiment shall, respectively, take rank according to their numbers, reckoning the first or lowest number highest in rank. That, if the same be convenient, each brigade shall consist of four regiments; each regiment of two battalions; each battalion of five companies; each company of sixty-four privates. That the said militia shall be officered by the respective states, as follows: To each division, one major-general and two aids-de-camp, with the rank of major; to each brigade, one brigadier-general, with one brigade-inspector, to serve also as brigade-major, with the rank of a major; to each regiment, one lieutenant-colonel commandant; and to each battalion, one major; to each company, one captain, one lieutenant, one ensign, four sergeants, four corporals, one drummer, and one fifer or bugler. That there shall be a regimental staff, to consist of one adjutant and one quartermaster, to rank as lieutenants; one paymaster; one surgeon, and one surgeon's mate; one surgeon-major; one drum-major, and one fife major.

Sec. 4. That out of the militia enrolled, as is herein directed, there shall be formed, for each battalion, at least one company of grenadiers, light infantry, or riflemen; and that, to each division, there shall be at least one company of artillery, and one troop of horse: there shall be to each company of artillery, one captain, two lieutenants, four sergeants, four corporals, six gunners, six bombardiers, one drummer, and one fifer. The officers to be armed with a sword, or hanger, a fusee, bayonet and belt, with a cartridge box, to contain twelve cartridges; and each private, or matross, shall furnish himself with all the equipments of a private in the infantry, until proper ordnance and field artillery is provided. There shall be, to each troop of horse, one captain, two lieutenants, one cornet, four sergeants, four corporals, one saddler, one farrier, and one trumpeter. The commissioned officers to furnish themselves with good horses, of at least, fourteen hands and an half high, and to be armed with a sword, and pair of pistols, the holsters of which to be covered with bearskin caps. Each dragoon to furnish himself with a serviceable horse, at least fourteen hands and a half high, a good saddle, bridle, mail pillion, and valies, holsters, and a breast plate and crupper, a pair of boots and spurs, a pair of pistols, a sabre, and a cartouch box, to contain twelve cartridges for pistols. That each company of artillery and troop of horse shall be formed of volunteers from the brigade, at the discretion of the commander-in-chief of the state, not exceeding one company of each to a regiment, nor more in number than one-eleventh part of the infantry, and shall be uniformly clothed in regimentals, to be furnished at their own expense; the color and fashion to be determined by the brigadier commanding the brigade to which they belong.

Sec. 5. That each battalion and regiment shall be provided with the state and regimental colors, by the field officers, and each company with a drum, and fife or bugle horn, by the commissioned officers of the company in such manner as the legislature of the respective states shall direct.

Sec. 6. That, there shall be an adjutant-general appointed in each state, whose duty it shall be to distribute all orders from the commander-in-chief of the state to the several corps; to attend all public reviews, when the commander-in-chief of the state shall review the militia, or any part thereof; to obey all orders from him, relative to carrying into execution and perfecting the system of military discipline established by this act; to furnish blank forms of different returns, that may be required, and to explain the principles on which they should be made; to receive from the several officers of the different corps, throughout the state, returns of the militia under their command, reporting the actual situation of their arms, accoutrements, and ammunition, their delinquencies, and every other thing which relates to the general advancement of good order and discipline: All which, the several officers of the divisions, brigades, regiments, and battalions, are hereby required to make, in the usual manner, so that the said adjutant-general may be furnished therewith: from all which returns, he shall make proper abstracts, and lay the same annually before the commander-in-chief of the state.

[Sec. 7. Rules of discipline, the same as in 1779; except, &c.]

Sec. 8. That all commissioned officers shall take rank according to the date of their commissions; and when two of the same grade bear an equal date, then their rank to be determined by lot, to be drawn, by them, before the commanding officer of the brigade, regiment, battalion, company, or detachment.

Sec. 9. That if any person, whether officer or soldier, belonging to the militia of any state, and called out into the service of the United States, be wounded or disabled while in actual service, he shall be taken care of and provided for at the public expense.

Sec. 10. That it shall be the duty of the brigade-inspector, to attend the regimental and battalion meetings of the militia composing their several brigades, during the time of their being under arms, to inspect their arms, ammunition, and accoutrements; superintend their exercise and maneuvers, and introduce the system of military discipline, before described, throughout the brigade, agreeable to law, and such orders as they shall, from time to time, receive from the commander-in-chief of the state; to make returns to the adjutant-general of the state, at least once in every year, of the militia of the brigade to which he belongs, reporting therein the actual situation of the arms, accoutrements, and ammunition, of the several corps, and every other thing which, in his judgment, may relate to their government and the general advancement of good order and military discipline; and the adjutant-general shall make a return of all the militia of the state, to the commander-in-chief of the said state, and a duplicate of the same to the President of the United States.

And whereas sundry corps of artillery, cavalry, and infantry, now exist in several of the said states, which by the laws, customs, or usages, thereof, have not been incorporated with, or subject to, the general regulations of the militia.

Sec. 11. That such corps retain their accustomed privileges, subject, nevertheless, to all other duties required by this act in like manner with the other militia.

[Approved, May 8, 1792.]

Design / Typesetting: Pam Pitzer, Coastal Type & Design

Index

Strategic Tools for Securing Your Constitutional Rights

Check out the following pages for the best in books, videos, bumper stickers and fact sheets developed to further your understanding of the rights granted to you in the United States Constitution.

BOOKS

Firearms Folly in Maryland: Official Corruption Overrides The Constitution

Pro-gun forces lost a gun-ban referendum in 1988. Jim Boulet, who worked for the Maryland Committee Against the Gun Ban, brings a first-hand account of how anti-gun politicians used the resources of the State of Maryland to promote the gun ban. Offers a discussion of what can be done in other states to prevent a repeat of Maryland.

FIREARMS: $7.95

That Every Man Be Armed: The Evolution of a Constitutional Right

Written by Second Amendment attorney Stephen P. Halbrook, this book provides a definitive account of

the individual right to keep and bear arms meaning of the Second Amendment. Must reading for those interested in defending our right to bear arms.

ARMED: $14.95

Bearing Arms: Our Rights, Our Duties, and Our Freedoms

BEARMS: $7.95

This book examines the right of self-defense, gives three means to preserve freedom, refutes four current myths prevalent in today's gun-control debates, and explores the Second Amendment's concept of an armed militia.

TO ORDER: Send checks or money orders to Gun Owners Foundation, 8001 Forbes Place, Suite 102, Springfield, VA 22151. Please add $3.00 for shipping to all orders.

For quantity discounts and credit card orders please call 1-800-417-1486.

Safeguarding Liberty: Constitutional Liberties and Citizen Militias

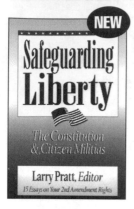

This collection of essays edited by Larry Pratt of Gun Owners of America focuses on the real issues concerning the 2nd Amendment and the militia: first, that the Constitution guarantees individual citizens to join together to protect life and property apart from the government, and second, the fact that people — *not guns* — kill people. Social commentator Walter Williams stated that: "Among our God-given rights is the right of self-defense. The Founders knew this well and charged Congress, through the Second Amendment, to protect (not grant) that right. *Safeguarding Liberty* reminds us of that; plus, if America is to remain free, we must not compromise with those who would strip us of our right to keep and bear arms."

SAFE: $14.00

From My Cold Dead Fingers

Sheriff Richard Mack has become a hero of the Second Amendment for his opposition to the Brady law. Mack has now written a book,

From My Cold Dead Fingers, that eloquently defends constitutional gun ownership in America. It ends with a powerful open letter to his fellow police officers urging them to be faithful the their oath of office to uphold the Constitution of the United States. Mack argues that not even an order from a superior can justify violating the Constitution of the United States.

MACK: $12.95

Armed People Victorious

Guatemala and the Philippines were near collapse when the organized militia repulsed the guerilla movement which had nearly brought down the governments.

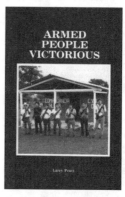

PEOPLE: $7.95

VIDEOS

Enemy Public Number One

Could the United States government actually declare war on its own people? Tyrants like Adolph Hitler have done that very thing with governmental power. In this video presentation, you will find out what happens when our leaders follow Hitler instead of our founding fathers, who spelled out very clearly what freedom was, what military firearms were for, and what militias were supposed to do. This is the video that defines the Second Amendment in all its clarity.

Arm yourself with this vital information.

VHS # EPNO: $19.95

The Waco Incident

This 2-hour documentary produced by TV station KPOC in Ponca City, Oklahoma, makes known information never before made public about what the government did in Waco.

Cyanide gas killed a number of Branch Dividians as a result of the tear gas used by the Federal Government.　VHS # WACOINC: $19.95

Breaking the Law... in the name of the law: The BATF Story

A documentary report by
Gun Owners Foundation

The right to "keep and bear arms" is an established protected provision of the United States Constitution. In recent years, this right has fallen under attack by do-gooders, leftists in the media, in state and national legislatures, and the uninformed. Now the attack is joined by certain agents of the U.S. Bureau of Alcohol, Tobacco and Firearms (BATF).

This video presentation documents the harassment and intimidation tactics employed by these agents. Live interviews with victims of the persecution reveal the shocking truth about the obvious anti-gun mentality of the bureaucrats, their arrogant disregard of the law, and how they have destroyed the lives of many innocent law-abiding citizens.

VHS # BATF: $19.99

The Assault on Semi-Automatic Firearms: Assault Rifles... Friend or Foe?

They are, in fact, neither. They are tools to be used in hunting, target shooting and for self-protection. Because they have been used illegally by criminals, there is an attempt to prohibit them nationwide. This video explores the history of the anti-gun movement and the

most recent effort to ban firearms.

This is an action-packed, 28-minute, made-for-TV video exposing the real passions behind the campaign to get rid of the so-called "assault weapons."

VHS # ASA: $19.95

A Matter of Common Sense

Would you put a sign in the front window telling all the world that there are no guns in your home? Of course not. You know that would literally invite a criminal into your home.

Whether you own a gun or not, few are foolish enough to advertise that they don't have one. Yet everyday, politicians are working to disarm law-abiding citizens. In effect, they are telling criminals that there are no guns in the home.

In this dramatic video, Senator H.L. Richardson, founder of Gun Owners of America, explores some of the myths which gun control advocates use to promote a ban on firearms. This is a must-see program for anyone who is interested in protecting the right to bear arms.

VHS # MCS: $19.95

The Truth About AK-47 Power

In this program the firepower of many different firearms is compared, and the ballistic characteristic of different ammunition is tested on watermelons. The slow motion results are astonishing, and refute the charges repeatedly made by AK-47 critics.

VHS # AK47: $14.95

Fatal Verdict: "Guilty as Charged"

What happens when a law-abiding American is charged with a crime that's really no crime at all? This explosive video shows how every American can fight back in the war against our Constitution.

VHS # FV: $19.95

Gun Control: Gateway to Genocide

A Capital Hill Briefing sponsored by Gun Owners Foundation and Jews for the Preservation of Firearms Ownership (JPFO). Dramatic evidence has been unearthed by Jay Simkin, Research Director of JPFO revealing the link between gun control and genocide.

Past gun control laws were passed by governments not intent on genocide, but their successors used these laws to carry out mass exterminations of their political enemies.

VHS # GTG: $14.95

A Way of Life

This 26-minute story details the multi-faceted world of hunting and why it is an integral part of many Americans' lives. The video is an excellent professional tool for the gun owner to use to combat anti-hunting propaganda. Written and narrated by former California Senator H.L. Richardson (Founder and Chairman of Gun Owners of America), the film was photographed and edited

by David McClain, renowned wildlife cameraman. The fantastic scenic and animal footage alone is worth the price.

A Way of Life is ideal for placement on cable TV outlets all across the nation. The film is an excellent program for service clubs, veterans organizations, mens clubs, hunting fraternities, and to give to friends and neighbors to be viewed on their home VCRs.

VHS # AWL: $19.95

Geraldo Live: Larry Pratt vs. former NJ Governor Jim Florio

Geraldo Live recently looked at gun control. It turned into a debate between Gun Owners of America Executive Director Larry Pratt and the nationally known gun-banning former governor of New Jersey, Jim Florio. Many issues in the firearms debate are covered in this program. The Brady bill, foreign crime statistics, the meaning of the Second Amendment and much more.

Also on the show is a pro-gun rape victim and an anti-gun survivor of the Long Island commuter train mass murder. This video is loaded with great information. The anti-gunners lost this one! Show this tape to your friends.

VHS # GL: $19.95

Jaquie Miller Statement

Jaquie Miller is the brave victim or four wounds from an AK-47. She is still wheelchair-bound, but has taped a powerful statement against banning semi-automatics and against waiting periods. Jim Brady has nothing on Jaquie Miller! This tape can be shown to elected officials even though Jaquie Miller cannot travel.

VHS #JMS: $14.95

TO ORDER

Send checks or money orders to: Gun Owners Foundation
8001 Forbes Place, Suite 102
Springfield, VA 22151

Please add $3.00 for shipping to all orders.

For quantity discounts and credit card orders please call 1-800-417-1486.